BOOKS BY EDWARD WEEKS

This Trade of Writing
The Open Heart
In Friendly Candor
Breaking into Print
Boston, Cradle of Liberty
The Lowells and Their Institute
Fresh Waters
The Moisie Salmon Club: A Chronicle
My Green Age
Writers and Friends

EDITED BY EDWARD WEEKS

Great Short Novels
The Pocket Atlantic
Jubilee: 100 Years of the Atlantic
(with Emily Flint)
Myopia, a Chronicle, 1875–1975
Selected Letters of James Thurber
(with Helen Thurber)

WRITERS AND FRIENDS

The Editor and his Associate, Charles Morton, in the mid 1940s

WRITERS

AND

FRIENDS

by

EDWARD WEEKS

An Atlantic Monthly Press Book

Little, Brown and Company   Boston/Toronto

FIRST EDITION

The author wishes to thank the following for permission to reprint material: George
Butterick, literary executor of the estate of Charles Olson, for "Pacific Lament." John
Ciardi for his poem "Elegy Just in Case." Robert Graves for his poem "The Persian
Version." Viking Penguin, Inc., for "A Little Night Music" from *Times Three* by Phyllis
McGinley. Copyright © 1958 by Phyllis McGinley. Little, Brown & Company for excerpts
from *History of United States Naval Operations in World War Two* by Samuel Eliot
Morison; from *The Two-Ocean War: A Short History of the United States Navy in the
Second World War* by Samuel Eliot Morison. Copyright © 1963 by Samuel Eliot Morison;
from *The Last Hurrah* by Edwin O'Connor. Copyright © 1956 by Edwin O'Connor; from
Drive by Charles Codman. Copyright © 1957 by Theodora Duer Codman. The *Boston
Globe* for excerpts from Laurence Winship's article "The Raunchy Wolf." Alfred Rice
and the Ernest Hemingway Foundation for letters of Ernest Hemingway. R. P. Lister for
his poem "The Owlet and the Gamekeeper." Macmillan Publishing Co., Inc. for lines
from "Wonderings." Copyright 1943 by John Masefield, renewed 1971 by Judith Masefield.
New Directions for opening lines from "In the White Giant's Thigh" from *The Poems of
Dylan Thomas.* Copyright 1952 by Dylan Thomas; for excerpt from "How to Be a Poet"
from *Quite Early One Morning* by Dylan Thomas. Copyright 1954 by New Directions
Publishing Corporation. David Higham Associates Limited for excerpts from letters and
cables of Edith Sitwell. Helga Green for the Raymond Chandler letters. From pp. 37 and
46 in "Bedfellows" from *The Points of My Compass* by E. B. White. Copyright © 1956
by E. B. White. Reprinted by permission of Harper & Row, Publishers, Inc. Mark Twain's
letter to William Dean Howells. From *The Love Letters of Mark Twain*, edited by Dixon
Wecter. Copyright 1947, 1949 by The Mark Twain Company. Reprinted by permission of
Harper & Row, Publishers, Inc.

Library of Congress Cataloging in Publication Data

Weeks, Edward, 1898-
Writers and friends.

"An Atlantic Monthly Press book."
Includes index.
1. Weeks, Edward, 1898-   . 2. Journalists—United
States—Biography. 3. Editors—United States—
Biography. 4. Authors, American—20th century—Biography.
5. Atlantic (Boston, Mass.: 1932) I. Title.
PN4874.W369A33 070.4'1'0924 [B] 81-19383
ISBN 0-316-92791-0   AACR2

ATLANTIC–LITTLE, BROWN BOOKS
ARE PUBLISHED BY
LITTLE, BROWN AND COMPANY
IN ASSOCIATION WITH
THE ATLANTIC MONTHLY PRESS

Designed by Janis Capone

*Published simultaneously in Canada
by Little, Brown & Company (Canada) Limited*

PRINTED IN THE UNITED STATES OF AMERICA

DEDICATION

A writer at work is difficult to live with, absentmindedly leaving mounds of paper in room after room, forever misplacing his glasses case, or demanding an audience while he reads aloud passages that defy him. Phoebe-Lou Adams, whom I married after the death of my first wife, has sustained me in the writing of three books since our wedding in 1971. She deserves the dedication of this one, in words she never failed to respond to:

"Phoebe, are you there?"

CONTENTS

Marion Danielson Campbell; Robert J. Manning; Joseph Wambaugh; James Alan McPherson; E. B. White; Thornton Wilder; Walter Lippmann; Leverett Saltonstall

AFTERWORD / 308

Bennett Cerf; John Walcott; Chester Kerr; Seymour Lawrence; Curtis Cate; Peter Davison; Upton B. Brady

Index / 315

WRITERS AND FRIENDS

CHAPTER

I

When we were driving ambulances with the French in 1917–1918 and our division went "en repos" we played cards. My luck was usually good and I liked to fancy that in an earlier existence I had been a gambler on a Mississippi riverboat, and a good one. Perhaps there was something to the notion, for in my own time and place I reverted to the gambler's trade; I became an editor.

I needed luck and sound hunches when I became editor-in-chief of the *Atlantic Monthly* in June of 1938 as the magazine was just barely solvent. From my predecessor, Ellery Sedgwick, I inherited three distinguished authors, Walter Lippmann, Charles Nordhoff, and James Norman Hall, but I had to find new, younger talent if we were to have new readers. Eudora Welty, Vladimir Nabokov, Geoffrey Household, and Jessamyn West were four whose short stories brightened my early issues. I intended to feature biographies and some of the best to come to me were written by women: Catherine Drinker Bowen, Agnes de Mille, Kathryn Hulme, who told *The Nun's Story*, and Agnes Newton Keith, all had their work published under the Atlantic colophon. The war brought me close to Vannevar Bush and Samuel Eliot Morison. I learned about Black America from long involvement with the United Negro Colleges, and, individually, from Roland Hayes, later in my twelve-year pursuit of *The South and the Southerner* by Ralph McGill, and recently as I encouraged our most gifted black author, James Alan McPherson. I met George Kennan as his star was rising, and our friendship deepened as I edited five of his books. Comedy, so rare at any time, came to us in manuscripts by Fred Allen, Raymond Chandler, Edwin O'Connor, James Thurber, and Peter Ustinov. I was fortunate in my proximity to Harvard and the Massachusetts Institute of Technology and in my friendship with three distinguished presidents, James Bryant Conant of Harvard, James R. Killian, Jr., of M.I.T. and John Dickey of Dartmouth, and with Harvard's great classicist, John Finley. Editing is the friendliest of professions, as I hope this book will show.

Magazines are an American institution. No other country reads anything like the diversity of the more than 8,000 which we produce. But the competition is killing and in the long run it has proven more profitable to launch a new periodical than to preserve an old one. I can think of only three in the English-speaking world that have been in continuous circulation for well over a century.

Magazines die from one of two causes: either, like *Scribner's*, they fall behind because the editor has been too long in control and has lost touch with the upcoming generation, or they are put down by competitors who are opening up new vistas of more timely interest. In the 1890s, when American corporations were corrupting Congress and defying regulation, S. S. McClure, a daring editor, challenged corporate power with a series of muckraking articles by reliable investigators such as Ida Tarbell, Lincoln Steffens, and Ray Stannard Baker. *McClure's* shot up like a rocket, widely read throughout the country. Two decades later, when Congressional investigations and the Sherman Anti-Trust Act had brought about reform, *McClure's* fizzled out. By 1907 Sam McClure had accomplished one mission, could not find a second, and was deep in debt.

Each generation of readers sees the world in a different light. In 1922 when Brit Haddon and Henry Luce were writing a prospectus to attract backers for their new periodical (they figured they would need $100,000; they had $85,675 when they printed the first issue of *Time*), they cited four magazines which they believed *Time* would surpass: the *World's Work*, the *Century*, the *Literary Digest*, and *Outlook*. The *Literary Digest* was the giant of the four with a circulation of 1,200,000 and advertising second only to that of the *Saturday Evening Post*. Fifteen years later, when *Time* had lived up to its billing, that quartet was dead. In the same period and with the same celerity, the *New Yorker*, lively, sophisticated, brilliantly edited, had buried the humorous magazines, *Judge* and *Life*, and the fashionable *Vanity Fair*.

I was aware of these casualties but we had a backlog. In 1917 the *Atlantic* published its first book by an *Atlantic* contributor. In 1927 and through the Depression I edited the Atlantic Monthly Press books, a source of revenue which, thanks to our collaboration with

4

Little, Brown and Company, was a lifesaver. In June 1938, I became the ninth editor of the *Atlantic*. The *Century*, the leader of the "quality group," had perished, so had the *Forum* and the *Bookman*; *Scribner's* was about to fail, *Harper's* and ourselves were running in the red, kept alive, as I say, by the earnings of the books we published. *Time*, in alluding to my promotion, described me as "wiry and effervescent" (I resented being called effervescent), and accurately pointed out that Ellery Sedgwick, under whom I had served for fourteen years, still owned the magazine and could sell it out from under me, the inference being that I was a stopgap. The *Atlantic*, ever since it was founded in 1857, had been published in Boston and there were two immediate problems that troubled my sleep: to hold off the bids that were coming in from New York, most pressingly from William Randolph Hearst, until I found the capital to keep the magazine in Boston, and to stop the decline in our circulation and advertising. (Our pages of advertising for the twelve issues of 1938 grossed $352,000 and I should hate to say how many dollars of promotion we spent to get that pitiful total.)

The new capital came out of the blue at a dinner party the evening of September fourth, 1939, the day after war was declared. Our hostess turned to me. "What am I going to do about my Dick?" she said. It took time for the full implication to sink in. "I wish he would come with me," I said. "Can you make a go of it? Dick couldn't stand another failure." "I can," I said. "I know I can."

In ninety days, Richard and Barbara Danielson purchased the magazine at seven times the $50,000 Sedgwick paid for it in 1908 — and I was confirmed as editor-in-chief. Dick, who had edited the *Independent* with Christian Herter during the 1920s and been editor of the *Sportsman* for the nine years of its handsome but expensive existence, became president of the Atlantic Monthly Company, Barbara, a vigilant director, and thereafter I was to have their steadfast support.

I suppose that every executive who comes to the top as he turns forty begins by trying to do it all. I certainly did. I worked so late at the office that I felt dizzy as I walked home through the Public Garden. I read manuscripts for the magazine and on weekends edited books by *Atlantic* authors, wrote a monthly column of reviews, lectured at the drop of a hat — and was knocked flat by an excruciating attack of shingles.

Back in 1924 when Sedgwick invited me to become the First Reader, our editorial staff numbered just four: Ellery, editor and

5

arbiter (we had no editorial meetings), Florence Converse, his deputy who usually deferred difficult decisions when he was away; Caroline Church, an incomparable proofreader, and I, passing judgment on fifty to seventy-five manuscripts a day. Now it was for me to initiate and decide, to dictate letters so compelling they would make up for our small fees, to build a new staff — and learn to delegate.

Just as my future was determined on the second day of war, so the immediate fate of the *Atlantic* would depend on our policy about that war. Everything in my experience convinced me we would have to intervene if England and France were seriously threatened by Hitler. The fellowship I held at Trinity College, Cambridge, after my graduation from Harvard, strengthened my admiration of the British and my study of English constitutional history made me realize how closely our democracy had evolved from theirs. The British and the Commonwealth were our most dependable ally against the dictators, and we were bound to be theirs.

In the First World War, from July 1917 to June 1919, I had been an ambulance driver with the 37th "Algerian" Division of the French Army, and that attachment changed my ambition. Because of the *Atlantic*'s slight praise of my war letters (which were rejected) I came home believing that further study of English would open a door. Remembrance of the mutilated and dying *blessés* I had carried left me with a loathing for war but rather than see Hitler enslave Europe, as he was enslaving the Jews, I knew we would have to fight.

The *Atlantic* had had plenty of warning from our contributors that war was inevitable. My most dependable correspondent in London was David L. Cohn, from Greenville, Mississippi: the county that produced William Faulkner, Eudora Welty, and the legendary Will Percy, author of *Lanterns on the Levee*, who had helped Dave through college. Dave had known poverty and race prejudice and was a freelance any editor would covet, for he wrote with humor but without rancor and gave his feelings full blast. He had many friends in England, one of them Jacob Epstein, the sculptor, whose bust of Cohn brings out his intellectual power, his wide brow, blunt nose, and deep-set eyes; what it cannot convey is the animation of those features when Dave was stirred to anger or mirth. On an afternoon in November 1937, as he wrote in an article for us, Dave walked into the gallery of a London art dealer with Edward Wolfe, the South African painter. A droopingly tall man stood there looking at Wolfe's paintings, and on being introduced to him Cohn impetuously asked, "When do you think war will begin in Europe?" The tall man was so aroused that he shouted, "Only Americans think there will be a war in Europe!" That man was John Maynard Keynes. Whether Keynes was covering up, mortified by his knowledge of Britain's unpreparedness, or whether he believed at the time that appeasement would prevent hostilities, I have long wondered.

A year later Dave was invited to Cliveden, where his hostess, Nancy Astor, and her other guests seemed sure that Hitler, having consolidated his grip on Czechoslovakia, would turn against Russia, and that England had no cause for alarm. Dave was shocked at such complacency. I could not believe it was typical of the Chamberlain government. But it was. So over-confident was Mr. Leslie Hore-Belisha, Secretary of State for War, that British rearmament was soft-pedaled lest it disturb *der Führer*.

The political demoralization in Paris gravely troubled my friend Raoul de Roussy de Sales, the Washington correspondent for *Paris-Soir* and *Havas*. Raoul was the most brilliant Frenchman I knew, skeptical, searching and witty. One of his grandmothers was American, his father a Parisian aristocrat, and Raoul himself was bilingual with a sympathetic understanding of the American temperament. I had urged him to write a book contrasting our two democracies, and the early chapters — my favorite one was "Love in America" — were appearing in the *Atlantic* when the war distracted him.

He spent his holiday in France every summer and when I met him on his return in 1938 he seemed bleakly pessimistic. "You have no idea what a relief it is to get back to New York," he said. "Here no one is looking over his shoulder. Europe is sick with fear." He had read *Mein Kampf* as soon as it was in translation and did not dismiss it as bombast; he took the threat seriously and began writing a commentary on the complete text which, alas, was not published in America until 1939. From his friend the writer-pilot Antoine de Saint-Exupéry, he well knew how powerless was the French Air Force.

Like most Americans I was slow to realize the malevolence of Hitler. After the rape of Poland, there was a pause of six months. Britain was now manufacturing, around the clock, Spitfires and Hurricanes, which were to defend it from Göring's armada and in the United States the double shifts working on armament were offset by the overheated oratory of "America First," our isolationists. Raoul derided the paradox. "This violent outbreak of America impartiality," he wrote in the *Atlantic*, "reached its peak precisely at the moment when the English and French finally made up their minds to accept the consequences of doing what nine Americans out of ten had urged them to do," namely, to resist Hitler. His article appeared in the interlude known as "the phony war" and in his conclusion he ob-

served that many Americans were anxious to stop the fighting immediately, "Before we have even started the wrecking of civilization in
Europe we are discussing the new world which will arise from the
smoking ruins-to-be." Well, why not, if there's time? I thought. I
asked Raoul if he could persuade Paul Reynaud, a leading member
of the French cabinet, to define France's war aims. Reynaud agreed
and his "Program for Peace" (which Raoul probably wrote) led our
issue for April 1940, appearing on the very day Reynaud became
the new Premier. "How the hell did you know Reynaud was going
to take over the government?" asked the night editor of the *New York
Times* as he requested permission to reprint it. Raoul knew.

One of the last happy-go-lucky manuscripts we accepted before
the invasion of Poland was a piece by a pleasant Englishman, entitled "By Canoe to Mandalay." In this tense interlude it no longer
was appropriate and at subsequent editorial meetings, "By Canoe to
Mandalay" came to symbolize a lost world, and was never printed.
In India, however, Nehru was making himself obstreperous and,
acting on the same impulse that turned me to Reynaud, I asked
Jawaharlal Nehru to describe for us the India which he saw emerging
after the war. He finished his blueprint for Indian independence just
before he was put in jail. It was entitled "India's Demand and England's Answer" and a powerful forecast it was: "The British Government's answer," he wrote, "was an affront to the people of India,
who saw in it the desire to consolidate the imperialist regime in
India and elsewhere. If this was so, the war in Europe became obviously a war of rival imperialisms and India could be no party to
it. . . . The tragedy is that Britain should have encouraged, and
should continue to encourage, disruptive and reactionary tendencies
in India in order to preserve her imperial interests. She will not preserve them for they are destined to go, but they will go in hostility
and conflict if no better way is found. The day when India could
submit to external impositions is past." Nehru's manuscript was un-
censored but our check for it, which he endorsed to his London bank,
disappeared and his daughter, Indira, asked that we send a second to
his American publisher, which was done. We published the article,
expecting widespread editorial comment, but it went unnoticed except
by the *New Masses*, which reprinted it in full. Evidently we were too
far ahead of time.

Our source in the Soviet Union had long been William Henry
Chamberlin, the Moscow correspondent for the *Christian Science
Monitor* from 1922 to 1934. "William Henry," as his contemporaries
called him, graduated from Haverford College with honors in 1917.

He was small, round-faced, with large dark eyes and an habitual half-smile, a deceptively youthful appearance for one with a penetrating mind and such swift grasp of the essentials. A Quaker who neither smoked nor drank, he had a fondness for sweet chocolate, of which he ate his weight annually (frequently half a pound a day). No records survive of how many wooden boxes of chocolate we dispatched to the Soviet Union — or how many were intercepted by the censor. We knew they were essential and enough got through to keep him happy. During his years in Moscow he had shrewdly observed the Five Year Plans of the Politburo to industrialize the nation and the inevitable shortages which resulted, year after year. This was the subject of the first book he wrote for us, *Soviet Russia* (1930), and even more emphatically in *Russia's Iron Age* (1934). He departed from the Soviet Union appalled by the effect of Stalin's trials and purges.

In 1938 Chamberlin was reassigned to Paris, where he was depressed by the hopeless drift of the Third Republic and by the unconcealed belligerence of the Third Reich. Like Raoul he believed Hitler meant what he said: "It will be my duty to fight the next war in such a terrible manner that my enemies cannot endure it. Each country will imagine that it alone will escape. I shall not even need to destroy them, one by one. Selfishness and lack of foresight will prevent each one fighting until it is too late."

William Henry remained in Paris until two days before the Germans marched in. On his return to Boston I asked him to attend our weekly editorial meetings as a consultant. He was the first experienced correspondent to predict that once Hitler had embarked on conquest he could not stop. His article "Hitler's Alternatives," which led our January issue in 1941, was prophetic. He drew a fascinating comparison of Napoleon's Europe with that which Hitler had conquered, and concluded, "Strategic minerals, fuels and fats are much more important for Hitler than Napoleon because modern warfare is so highly industrialized." In the very first year of conquest, from Norway, through the Low Countries, in the Reich itself, in France and south to the Balkans, people were living on short rations. "Hitler's empire," he continued, "was oversupplied with men and machines, undersupplied with foodstuffs and essential raw materials. . . . He must find a means of covering Europe's deficits." The argument seemed undeniable when Chamberlin examined the three alternatives for breaking out of this bind. The enslavement of the Soviet Union was clearly the most tempting — although German technicians in number would be needed to extract the desired food and oil. It was the most explicit prediction we published of the invasion that followed six months later. At the time, William Henry and I had only one serious disagreement: he did not believe the Soviets could repel the German invasion, and he preferred it that way. I believed the Russians would hold.

Magazines are most widely read at the approach of war and during the conflict. The first issue of the *Atlantic* appeared in November 1857, when most of the best writers in America lived within thirty miles of the Massachusetts State House. The founding editor, James Russell Lowell, was a passionate advocate of Lincoln, and those who wrote for him believed, almost without exception, in the abolition of slavery. They were Thoreau, Longfellow, Emerson, Harriet Beecher Stowe, Hawthorne, Oliver Wendell Holmes, Thomas Wentworth Higginson, Julia Ward Howe, and Whittier, who was a demanding poet, never satisfied with less than $150 for a poem. Such were our charter contributors, and never again would we have such a monopoly of talent.

Our third editor, from 1871 to 1881, was William Dean Howells. He introduced the Westerners and in an outrageous gamble paid Bret Harte $10,000 — more like $100,000 in today's currency — for the exclusive right to publish everything Harte wrote in the year 1872. Harte did not overexert himself; he started a novel, never finished, and his best offering was a story, "How Santa Claus Came to Simpson's Bar." The offer was not renewed.

Howells was beginning to publish Mark Twain, at a much smaller fee — $16 for every thousand words — but the price went up as they became friends. The *Atlantic* liked to feature a new serial in the January issue and Mark promised to write one, but by November 1874 no manuscript had appeared, and the author reported he had no new idea despite constant reminders from Mrs. Clemens. Then came this reprieve:

Home, 24th '74

Dear Mr. Howells,

I take back the remark that I can't write for the Jan. number. For Twichell and I have had a long walk in the woods and I got to telling him about old Mississippi days of steam-boating glory and grandeur as I saw them (during 5 years) from the pilot-house. He said "What a virgin subject to hurl into a magazine!" I hadn't thought of that before. Would you like a series of papers to run through 3 months or 6 or 9? — or about 4 months, say?

Yrs Ever
Mark

Howells did want them, and they soon appeared monthly (January through August 1875) as "Old Times on the Mississippi," so realistic, as Howells claimed, that they turned the ice-water in his pitcher muddy.

There has been a fortuitous streak all through our past: manuscripts tossed "over the transom" by unknown writers have occasionally proved to be unexpectedly good. Gradually we gained a reputation for making "discoveries" although there were times when we did not know we had one.

Early in 1862 while he was endeavoring to recruit a regiment, Thomas Wentworth Higginson wrote two essays for the *Atlantic*, the second of which, entitled "A Letter to a Young Contributor," he considered a potboiler. But, as his biographer, Anna Mary Wells, says in her discerning book *Dear Preceptor*, it was to have a more profound effect than anything he would live to write. Higginson emphasized the painstaking effort in forming a style: "Often times a word shall speak what accumulated volumes have labored in vain to utter; there may be years of crowded passion in a word, and half a life in a sentence. . . ." This spoke directly to Emily Dickinson, a recluse in Amherst, who wrote to him at once, the envelope enclosing a card, bearing her signature, and four poems. Higginson with his characteristic good sense said they gave him "the impression of a wholly new and original poetic genius." When he showed them to his wife, Mary, she thought the woman was insane.

Higginson was then thirty-eight, Emily thirty-one; their correspondence continued for twenty-five years; she sent him her poems in their final version and so valued his judgment that she addressed him as "Dear Preceptor." As Colonel Higginson continued to be a contributor to the *Atlantic*, I assume he must have shown them to the second editor, James T. Fields, and probably to his successor, William Dean Howells. But Emily's poems were elliptical and unconventional when verse was supposed to be foursquare and lucid, so I, also, assume they were rejected. Not until six years after Emily's death, when the *Atlantic* published the letters of Colonel Higginson, including her accompanying poems, did Emily appear in our pages. That was a superb "discovery" which we muffed.

"Read the unsolicited manuscripts" was an office edict; "one of them may be a find!" We still do and this accounts for the byword "Why don't you send it to the *Atlantic*?" Professors of English favoring a precocious pupil, the mother of a daughter threatening to be a poet, advise, "Send it to the *Atlantic*"; in they come and maybe one in five hundred is accepted. Our fees, particularly for the newcomer, have seldom been excessive — Julia Ward Howe received $4.00 for her poem "The Battle Hymn of the Republic" — but from her day to mine the *Atlantic* has been a good place to begin.

The amenities are in short supply in times of crisis, so it was good luck when in 1941 I met Vladimir Nabokov, then lecturing on comparative literature at Wellesley College. Vladimir was an Elegant, in baggy flannels and a worn tweed jacket. When I think of him I remember first his beautiful hazel eyes, which so perfectly mirrored every mood, his mirth, his serious concern, or wry amusement. Hair brushed back from a brow unmarked by loss and poverty, he had a distinction that set him off in any company. And he was such fun! Of a noble family, brought up in the wealth of St. Petersburg, heir to a rich uncle whose fortune, as he said, was given just before the Revolution had taken it away, he alluded to that vanished world with affection, not bitterness. Butterflies were his passion. He lost his first collection in St. Petersburg when fleeing from the Bolsheviks, his second when he escaped from the Crimea; and his third one he abandoned in Paris in 1940. Since then he had never started another. In Berlin he had supported his wife and young son, translating, tutoring, giving tennis lessons and with the meager royalties of his novels, written and published in Russian and read mainly by the refugees.

In the war and post-war years the *Atlantic* published seven of his short stories, and they were unique. The first two were thought out and written in Russian; a friend made a literal translation, which Vladimir then went over, line by line, inserting his magic figures of speech, similes like, "the [wet]-asphalt shining like the back of a seal" or "a whitish moth had dashed in and was kissing its shadow all over the ceiling." The second story, entitled "The Aurelian," is particularly touching because it embraces one of his dearest loves, butterflies. It, too, was set in Berlin, in a curiosity shop where the aging Herr Pilgram sells school supplies and, on rare occasions, a few of his preciously preserved butterflies, dreaming of the day when a windfall will permit him to close up and travel far out, netting and collecting for his very own the beauties he dreams of, "velvety black butterflies soaring over the jungle, and a tiny moth in Tasmania, and that Chinese 'Skipper' said to smell of crushed roses when alive, and the short-clubbed beauty that a Mr. Baron had just discovered in Mexico." But when at last Herr Pilgram had the money and had written the terse farewell to the wife he was about to leave, he blacked out.

"The Aurelian" has a special significance as it concluded his writing in Russian. A week after I had accepted it he sent me a short poem

which expresses his love of his native tongue, as well as the buffeting
so many refugees have suffered.

SOFTEST OF TONGUES

To many things I've said the word that cheats
the lips and leaves them parted (thus: prash-chai
which means "good-bye") — to furnished flats, to streets,
to milk-white letters melting in the sky;
to drab designs that habit seldom sees,
to novels interrupted by the din
of tunnels, annotated by quick trees,
abandoned with a squashed banana skin;
to a dim waiter in a dimmer town,
to cuts that healed and to a thumbless glove;
also to things of lyrical renown
perhaps more universal, such as love.
Thus life has been an endless line of land
receding endlessly. . . . And so that's that,
you say under your breath, and wave your hand,
and then your handkerchief, and then your hat.
To all these things I've said the fatal word,
using a tongue I had so tuned and tamed
that — like some ancient sonneteer — I heard
its echoes by posterity acclaimed.
But now thou too must go; just here we part,
softest of tongues, my true one, all my own. . . .
And I am left to grope for heart and art
and start anew with clumsy tools of stone.

Henceforth, Vladimir would write his novels and poems in English,
but not in words "of stone."

For six months he worked one day a week at the Harvard Museum
of Comparative Zoology, rearranging a famous collection of butterflies, and that summer the museum sent him west to capture what he
could. At Alta, Utah, in the surrounding lovely meadows he discovered the haunts of certain long-lost species of butterflies. On his
return in September he wrote me from Wellesley, "It is pathetically
dull to watch the good old eastern combination of butterflies on the
College lawns here — after my Western orgies: rather like a garden
in Cambridgeshire after a summer in the mountains of Spain. Otherwise I feel much more at home in New England than I did in fair but
somehow unreal California, among those blond hills (or shall I compare them to old white bears with a dirty tawny tinge?)"

13

We used to lunch together in the little café at the Ritz before his afternoon class at Wellesley, and on one occasion both pockets of his coat were bulging with papers. "What in the world have you got there?" I asked. "Tolstoy," he replied. "You people simply don't realize what dreadful translations of Tolstoy you put up with! I think you must supply your own verbs and adjectives. Garnett and Maude are both wooden. To show my girls, I've been properly translating some chapters of *War and Peace*." His eyes were alight.

The Russians are masters at translating and Vladimir was one of the very best. In 1944 we published his translation of three poems by Tyutchev, and a year later, Lermontov's eloquent poem, "Thanksgiving." By now we were paying him our top fees and I was saddened but could not begrudge it when the *New Yorker* came knocking at his door. Our showcase would not have such sparkle without him but I was grateful for the years we had him in it.

Manuscripts from a remote country always aroused our appetite. Such was the case with an article, "The Story of Saudin," submitted by a Mrs. Agnes Newton Keith of Sandakan, North Borneo. Saudin Bin Labutau was a member of the Murut tribe whom Mr. and Mrs. Martin Johnson had borrowed from the Keiths to care for the wild animals they had collected while making a film in the Borneo rain forests. He shared their long voyage back to the States, feeding and tending the beasts, and remained for three months in New York City, living in the basement of the Johnsons' apartment house and, of course, in their charge. Since Saudin spoke not a word of English and liked to roam, he carried a label, "If lost, please direct to . . ." On his return to Sandakan he stopped at the Keith compound to tell his friends the wonders he had seen and Mrs. Keith, hearing he was there, got him to repeat his story, in Malay, which she translated, retaining the amazement with which he spoke. Two paragraphs will give the flavor of Manhattan as it appeared to this observant wild man of Borneo:

I was so astonished by New York that I just wanted to look and look and look at it. I forgot all about feeding the animals and my work. Every night men had their names put in the sky with bright lights so that they would not be forgotten, because there are so many people in New York that it would be easy to forget some of them. All the time there was a great noise made by motorcars and buses and trains. There were trains above me on bridges, there were trains below us, and there were more trains that were below the trains that were below. Always the trains were very full of people. I think if the trains all stopped and the people got off them there would be no space in New York for all the people. So the people take turns living in the trains. I used to walk and walk because I was afraid to get on those trains to ride, as I did not know how to get off or where I should be when I did, or if I might have to live on one.

Mr. Johnson took me to eat at a place where you put money in a hole and take out a plate of food. The different holes have names on them to tell you what foods are concealed within. We had vegetables and potato and meat all cooked together in a flour wrapping which they call a pie. I think this place was very cunning indeed, because the hole to receive a ten-cent piece was so small that you could not put in a five-cent piece, and the hole for a five-cent piece did not answer if you put in a one-cent piece.

Mrs. Keith, it appeared, was a native Californian married to a Canadian, Harry Keith, then Conservator of Forests for British North Borneo. It took six weeks for my letter of acceptance to reach Sandakan and by return post came a second manuscript accompanied by this message: "Saudin visits us occasionally, and I give him news of America. His natural niceness has not been spoiled by his travels. He does not work energetically, but why should he? His bank account will last him a lifetime, as a Murut spends money. His store clothes have been much admired. A few years ago the popular picture postal card in Borneo was Mensaring, the Murut Chief in loin cloth. Now it is any Murut in Saudin's borrowed New York suit." The letter went on: "The natives of this country are a saddening, maddening, lovable, heartbreaking lot. They are a gentle and courteous people yet one from whom the zest of life seems to have been taken since the ancient rite of Headhunting has been banned by Government. . . ."

I sent her the announcement of the Atlantic $5,000 Prize which we were offering for the best book of nonfiction to reach us by February 1939. "What I want you to do," I wrote her, "is to tell the story of your daily life in Sandakan, the scope of your husband's activity; tell us about your compound and its staff — your presence in every chapter is required as referee, partisan, and wife. Where do you go for a hair-do in Sandakan? [To the Chinese, she replied.] How does your husband protect his library from the damp heat? [They had built an inner room, she said, to seal off the effect of the rains.] How many Europeans were there in the colony and what was their attitude toward the Eurasians?" This was needling, though no more than I would have given any other far-out contestant, and I applied the pressure since I was doubtful that she could finish the manuscript in the time that remained.

A large parcel from Borneo arrived in the closing days of January 1939; when the wrapping with its stamps was removed here was a mound of white paper, tied up in a sarong of striking blue and brown design (which we later reproduced for the binding). The top page bore the title, *Land Below the Wind*, and beneath the last page, separated by tissue, were pencil sketches of Sandakan, the houseboys, the apes who were the family pets, a tent in a dripping jungle and the author propped up on a cot, writing under an open umbrella — casual drawings which conveyed amusingly what Agnes's life was like. The title, *Land Below the Wind*, we were told, was the translation of the Malay name for Borneo; "To journey together is happiness" was the theme, and these points clarified, the judges went on to read it and some seven hundred other competitors. It was different from any other book we had published and I was elated when the Award went to Keith by a vote of 6 to 1.

All this time, because North Borneo was a British chartered company, I had pictured Mrs. Keith as a short sturdy woman in a cloche and tweeds. In June 1939, the Keiths flew to America for a family reunion on the Coast and then on to Boston to receive the prize, be photographed and interviewed. When Agnes stepped off the plane I had my first sight of that slender, long-legged Californian whose high cheekbones, dark almond eyes, and lovely throat reminded me instantly of Queen Nefertiti. I could tell from the glances of the reporters and the way people turned to look at her in the Ritz that we had won not only a writer but a beauty.

She spent the mornings with me, fitting the manuscript together chronologically, the afternoons in her room inking in her drawings or buying new clothes, for she and Harry were to spend the late summer and autumn in Oxford, where he would be lecturing. But the exhilaration in Boston was the high point; the outbreak of war cut short their holiday; they never did get to England, and Agnes took back to Sandakan the Atlantic trousseau, much of which she was never to wear. *Land Below the Wind* was serialized in the magazine, then chosen by the Book-of-the-Month Club. The mounting royalties she asked to be spread over the years for she had serious misgivings about the immediate future The first royalty check assisted in the arrival of Henry George Keith II, who was born in Sandakan on April 5, 1940.

Like most of us Agnes underestimated the striking power of the Japanese. After the fall of Singapore she was offered her last chance to return to California with her baby. Instead she built up a lifesaving kit of drugs for Harry, young George, and herself, and in an article which reached me shortly before Pearl Harbor she foretold how the three of them might retreat by canoe into the interior to hide away with friendly natives until the Japanese were driven off. We published "Before Invasion, A Letter from Borneo," and the week after it appeared the Japanese landed; the three Keiths were taken prisoners and separated, she and George confined in the camp for women. What happened to them during the ensuing three and a half years we were not to know till peace; only three times during that spirit-cracking degradation was the curtain lifted by prisoner-of-war postcards, the first to Agnes's mother; the other two to me. Her message, dated "Xmas Day, 1944" read:

"Dear Ted: Quote Sherman reference war. What about Red Cross? Resources this country limited. Our one hope peace soon. All three ragged, tired, homesick, but surviving. Love, Agnes, Harry & George Keith."

Her colonial life in the big house at Sandakan did not make Agnes race-conscious nor did the beatings before liberation, which broke three ribs and a vertebra. In *Three Came Home*, her fine, valiant book, written from notes stuffed into George's teddybear, she tells what she sacrificed to get nourishment for her child, and in her struggle for survival one feels her detestation of war and the absence of bitterness toward her captors. Her epitome of Freedom speaks for prisoners — for hostages — everywhere.

I know now the value of freedom. In all of my life before I had existed as a free woman, and didn't know it.

This is what freedom means to me. The right to live with, to touch and to love, my husband and my children. The right to look about me without fear of seeing people beaten. The capacity to work for ourselves and our children.

The possession of a door, and a key with which to lock it. Moments of silence. A place in which to weep, with no one to see me doing so.

The freedom of my eyes to scan the face of the earth, the mountains, trees, fields, and sea, without barbed wire across my vision. The freedom of my body to walk with the wind, and no sentry to stop me. Opportunity to earn the food to keep me strong. The ability to look each month at a new moon without asking, How many more times must this beauty shine on my captivity?

I will never give up these rights again. There may be more to life than these things. But there is no life without them.

As soon as Agnes and Harry were able to travel (just five months after liberation) they returned to North Borneo, Harry's duty to promote food production in a starving country. They found their home and his irreplaceable library wiped out by the bombing; they found welcoming natives and uppermost, the new aspiration, "Asia for the Asians." In 1952 he joined the United Nations as an expert in tropical forestry and agriculture. In each step thereafter, as in each book, Agnes recorded their mission to the Philippines, their nine years in Libya, and, finally, in 1974, on a grant I secured from the Japanese government, they returned to Japan, which she and Harry had first visited on their honeymoon, to describe the renaissance in the country which had never broken their spirit. This is what American reconciliation should be.

CHAPTER

II

During the Depression Americans had to decide what they could do without; families which had formerly subscribed to several magazines cut back to one, and the decline in our circulation, before my promotion, showed we were among the discards. At a directors' meeting Reginald Washburn of Worcester, after listening to the lugubrious report of the circulation manager, remarked dryly, "Wouldn't it really be cheaper to mail five thousand one dollar bills to a list of former subscribers, saying, 'If you return this we will send you five issues of the NEW *Atlantic?*' " The implication after the laughter was plain: somehow I had to drum up fresh interest without spending money.

As "The Town Crier" Alexander Woollcott had created one of the highest rated programs in radio. It was a mélange of anecdotes, hero worship — of Lincoln, Mr. Justice Holmes, Helen Keller — and rapture over books which appealed to him, skillfully worded and delivered with a throb. When Alec went "quietly mad" over *Lost Horizon*, by James Hilton, that fine novel by an unknown became a best seller. Woollcott's fee had risen to $2,500 a week before heart trouble slowed him down. (He was to have his last attack while delivering a Christmas broadcast to Britain.)

Before that occurred the networks were looking for another "literary" voice, and it was probably my success in lecturing — at nearby colleges and the New York Town Hall — that prompted an invitation from NBC. They asked for a thirty-minute broadcast on "The Human Side of Literature." I would follow "Information Please" in the same studio before a live audience in Radio City on Tuesday evenings, on the Red Network, with the title "Meet Mr. Weeks." Well, it was a priceless chance for coast-to-coast promotion and for listeners to hear what the new editor was like. The office was elated; the only misgiving came from my very able secretary, Jeannette Cloud, who foresaw endless hours of dictation. "If you don't keep two programs ahead," she said, "we'll go crazy."

I sought Woollcott's advice. He and I had had our differences, but he had buried the hatchet: he was then living at the Hotel Gotham, where he received my news with mock approval.

"Since they've been fool enough to ask you, you surely aren't going to be a Goddamn fool and decline! What will they pay?"

"One hundred and fifty dollars for me and fifty dollars for a guest."

A grunt. "Have you a list of your programs?"

I had blocked out thirteen, not naming the guests, and this I showed him.

" 'Children Who Live Forever,' " he read. "You mean Alice, Mowgli, David Copperfield, Tom Sawyer — ?"

"Yes," I said. "I've thought of eight."

"Well," he said, "that might be fun. I'll be your guest then if you like." I grinned in gratitude.

"Great! Now — is there a book that will help me write my scripts?"

"No. And you don't write them: you make notes and then talk aloud to someone with good ears and repeat until it sounds like talk. The curse of radio is professors who read. Radio has its own vocabulary — you depend on the vowels — the short words, 'scream,' 'kick,' 'fight,' 'love,' 'bite,' 'loiter' — they come over so much more sharply than the consonants — the *s*'s and *ch*'s always blur. If you notice, I slow down for a word like 'successively.' It's so easy to dry up on the air. Keep paper cups of water handy. And never say, 'You who' — it sounds like a yodel. You'll learn from your mistakes. . . ."

My first program took place on October 17, 1939, and by my third, with Pearl Buck, my mail was running strong. I continued through the spring of 1941, thirty-nine in all, fitting one in at Pontiac, Michigan, a few at Boston, or wherever my lectures necessitated. The war, as it worsened in Europe, was a period of deep anxiety for which I suppose I supplied a distraction. The guests were willing: Sherwood Anderson told of his early days in Greenwich Village and of how Liveright's advance of $100 every Monday nearly ruined him; Bernard de Voto brought Mark Twain to life, David McCord, speaking of light verse, sang "The Owl and the Pussycat"; Ruth Gordon went back to her impecunious girlhood in Wollaston, Massachusetts, and her New England sketches of father, mother, and the family cat were hilarious; Archibald MacLeish, Carl Sandburg, John Marquand, André Maurois — each spoke characteristically of his work.

The scripts were prepared a fortnight in advance. I dubbed in the dialogue and sent it to the guest to revise and we rehearsed at Radio City Tuesday afternoons until it was time to dress (a boiled shirt and black tie for the live audience). I took the guest to dinner and we appeared at the studio as Clifton Fadiman, John Kieran, and Franklin P. Adams were finishing "Information Please."

Somerset Maugham was the wealthiest of British authors, but all the money in the world could not cure his stutter and NBC was wary of him on that account. His autobiography, *The Summing Up,* I much admired, and I planned to draw material from it about his early training as a doctor in the London slums to demonstrate that until one passed thirty, few writers had seen enough of life to write a first-rate novel. The network finally conceded.

But after our rehearsal Tuesday afternoon I wasn't so sure. Maugham had escaped from France and arrived in New York so recently that he had not glanced at the dialogue, which was based on what he had written in his book; he stumbled over his own sentences, he stuttered and perspired, and when we let him up from the mat at five o'clock and he had departed, Ben Grauer, my director, looked at me: "If he does no worse than that," Ben said, "you'll fill. But just in case he improves, we'd better time some rubber numbers." A "rubber number" is the extra material you keep at hand in case you're running short. We timed three minutes of the letters in response to my "Children" program, and separated with misgivings.

At Voisin, where his publisher joined us for dinner, Maugham was again his suave self. He wore his clothes well and with his hooded eyes, dark hair swept back, and deeply creased cheeks, he looked the world-weary sophisticate. He told us of what he had done to protect his villa at Cap Ferrat against the German occupation and of his present negotiations with Hollywood to produce short films of four of his short stories. I asked him to choose the wine, and the steak was tender. Over the demitasse he turned to me. "My dear Weeks," he said, "after my b-b-baarth I re-re-rewrote our dialogue."

"Oh."

"Yes, your di-director sent for it, and we shall have fr-fr-fresh copies."

Fresh they were, the long pages in large type, one page to a minute. I warmed up the audience before we went on the air while Maugham, seated to my right, paged through the script, then I took my place before the mike and waited for Ben Grauer's opening.

I began talking about a compulsive gambler (name withheld), a young Englishman who lost as much as $7,000 a night to card sharks. In Paris he aspired to be an artist, but no one would buy his drawings. When his inheritance was gone, so was his marriage, his wife hopelessly insane, their two little daughters shipped off to the grandparents. In London, now a journalist, he bobbed up with an idea for a serial story; only two chapters were written, the rest in his head. He called it "Pen and Pencil Sketches of English Society," and for once a publisher was enthusiastic. The first part, in a yellow paper cover, with illustrations, appeared on New Year's Day, 1847; written month by month, the story ran through twenty installments, until all London was talking about it; such was the origin of *Vanity Fair*, the great novel Thackeray finished in his thirty-seventh year. I was about to add that Leo Tolstoy, also a notorious gambler, had finished his greatest novel, *War and Peace*, at thirty-seven when I heard our engineer, offstage, ask "What's that creaking?"

"Weeks's stiff shirt when he leans over," said Ben, also offstage. "Tell him to sit still." A note fell on my table.

I came to our first dialogue and in answer to my questions I was gratified by Maugham's calm, unfluffed reply. Nor in the exchange that followed was there noticeable hesitation nor any of that agonized stuttering we had timed. Evidently in his revision he had removed the words that tripped him and substituted those that came easier. Fresh material, too: how at twenty-three he had struggled with a novel whose characters were beyond him; it was very immature and when his publisher would not give him a hundred pounds for it he turned to writing plays. But he kept the manuscript and in maturity rewrote *Of Human Bondage*, the book which was to become his best known.

Ben Grauer was spreading his hands in the signal that means "Slow it down!" But there was no slowing Maugham. At the end of our second exchange a note dropped before me reading, "More than 3 minutes short," and as I was finishing the letters, the last of my rubber numbers, another "Ad lib until I signal."

"Mr. Maugham," I said, "there'll be a great many novels written about this war. Where do you think the best one will come from?"

"Well, Mr. Weeks," he ruminated, "Every novelist would rather write about defeat than victory." Now he *was* stuttering. "And j-j-just as the b-b-best novel about the First World War, *All Quiet on the Western Front*, came out of Germany's defeat, so I hope and b-b-believe the best book about this war will come from the same source, and f-f-for the same reason!" It was a bold answer in 1940, and with the outburst of applause from the audience that followed, it filled.

Broadcasting made me more nervous than lecturing; to avoid drying up I had cups of water for the guest and myself and one evening a quick gulp, just as we went on the air, choked my windpipe. I turned away from the mike and Ben Grauer kept on talking until I squeaked out, "Good evening," and the voice returned. I never had a sponsor, although a major oil company did make a flattering offer some time later. The two immediate effects were the aroused interest in the magazine and my appointment as a judge of the George Foster Peabody Awards, in radio and ultimately in TV. For fifteen years I was chairman of that jury.

Of the many hundreds of letters (and a basket of Christmas cards) about my program there are three, one from a friend, the other two from strangers, which I particularly cherish:

SUPREME COURT OF THE UNITED STATES
WASHINGTON, D.C.

Chambers of
Justice Felix Frankfurter   November 16, 1939

Dear Ted:

I quote: "Don't you think we ought to get the Atlantic?" Believe it or not, such was the question put to me by my wife. I cannot imagine that you have had a greater triumph than to have overcome her deep skepticism. So please regard this as a subscription to the Atlantic. Have it sent to 1511 — 30th Street, and send me the bill.

We heard at least part of your talk last Tuesday and rejoice at any such inroad on the normal tripe that comes over the radio. I shall listen in from time to time, but I do not promise to do so regularly,

With warm regards,

Ever yours,
F.F.

HENRY E. HUNTINGTON LIBRARY AND ART GALLERY
SAN MARINO, CALIFORNIA

31 January 1940

Dear Mr. Weeks:

In spite of the fact that I have a longstanding habit to break in writing almost my first fan letter, I can't help saying bravo and congratulations for your splendid program last night. A good many times during the past three months I have been upon the point of writing you; among recent programs, for instance, that on light verse and nonsense verse was so engaging that I felt sure you would be blanketed in fan mail. But last night's half-hour with Archibald MacLeish was, for me, one of the very finest you have given — with beautiful speech, wisdom, and deep penetration into the aspirations of American life. Incidentally, I've learned to listen to your *causeries de mardi* with a pencil at hand: last night's story about Mr. Ford and family cooking was so apt that I nailed it at once. (In the book about heroes and hero-worship in America, which Howard [Mumford] Jones mentioned to you last year, I'm trying to write a chapter on the self-made man and his appeal to the American public — and the remark was perfect in this context.) So please accept my very hearty congratulations, and thanks. . . .

With best greetings, I am

> Faithfully yours,
> Dixon Wecter

And the last, a year later, a telegram:

Old Greenwich, Conn.   1940 FEB 21
WEEKS-ATLANTIC MONTHLY BSN
NOW WHY IN THE NAME OF THE WESTERN UNION DO YOU GO OFF THE AIR WHEN IT WAS ABOUT THE ONLY CIVILIZED THING LEFT ON OUR LONG SUFFERING AIR. I AM SORRY BUT GRATEFUL=

HENDRIK WILLEM VAN LOON

A serious wildfire was spreading in the Northeast which the *Atlantic* could not ignore: the outburst of anti-Semitism fanned by the war in Europe, by Father Coughlin, "America First," and by Nazi propaganda. It had been latent during the period 1881–1929 (when 2,304,668 Jews passed through Ellis Island), partly sublimated by good nature, the comedy of Weber and Fields, the "Potash and Perlmutter" stories Montague Glass wrote for the *Saturday Evening Post* and subsequently brought out in three volumes, and the Yiddish jokes in vaudeville which were no more offensive than a parody of the Swedes' inability to pronounce the letter *j*. In thirty years Mr. Sedgwick had never had to cope with violent American anti-Semitism. Now it was in the open, invidious and ugly.

I invited Albert Jay Nock to sound the alarm. The former editor of the *Freeman*, white-haired, irreverent, and in his mid-seventies, Nock was a disciple of Herbert Spencer. His argument, "The Jewish Problem in America," was urbane, steeped in history, and so long it had to be printed in the June and July issues, 1941. He began by reproaching the country for not being aware of what was going on and cited the anti-Jewish demonstrations — beatings, baitings, intimidations, picketing — which had taken place in Brooklyn, Jackson Heights, the Bronx, and Yorkville, as many as fifty or sixty a week in the summer of 1939. "It must be constantly kept in mind," he wrote, "that a general resentment against any minority is always of proletarian or sub-proletarian origin; and therefore the evidences of it are slow in coming to the notice of society's more reflective elements." He quoted an exchange at the beginning of the Nazi persecution of the Jews when an American asked Hitler why he was making it so ruthless. "The Reichskanzler replied that he had got the idea from us. Americans, he said, are the great rope and lamppost artists of the world, known to all men as such." Nock, who had little admiration for FDR, then made a forecast: he declared that he expected "credit inflation, currency inflation, repudiation, and perhaps great civil disturbances." He deplored the ethnic differences between Oriental and Occidental which through the centuries had prevented assimilation and concluded, "If I keep up to my family's record of longevity I think it is not impossible that I shall live to see the Nürnberg laws reenacted in this country and enforced with vigor."

That opened the floodgates. In came too many letters for our correspondence column, one of the first by Alfred A. Knopf, who wrote:

My congratulations on your June issue. The articles by [Carl] Friedrich and Mrs. Lindbergh are well worth reading. But I am particularly pleased to see you tackling the question of anti-Semitism with such boldness and frankness. Nock makes an extremely good opening.

Others, by Congressman Emanuel Celler, Frances Strauss, and Dr. Louis Finkelstein, we published in an immediate symposium. The argument showed how troubled people were, and it continued. James Marshall scoffed at Nock's Olympian calm, his apparent air of irresponsibility, and, especially for calling it "an Oriental problem." "Nonsense! It is 'The Anti-Semitic Problem in America' with which we are plagued. I believe," wrote Marshall, under that title, "that the *modus vivendi* for which Mr. Nock sought, and which he failed to find between the American Jew and his fellow citizens is the identical *modus vivendi* which the entire American people must find to assure survival of democratic processes and democratic approaches to life. If with our varying interests, capacities, and backgrounds we cannot have a common faith in democratic aims and make common cause of those ends through democratic procedures and mechanisms, then our American institutions will fall. Then the programless defeatism of our Junkers will leave us nothing but the totalitarian alternative."

In December, the month of Pearl Harbor, Arthur H. Compton in his *Atlantic* paper "The Jews: A Problem or an Asset?" began by reminding readers "that in the 'Great' war the Jews supplied 40% more than their proportionate quota of soldiers in the U.S. Army; 18% of them were volunteers, half of the volunteers were in the Marine Corps and six of the 78 Congressional Medals of Honor were awarded to Jews." (That was prophetic of things to come.) Compton continued: "Of the hundreds of organizations openly anti-Semitic that have recently been active in the U.S. one of the most important bears a German name and is unquestionably a part of the Nazi propaganda machine. Perhaps more dangerous, however, are those that work under a cloak of religion or of 'America for the Americans.' "

With our entry into the war the wildfire of anti-Semitism died down. But not entirely. In the spring of 1943 it flared up again during the "dim-out" on the Eastern seaboard, most noticeably in Dorchester, Massachusetts, a suburb of Boston. Ward 14 of Dorchester was then the most solidly Jewish neighborhood in the United States, with only 2 percent gentiles. It was surrounded on all but the water side by the Boston Irish, and a target for attack. The Catholic agitator and Jew-baiter Father Coughlin had testified to a group of Internal Revenue agents that he drew most of his funds from Boston and unquestionably his inflammatory radio talks and his periodical, *Social Justice*, had a pernicious effect. The trouble in Dorchester was dismissed as "kid stuff," but it clearly went deeper.

Wallace Stegner, who was then teaching English at Harvard, had been following the "beat-ups" and in a long, impressive letter to me he outlined the article he proposed to write. These were the main points:

That hoodlumism broke out very suddenly and very savagely the moment the dimout made it safe and easy; that from the beginning it had a very definite direction — nobody but Jew kids got beaten up; that it even could have been a planned and directed scheme, since apparently the gangs had a system of lying in wait around Hecht House and collaring ones and twos and threes as they came out at night; that the police, who almost certainly knew of it, did nothing about it; that on November 9, when they finally arrested a gang of kids, they were out to make an example of very definite people . . . that though they arrested three Gentiles along with the four Jew boys, the three Gentiles had somehow evaporated before the prowl car got to the station. The two Jewish boys old enough to be tried in open court were finally fined ten dollars apiece, and the district attorney later nol prossed the trial.

In other words, the anti-Semitism of Boston, at least in its violent aspects, is something of an Irish monopoly, though the Jews themselves will not say so because they do not want an internecine race war and because there are plenty of Boston Irish-Catholic laymen who are enlisted on the right side. . . .

I think it can be demonstrated that the Irish in Boston have had a profound psychological reason for scapegoating the Jews; that on the one hand they are resentful over the discrimination shown against themselves by the "codfish aristocracy," and that on the other they probably have, or ought to have, a sense of guilt over the messiness of their own political machines. Boston and the surrounding towns controlled by the Irish have the reputation, and have had it for a long time, of being the worst administered cities on the continent, and knowing that, Irishmen are put more on the defensive than ever. So far as I can see they are psychologically ripe to scapegoat a minority group. . . . I'd like to suggest finally not only what certain neighborhood groups are doing about the problem, but what they *might* do. . . .

Stegner investigated Ward 14; assured himself that the gangs were predominately composed of young toughs bearing Irish names; that the beatings were harmful and that the raids, which had averaged two or three a month in the spring of 1943, had jumped to eight in July and to eleven by September. The police had looked the other way. His article, "Who Persecutes Boston?" was firm and fair; he traced the persecution which the Irish immigrants had suffered after they landed and why their motive for revenge lingered on, and he concluded, "The Roman Catholic Church is not in the least responsible for the anti-Semitic outbreaks in Boston. But it could do more than any other single agency or institution to stop them, if it would."

When his article was accepted and ready for copyediting I had a revolution on my hands. Margaret Mutch, our head copyeditor, was a loyal Catholic, so was Teresa S. Fitzpatrick, our circulation manager and the boss of fifty women we employed. Short, dynamic, beautifully turned out, "T. S. F." was my constant ally on most questions, but not when a writer pointed a finger at the Hierarchy. She backed up Miss Mutch, told her not to touch the manuscript. I asked Miss Mutch to come to my office. "I think you misunderstand," I said. "Mr. Stegner is appealing for help in a dangerous situation. If you refuse to copyedit it I shall, for we intend to publish it just as soon as possible." She did as I insisted and sent it to press.

27

There was resentment when "Who Persecutes Boston?" was read and digested. Archbishop Richard Cushing of Boston, soon to become Cardinal, denounced "one Wallace Stegner" over the Yankee Network and there was quite a bit of flak from the *Pilot,* and other parochial papers. But I have always supposed that word had gone out to the priests in South Boston and Dorchester "to cool it," for ten days after Stegner's article appeared on the newsstands the raids ceased.

I have said that during the Depression the *Atlantic* was kept afloat by the success of our books which I was then editing. Among the novelists, like Mazo de la Roche, Walter D. Edmonds, and James Hilton, who sustained our solvency, were two whom we rarely saw: Charles Nordhoff and James Norman Hall. When France was overwhelmed in 1940 they wrote me that they were leaving Tahiti and, to my dismay, that their partnership was at an end. Papeete had been their home for nearly twenty years and there, in a unique collaboration they had co-authored seven books.

I can think of many successful collaborations in the theater but in American fiction of this century only that of Nordhoff and Hall. Four of their novels, *Mutiny on the Bounty, Men Against the Sea, Pitcairn's Island,* and *Hurricane,* are now classics of the sea.

They were of the same age and had graduated from college the same year, 1910, Nordy from Harvard, Jim from Grinnell College. But physically and in temperament there was a striking difference: Nordhoff, a tall, ash-blond Californian, reserved, skeptical, and determined; Hall, who believed in the good, the most modest writer I have known, black-haired, his eyes gentle, his long nose broken on the control panel when his plane, hit by an anti-aircraft shell, made a miraculous landing within the German lines in May 1918. After his escape from Germany Hall met Nordhoff in Paris; they were asked to prepare the official history of the Lafayette Escadrille, and in so doing they became friends, eager to find an island where they could live cheaply, and write. Mr. Sedgwick, who had been publishing Hall's war material, helped them settle in Papeete, Tahiti, and with *Harper's* he put up the money to get them there.

Papeete in 1921 was still in the age of innocence. At Paré's Retreat, a ramshackle hotel overlooking the lagoon, they lived in adjoining rooms opening "on the upstairs veranda, with brass bedsteads, mosquito nets, chamber pot and a tin bucket for slops." This was to be their workshop and here at the outset they developed their individual talents: Nordhoff, his skill in narration in his two books for boys,

The Pearl Lagoon and *The Derelict,* and Hall, his talent for descriptive essays, his poetry, and the occasional short story he sold to the *Atlantic.* I doubt if either earned more than $3,000 a year, but they were teaching each other more than they realized.

It was Nordhoff who suggested that they collaborate in writing an adventure story about the Lafayette Escadrille, in alternate chapters, each to be signed with their initials (the initials I ruled out), and when half done they sent the manuscript to me for encouragement. It was exciting and authentic; clearly Nordhoff was providing the motor, the driving power and Hall, who had been in a number of "dog fights," the poetic descriptions. (Hall's delight in being airborne made him an erratic member of any patrol; he constantly got lost and, returning alone on one occasion, remarked at mess, "I know now why birds sing," for which he was mercilessly ribbed thereafter.)

After the success of *Falcons of France,* Hall proposed that they write about the mutiny on the *Bounty,* the most dramatic mutiny in the British Navy, which occurred in the South Seas. After months of assimilation Hall was to tell what happened on shipboard, Nordhoff of the enchanted days on Tahiti, but as they read their chapters aloud, revision took them into each other's work and Hall dominated the emotional scenes. *Hurricane,* their fifth novel, is to me their most beautiful, the force of the storm is Nordhoff at his best, and Hall's delineation of the lonely fear of the heroine as she clings to the swaying tree, a scene one cannot forget. I was touched that they dedicated it to me.

The threat that the Japanese might seize Tahiti brought Nordhoff and Hall with his family to Boston in the spring of 1942. At our first luncheon together Nordy showed me a clipping telling of three convicts who had escaped from the French penal colony, Devil's Island, and had been picked up far at sea, on the point of death, their one ambition to join the Free French and drive out "le Boche." "God, what a spirit!" he said. "I wish Jim and I were young enough to do the same. We're thinking of writing a short book about them." The clipping revived their collaboration. That summer they wrote *Men without Country,* and then they moved to California, where they settled in for the duration, working together on the more substantial novel *Botany Bay.* Nordhoff was once more his resolute self; his second marriage in California was a happy one and he was never to return to Tahiti. But Papeete was the Halls' island home and, with the coming of peace, there they returned.

Nordhoff's sudden death in 1947 was a shock and an inconsolable loss to his partner. Hall had been researching for a book about the earliest Polynesian migrations of which so little is known and I felt it would be tonic if he put aside a theme he had often discussed with Nordy and switch to writing his memoirs about his boyhood in Iowa, the happy years at Grinnell, and the circumstances that brought him to Boston and, at the end of his first trip abroad, as a "Canadian" volunteer in the British Army the summer of 1914. He replied:

"Now that Nordy is dead, I write in a vacuum, so to speak. There is, actually, no one here to whom I can appeal for criticism and advice, and as I read over my stuff I often get deeply discouraged and disheartened. I wish that you might have time to give me some criticism in detail."

In *Return to Paradise* James Michener wrote, "James Norman Hall . . . is the most universally loved American ever to have lived in Tahiti, and one might safely include all Europeans in the comparison. His work is a kind of tribal accomplishment. Boys in Papeete will tell you sorrowfully, 'Jimmy is bogged down on Chapter 18.' A Chinese adds, 'I hear Hall is going through hell on Chapter 18. . . .' " But he persisted and I had more than half the manuscript by June 1950, when Jim visited Boston. He was in buoyant spirits, fresh from his Fortieth Reunion at Grinnell where he had received an honorary degree. He mentioned that his left leg felt numb on the flight east and that he was to have a check-up at the Massachusetts General Hospital. My momentary anxiety was forgotten in the affectionate luncheon with Harold Willis and Charlie Codman, who had flown with him in France, but that numbness was a fatal warning. Jim died of a sudden coronary collapse July 6, 1951, and I had to write the epilogue of his unfinished autobiography, *My Island Home*, and of that devoted partnership he never lived to describe.

Among the letters which praised our criticism of anti-Semitism was one from Anne Morrow Lindbergh, written from Vineyard Haven, where she and Charles were temporarily in seclusion.

We are now left virtually alone on this beautiful island and I am having a little more time to catch up on my reading. I have gone through the last Atlantics with much interest. The articles you have been publishing on the Jewish question in America seem to me of outstanding merit and value. Your courageous, dispassionate, and completely sympathetic handling of the whole difficult problem is certainly an important step forward to its possible solution. Many people — like a Jewish friend of mine with whom I was discussing the articles last week — will be grateful to you for the bridge you are attempting to make between age-old misunderstandings. I was particularly impressed by the letters you have published, chosen — from thousands no doubt — with unusual discrimination. The Jewish ones especially are wonderful, some of them so fair, so generous and very moving. I do hope your open and tolerant attitude will have a constructive effect in these intolerant times.

I much admired the way Anne wrote: her early books, *Listen! The Wind*, and *North to the Orient*, in which, serving as her husband's radio operator, she described Charles in his pioneering of the air routes overseas, quelling her fear when fog closed in and forced them to spend the night in the cockpit of their seaplane, were such a brave record of trust. I accepted three poems she wrote of that experience, but could not put them in print before the bombs were falling on London and we agreed to defer their publication until the war's end, when they did appear. In time we printed more than a score of her poems. This brought us together, and my wife and I looked forward to an occasional luncheon with the Lindberghs in New York.

Charles Lindbergh reached the top in one stupendous exploit and stayed there. "No man before me," he wrote in his posthumously published *Autobiography of Values*, "had commanded such freedom over earth," and the words are true, not vainglory. For twenty-five years, from 1925 to 1950, he was continuously airborne and learning. Until I read the *Autobiography* I had not realized that he spent twenty-three hours without sleep before his historic takeoff from Long Island, *and fought to keep himself awake for another thirty-three hours*, "sometimes in a daze in which I saw mirages as real as reality and talked with ghosts riding with me in the fuselage. But the wish for sleep had left by the time I crossed green Ireland's coast, within three miles of my plotted course."

Such superb resourcefulness preserved him: on the goodwill flights over North and South America in the course of which he proved his skill under the most primitive conditions (and won Anne); then, plotting the overseas routes for Juan Trippe and Pan-American, conferring with Robert Goddard, the inventor of jet-propulsion, to whom few others would listen so attentively in 1929, and then gaining the confidence of Henry Ford, who was determined to manufacture airplanes that would not crack up.

In Lindbergh, as in his father, cool Swedish blood predominated — Nancy Astor's nickname for him was "the Swede." His father, whom he worshipped, was one of the members of Congress who voted against our entry into World War I and this same conviction compelled Charles to resign his colonelcy and take the leadership in "America First," which, without him, could never have mustered such popularity.

From 1936 to 1938 he had the opportunity to inspect the air forces of Germany, France, Britain, and the Soviet Union and had no doubt of the Nazis' overwhelming superiority.

When war was declared, Lindbergh stumped the country for non-intervention. His speeches, before tumultuous audiences, filled me with dismay but I asked him to state his case in the *Atlantic*, which he did. He felt no such attachment to Britain as I did and I disagreed with his views. His motivation is plainly stated in the *Autobiography*: "I believed a victory by Germany's European peoples would be preferable to one by Russia's semi-Asiatic Soviet Union. Hitler would not live forever, and I felt sure the Germans would eventually moderate the excesses of his Nazi regime." Neither of us then knew the enormity of the horror being perpetrated on the Jews, but I deplored the fact that he made no mention of their suffering, when he was carried away in oratory. And professionally he underestimated, but by a narrow margin, the supremacy of the Spitfire and the British fighter pilots over Göring's armada.

The bitter division of the country, forced by "America First," was subdued after Pearl Harbor and has shrunk to a small footnote in history. No American will ever forget where he was that Sunday afternoon, December 7, 1941 (in my case, in New Jersey, listening, as the shocking news broke into a radio broadcast of professional football). In the fighting that followed in the Pacific, "test pilot" Lindbergh flew sixty missions; shot down one Japanese plane and was very nearly shot down himself; the experience made him realize "how vulnerable my profession — aviation — had made all peoples . . . the centers of civilization, like Hiroshima, were now the centers of targets." Like other veterans he came home aware of how thin the skin of our civilization is, and himself a much more reflective man. Once again Anne's poetry, which was appearing in the magazine, brought us together. Like his open countenance, Charles's open-mindedness was characteristic and now the spirit of inquiry took him to the Masai in East Africa and to the remote mountain people in Mindanao to confer with tribal leaders and to wonder if they would be "the carriers of evolution." The truth is that Anne, not Charles, was the pacifist, appalled at the thought of the devastation that was coming in 1940, and might come again.

I sent the foregoing pages to Anne with the request that she make any corrections and her reply was so revealing that I asked if I might reprint it for the public record:

I only found one inaccuracy, or wording that implied a position that Charles never took. . . . I was the pacifist; Charles never really was a pacifist and denied being one. You have been very fair and honest about his position during the "American First" anti-war speech-making period, and your dismay over it. It is true, as you say, that he was "appalled at the thought of the devastation that was coming in 1940." In many of his speeches and as early as September 9, 1938, he stated that a war would "throw Europe into chaos. It would be much worse than the last war and would probably result in a communist Europe" (p. 70, *Wartime Journals*). To my mind — as well as to yours — he never expressed enough sympathy with the British, although in one of his later speeches he denied that he wanted a German victory and said he believed it would be a tragedy to the whole world if Britain were defeated. (See Cole's *America First.*) I also, as you know, deplored the Des Moines speech and urged him not to give it. He did not know — nor did many of us — as you fairly state, "the enormity of the horror being perpetrated on the Jews." But he saw the evidence of it with his own eyes when he witnessed the remains of Camp Dora shortly after the war on his mission to inspect the rocket factories at Nordhausen and then wrote in his *Journals* (p. 995), "Here was a place where men and life and death had reached the lowest form of degradation." So he did indeed learn by his war experience, as you put it succinctly, "how thin the skin of our civilization is."

CHAPTER

III

The attack on Pearl Harbor swept away all but one illusion. Roosevelt haters have claimed that the President deliberately provoked it and expected it. The fact is that on December 5 Admiral Hart, Commander of our Asiatic Fleet, Vice-Admiral Tom Phillips of the British Navy, and General MacArthur, at a precautionary meeting in Manila, discussed the grave situation, unanimous in the belief that Pearl Harbor lay beyond the reach of Japanese war planes. This World War I credulity was still in MacArthur's mind when he was caught with his planes down in the Philippines *five hours after* he had been warned of our losses at Pearl. In truth, the Japanese were at the outset farsighted and clever, and the Allies confused and overconfident, as Churchill admitted. Ten days after the attack I lunched with Eric Hodgins, the boisterous editor of *Fortune*, at the University Club in New York. He paused at the threshold of the dining room and pointed to the floor. "Here," he said, "a plaque should be inserted saying, 'On this spot the evening of December 6, 1941, Admiral Barnacle, U.S.N., stated that under no circumstances would the Japs dare to attack Pearl Harbor.' I heard him."

It took time to put the *Atlantic* on a war footing, although we did expect that paper would be rationed. As a result of our rising circulation — my radio program helped that — and an increase in advertising, our president, Dick Danielson, declared a Christmas bonus for all employees, and my "honorarium," as Mr. Sedgwick used to call it, which had been pegged at $9,500, was increased by a thousand. It was my first bonus and an indication that the magazine was beginning to recover.

Dick had served in Europe in Military Intelligence in the First

World War, and shortly he and Barbara moved to Washington, where he was recommissioned in the same branch and assigned to the African desk. He was twelve years my senior and his decision intensified my irresolution. Should I follow him? "It is required of a man," said Justice Oliver Wendell Holmes, who had been three times wounded in the Civil War, "that he should share the action and passion of his time at the peril of being judged not to have lived." That great truth troubled me.

Several of my younger friends were already in the Army Air Force, being trained for Intelligence. I should have preferred that to writing speeches in Washington. But what was binding was my promise to Barbara when she had asked if I could really make a go of the *Atlantic*. At the age of forty-four, and after only a two-year trial, could I walk away from that pledge? One's shortcomings are magnified in the dark. One of mine was money. Fritzy, my dear wife, and I had no inheritance to fall back on, our families had lost everything in the Depression; my savings were $10,000 in a mutual fund and two hundred shares of Atlantic stock, which I had borrowed the money to buy. Sara, our daughter, was a year away from college, and young Ted, age seven, in day school. Most of my lecture fees went to support my mother. In the watches of the night I worried over the right decision. I cared deeply about the survival of the *Atlantic*.

In June 1942, my Harvard class held its Twentieth Reunion, a one-day affair at the Dedham Country Club. It would be more serious than alcoholic and the Committee had asked me to arrange a seminar, morning and afternoon, in which each speaker had ten minutes to tell what he was doing: I called on our doctors in uniform, one just back from Guadalcanal, another from the Chelsea Naval Hospital, where he'd been caring for seamen whose ships had been torpedoed; there were lawyers serving under the Judge Advocate General, architects now devising camouflage, lieutenant colonels in Procurement, and the uncommitted.

It was Judge Charles C. Cabot of Boston who spoke for the last. "Each one of us has been struggling to determine where his duty lies. I admire those of you who have gone immediately into the service. I envy you. But we cannot have a strong fist without a strong arm back of it. I, for one, believe it is my responsibility to stay here and do what I can to strengthen that fist." Uttered with such quiet conviction, Charlie's words helped me decide. I would stand by my promise and do my utmost to make the *Atlantic* a vital force.

*　*　*

Our publisher, Donald B. Synder, had vision; he anticipated the reader's reaction and he now proposed three changes that would make the *Atlantic* more serviceable. First, it was imperative to enlarge the size of the pages and the size of the type. He asked for an 11-point (in the past it had been as small as 8), and wider spacing. On the enlarged page we could print, with minute trimming, the same advertisements that were scheduled for *Time* and *Newsweek* (and they flowed in beyond expectation).

Next, he suggested four "Atlantic Reports," which would be the first editorial matter in each issue. They would summarize where we stood and then forecast what to expect; they must be authoritative, anonymous, and the last copy to go to press. We opened with "The European Front"; as this was most subject to change I wanted the writer to be nearby and chose the dependable James Powers of the *Boston Globe*. Second, "The Pacific War" by George Taylor of the University of Washington, who had followed Mao in his march across China, and was untainted by the "China Lobby." For "Latin America" there was only one knowledgeable specialist, Duncan Aikman, and only his employer, Nelson Rockefeller, the Coordinator of Inter-American Affairs, knew that he wrote it. And for "Washington" I had to have Herbert Elliston, the tireless and confidential editor of the *Washington Post*. The Reports were a war expedient that took some of the pressure off the saddle of the magazine; they were frankly envied by *Harper's*, and advertisers began to ask for a position facing them. A monthly poll of our subscribers during the years 1942–1944, querying what they liked — or disliked — showed that the first thing men turned to was "The Washington Report."

Don's third innovation was a new department he called "Accent on Living" — he said they were the only three words he ever published in the *Atlantic* — a department of short pieces, prose and verse, satirical, appetizing, and a relief from death and destruction. Traditionally, the magazine had never accepted pictures, but we needed comic relief! He went looking for the right artist.

Meanwhile, I was recruiting my staff, beginning with an associate editor. I spoke to Louis Lyons, Curator of the Nieman Fellows, the hand-picked journalists in mid-career who came to Harvard for a year to study what they pleased; as their advisor Louis might know if one was looking for a different pitch. Lyons mentioned the opening to Charles W. Morton, one of the bright lights on the *Boston Evening Transcript* in its last years, adding his own qualification for the job: "The rest of the staff is mostly women. I believe they pay very little."

Morton applied and my good friend David McCord seconded his application. "Charlie's published a number of pieces in the *New Yorker*," he said. "Ross even gave him a tryout as a managing editor. He's frank and sometimes cantankerous, but if you two can hit it off, I think you'll find him valuable." I asked Morton to lunch with Don and me at the St. Botolph Club, where I'd known him casually but had never thought of putting one and one together. For a month I equivocated, looking over other possibilities, then telephoned him that he'd been elected and that I'd like to talk terms with him at the Club. Charlie describes what followed, in words I cherish, at the close of his autobiography, *It Has Its Charm*:

We sat down together that Sunday afternoon and quickly came to an agreement. The starting salary was not at all what I needed, but I was sure it was the right place for me. Much better days would come, I thought, and they did. The quarter-century from that time to this was all that I could have wished it to be. There never was a moment when I would have changed places with anyone, anywhere.

We complemented each other: where I was a believer, he was a skeptic. His years on the *Transcript* had convinced him that the authorities were usually to be mistrusted, society people were always gullible, and that the police hadn't yet caught the criminal. He was sure all professional sports were fixed, except the Indianapolis "500" and if he could find the money to get there each May, go he would. He had no patience with the pompous and scoffed at the long literary revaluations which in dull times had been the *Atlantic*'s stock-in-trade: He called them "On Rereading Doakes."

Charlie was my age, a smallish man, fastidiously dressed, with an original, sharply amusing mind behind a scowling countenance. But when the scowl broke and he relaxed, screwing his features into disbelief with that flat, taunting laughter, no one could resist him. He was a native of Omaha, Nebraska, and it was impossible to fool him about the West. He knew the ranches, real and dude; was expert at stud poker ("Poker is no fun unless it hurts if you lose"); and had a soft heart for bull terriers and fast cars. He had been sent east to school and to Williams College, but did not tarry for a degree after he fell in love with Mildred "of the violet eyes," to whom he dedicated his books. They were married and took their honeymoon on his Indian motorcycle and sidecar (the trunk of which held what they couldn't stuff into their one bag), riding it from Omaha to the New York pier of the *Mauritania*, and, after the crossing, on to Paris and the south of France until they ran out of money in Marseilles. There they waited, hoarding their last francs, living on French bread and *vin du pays* until at last cash was cabled from home.

Charlie joined me in 1941 as Associate Editor and was ever after indispensable. At the outset I did not find it easy to give him a tough assignment, and when it was unavoidable, would preface my request with "Doc." "Doc, would you mind . . . ?" "I wish you wouldn't call me that," Charlie said one day. "Every time I hear that word I know something unpleasant is coming." He was more of a worrier than I. He was the most overpunctual man I have ever worked with: in the summer by three-fifteen he'd start worrying about catching the four-fifty-six train to Rockport, and not infrequently boarded an earlier one, then waited patiently for Mildred to pick him up. He continually worried about the *Atlantic*'s inventory. Manuscripts lose their zest if they are held too long unpublished, and the authors, naturally, grow impatient. Except for poetry I kept a lean cupboard, and I remember once on my return from England how dolefully he greeted me with "Ted, we really haven't received a *single decent* piece since you left." "Great!" I said. "Our hands are free. I brought back a couple of good things that can go right in and let's telephone the agents to see what's new." He used to rib me about this.

He had served at the *New Yorker* long enough to know Harold Ross's four indispensables: E. B. and Katharine White, Wolcott Gibbs, and James Thurber. In New York Charlie and John Mosher had read manuscripts, writing on each rejection slip in longhand the word "Sorry," and a meaningless initial beneath, to supply the personal touch Ross wanted. With this in mind Charlie composed rejection letters of no more than three sentences, so pithy that he left behind him a bare desk at day's end.

It was Charlie's assortment of prejudices that made him the ideal editor of our new "Accent on Living." He could be as persuasive about what he liked as he was derisive about what he didn't. He was an exquisite, if finicky, cook, had long collected recipes from his favorite restaurants, and now began to serve up these delicacies to *Atlantic* readers. There was only one proper clam chowder, Charlie proclaimed, as it was served at Locke-Ober's in Boston; the Philadelphia chowder with tomato in it was a thin fraud. (Many letters surged in from amateur chefs describing their chowders.)

On a July morning, after having dined the night before at his favorite rathskeller in New York, he flew back to Boston with a strudel stuffed with cheese. The plane had been standing on the runway in the heat, and Charlie, among the first passengers to enter, deposited his parcel, unobserved, in the overhead compartment to the right and then seated himself at the rear. As the cheese warmed up, the odor was pervasive, even in flight, but neither stewardess could locate it. In Boston the last to depart, Charlie reached up for his trophy and was caught in the act. "You bastard!" said the two stewardesses.

Off on a summer holiday he and Mildred drove to Nova Scotia and happened upon an inn with outlying cottages on a chain of lakes at South Milford. The cuisine was so delectable that they stopped to spend the rest of their vacation there and the appetizing piece he wrote about it for "Accent" drew in more than sixty other couples in the next two years, including the Weekses and the E. B. Whites.

Charlie had a sharp eye for pretentious English and he exploded when a reporter on the *Boston Globe* referred to the banana as "that elongated yellow fruit." He declared war on this nonsense and thereafter kept a file of such absurdities for "Accent." He was just as merciless about the clichés with which people describe their favorite hobbies: fishing, hunting, pets, or antiques, and he invented a form of parody that I probably inspired with my delight in fly-fishing.

It went like this, leaving blanks for the reader to fill in:

The fishing story must begin with a modest statement of the author's credentials: "I've fished for the mighty_____off Acapulco and the battling_____along the Florida Keys. I've seen a maddened_____ swamp a dory off Wedgeport, but for sheer power and gameness I've seen nothing that can equal, pound for pound, a_____."

That's a perfectly workable opening paragraph for any fishing story. . . . Guides are always terse, monosyllabic men — which saves the author from writing much improbable dialogue and dialect. They grunt or they gesture, but that's about all. . . . ("We never did learn Joe's last name, but he taught us all there was to know about_____s.") . . . And so on to that mysterious locality known only to Joe. . . . "It looked like the last place in the world to try for_____s, but Joe merely grunted and gestured vaguely at the water. "_____here," he said. "Big one." (Any angler can take it from there.) . . . DOWN goes the rod again, OUT screams the line. . . . I tried to brake it with my thumb. Naturally enough, he gets a bad burn on his thumb. More leaps, lunges, a page or so of them. Suddenly, my line went ominously slack. I began frantically reeling in. "_____ gone," Joe grunted.

Charlie used this formula, just often enough, and it always brought down the house.

In Carl Rose Charlie found the ideal illustrator to point up

"Accent." For the fish story he drew Charlie at his typewriter, and, looking down at him from the wall above, a gigantic stuffed fish with a cynical eye. Charlie's pieces set the pace for other gaieties, from John Gould in Maine, Gilbert Seldes in New York, Wallace Stegner describing the antics of his pet turtle, Achilles. Charlie's deadpan account of some wealthy New Yorkers, professing to enjoy a summer without modern conveniences, on Little Chokeberry Island — these provided the amusement we needed.

Phoebe-Lou Adams, a keen, irreverent reader, went scouting for light verse, of which we had printed far too little. She selected first this by Robert Graves, delightful and prolific after his long and profitable absence in fiction.

THE PERSIAN VERSION

Truth-loving Persians do not dwell upon
The trivial skirmish fought near Marathon.
As for the Greek theatrical tradition
Which represents that summer's expedition
Not as a mere reconnaissance in force
By three brigades of foot and one of horse
(Their left flank covered by some obsolete
Light craft detached from the main Persian fleet)
But as a grandiose, ill-starred attempt
To conquer Greece — they treat it with contempt;
And only incidentally refute
Major Greek claims, by stressing what repute
The Persian monarch and the Persian nation
Won by this salutary demonstration:
Despite a strong defense and adverse weather
All arms combined magnificently together.

Then she discovered another Englishman, R. P. Lister, so amusing and versatile that in all we printed sixty-five of his deft lyrics. After his first two and a half years the *New Yorker* cut in on us, and he divided his work between the two magazines until 1971. Here is a good Lister:

THE OWLET AND THE GAMEKEEPER

A little fluffy owlet, short and fat,
Upon the topknot of a fir tree sat;
He thought of baby rabbits and of mice,
He thought of human beings once or twice.
It can be said, and said without demur,
He was a most profound philosopher.

A keeper passed, a sturdy realist;
He raised his gun and aimed; and fired; and missed.

And so, my dearest pillicocks, we see
Two kinds of creature on this earth there be;
One thinks and dreams and idles in the sun,
The other Works and Acts and Gets Things Done.
Without the Keeper we'd be in a mess;
We would not miss the owl; yet none the less
The keeper missed him. Oftener than not
The man of action's such a rotten shot.

The mass of unsolicited manuscripts known as "The Generals" also yielded unexpected trophies, such as the page of haiku by a young naval officer stationed in Japan, who wrote, among others:

The Admiral is being court-martialed
How refreshing
The wind from the mountain.

He insisted on anonymity because, as he put it, "The Navy's eye is bloodshot but keen."

Or again, this charmer by Winona McClintic:

LAMENT FOR A DEAD SEA-OTTER

Heedless of dirt and uncombed whiskers
She keeps her lone regard
Not for those dream-attended baskers
Or romping herd.

Mindful of the search over the water,
No familiar yelp,
Seeking the furred and watchful lover
Through the kelp.

Asleep in the island-lapping shallow
Where the waters suck,
Lying with crossed paws in a hollow
Is Amikuk.

Rather than return to wave with the others
A clever, lonely paw,
She would be where the gull its sea-hoard gathers,
Where he is now.

Charlie was fussy about secretaries until he got a good one. His best was Kay Ellis and I ruthlessly appropriated her after her first year in the office. Kay, in her twenties, was slim and dark-haired, with a Tennessee accent. She came with a superlative recommendation from her former boss in Nashville and we were unaware of how dubious she was whether she could follow the barbarous Yankee way of talking. The night before her trial run for Charlie she persuaded an alcoholic Bostonian in her boardinghouse to read aloud while she tried to convert the alien sounds into shorthand. No fear; she had good ears and learned fast.

My desk was the last stop for those manuscripts we were pleased to accept and the many others about which there were divided opinions. We offered suggestions, and, not infrequently, accepted the revision. Either way Kay was determined not to let them hover; somehow she found time to read the problems and with a "Don't you think we might send back old Mr. Peabody's recollections before they become a bore?" she'd poke me to decide. My correspondence was large and it surprised me that she could cope with it and still read so much. Once, as I was dictating my suggestions for a controversial piece, I paused, and asked, "Kay, what do you think?" Her eyes widened, but her judgment was so pertinent that I knew we had a Reader ready for promotion.

An editorial secretary is a woman who enjoys being involved, not emotionally but vigilantly in the multitude of decisions that are hanging fire. She must know what promising manuscripts are expected, and if they're late; she keeps in mind what the boss is planning for the next issue, and his hopes beyond. She has accustomed herself to the rhythm of his dictation, catches his repetitions when he is struggling with a difficult letter, and consults the dictionary if he surprises her with an unfamiliar word. Letters of rejection are her most sensitive concern and a dreaded error occurs if the readers' report — ours were summarized on a single sheet — with candid, denigrating comments, is inadvertently enclosed between the pages of a rejected contribution. This does occur occasionally, with resulting fury at one end and apology from the other.

Washington in the months after Pearl Harbor was a place of nervous intensity, crowded with men in uniform and new civilian administrators, working eighteen hours a day. After the news of Rommel's defeat of the British in Libya the mood was bleak; it was our defeat, too, because the light Stuart tank and the cumbersome Grant tanks with the gun on the side, which we supplied to the British 8th Army, were both vulnerable, as Major Henry Cabot Lodge reported from the front. One heard but did not print that our submarine commanders were returning to base outraged at the high percentage of duds in our stale torpedoes. Our failures led Anne O'Hare McCormick to say that we might not have a better military brain than Germany but our industrial brain was unrivaled — and we'd better prove it. The furious fighting with which the 2nd Division of Marines won their foothold on Guadalcanal was our only word of cheer from the Pacific.

An editor looking for tips must avoid being a nuisance, and there were only three friends I could hope to see before noon. Herbert Elliston didn't object to my talking to him at ten o'clock, before he began planning the editorials for the *Washington Post*. Herb was a Yorkshireman with a thick burr in his accent, who had represented the *Manchester Guardian* in China and later had been called to Boston as economics editor of the *Christian Science Monitor*. My wife, Fritzy, and I had seen a good deal of him and his beautiful wife, Joanne, and he sought my advice when Eugene Meyer offered him the editorship of the *Post*, then second-rate.

I told him it was the chance of a lifetime. Mr. Meyer once remarked to me that to be happy a man ought to change his job every twenty-five years. He had made his fortune on Wall Street at an early age and when President Wilson appointed him head of the Federal Reserve in 1917, Meyer plunged into national finance and was drawn to Washington. Sagacious and public-spirited, he and his great-hearted, intelligent wife, Agnes, maintained a "house of truth" that was a delight to visit. Together they gave Herbert advice and the backing which helped him lift the *Post* to its prestige in ten years. Herbert's burly stamina kept him keenly alert at cocktail and dinner parties; he met everyone who was coming or going, and could tell me of those who were in a position to write. He was making our Washington Report a scintillating reflection of the mood of the Capital and he was my most helpful scout. I frequently stayed with him, especially in the torrid months when Joanne was cooling off in Peterborough, New Hampshire.

While he was Librarian of Congress Archibald MacLeish instilled new life in that ancient institution. He widened the search for historic photographs; he set up a collection of recordings, such as Will Lomax of Texas had made of the cowboy ballads and songs of the chain gang sung by that talented black lifer, "Leadbelly." Also he established fellowships for writers-in-exile, like Aléxis Léger (St.-John Perse) and Thomas Mann. These, of course, were additions to the traditional budget and Archie had to hold his temper when the appropriation for such novelties was questioned at the Congressional hearings. "When you become so attached to an institution that you bleed when it's criticized," he told me, "it's time to get out."

MacLeish went on to serve in the Office of War Information, then the State Department, and eventually as our representative to UNESCO. He was a valuable literary adviser and in critical times his prose and poetry could stir, as no one else's, the adrenalin of patriotism.

My visits to Walter Lippmann were timed for the late morning when I was sure he had finished writing his column, "Today and Tomorrow." He was an early riser so I would usually appear after eleven and sit opposite him at his desk in the library. He was relaxed in an old sweater, shirt open at the throat, and in answer to my somewhat nervous questioning his face would be alight and the "O-ho, ho" of his laugh put me more at ease.

In the spring of 1936 Mr. Sedgwick caught Lippmann in a receptive mood and, at recurring meetings at the Century Club in New York, gave him the essential encouragement to write *The Good Society*, a book we published in part in the magazine and then under the Atlantic–Little, Brown imprint.

In Walter's words, "It was written to be read after a war that had not yet taken place," and I had misgivings about it. The book was divided into two parts, and they did not meld. In the first half he analyzed the complacency and bad judgment which had demoralized Britain and France and left us unarmed in the face of the ever-increasing power of the dictators, and this was sharp as a cleaver. In the second half he proposed the reforms (not much dissimilar from those in the New Deal he had accepted with a pinch of salt), which would shape a "good society" if the democracies prevailed. But what mainly concerned him was the demoralization of democracy. The sale was disappointing — 16,000 copies — and the revised edition in 1941 found few takers; the public by then being too engrossed in the war he had prophesied. He had left his New York publishers to become an *Atlantic* author and it was my responsibility to keep him one.

I held him in awe, was fearful of seeming naive and fascinated by his looks. His wife, Helen, said he looked like an owl and with that fine head of hair, the high cheekbones, and widely spaced eyes, perhaps he did — but a handsome one. I, who after a false start in mechanical engineering had been reading all my life to catch up, marveled at one who had mastered the classics at twenty, with a memory that led him precisely to the book or reference he needed.

Our intimacy began when he questioned me about the finances of the *Atlantic*. "Yes, you're right," he said, "the magazine must never leave Boston. Your New England heritage still has a hold on families that once lived there. I'm surprised that you can still depend more on your subscribers than on advertising. . . ." and he went on to compare our economy with that of the *New Republic*, which he had founded with Herbert Croly.

When I was in town Helen would sometimes include me in one of their parties, taking me with them for cocktails or at their own table. Wartime dinners ended promptly at ten o'clock, and at five minutes before ten the Lippmann poodles, very large for their breed, would rouse themselves from beneath the piano, where they had been sleeping, and walking over to one or another of the guests, stretch themselves with an alligator yawn. On one occasion, "Courage," the male, addressed himself to Mr. Nabuco, the Brazilian Ambassador, who had been talking to our hostess. "I get the signal," he said. "But, Helen, before I go I wonder if you've heard of the recent poll on why Frenchmen get up at night?"

"No," Helen hadn't.

"Four percent," he said, "get up for natural causes. Five percent get up to shut the window. And ninety-one percent get up to go home. Good-night."

In the early spring I wrote Lippmann that I was trying to get an article by Stalin, and was coming down for an appointment with Maxim Litvinov, the Soviet Ambassador. At that time when the Russians were taking such punishment there was mounting sympathy here as we realized they would have to bear the brunt until we had gathered our strength. Gardner Cowles, the editor of *Look*, on his trip around the world with Wendell Willkie, had brought several questions with him to an interview with Stalin, and the replies, which were not sensational, he received permission to print. The interview, with a gee-whiz foreword, produced a phenomenal sale of *Look* on the newsstands. If Mike could do it, so perhaps could I, and after reading some of Stalin's recent speeches, I framed five leading questions, predicated on Hitler's defeat, and sent a copy of them ahead to the Soviet Embassy.

My appointment with Litvinov was set for April 1, 1942, and the evening before I accompanied the Lippmanns to a concert by the Boston Symphony Orchestra in Constitution Hall for the benefit of the Russian War Relief. The place was packed. We stood, first, for the playing of the national anthem of the USSR and then the "Star-Spangled Banner," after which Koussevitzky, at his best, conducted an all-Russian program: Prokofiev's "Classical Symphony," the 6th Symphony of Shostakovich, and Symphony No. 5 in E Minor by Tchaikovsky. It was stirring, the applause recalled "K" again and again, and when it was over many of us went on to a reception at the Russian Embassy. Refreshments were served on the old gold plate, and emotion had left us ready for the vodka and the delectable caviar on black bread. Madame Litvinov was a Scot, and I had an appreciative word with her and the English-speaking Ambassador before returning to the vodka.

The following morning I went off jauntily to the Soviet Consulate. There was not the slightest recognition of last evening's pleasantry as Litvinov shook my hand and motioned me to a seat. My letter was on his desk, and swiftly he brushed me off. "Mr. Weeks, I could not possibly forward your request to Moscow. Like most Americans you do not seem to realize how desperate, how very hard pressed we are. The British won't fight and we fear you won't be ready in time." He rose and the interview was over.

When I related this to Walter, he burst out laughing. "Well, I don't think I'd try that again."

But the British were fighting, more effectively than the Russian would admit. One humid evening that June the four of us, Walter, Helen, Air Chief Marshal Peter Portal, and I, sat in the Lippmanns' garden after dinner, enjoying the cool while the airman described the audacity and exhaustion of the RAF during the Battle of Britain. They had the advantage of radar but the fighter pilots went up on five or six combat missions a day, and when the "wastage" (his word) rose to more than 700 pilots a month, they relied on the ablest sergeants who had been servicing the planes. "Good men, too. And by that margin we drove off Göring's bombers."

In the first week of December 1942 I was on my way to Detroit on a lecture trip, traveling in a Pullman, all the other seats of which were occupied by members of the National Association of Manufacturers, homeward bound from a convention. They were drinking and, in strident voices, jeering at the defeat of the British in the desert. "That'll teach the Limeys," said one of them, and their laughter betrayed their ignorance of what Britain — and its fleet — meant to us. It was such an infuriating revelation of Isolationism that I boiled, and that evening from my hotel I wired Lippmann saying that I must see him at the end of my trip.

When we met in his library I described what I had overheard in the Pullman. "You're the only man in the country those damn baboons will listen to," I said. "Walter, you really must spell out for people like that what our foreign policy is, and why the survival of Britain is so crucial."

He reached down to the lower drawer of the desk. "I began writing this last summer," he said as he handed me a manuscript. "There are two chapters and they haven't been typed. If you can read my handwriting, see what you think." Walter's handwriting was so minute that I often wished for a magnifying glass. He left me alone and as I read, slowly, I realized that this was what I wanted him to write. On my return to Boston I sent this memorandum to our publishing partners at Little, Brown:

WALTER LIPPMANN'S BOOK: — 1/8/43

. . . The recent Convention of the National Association of Manufacturers revealed how many of the leaders in Big Business still hanker for our return to an unfettered economy and how little they think of the reciprocal trade treaties. . . . On my recent swing through the Middle West, I rode . . . through five states and was both impressed and depressed by the suspicion of Willkie, by the Republican complaints of "regulation" and by the vagueness with which they viewed our foreign commitments after the war. I think the idea is widespread throughout the country that it is up to us to take a leading part in the post-war reconstruction. But I think it is equally true that people have only a vague notion of what this involves and that unless someone can produce immediately a practical demonstration of the foreign and economic policies we need, the feeling of commitment may give way to an exasperating desire to get back into our own cyclone cellar. In short, what I am seeking is an American "Economic Consequences of the Peace," to be written this year. . . .

Lippmann has the most direct access to industrialists, management and labor. . . . The question is, do these two chapters of a book which he projected last summer have in them source material which bears upon this urgent need which I have tried to outline.

Alfred McIntyre, the President of Little, Brown, and Raymond Everitt, his understudy, caught fire as I hoped they would; they told me that if Walter could complete the manuscript in three months we could have bound books in May. I wired him: "Can't exaggerate importance we attach to your opening chapters. Am confident you have it in your power to develop this argument into a short book of immense and immediate influence. . . ."

Lippmann cut his column to two a week and because so much of the argument had been in mind since summer, the writing was fast and incisive. His title was *U.S. Foreign Policy, Shield of the Republic.* The complete manuscript of 45,000 words was in my hands in mid-March and copies of it were submitted to Dean Paul Buck of Harvard, Robert Lee Wolff in the O.S.S., and Assistant Professor Ruhl J. Bartlett of Tufts for their scrutiny.

Meanwhile, in several pages of notes, I was shaving down the text, knocking out the dead word "thesis," and a couple of dozen "I submits" and "in our inquiry" and cheering when Lippmann predicted that if in the coming election of 1944 "we again fail to form a national policy, the acid of that failure will be with us for ages to come, corroding our self-confidence and our self-respect." The historians' suggestions and mine were sped to Washington and after Walter's revision the manuscript went to press. We had bound books in May.

Unlike *The Good Society* this was a strong and very personal book, and the more appealing because of his admission at the outset of his mistaken acceptance of our foreign policy which since 1900 had left the nation "unprepared to wage war or make peace and divided within itself. . . ." His new conclusions, he said, "came slowly over thirty years and as a result of many false starts, mistaken judgments, and serious disappointments. They represent what I now think I have learned, not at all what I always knew."

The success of *U.S. Foreign Policy* was due in part to the timing: so many people, at home, and the world over, wanted to know what course we had in mind. It must also have come as a jolt to many Americans, particularly those in the midlands, to realize that beginning with Theodore Roosevelt our "empire" had in fact emerged, calling for commitments to protect the Philippines, some 7,000 miles away, Hawaii, Cuba, and Puerto Rico, as well as Alaska, our vast province at the back door of the Soviet Union. It must have come as a revelation to some foreign readers to hear with what innocence and ineptitude we had disengaged from our allies after the Treaty of Versailles, and disarmed as if we had not a care in the world.

We could not keep the book in stock; there were six printings in June. The Book-of-the-Month Club made it a special selection, distributing 320,000 copies; it was syndicated in over two hundred newspapers in the United States and abroad, and after publication it was again serialized in the *Reader's Digest*. The foreign rights were sold to Britain, Spain, Portugal, Sweden, France, Norway, Italy, China, even for a German edition. In all I estimated that *U.S. Foreign Policy* had been shown to and, I hoped, taken seriously by 13,000,000 readers. It was Lippmann's most popular book.

As *U.S. Foreign Policy* was going to press William Allen White, the newspaper editor in Emporia, Kansas, who expressed the thinking of the prairie states better than any other, telephoned Lippmann urging him to add another chapter showing how the alliance of the four great powers, Russia, Britain, China, and ourselves, could become the means of a lasting peace. Walter replied that he could not write that chapter while the outcome of the war was still uncertain and until we could understand "in its grand outlines how it would be won." But with this prodding, *U.S. War Aims* was written and went on sale three months after "Operation Overlord" had breached Hitler's stronghold.

Of Lippmann's warnings two were disturbing: "For if the worst that men fear is going to happen, it will be upon the solidarity of Western Europe and the Americas that we shall have to rely" and, secondly, "Fate has brought it about that America is at the center, no longer on the edges, of Western civilization. In this resides the American destiny. We could refuse it. If we do, Western civilization, which is the glory of our world, will become a disorganized and decaying fringe around the Soviet Union and the emergent peoples of Asia. We shall be equal to our destiny if we comprehend it. The vision is there and our people need not perish."

My help with the two books brought us closer. Walter thanked me in print and he began to take me with him to restricted press conferences. I remember that sweltering day later when we listened to General Wavell's account of his retreat in Burma. He seemed haggard with fatigue as he spoke to us morosely, brightening when he praised the Gurkhas' heroism, darkening when he mentioned certain Indian divisions which had failed him, all this told in the presence of Indian staff officers, their faces impassive.

In summer Washington is tropical; one stepped out of the hotel into heat like that of a furnace. There was a restaurant not far from the Mayflower, air-conditioned and known for its delicious crabmeat and salads. Here I used to lunch with Betty Woods, the lovely receptionist at the British Embassy, when I could catch her, or with Milo Perkins — Milo was a no-nonsense Texan who had built up the Board of Economic Warfare into a powerful, well-run agency. I remember his telling me of a meeting with the top officials of the United Automobile Workers. After their business was settled Milo said to them casually, "You know, if you boys invested your pension funds in General Motors stock, it wouldn't be long before you'd have quite a say in the management." They looked at him steadily for a moment before one of them replied, "That's not the sort of responsibility we're after."

Archie MacLeish, once speaking of his work at the Library of Congress, had said, "This is a lonely job." When I mentioned this to

Walter, he repeated, rather somberly, *"This* is a lonely job," yet I felt that in the crescendo of the war he wanted no other, certainly nothing official. The position he had created for himself in the Capital was unique. In a shy way he became very kind to me and it was a god-send one evening when Helen said, "Ted, it must be awfully sticky in your hotel. Why don't you stay here in our guest room? It will be cooler — and I'll be frank if we can't have you." I could not have asked for a happier invitation: I came and went, and ofter joined them in their afternoon walks along the Old Canal, with the poodles, "Courage" and "Victoria," who would plunge into the water until cool, then dash to catch up and shake themselves off at our feet.

I became a come-and-go guest, having the fun of sitting beside Clover Dulles or Alice Longworth at dinner or the not-so-much-fun of being teased by Dean Acheson. The sight of Walter, with whom he frequently disagreed, brought on Dean's hauteur, the hauteur with which he was born and which made him so uncomfortable for Congress to deal with. "Well, Ted, how are the women's clubs?" was his invariable taunt, never "How is the magazine?" Useless to explain that I was lecturing as often at universities — just grin and bear it!

On every Washington visit I reported to Dick and Barbara Danielson about how the *Atlantic* was faring. The War Rationing Board had allocated a maximum tonnage of paper for every periodical and with our larger page our ration was just sufficient for a monthly edition of 120,000 copies. Our subscribers were considerably under that figure when I took over the magazine, but now there was a steady increase and, as the number went up, the copies we put on the newsstands went down.

They were elated at the success of Walter's *U.S. Foreign Policy.* I could see that Dick was itching to get away from the Pentagon, and he swore me to secrecy when he confided that he might soon be outward bound for Africa.

In June 1943, a letter from Harold Butler of the British Embassy informed me that the Ministry of Information was inviting a small number of American editors to observe the British war effort, and that he hoped I could arrange to be one of the first quartet in early July. Space would be reserved for us on a British aircraft and we would be guests of the Ministry for six weeks. I had not seen England since my Fiske Fellowship at Trinity College, Cambridge, twenty years earlier, and I accepted, happy to learn that my companions would be Laurence Winship of the *Boston Globe*, an old friend; Ralph McGill of the *Atlanta Constitution*, whom I had heard speak at Harvard, and Oliver

C. Keller of the *Pittsburgh Post-Gazette*, for whom Winship had a high regard.

This would be my first flight across the Atlantic, traveling in an unheated seaplane, and I was told that it would be plenty cold when we reached an altitude of 10,000 feet, so I decided to wear a heavy tweed jacket and advised Winship to do the same. In my boyhood I could get seasick on a swaying trolley, traveling from Elizabeth to Newark, New Jersey, a distance of six miles. But, like Will Rogers, I had learned to tranquilize my stomach (and imagination) for longer and longer flights. Still, it might be a precaution to carry some Dramamine.

Remembering how the English sanctify their weekends, I expected that the Ministry would arrange our schedule through the week but leave us to our own devices Saturday and Sunday. Walter Lippmann had given me letters to three friends, one of them Lady Sybil Colefax, whose dinners were famous. I wrote ahead to *Atlantic* contributors H. M. Tomlinson, Rebecca West, H. E. Bates, and Nora Waln, and to Dick Creswick, with whom I had shared rooms at Trinity in 1923. Dick, an ardent bookman, had gained distinction as the director of the Bodleian Library, and I asked if he and Agnes could put me up for a weekend in Oxford. I assumed that we would be traveling much of the time and so purchased drip-dry shirts, and nylons, lipsticks, soap, and cigarettes with which to thank my British hosts.

Winship and I flew down to Baltimore together where the temperature in the early evening was 90°. Larry, who was short and solid, was perspiring in his heavy tweed; I too, and I could not avoid his look of reproach. We had been directed to an inconspicuous hotel and in a large private room met and had drinks with our fellow editors. Ralph McGill, the courageous Southern liberal, who had a fine head on broad shoulders, rumpled black hair, an appealing smile, and a creaky voice. Keller, the youngest of us, was tall and reserved. We speculated about our English shipmates who were beginning to fill the room; some were authoritative, all in mufti, many of them carrying large bundles in brown paper concealing their military equipment as Eire, where we would pause for fuel, was neutral, and did not admit combatants in uniform. A Parliamentary Commission, headed by Lord Penny, was returning from Washington, and took precedence. There were forty-one of us, and about 11 P.M. our gear was stowed into a bus which took us to a dimly lit marina — these precautions ostensibly to avoid any watchful German agent.

The white seaplane was furnished with low iron-leg canvas benches and those who had been aboard before swiftly preempted the corners where one could lounge on one's side. Outwitted, I shared a center seat in upright contact with Henry Clay, a British economist; Winship, still scowling, kept his distance. Engineers in coveralls fiddled about and disappeared; the motors purred, roared, and throttled down. After midnight while Clay and I were chatting I discovered that we were airborne. It grew cold and colder; my Harris tweed wasn't enough; I saw Larry wave as he put on his raincoat. A steward appeared, doling out tiny pillows and thin strips of blanket; the one provided for the economist and myself covered both laps — if it was not monopolized. The cabin was piercingly cold. "Mr. Clay," I said, "have you ever heard of the American custom of 'bundling'?" "No, can't say I have." "Well, first you take off your shoes," and I began to do so. "Yes, you too — and then we lie side by side, with the blanket and raincoats on top." Our feet had to hang over but it was warmer, soon sleepily so. We awoke as the seaplane made its approach to Gander. "I say, that's not bad!" exclaimed Henry Clay.

It was a bright Labrador morning with a north wind ruffling the very blue water. Except for the airport, Gander was desolate. I chatted with a Canadian fighter pilot, convalescing on clerical duty, who said the salmon fishing wasn't bad if you didn't mind being eaten by black flies. In the shanty dining room we were served steak — "the last for some time!" — and then resumed our places for the second night's crossing. I had with me a pamphlet put out by the American Iron and Steel Institute which spoke quite critically, not of the quality of British production but of the lack of inventiveness which had overtaken their British competitors early in this century. The writer attributed this slowdown to absentee ownership and dated it before 1910 when the abler administrators, like Lord Cromer, were sent out to the Empire instead of staying to mind the shop. Henry Clay agreed, rather ruefully, that this might be true of certain companies but he distrusted the generality; talk slowed down as the cold set in and he seemed quite agreeable to bundling again.

We saw the fields of Irish green beneath us as we descended and were the first of four seaplanes to foam up the estuary of the River Shannon, closely followed by two from the British 8th Army in Libya, and the last from New York. A small tender came out to meet us with an Irish officer in the prow, immaculate in his dove-gray britches and tunic without ribbons. The towering Lord Penny went to the door. "Dr. Livingstone, I presume," he said. "What a spotless uniform!" and the taunt in his voice made the young lieutenant flush. We went ashore as the sun rose, for a breakfast of fresh eggs, Irish bacon, plenty of toast, tea, and marmalade. The passengers from the army

52

planes, in mufti, trooped in and were greeted by the British. While we were still eating, Victorian thunderheads closed the sky and after the lightning, heavy rain set in and the wind howled. Above the din our captain announced that there'd be no more flying that day and we should be bused to the villages of Foynes and Limerick where we'd double up for the night. I recalled aloud that Archie MacLeish had been caught in the same predicament and on being pressed for a new limerick had improvised:

> *There was a young lady of Foynes*
> *An ardent collector of coins*
> *She took thripenny bits*
> *with the quick of her wits*
> *And pounds with the quick of her loins.*

Before our takeoff from Shannon the next morning there came aboard twenty-five RAF pilots and bombardiers from the 8th Army. One of them had been released by the Italians and was coming home to have new skin grafted on his scarred face; all were in their twenties, with that steady gaze a contrast to their horseplay. They had all come through twoscore or more missions; their days in the desert were over and after home leave they could fly again or be seconded to Intelligence. When they squeezed in amongst us the cabin was crowded.

We civilians had come to admire our pilot, Captain Peacock, who had flown Mr. Churchill back to England shortly before our trip. But the presence of these younger airmen seemed to make him self-conscious. Because of their additional weight he had difficulty getting off the water, and in his approach to Poole in England he overshot the harbor and had to climb and circle for a second descent. The fighters were squirming. "Now, what's the bloody fool up to?" At last we were taxiing safely across the water and one turned and said laughingly, "And you endured eleven hours of this!" In fact, it had taken us three nights and most of the third day to reach England.

London was still bathed in the sunny evening haze as we drove to the Savoy Hotel. The London I had first seen as an impecunious student in 1922 was majestic, the capital of the world, whose shops and public buildings, whose enormous parks and handsome mansions preserved the varied styles of centuries. But all I had read about the Blitz had left me unprepared for the savagery of London bombed; the rows of gutted little houses in Bethnal Green with the odd survivor flaunting its tiny garden, the faceless apartments in Westminster with a fireplace and a flapping tatter of drapery three flights up. The clocks in the steeples had been silenced at different times. Beds of cerise willow herb, seeded everywhere by the birds, had overgrown the ruins. The shattered windows of homes in the West End were covered with oilcloth, and in the west wing of Buckingham Palace, where a bomb struck, the fragments of carving and masonry now stood neatly in the yard awaiting the day of restoration. This was as close to "the action" as I would ever be, and I was intent on making the most of it.

CHAPTER

IV

The ginger-haired Minister of Information, Brendan Bracken, in his welcome made it clear that we were to see and judge for ourselves. He suggested we spend the first few days in the city — a car and driver would take us where we wished. Later, trips would be laid on to Coventry, Liverpool, Hull, and Scotland. The weekends were open — we would surely wish to visit American air bases — and now come and meet his staff, among whom I recognized an old friend, the publisher Hamish Hamilton.

The following morning Winship and I, driven by a pretty WREN, were on our way. With us was H. M. Tomlinson, who, in 1940 when Britain stood alone, had written an eloquent series describing the fortitude of the British during the Blitz. We were to pick up Tommy's friend, James Bone, at the Inner Temple. He was waiting for us at the gateway, a chunky Scot whose high coloring was in contrast to Tomlinson's gray, furrowed features. Both were in their seventies, both loved the city, Bone having covered it for four decades as the correspondent of the *Manchester Guardian*. In his picturesque book, *The London Perambulator*, he has preserved what was ancient and lovely in Edwardian London. He beckoned us in.

The Temple is the largest of the four Inns which have provided learning and lodgings for lawyers for over five centuries. The old red brick buildings, used more as offices than dwellings today, formed courts presided over by the Master's Lodge, and broad walks led to the Norman Church and the famous Tudor Hall. Writers were also permitted to dwell here, and Chaucer, Fielding, Goldsmith, Johnson, Dickens, Thackeray, and Charles Lamb (who was born in the Temple) contributed a Bohemian air to its austerity. Bone spoke of a Master

who, incensed by scandal, set a new rule that ladies entering after
the doors were closed at night must write their names in a book and
that of the person they were visiting. On the first night of enforcement
so they did, giving names "romantically unreal," and each had put
down the Master's name as the person they were visiting. The rule
was withdrawn.

James led us through the Inner Courts: we paused before the ancient sundial with its reminder

> *Shadows we are and*
> *Like shadows depart*

and were silenced by the rubble of the great Hall where Shakespeare
was said to have played in *Twelfth Night*. It had been demolished by
a direct hit. Bone pointed up to his own rooms on the top floor of an
adjacent building where his books were safe but the structure so damaged that it was padlocked until peace. As we stood gazing an elderly
barrister was hailed and introduced. Sir Ronald Somebody, "our
most eminent authority on Libel." I noticed how ragged were his
cuffs and that a button was missing on his vest; it seemed that having
made up their minds to gamble everything, these people were unashamed of shabbiness and unsentimental about their ruins.

Back in the car Bone spoke of how Sir Christopher Wren had rebuilt London after the Great Fire of 1666, his supreme achievement
being St. Paul's. We drove past the Bank of England and other sooty
granite buildings and came suddenly to the clearing in which the
Cathedral stood. St. Paul's had been encircled by bombs, ringed by
fire, yet only slightly damaged, though its surrounding neighbors had
been obliterated. "You're seeing it as Wren saw it," said Bone, "in
dusty splendor and in the clear." The great dome reached up and up
into the blue; there was nothing to encroach on such grandeur. We
entered the nave. "At the end of the funeral service for Lord Nelson,"
Bone told us, "the coffin was borne out by men from the crew of his
flagship, the *Victory*; they were weeping, and when they had placed
it on the gun carriage out of love they tore the Union Jack to shreds,
each man demanding a bit of it for a keepsake." It was a picture to
remember: the packed Cathedral with the organ thundering, and the
adoration of that slight, heroic admiral; I thought of it again weeks
later when I was shown a painting of St. Paul's after the fire of 1941,
painted from the opposite bank of the Thames, by John Spencer
Churchill, the P.M.'s nephew, and I bought it.

In all, Sir Christopher built fifty churches in London, of which nineteen had been dismantled, for new churches in the suburbs, and another fifteen presently destroyed by German bombs. "Before Göring began his demolition," said Bone, "Wren's genius was being driven out of the City by the money-changers. Now we shall have to raise funds for those that can be restored." We paused before two cripples, St. Bride's in Fleet Street, and on the little island in the Strand, St. Clement Danes, where Samuel Johnson once worshipped (gutted 1941, restored 1958).

Tomlinson took charge as we were driven to his birthplace nearby St. Katherine's Dock. I wrote these notes that night. "Look," said Tommy, pointing to a large quadrangle of bare quays into which ships passed, through a narrow lock. "American clippers used to dock there. On those quays stood three-storied warehouses with arcades and pillars. Ships lay beside the arcades, so many ships you could walk from deck to deck, half across the water." But there was not a ship in sight. "Gone — it's all gone. . . . Over yonder is where the *Torrens* was moored when Conrad was her mate. I have seen her there. All the warehouses have been bombed; now they unload in the open and move it away fast."

At the Crescent Wine Vaults we descended into cool corridors sixty feet down. Like the Catacombs, but vast, twenty acres underground, many cellars connected by a narrow gauge railway. We were given candles half a yard long, set on pieces of polished wood. Said the caretaker, 'A man could get lost down here. Forty miles of track. That's why we give you a candle. Can tell you're missing if you don't return it.' The vaults depleted now; tuns of old madeira and sherry, soft and mossy to the touch, with sugary stalagmites at the bottom, showing the age. Temperature 60° — port fifty years old, owned by Oxford and Cambridge colleges, and Parliament. Many private vaults but Claret in short supply. Nothing alters here.

"We drove to the oldest seafaring site in London, the Isle of Dogs, in the middle of London River. Harbormaster wanted to know our business then recognized Tommy. A little man whose shiny blue jacket showed rank of Commander and ribbons from First World War. Became dryly communicative, pointed to the basins out of which he — they — had warped ships, some loaded with explosives, ship after ship, during the worst nights of the Blitz. 'What? Big ships shifted from that limited space, hurriedly? At night?' 'We had plenty of light' was all he said."

Leaving the docks we drove through narrow streets past the rows of small stone dwellings where thousands of dock workers once lived, jagged, deserted now, the occupants long since evacuated. Tommy was looking for something. "Slow down, please. . . . I can't think it has survived." But it had. A little old pub to which Dickens once came. "That's it! My father brought me here when I was a boy." The neat burnished taproom was still in use. He led us along the corridor and out upon a little balcony hanging over the water. "Now look," he said. "There's Limehouse Reach. And this is where Whistler made his drawings." The tide was running out, below us lay the Whistler barges. But the ships were missing.

It takes time for a visitor to appreciate the enormity of Britain's loss. Tomlinson had no illusions: a letter he wrote me after reading proofs of my article on this trip touched me:

How you kept in mind the information dropped about those uptown docks and Limehouse I don't know. It seemed to me at the time that it was no good at all pointing to a fact or two in Chaos. For all *I* felt — except the warm satisfaction of having you by me — was a dull ache in my soul. But I note you divined that, Weeks, I tell you our bowels have been riven, and there hasn't been a murmur; we stood up to it when the day seemed without help and gave everything. But, when Victory comes, little England will be spent — all poured out. Keep that in mind, you big people, you Americans and Russians. But we can count on *you*. You've *seen;* and clearly are as much a native of our soil as the hawthorn in the garden here. If only we could count on all American writers feeling, as you did, the ache in the memory of this scene. Two major wars, the sons following the fathers!

It was with gratitude that Winship and I invited Bone and Tomlinson to dine with us that night at Simpson's. "We must come early," Tommy said, "if there's any hope of getting a sliver of their famous mutton." We did and each had — a souvenir of a great restaurant — a bit of the fat, a bit of the lean, thin as a wafer, carved from the joint on the large silver platter.

The following afternoon I had an appointment with one of the younger executives at the Bank of England and arrived just as the tea trolley was passing his door. "Better have a cup," he said. "It's our life preserver. We work late here — and most of us are fire-wardens every third night." I spoke of my visit to St. Paul's and of how splendidly it reared up above the ruins. I had seen in the papers that a track meet — three-legged races, broad jump and sprints — was to be held there on Bank Holiday, "run on the most expensive cinders in Britain!" It set him ruminating. "One can't help wondering about the future of the City," he said. "That land was once valued at one thousand pounds a foot, and certainly it will be rebuilt when the war is over. But I wonder about the wreckage beneath. The bombing has done immeasurable damage to the intestines of London — the cables, the wiring, the water mains, the sewerage, the whole skeleton is held together now by Scotch tape and make-do — and can private capital be found to set it right when the last bomb has been dropped? Our reserves are gone, you know, we even owe India. . . ."

What an American male scrutinizes in any strange land are first the women, then the food (he knows the plumbing will be inferior). The British women are not as long-legged as ours, nor are their legs as well articulated ("Oh, those beautiful long legs!" my companion exclaimed as she watched a company of our WAACs swing past Trafalgar Square), but they are full-bosomed and, thanks to the damp, salty air, their cheeks are naturally highly colored. Apparently they number a greater percentage of blondes, though whether this be due to their bleach or their Saxon blood I am uncertain, and, of course, in the Celtic north brunettes predominate. In London the classic beauty is fair, with a peaches-and-cream complexion. Their differences, their voices, and the common bond of language make them more attractive to me than any other women of Europe.

To free the men for fighting, women between the ages of eighteen and forty were drafted. They were the clerical backbone in every branch of the service; they supplemented the police, operated the buses, oiled the locomotives, tended the aircraft batteries (though not permitted to aim the gun), handled the captive balloons which protected London from low-flying bombers, drove ambulances and mobile kitchens to the bombed districts; "plotted" the incoming enemy aircraft, flew the ferry command, and composed from 50 percent to 90 percent of the force in factories. In one munitions plant I visited north of Coventry, of a total force of 12,000 workers, on three shifts, 11,200 were women. At the end of an eight-hour shift, those who were married had to queue up for food, feed the kids, and bring cheer to a home whose man was gone. After three years of this, lining up patiently for everything but toil, they were weary.

The rations, as restricted by Lord Woolton, were sufficient for vitality but never enough for the appetite. The weekly ration of meat was less than what a professional soccer player would eat at one sitting; eggs were fresh for those who could keep hens, powdered otherwise, and the universal tea cake was khaki-colored and unsweetened. In a London shop a small bowl of peaches caught my eye, priced at 12 shillings: that is, $2.40 a peach.

Winship and I shared a double room and on the Monday morning of our second week were surprised when the bellboy delivered to me a woman's hatbox, surprisingly heavy. Beneath the tissue paper was a layer of well-ripened grapes, then a layer of purple plums, each set apart in cardboard, and beneath them espalier peaches. The card was signed, "Affectionately, Nora." No, said Buttons, the lady had not waited.

Nora Waln was the first Orientalist whose books I secured for the Press. In the spring of 1924 we accepted a short paper of hers posted from Canton, so knowledgeable that I asked for more, and to tell me what she was doing in China. This was her story, confided as our friendship grew. The Walns were of Swedish descent, who had dwelt in Pennsylvania as early as the Penns; for generations they carried on a trusting and prosperous business with the Lin family in Canton. Nora graduated from Swarthmore and when her fiancé was killed in action in 1918, she turned to writing. The China connection offered her an escape from grief; she went to Canton, where she was welcomed, first as a guest, then as an adopted daughter of the Lins in their rich ancestral compound which Nora called "The House of Exile." In 1924 she left them to marry a tall, reserved Englishman, Edward Osland-Hill, who was administering the Chinese Postal Service. They lived in Peking during the years when Borodin, the Soviet envoy, was feuding with Chiang. With her husband's influence she was passed through the armies of the War Lords to gather book material about Mongolia. It was there that a letter of mine caught up with her, urging that she write her loving, picturesque account of Chinese family life. We published it under the title of *The House of Exile* and it was widely read in 1933.

To thank her for that luscious gift of fruit I took Nora to the exhibit of war paintings at the National Gallery. Their more precious paintings, of course, had long been hidden in Wales. We were in time to get a front place to eat our sandwiches, seated on straw mats on the floor of the largest gallery, listening to Myra Hess's noon-hour concert. I cannot remember how many hundred such performances that artist had given for the office workers who crowded in; it was Miss Hess's "war work" and a joy. In mid-afternoon we boarded the train to Fulmer in Buckinghamshire, where Nora and her husband were living in retirement, and I met and congratulated that austere gentleman on his skill as a gardener. After supper we talked about Nora's next book, *The Children of Light*, an historic study of the English Quakers, which, alas, like so many of her projects, was never finished.

A week later came another and larger packet of fruit to be shared with my friends. Deep in the box I discovered a small ivory and silver wine cup with this note:

Down in one corner of the fruit I've put a Mongol wine cup. It is one of a pair given me by the ruler of Sunit to divide with you. When your first letter asking me to write a book reached me I was at Sunit in Inner Mongolia. You gave me joy. I could scarcely believe that the Atlantic was asking me to write a whole book. I could not keep the news. As soon as I told her, the Princess Sunit ordered a celebration. I wish you could have been there. . . .

It was a concert by an orchestra: from all round the palace came notes — now far, now near, and far again; flutes in separate voice and in chorus. While the chorus continued two bearers in green and blue brought the cups, carrying them high. The bearers stood on either side of Prince Sunit. He had on a robe he used to wear in the Manchu Court at Peking and a hat with a peacock feather. He is tall and lean with a hard but handsome face, and he took the cups in his own hands. He had to command me twice before I comprehended that I was to rise and read your letter. I did in English as you wrote it. In meaning it was a high point in my life and in Mongol it is a dramatic letter. At my finish, Prince Sunit spoke. He mentioned the ivory, worn and cracked, and the silver lining; he felt it good that Mongol treaty cups should be held together with silver taken from the plateau's own earth. Prince Sunit was confident that any bargain made with them — no matter how wide the geography that separates those in the bargain — will prosper both parties to it. He drank to you.

I could never tell how much Nora was embellishing, nor did I care. She herself was genuine, a Quaker with a gift for language and a disarming friendliness that kept her traveling, writing and giving her royalties to charity to the end of her days.

I was eager to spend a weekend with our Fortresses, the B-17s, and as a first step I had a Friday afternoon session with Major General Ira Eaker, Commander of the U.S. 8th Air Force. To spruce up I went down to the Savoy barber shop for a haircut and recognized, in the chair next to me, Eddie Rickenbacker, deep in thought and continually rubbing his knees. I had read about his crash landing in the Pacific and the miraculous rescue after many days on a life raft on a diet of one captured seagull. "I'm Ted Weeks," I said. "Those legs still bothering you?" He grinned. "Yeah," he said. "But I'm all right. Just returned from the Soviet Union, where I saw their fighter-pilots. They're a tough lot. Got in last night." I told him I was going to see Eaker that afternoon at three. "I'll be there a little ahead of you."

Rickenbacker was with the General when I reached headquarters and waved as he came out. Evidently Eaker had been showing him the results of our bombing, for he led me to a long table covered with enlarged photographs of a city taken at very high altitude before our planes attacked. On each was an overlay with the targets marked, showing the destruction of our bombs. "Where you see roofs doesn't necessarily mean that the factories or houses are now habitable." Then Eaker spoke about the fire power of the Messerschmitts when our fighter-escorts had to turn back for lack of gasoline. From aerial reconnaissance, from crew sightings and our agents in the Resistance, he told me, our Intelligence kept track of the German interceptors and with this information feints are plotted to lead the fighters away from our real objective. "One of my men here is an expert in this. I'd like him to show you around." Over the intercom, he asked Captain Haines to come in. A trim, dark-haired officer entered, saluted, and as he saw me, winked. "Captain Haines," said the General, "this is Mr. Weeks, editor of the *Atlantic Monthly*. I'd like you to show him the War Room and tell him something about the German fighters." "Yes, sir," said Bill Haines. "Mr. Weeks and I are old friends. He's my publisher."

Bill had worked his way through college, one of several crews electrifying the Pennsylvania Railroad from Washington to New York and from his experiences in those hazardous summers working over the "hot wire" had come his first book, *Slim*, a pre-war finalist for the Atlantic Novel Prize. I knew he had been commissioned in Air Force Intelligence, and it was a happy surprise to find him here. The War Room with its huge maps was impressive, but what sank in were Bill's words: "What I and a sizable staff do is to tell our boys, and those planning their attack routes, about how many planes they would have to expect to fight and, roughly or precisely, where the German fighters are based. The most important targets are of course aircraft and ball-bearing factories, and oil tanks, which are bitterly defended. Remember that once our bombers have passed beyond the support of their fighter-escorts, they just have to keep their course and take what comes, and they do."

I had asked the General and now asked Bill if Winship and I could be given passes to spend a night at a bomber base. He thought it would be possible: "How about this weekend?" he said. "The weather's clear. They'll be flying." That evening word came that on Saturday Larry and I were to take the afternoon train to Thetford in Norfolk, where we would be met. There would be accommodations for us for the night.

The train was so jammed with air personnel and civilians that we could find no seats and stood in the corridor chatting with a couple of pilots returning from leave. At Thetford, where the airmen stowed themselves in jeeps, trucks, and staff cars, a sergeant spotted us and, as he drove, explained that we would be visiting a freshman Group of 27 Forts, six of which had just returned without a scratch from their third mission. We were welcomed by a public relations officer who showed us to our rooms in a Nissen hut, and then led the way to the bar, introduced us and ordered drinks. The crews going out tomorrow had already been alerted that they would be part of the first attack on Hamburg. Over in a corner I noticed three flyers shooting craps on a high table, not rolling the dice but bouncing them off the backboard; as in their flying, they gambled on luck. "How well do you sleep when you know what's coming up?" I asked my neighbor. "Kind of jumpily," was his answer.

Again, on that long Sabbath I took note:

Sunday 7:00 A.M. The gunners who have had their breakfasts (fresh eggs before a mission) are being briefed. Through the windows of the camouflaged headquarters you see the knots of men at the six tables, leaning attentively toward the officer who is speaking. One imagines what he is saying. "The escorts will leave you here. . . . Watch out for interceptors from this point on. . . . They may be waiting here as you return." As fast as one knot dissolved, another took its place. Nineteen Flying Fortresses are going up from this field — and that's 57 gunners.

Outside, the sun feels hotter; it's going to be a perfect summer day. The roads, converging where we stand, are alive with bicycles, jeeps, and trucks, for now the pilots and navigators are beginning to arrive and their briefing will take longer. . . . We talk to the colonel who is to lead them in — a veteran at 26. He flew 18 missions in the Pacific and brought the last Fortress out of Java; I wondered how much longer he'd be flying. His soft mustache doesn't conceal the firm lines of the mouth, and he speaks with a quiet authority. As the men are re-emerging from the brick building, he turns us over to a master mechanic.

Joe drives us in his jeep and it's quite a way. The realization suddenly hits me of how much space these B-17s need, a two-mile enclosure, the turf crisscrossed with runways. The Forts are dispersed in small, oil-stained islands on the perimeter; some are in blast pens, others snuggle right against the hedgerows; their wingtips ten yards away from the ripening wheat. Farmers live beside all this, and the church bells are ringing just as Joe curves us in a swoop beneath "The Raunchy Wolf."

The ground crew, who service the plane, are suspicious of us: we might bring bad luck; they wish we'd get the hell out. But Joe is a good chaperon; he introduces us to the pilot, Lieutenant Irving Frank, who casually cuts us into the conversation. Most of the crew have stripped to their shorts — it's that hot. I was talking to the navigator, just as a tail gunner rides by. "He's a real Indian," says the navigator. And he is — a full-blooded American Indian, a lieutenant, riding on an English woman's bicycle with a 50 mm machine gun on his shoulder. He stops at the next island and leans the bicycle against the hedge.

Time is getting short — and how they hate the wait! One of the crew begins to clown — the burly guy with the ham hands. He has climbed into his electrified suit and he does a monkey act with a plug wire as his tail. Now the rest of them are pulling on their flying clothes, and the boots, and the parachute harness, and the helmets and the Mae Wests — and the pilot is dealing out flat cellophane packets containing drugs, concentrated food, what they will need if they have to bail out.

"Better go," says Joe. And in the jeep we scurry down to the crossroads where the feedway joins the main take-off. We drive into the grass and park beside the radio control, a little boxcar painted in yellow and black squares. Next to it is an ambulance and beyond that a fire-fighting crew. "Move those people away from that hedge, will you?" says the sergeant with the earphones, and as he directs the MP I notice the English villagers who are standing with their youngsters all down the hedgerows. Church is over and they have come to see the boys take off — the Yanks who sometimes help them with the reaper, to whom they sell their eggs, and to whom their daughters are kind.

The props begin to turn and suddenly the air is shuddering. We stand beside Joe on the seat of the jeep and watch as the 19 Fortresses file into line and come taxiing toward us down the runway. The four motors are roaring now, and as the pilots go by, they give us thumbs up. I saw one radio operator leaning out clasping his hands in the old prize-fighter gesture to a buddy. You can't hear yourself shout. The first five are Joe's special charge and I watch him as they come up to the line — "The Raunchy Wolf," "Big Stink," "Hesitating Hussy," "Grim Reaper," "Yank and Reb." They halt thirty yards from us and all turn at an angle to keep the slip stream out of each other's teeth. The waist gunners lean out of their open bays and thumb their noses.

And then with a roar the first takes off — and the flight goes up.

One of the nineteen never makes the run; it turns off to the left and goes slowly back, one motor dead. "Aborted," said Joe. "Tough."

I look away, up at our planes as they circle and circle the field, gaining altitude. Other flights are rising to the west and south of us, and from where we stood we could see the beginning of that great formation, a flying arrow-head with height and depth, which was weaving together higher and closer as it neared the sea. Then they were all gone from sight, their fighter escort 10,000 feet above them.

"Now you'll know what it is to sweat it out," said the doctor as we sat together at mess. Lunching with us were the crews who had come in the night before from Norway and were being rested.

Time dragged that afternoon. I spent most of it with the mechanics (there were over two thousand ground men on this field) watching them salvaging parts from a damaged ship — "cannibalizing" they called it. I saw a new tail being fitted on to "The Careful Virgin" while on a platform up at the nose the artist of the outfit stood, brush in hand, painting a large "X" over that word "Careful." She would be the "X-Virgin" from that time on.

By six in the evening the camp is restive and the exodus begins — on jeep, bicycles, on trucks — to the vantage points, to see the boys come in. Joe drove us back to the crossroads. I noticed that the silent English had returned.

"Here they come!" called the radio operator to the hedgerow, and swiftly, straight out of the horizon there swept over us in formation twelve of the great planes. Everywhere I could see the faces upturned, the fingers counting. Twice they circled the field. "Now, watch," said the radio voice. And with that, one of the Forts peeled off, rose sharply to break its speed, leveled out of sight and then came in, smooth as cream from a jug. "They're coming in hot," Joe said. "Hot?" I asked. "Yes, fast — and thank God they're turning left, — ambulances are up there to the right," he added for my benefit.

And now the second formation swung into view, another five. One after the other they peeled off, swung out, and came in on the run. We had sent up eighteen. Where was the other? was the question as we raced back across the field. (Not for an hour did we have the answer; slow, crippled, it had made a forced landing nearer the coast.)

The taxi line was forming coming in like elephants. "The Raunchy Wolf" settled into the center of her space, the pilot cut the motors, and after an instant long legs began to dangle from the hatches. Stiff-kneed, their faces flushed and sweaty from the seven hours on oxygen, damp curls at their temples, their eyes tired, reflective, the crews came back to earth. Joe had the first crack at each pilot as he came out. "Anything wrong?" he asked. He took down their answers on his clip pad, and then raced to the next island.

The weary men with their heavy gear over their shoulders sat down on the hardpan to wait for a lift. The Indian with his gun barrel mounted his bicycle, and rode by. Crew by crew they would go back to headquarters to be interrogated until every last scrap of information had been gleaned about their mission. And then some of them might be put on notice for the next day's raid.

At headquarters Larry and I talked with a number of the airmen from New England. "Cold up there?" "Forty below." "Ack-ack bad?"

"Worst we've seen." "Coming up like Roman candles," said one. "Like trying to walk on a bead curtain," said another. We began to jot down messages for their folks at home, and I remember one boy, Jack Leahy from Norwood, Massachusetts, pausing before he spoke. He had given me his mother's address. "Tell her I like it over here," he said. "Tell her there are the same kind of people to fight for we have back home."

There was a miraculous postscript to that trip which Larry Winship wrote about eight months later, when Lieutenant Frank, the tall, slim red-headed pilot of "The Raunchy Wolf" walked into his office at the *Boston Globe* to tell, with a shy grin, what had happened to him and his crew after our first meeting. Lieutenant Frank, who was from Boston, had, in Larry's words, trained with his crew of ten in Boise, Idaho, flown them to England, piloted them on more than a score of bombing attacks over Hitler's Europe and when their tour of bombing was completed, brought every one of the men home without a scratch.

"What!"

"That's right! Not a Purple Heart on the ship."

Winship was a great reporter before he became editor, and this is one of the best stories he ever wrote. He asked the young pilot what their longest flight was and the answer: "Regensburg, on August 17, 1943."

"The one no man who was on it will ever forget," says Lieutenant Frank. "They woke us up at 2 in the morning and told us to take two blankets apiece and enough equipment to last us awhile at another base. That was our first clue that it was something new. We weren't coming back. We had bacon and eggs, and went over to the briefing room, where Major Jim Lewis, who used to be a bond salesman in Boston — lives on Norway St. — told us where and how we were going. It was an anniversary, just one year to the day the 8th Air Force landed in England. Major Lewis told us we were going to celebrate by lambasting the No. 1 aircraft factory of Germany, at Regensburg.

"Then Major Jim MacDonald of Revere, who had been captain of the B.U. football team, talked to us as I bet he never talked to a football team. It was wonderful.

"Then we took our parachutes and stuff and walked over to the 'Raunchy Wolf,' and we certainly looked it over. It was going to be a long hop and a rough one.

"We took off at daybreak, and I think we fooled the Germans by the route we took for the first 50 or 60 miles. But as soon as our fighter escort left the enemy jumped us. [They] came in, head on, with 20 mm. cannons winking, their 303 machine gun tracer bullets streaming by on all sides.

"Suddenly the windshield shattered in front of Jim Watson, my co-pilot from Brattleboro, Vermont, a pre-med student before the war. Jim felt of himself to make sure he was not hit. Our luck was holding and no one was hit. ME 210's and VO 217's joined the pack. They usually save those for bombing and reconnaissance. But the Hun was putting up everything to keep us away from the target that day.

"It was a running battle for four hours. The Germans scored a few fast victories, and the sky was full of burning B 17's. (We lost 59 Fortresses before the day was over.) So many parachutes, with jumping airmen, were in the air that it looked as if we were pulling an invasion. They attacked us head on, with cannon and machine guns. They never seemed to quit.

"Then the most wonderful thing I ever heard of happened, when we were still half an hour away from the target. Aubrey Bartholomew, the lumberman from Danforth, Maine, right up near the Canadian border, was riding in the ball turret, on the underside of the ship. He was shooting like mad when a shell from a Focke-Wulf shot off the door of the ball turret. There was nothing between Aubrey and the ground. He didn't have a parachute, because you don't have room for a parachute, scrunched up in that little space where he has to ride.

"But when Aubrey slipped out, by a miracle, he had his toes of one foot caught solidly in the range pedals. There he was dangling in the air. But he grabbed hold of the guns and pulled himself back in. Maybe he was saved because his back was towards the slip stream, the force of the wind which helped him get up and get hold of the guns and crawl back in. I think it was some super-human strength, and Aubrey thinks so, too.

"When he got back in, he didn't say a word about what had happened. He just called to me over the phone: 'Lt. Frank, I'm going to have to leave the ball turret.'

"I asked him if he was nuts. He said, 'Well, the damn door is shot off, and I can't stay here!' He came up and rode the rest of the way in the nose. . . .

"I don't know whether to tell you about the rest of the run, or about Aubrey."

We said we'd like to hear the rest about Aubrey.

"Well, he was a Canadian. He'd come over the border to work in a lumber mill on the banks of Lake Baskahegan because he likes to fish and hunt. His parents are dead and he lives with his sister.

"When we finished our run that day and landed in Africa, he was kind of shaky. He got us all together and said we had to go to church with him and we all felt so good we said sure, and we hunted all over for a church. We found one and we went in and he went every morning that week we were there.

"When he stepped out of the plane he had said he'd never ride in that ball turret position again as long as he lived. But after going to church every day that week and talking with the padre, he told me the day we were ready to start back, 'Lieutenant, I guess I'll ride in the old spot.' And when we got back to England he found a message saying the United States citizenship he'd been waiting for four years had come through."

Although I reached Waterloo Station well ahead of time, the train for Oxford was jam-packed. When Hitler threatened to invade, the Admiralty and other government departments moved down from London. Naval personnel, American airmen, and civilians left not an empty seat. I walked toward the engine and in the very first carriage spotted a young boy seated beside his mother. "Ma'am," I asked, "would your son mind if I took him on my lap?" He stood up obediently and I put my overnight bag on the rack and squeezed in. I was carrying some oranges for the Creswicks and it seemed only fair to give the boy one. He gazed at it. "We shan't eat it now, shall we," said his mother. "Better save it for supper. It's the first he's ever had," she added.

Dick Creswick, who seized my bag at Oxford, was the same trim, dedicated bookman with whom in 1923 I had shared rooms at Cambridge, he as an undergraduate and I a graduate student. We were fond of each other, and as we drove to his home in Old Headlington I told him of those I hoped to see on the morrow: Salvador de Madariaga, the Spanish exile; Sir Richard Livingstone; C. S. Lewis; Lord Elton. When I said I had a date for tea with John Masefield, Dick hooted. "My dear Weeks, you're doing a literary pub-crawl!" "Well, time is short, but I want you to come with me to see Masefield."

I had arrived in the midst of examinations, as I found the next morning when I called on Sir Richard Livingstone. Corpus Christi, his college, was half full of schoolboys trying for scholarships. "But won't they be going straight into the Army?" I asked. "Not quite. Those of eighteen will have six months of intensive study here before they go into uniform; we work them on two shifts. You see we want to be sure that the true scholars will come back to us afterwards. Their scholarships will wait."

Sir Richard was tall, spare, and invigorating, a classicist and, like Sir William Beveridge, an advocate of the reforms that were promised when the fighting ceased. He was disturbed by the inequalities in

68

education which, in Disraeli's words, had divided Britain into "two nations." Somehow he found time (out of sleep, I imagined) to write his new book, *Education for a World Adrift*, to administer a cramming curriculum, and go up and down the country speaking to those in uniform, to munition workers, and to teachers about the humanistic and technical education to be inaugurated in the new universities to come. He agreed to send me an article he was working on and he gave me a pointer:

"Do be sure to see Mr. Williams, the Welshman in charge of the Army Bureau of Current Affairs. Not many realize what a profound effect he is having upon our troops." As we parted Sir Richard pointed to two hencoops nestling in one corner of the entrance to the Master's Lodge — "Our occasional source of fresh eggs," he said.

C. S. Lewis I found grubbing in his rose garden. He rose and shook my hand. "Stand by for a moment while I finish this job. Then we'll have a cup of tea." Job done, we went into his study, a maze of books and papers. Lewis was too evangelistic for Oxford; they looked down their noses at his popular books, *The Screwtape Letters* and its more spiritual successor, *The Problem of Pain*, but his following had grown. I asked what he was up to. "At the moment, nothing but the Examinations; they squeeze one dry." But on his desk was a poem, handwritten. "Is that yours?" "Oh, some giddy verses I wrote when I couldn't sleep, 'An Examiner's Nightmare.' Do read it." I did. I bought the manuscript and carried it off with the promise that he would show us chapters of his next book.

In mid-afternoon Creswick and I set out for Abingdon, where the Masefields lived. Our bus dominated the narrow Oxford streets, parting its way through the swarm of cyclists; we came into open country, passing by airfields, vibrant with planes marked with the American star, and on to a crossroads, where we dismounted. At the foot of a dusty lane a driveway led us to "Burcote Brook," a rambling dwelling whose modesty reminded me that the annual reward of England's Poet Laureate was only £16.

The *Atlantic* had published Masefield's sea ballads early in the century and in 1919 a poem, "On Growing Old," thereafter nothing. But the poet who opened the door did not look that ancient; he was in the pink. He told us he had just come in from boating, and his flushed cheeks, dark eyes, and thatch of white hair were a picture of health. His voice was unusually deep and melodious.

Mrs. Masefield was older than he, older and grayer; she served the tea silently while her husband was questioning me about American writers of new repute. Certainly William Faulkner, I said, and John Steinbeck — but with us, as over here, the war had absorbed the younger.

Dick, who had been listening, made a request. A new association, "Friends of the Bodleian," had been formed and was seeking the manuscripts of celebrated authors for the Library. Would Mr. Masefield grant them one of his? The Laureate flushed. "You hear that, my dear?" he said turning to his wife. "Which one do you think?" They agreed on *Reynard the Fox*. He leaned back reflectively and began to speak of his friendship with Thomas Hardy; they had written to each other with regularity; he had kept Hardy's letters and at the novelist's death his had been returned to him by Mrs. Hardy. He anticipated my question. He felt very strongly, he said, that private letters should not be made public during the lifetime of those who wrote them. (Nor were these ever shown to me or given to the Bodleian.)

As we were talking, a flight of bombers thundered over the house and this drew us out of the library to the lawn sloping down to the Isis. In the center of airfields as they were, I wondered if they had been blitzed. "The Germans had been over, time and again," said Masefield. "I remember one night when my wife and I were in there and the room as black as pitch. We could hear a single raider circling around and around, looking for a target, but the whole countryside was blacked out. Finally, as if in exasperation he let her go — right across the river beyond the bend. It broke every window on that side."

It was after six when we took our departure. Masefield had given me permission to publish as much as I liked of his new long poem, "Wonderings," gave me the corrected proofs; I ran the whole of it — 1,300 lines — in our November and Christmas issues. This reminiscence, in rhymed couplets, is of a sensitive boy's awakening to the daily life, to the beauty and to what was fearful in a little market town of the 1880s, the mail coach, the barges on the horse canal, the Bargemen's Inn, a rampaging bull that had killed a man, the gypsies, old Joseph who once rang the bells for Waterloo — a pastoral picture with passages such as this:

> *Great floods were out; the hedges in black lines*
> *Wallowed like water-snakes with bony spines,*
> *Within the channel, full of swirl in swill,*
> *A six-mile current romped towards the mill.*
> *I was then three; two half-remembered men*
> *Launched with me forth and brought me back agen,*

But half a century later, I was told
What risks beset us in that bliss of old.
The boat was crazy, like her merry crew,
And many drowned men's deaths that mill-race knew.
Life, looking on her lamb, postponed the slaughter
And stamped within my soul delight in water.

On a Monday Winship and I received our tickets and the itinerary for a week's inspection of war plants. At Coventry, whose cathedral was a shambles, we lunched at the gauge and tool company and were impressed by the precision work of the women; we joined in applauding a team of vaudevillians whose thirty-minute show had them all singing in the noon break. That afternoon at Rootes Factory, No. 2, we were informed of how much piecework on airplane parts was being done by *skilled women at home*. The docks we saw at Liverpool had been bombed to their foundations, as in London, but ships and cargoes were moving more securely here now that the U-boats were being accurately tracked. We were silent observers at a Convoy Conference, and then took the train to Glasgow, where we joined Ralph McGill and Keller.

The famous shipyards on the Clyde were antiquated compared to the prefabricated, three-part welding which Kaiser had innovated in California. One frigate was nearing completion, the skeleton of a destroyer was in another cradle but, as they showed us, patterns were still being laid out on the old wooden floor. "Are you working at capacity?" I asked. "Bless you, sir, we've been working at capacity since 1920!" (Had we been shown the docks that were to be floated across the Channel to "Omaha" beachhead, we might not have been so critical.) In Edinburgh we witnessed a remarkable civil obedience in the Land Court. With American troops pouring in and the immense preparations for "Overlord," more coal was needed and young miners, who had been serving in the Army and Navy, were now being called back to the pits. Many of them were reluctant to leave their units and had appealed to remain where they were; the judge listened, but except for one case, said quietly, "No, I understand but the need is imperative," and down they went.

It was Hull that really stirred the four of us. The city had been bombed the night before by German pilots flying so low the radar could not give sufficient warning. We were received by the Lord Mayor, who drove us to the ruins, pathetic for being so fresh. That evening before sunset we watched the doubledecker buses take aboard the elderly, wives pregnant or with infants, and masses of children to be driven to the A.R.P. post out of town where they could eat and sleep in safety. When they had time to settle we were driven to see them in their underground community: dormitories, dining rooms, and kitchens, an infirmary and a large commons where the teen-agers were dancing "Bump-de-doodle" to an accordion, and the elders sat nodding in time. I, who am usually voluble, was taken shy; it was Ralph McGill who, as the music ceased, stepped into their midst, saying how much America admired their pluck and how humble we felt to see at first hand the valor and discipline with which they defied Hitler. They would find that our boys — the Yanks — talked with a different accent but fought with the very same loyalty as their cousins in Canada and Australia. He went on to tell stories about our training camps and they couldn't have enough of him.

We had all been reading about "the Battle of Britain," and we compared notes about the individuals who were responsible, beside the dogged pilots, for the desperate defense: Robert Watson-Watt, the scientist who during appeasement had perfected British radar in such essential speed; Lord Beaverbrook, who, once Churchill placed him in charge of procurement, produced new planes in numbers beyond the German calculation, and, finally, the head of Fighter Command at the crisis, austere Sir Hugh Dowding, who shepherded, dispersed, and directed his overtaxed squadrons with cool efficiency.

Winship and I had a timely demonstration at a weekend we spent with a squadron of Mustangs, the American fighter plane, which thanks in part to the persistence of Tommy Hitchcock, polo player and former pilot in the Lafayette Escadrille, had been powered in Europe with the Rolls-Royce-Merlin engines. The Mustangs were also equipped with disposable gasoline tanks — "Tokyo-Tanks" which could be dropped when used and which added about three hundred miles to the range of our fighter escorts. We witnessed their takeoff on a mission and after the twenty-one fighters had roared away and were climbing to cover the Fortresses we were allowed in the control tower where their radio was beginning to come in. The Mustangs were flying at a height and in deeper penetration than the Germans had expected and as the Messerschmitts rose to intercept the bombers the Mustangs tore down on them. Surprise was complete. Through earphones Larry and I were given a turn to listen to the warnings, profanity, disgust, and glee that came over the air from our pilots, who were having a field day. I do not recall how many kills they reported; what I do remember is their jubilation as they came back later — all twenty-one of them — when, wheels down, they chased each other like young colts along the landing strip. That picture, and the brimming confidence in the mess that night were unforgettable.

Back in London I sought out W. E. Williams, the Welshman responsible for lifting the morale of the British Army after Dunkirk. The survivors who were rescued from the beaches came back without arms, exhausted, and angry. The War Office, knowing how long it would be before they could be rearmed, and eager to relieve any festering resentment, called on Williams, who had a profound belief in adult education, to organize the Army Bureau of Current Affairs. Urged to move quickly, he outlined a series of seminars, compulsory for every regiment: speakers were to be provided by ABCA, the meetings would be conducted not by the colonel but by an articulate junior officer, and questions were encouraged from all ranks, with no holds barred. Printed guides were prepared for the presiding officer, the topics, in the main non-military, dealt with future expectations in education, housing, health, automation — the promise of better living conditions in a victorious Britain. Of all my interviews I think this one was the most prophetic: the many speakers Williams enlisted were as eloquent as Harold Laski, Sir Richard Livingstone, and Sir William Beveridge. Their words indoctrinated definite hopes for reform in a class-conscious army and it was to fulfill those hopes that Labour, not Churchill's Tories, was elected at the war's end.

There were three London editors I was eager to meet: Geoffrey Crowther of the *Economist*, Wilson Harris of the *Spectator*, and Cyril Connolly, who had founded the new literary review, *Horizon*. Crowther's task was the most difficult: with two assistants — Donald Tyerman and Barbara Ward — and despite the bombing which had damaged their London office, he was putting together an anonymous, well-balanced weekly survey of world economy. I was introduced to him by Miss Ward, who wrote most of the comments on foreign affairs; she was just thirty, lovely and unwed.

Reminiscing about the *Economist* years later Barbara wrote:

The weekly scramble to get the paper out was a little longer than you suggest: Wednesday midnight was the last moment for copy and we could still snick little bits in on Thursdays. Our network of correspondents . . . was excellent in North America . . . but . . . in some of the most important parts of the globe — for instance, Stalingrad — we were reduced, like everyone else, to guesswork. . . . In fact, during the war we enjoyed a freedom from facts which is probably the best foundation for creative journalism.

I do not remember that we were either very interested in or well represented in India, nor was Africa a matter of burning interest. The whole colonial structure seemed to be so embedded in the war effort that the countries seemed to lose their individual identity. It was very much a time of the total concentration of attention on North America and the warring states. This was where survival lay — as the bombs which fell on us at regular intervals were enough to remind us.

(The circulation during the war was 70,000; today it is 180,000 and still growing.)

Wilson Harris, editor of the *Spectator*, invited me to his country place with the promise of having tea with Sir Max Beerbohm. To my generation Max was inimitable — and we had never published him. On the train Harris and I talked of Max's caricatures. His most famous drawing is of Queen Victoria, seated in black in the foreground, holding a handkerchief in her lap, her eyes closed in revulsion, while in the far corner stands her bulky son, face to the corner, his hands twisting behind his back, and the caption spoke for both: "The rare, the rather awful visits of Edward, Prince of Wales, to Windsor." Another favorite of mine is of Walt Whitman, chesty, heavily bearded, waving his arms in ecstasy before a supercilious eagle. Caption: "Walt Whitman inciting the bird of freedom to soar."

Having stowed our bags in his cottage, Wilson took me through a famous beech woods in Surrey, beneath whose dense foliage were stacked rows of munitions, hidden when invasion was expected. We emerged into a Constable landscape and came to the tiny stone gatehouse at the entrance to a large estate. Thanks to a wealthy friend, this had been Max's sanctuary ever since the Beerbohms had fled their home in Rapallo. The gatehouse was of two rooms and I assume a bath, and everything about it was diminutive. The paintings on the wall were small, and the ceiling low. Max himself was small, debonair in brown tweeds, Canton silk shirt, dark tie, and comfortable old pumps. Lady Beerbohm made our tea and there were watercress sandwiches.

I remarked what a lovely view of the great park they had from their front windows. It was an unexpected cue and Max began to expatiate on the dramatic effect of a window. He said his most vivid memory of Mrs. Patrick Campbell is as she appeared in the window in Maeterlinck's *Pelléas et Mélisande*. "It rivets me," he said. "In fact, it's a magic casement." He told of passing through the Place Pigalle in Paris forty years ago with a friend who pointed to an open window high up on a tall building and said, "There's Degas." And there, in the distance, were the head and shoulders of a gray-bearded man in a red beret, leaning across the sill. There Degas was, and behind him, his studio.

Max said he was writing a paper about windows to be broadcast over BBC. "You've been on the air?" I asked in surprise. "Indeed, he has," Lady Beerbohm replied, "and he enjoys it. He's been talking about the old music halls and actually singing some of the songs that were once so popular." I could imagine what that meant to blacked out and depressed listeners. Before we left I had the promise of his essay on "Fenestralia"; his broadcast and, still to be written, his reminiscences of George Moore and W. B. Yeats.

In our final days I was invited to supper by Logan Pearsall Smith. His parents were wealthy Quakers of Philadelphia, friends of Walt Whitman. After studying at Balliol Logan became as anglicized as his mentor, Henry James; *Trivia*, a volume of short, impressionistic essays, published at his own expense in 1902, achieved a delicate success, was followed by a second, *More Trivia*, and thereafter he was referred to as "the Mandarin." The other guests were two of his protégés, Raymond Mortimer, the critic, and witty, snub-nosed Cyril Connolly. Over the sherry the teasing centered on Logan. On a visit to Iceland he had been reported as having died of pneumonia and, while convalescing, had the satisfaction of reading a quite flattering obituary in the *Times*. Cyril invented a couple of plaudits that had been omitted.

Then, as we sat down to Dover sole and Chablis, I became the target. Mortimer, a master of French literature, and Cyril, a prodigy at Eton, began vying with each other in quotations, allusions of which I could hardly identify a third. The English enjoy such baiting of visiting "Ameddicans"; Andrew Marvell, whom I'd been reading lately, was my only ace. When the game subsided we got Logan going on Henry James. He told us that James toward of the end of his life laboriously began to revise his novels, and said that he, Logan, was perhaps the only living soul who had compared the two versions, page by page. I asked what was the most notable alteration, and he replied that it was the insertion of adverbs — James had come to believe that adverbs, not adjectives, were often the muscle of a sentence.

We broke up early as it would be a long walk in the blackout. Before we departed Logan drew me aside. "These are the proofs of a new work by a friend of mine whom I much admire," he said, "the first volume of Sir Osbert Sitwell's autobiography, *Left Hand, Right Hand*. No arrangements have been made for its publication in America. If you like it, I think perhaps Osbert would enjoy having you talk to him about it this weekend at 'Renishaw,' his country place in Derbyshire."

My room at the Savoy was on the Thames side with a superb view of St. Paul's and the sweeping curve of the river. I began reading at eleven, munching on the grapes which Nora had brought me, and I kept going until 3 A.M., captivated by the beauty of the prose, the pageantry of the family, and Osbert's sardonic humor. No one since Proust had written like this. I was cutting as I read and had blocked out four installments for the magazine before I turned off the light.

Logan was elated when I told him that I was eager to publish the book and excerpts of it in the magazine. I cabled Boston to suggest a suitable advance and before supper had the terms and an invitation, relayed by Logan, to spend the weekend at "Renishaw." Saturday I traveled north on the early morning train to Sheffield, and, unsuspecting, came under the scrutiny of Osbert and Edith, his older sister, as I stepped down from my compartment. They had their car so placed that they could watch the incoming passengers and were ready to drive off, so they told me, if they did not like the looks of the strange American. I was not yet familiar with Sitwell teasing, but evidently we took to each other on sight; it was easy to admire Osbert's blond good looks. He had the carriage of a Guardsman and his broad shoulders, the Sitwell long nose, and jaw were appropriate to his height. He was beautifully tailored.

I knew from my reading that "Renishaw Hall" had been the home of the Sitwells since 1623, and recognized it from a distance on the crest of a gently sloping hill. As we entered the gates I noticed that the park had been converted into a nine-hole golf course on which sheep were grazing, and golfers were interspersed. "It's open to the public," Osbert explained, "and the sheep keep down the turf." The house itself was of stone, yellowish in the bright sunlight, long three-storied wings extending either side of the center portal. Blake, the chauffeur who carried in my bag, had been Osbert's batman in the First World War, and, as I discovered, was now butler, valet, driver, and, for all I knew, cook as well. Most of the threescore rooms were, of course, closed off during the war, but of those in which I was entertained I remember the ancient polished furniture and the feeling of long use, an enormous collection of walking sticks in one large container in the hall, and the painting bright with youth that hung over the fireplace in the living room. "Who did it?" I exclaimed. "That's by your American artist Copley," said Edith. At supper there was a superb claret, which Blake poured for us. "My, that's good!" "It's a

Château Mouton Rothschild," said Osbert, "a present from Bernard Shaw."

"What he means," said Edith, "is that we were attacked by a miserable little reviewer in a provincial newspaper who wrote that our books had been a fad and were no longer being read. Naturally we sued for damages and before the trial Shaw wrote a letter to the *Times* saying such untruths were abominable and that authors should be protected against them. The paper was fined and we each were awarded three hundred and fifty pounds, which enabled us to lay down this wine."

Logan had told me that Sir George Sitwell, their father, had died that spring in Switzerland and that Osbert had inherited the title and "Renishaw." In the long lingering dusk he led me up three flights of stairs to the roof walk from which we could take in the panorama of the estate. Below, close to the west wing, I noticed the delicately pillared stables in canary yellow, which dated back, so he told me, to Charles II, but empty of horses now. "In all we have about twenty thousand acres," he said, "and every farm is productive. Our tenants have never been so well off but there's little profit — it all goes into the war effort." We turned south, looking over a small lake where an occasional glow of flame flared against the horizon. "That's our colliery," he said. "I'm beginning to learn what a vast responsibility one's property is."

Next morning at breakfast I paid attention to Edith. She was two years older than Osbert (who was six years my senior), and almost as tall, with the long Sitwell visage, pale skin without make-up and very beautiful hands, accentuated by large rings of green aquamarine. She dressed in black, usually with a black satin turban, and the effect was to fasten one's eyes on her pale features. Her eyes would flash with mirth when amused. There was an air of regality about her and when with her throaty chuckle she turned her head aside as she cut off the head of one of her victims, such as "poor Professor Leavis," I felt I had a mischievous glimpse of Queen Elizabeth the First. I asked her for a poem, and, pleased but shy, she said she was working on a new one and would send it to Boston.

Then Osbert led me through the garden which his father had laid out with such precision, into the Maze, past the Tiger's Den where he had played as a boy and on to the shore of the lake — all unkempt and overgrown for there was no gardener, much less the five his father had employed. "It's artificial," said Osbert, pointing to the water. "Father had it dug. At a pretty figure. Later, hearing that mushrooms were in demand, he determined to have it drained — it would be such a perfect mushroom bed, and he would be known as the Mushroom King of England. Fortunately he changed his mind; it was just one of his notions, like the Artificial Egg, which he invented and tried to sell to Selfridges." In my laughter I realized he was telling me of what was to come in his autobiography.

On the train ride back to London I had time to relive my stay at "Renishaw." In those thirty hours, in laughter and admiration, we formed a friendship which was to last until death. Ahead of us were the five magnificent books which crowned Osbert's career as they were reprinted in edition after edition; the many poems Edith — Dame Edith, she became — contributed to the *Atlantic*, and her books, the editing of which I shall describe later. For that Christmas of 1943 I sent to "Renishaw" checks for their contributions, together with a large American plum pudding and brandy butter. They were ecstatic and the puddings continued for five years.

At the Savoy the four of us gave a farewell cocktail party for Bracken and his staff. Our relations with them had been so genial that I had forgotten the watchdogs who lurk at the gates. Before we boarded the seaplane in Poole Harbor we were examined by Customs. "Will you open your bags, please." There, wrapped in my pajamas was the Mongolian drinking cup, ivory, silver and obviously ancient. Was it an antique or a work of art? It would have to be evaluated. Nora had also given me an old-fashioned silver brooch for my mother — it must be taxed. And why those Liberty scarves? For the girls in my office, I said. Customs snorted, and began to puzzle over the baffling contents of my briefcase. The handwritten comic poem by C. S. Lewis might perhaps be in code, despite my protest that it was written by an evangelical Oxford don. It was set aside, together with a typed article, "Need for Peace," by Sir William Beveridge. They would be read and mailed to me if cleared. The tax, when figured, embarrassed me, but a Canadian officer, who had been waiting patiently in line, took in the situation and loaned me £5.

CHAPTER

V

My time with Ralph McGill in England was intermittent as we so often followed different schedules, he with Keller and I with Winship. But when the four of us went north to Scotland I had the chance to study him in repose, to watch those dark eyes, now merry, now somber, and enjoy his creaky laughter. He had a way of pulling at his forelock when he spoke thoughtfully of the South. "The war," he said, "will finally break the grip of the Old South. The 'Separate but Equal' decision of the Supreme Court was just a legalism. There was never *anywhere* an effort to make the separation equal. Today we know there's integration in our Army. You see it here in London — the black servicemen on leave, carrying the shopping bag home with their white girls."

On our journeys the mail was forwarded, addressed in the English manner, to "Laurence Winship, Esq.," "Ralph McGill, Esq.," but mine was sent simply to "Mr. 'Ted' Weeks." "I declare," said Ralph, "it riles me to see how they address the editor of our most eminent monthly — as if he were a prizefighter." Three weeks after our homecoming I received from Atlanta a cardboard tube containing my commission as a Lieutenant Colonel in the Georgia National Guard, signed by Governor Ellis Arnall — Ralph was a friend of the Governor — and with it a letter explaining that Larry had been given a similar commission, "so that he would not have to salute you." Thereafter, McGill's letters to Winship and me always began with the salutation, "Dear Colonel."

Ralph had been in Vienna during the *Anschluss*, and the delirium of the mob, the burning of the books, and the suppression of the press he could not forget. This was what he wrote about in his first article for the *Atlantic* in September 1944. "I have worked for newspapers for almost a quarter of a century. . . . But never until I saw there in Austria the physical disappearance of that freedom, along with others, did it become something vital." In 1945 Carl Ackerman, Dean of the School of Journalism at Columbia, Wilbur Forrest of the *New York Herald Tribune*, and McGill were a committee of three sent by the American Society of Newspaper Editors on a world tour to report on "the freedom of the press." They traveled 50,000 miles and at the end Ralph wrote for our issue of April 1946 an account of their controversial reception in the Soviet Union. With Ambassador Averell Harriman the committee called on S. A. Lozovsky, Vice-Commissar of Foreign Affairs, an "old Bolshevik" who had fought in the Revolution. After the courtesies the Commissar began asking questions. Were the *Chicago Tribune* and the Hearst papers represented on their committee? No, they were not. Why not? He wished to know what they meant by "the free flow of news" and reminded them that until eight months before the war came, Russia had allowed dispatches to be sent out, even cabled, without censorship. "Our own concept is that our press here in Russia is free. Ours is the freest there is, since it serves the people, interpreting their wishes. . . ."

Then came the inevitable question: "You say American newspapers, too, reflect public opinion. How can you say that when, in every one of Mr. Roosevelt's elections, most of your press was against him and yet he won. It would not seem you reflected opinion or had any influence."

The committee called at Tass, the Russian news service which supplies 10,000 newspapers in the Soviet Union, and which daily reports some 15,000 words on the United States. The files, which were shown to them, obviously did not give a balanced picture of our affairs, and now it was the Americans' turn to ask why not? A Soviet representative when pressed with an embarrassing query rarely replies directly. He retorts by posing a related question, loaded in his favor. He could not understand, said this one, how an ally could permit such scurrilous lies as were told about Stalin and Russia by some sections of the American press.

Ralph's article "Free News and Russia" showed how difficult it was for the two sides to reach a common ground and with how much suspicion each viewed the other. At the time it appeared we had just negotiated a contract with Monsanto for six color pages of advertising. At the sight of McGill's article the contract was canceled. I learned that their advertising manager was a Southerner with a pathological hatred of Ralph, and I had the satisfaction of telling him to go to hell. In my twenty-eight years as editor of the *Atlantic*, this was the only instance I recall of advertising pressure on our editorial content.

My friendship with McGill did not fade. He came to Boston regularly to speak to the Nieman Fellows at Harvard, and Louis Lyons, the curator of the program, always invited Winship and me to the dinner for him. Listening to Ralph's conviction as he fielded their questions about the struggle for Civil Rights was an edification. He should say this in a book. What Southerner could do it as well? When I spoke to Ralph he was abashed. "Good Lord, let me think it over." When I told Larry, he was skeptical. "You'll never get it." Coming from one who knew us both intimately, this troubled me.

"What's wrong with the Yanks?" wrote a London columnist. "Why, they're overpaid, over-sexed and over here!" But let it be added that they were generous with their money, their cigarettes, and what they got from the PX; and in their loneliness they appealed to English women whose men were long gone, fighting in far places or in prison camps. Flesh and blood demanded relief and shacking-up was inevitable. The writer who put this in perspective for the *Atlantic* was Laurence Critchell, a Lieutenant in the 101st Airborne Division. His short story, which I entitled "Flesh and Blood," told of an American paratrooper training in England. He was married, torn between loyalty to his wife in the States and his prolonged loneliness abroad. Off-duty Saturday night he wanders into the village to queue up for a film he has seen before and notices the girl standing behind him. He liked her looks and could tell she was conscious of him. "Two, please," he says, and their affair begins. The key is in the next to last paragraph when he returns to the camp at midnight, after they have made love:

He lit a cigarette and inhaled it deeply. He felt more at peace than he had felt in months. He did not understand it, but it was so. He had done what he had promised himself never to do again, as long as he lived, and yet he felt at peace. The balance had been restored. What was stranger still, he had found his wife again. Already the incident of the evening was going back into that part of his mind where he kept the memory of the flesh and the blood, the quick and the dead — those things that would never be wholly understood by him and never understood at all by the people back home. In their place had come his wife. He had her back.

It was the most provocative and compassionate story we printed during the war. Other editors saw the truth in it, for it was featured in the O. Henry Memorial volume for 1944 and it brought us a flood of letters blaming us for condoning adultery, and two from the author, now fighting in Europe:

14 November 1944
Dear Mr. Weeks: The Front: Holland
You'll be amused to know what the enlisted men and officers who read "Flesh and Blood" think of you. When I sent it home their comment was, "The people back there won't know what you're talking about." When they heard the other day that you accepted it they decided (those who were still alive) that you were (1) an ex-soldier, (2) a soldier, (3) a foreign correspondent — somebody who knew what it was like over here. Nothing seems to touch them more deeply than to have a person at home understand how they often feel.
My own thanks are very sincere.
                                            Laurence Critchell
                                            1st Lt., 501st Prcht Inf Regt
                                            Asst. Regimental Adjutant
P.S. An alternate title was "Two, Please." "Flesh and Blood" was the GI's choice.

23 February 1945
Dear Mr. Weeks:
Your letter of January 27 was much better than sweaters or woolen underwear for keeping this particular soldier warm. A few letters had already come to me from people who had read and liked the story — and from my upright flier brother in the Air Corps, who took stout issue with the choice of theme — so I guessed that something odd had happened.
It would be hard for me to finish a book-length novel on the theme before this overlong war comes to an end. But if you feel that it would still hold interest when the fighting is over, I could make a start — would like to, as a matter of fact, more than any other theme. In Dorothy Canfield Fisher's letter she mentioned that she had never before seen it treated in English. I believe there is a paragraph or two in Axel Munthe that deals with the curious balance of such values in periods of universal death. But his period was the plague.
Writing is necessarily slow here. Almost the only free times are between midnights and dawns. The Bastogne story, which my wife should have by now, was written underground during messy periods of waiting between attacks. But if you will drop me a note, when you can, to say whether you think the "Flesh and Blood" theme will still have interest after the war, I'll start using the mess periods to start thinking about it.
Most appreciatively,
                                            Laurence Critchell
                                            1st Lt/501 Prcht Inf.

Looking back at the First World War Ernest Hemingway wrote in *Men at War*:

In the last war there were no really good true war books during the entire four years. The only true writing that came through during the war was in poetry. One reason for this is that poets are not arrested as quickly as prose writers would be if they wrote critically since the latter's meaning, if they are good writers, is too uncomfortably clear. The last war was the most colossal, murderous, mismanaged butchery that has ever taken place. Any writer who said otherwise lied. So the writers either wrote propaganda, shut up, or fought.

But after the war the good and true books started to come out. They were mostly by writers who had never written or published anything before the war.

So it was with us. After the Japanese surrendered, the *Atlantic* published a collection of war poems, of which I reproduce two: the first by John Ciardi, a machine gunner on a B-29 in the Pacific.

ELEGY JUST IN CASE

Here lie Ciardi's pearly bones
In their ripe organic mess.
Jungle-blown his chromosomes
Breed to a new address.

Progenies of orchids seek
The fracture's white spilled lymph.
And his heart's red valve will leak
Fountains for a protein nymph.

Was it bullets or a wind
Or a rip cord fouled with doom?
What artifacts the natives find
Failed and left no tomb.

Here lies the sergeant's mortal wreck
Lily-spiked and termite-kissed,
Spiders pendant from his neck,
And a beetle on his wrist.

Bring the tic and southern flies
Where the land crabs run unmourning,
Through a night of jungle skies
To a climeless morning.

And bring the chalked eraser here
Fresh from rubbing out his name.
Burn the crew-board for a bier.
(Also Colonel What's-his-name.)

Let no dice be stored and still.
Let no poker deck be torn.
But pour the smuggled rye until
The barracks' threshold is outworn.

File the papers, pack the clothes,
Send the coded word through air —
"We regret and no one knows
Where the sergeant goes from here."

*(No one but the jungle root
Fusing to a flare of bloom
And the anthill underfoot
In his stalked enormous room.)*

"Missing as of inst. oblige,
Deepest sorrow and remain — "
Shall I grin at persiflage?
Could I have my skin again,

Would I choose a business form
Stilted mute as a giraffe,
Or a pinstripe unicorn
Or a cashier's epitaph?

Darling, darling, just in case
Rivets fail or engines burn,
I forget the time and place,
But your flesh was sweet to learn.

In the grammar of not yet
Let me name one verb for chance,
Scholarly to one regret:
That I leave your mood and tense.

Swift and single as a shark
I have seen you churn my sleep.
Now if beetles hunt my dark,
What will beetles find to keep?

Fractured meat and open bone —
Nothing single or surprised;
Fragments of a written stone,
Undeciphered but surmised.

And this beautiful elegy for the dead by Charles Olson of Gloucester:

PACIFIC LAMENT

In memory of William Hickey, a member of the crew of the U.S.S.
Growler, lost at sea in February, 1944.

Black at that depth
turn, golden boy no more
white bone to bone, turn
hear who bore you weep
hear him who made you
deep there on ocean's floor
turn
as waters stir:
turn, bone of man

Cold as a planet is
cold, beat of blood no more
the salt sea's course
along the bone jaw white
stir, boy, stir
motion without motion
stir, and hear
love come down.

Down as you fell
sidewise, stair to green stair
without breath, down
the tumble of ocean
to find you, bone
cold and new among the ships
and men and fish askew.

You alone o golden boy no more
turn now and sleep
washed white by water
sleep in your black deep
by water out of which man came
to find his legs, arms, love, pain.
Sleep, boy, sleep
in older arms than hers,
rocked by an older father;
toss no more,
love;
sleep.

My friend Charles R. Codman had flown as an observer and bom-
bardier in the First World War and when shot down had escaped

85

from a German prison camp with an older pilot, our author, James Norman Hall. Charlie spoke perfect French, and in 1941 he went to Washington hoping to be a retread in our Air Force but to his surprise was commissioned as a liaison officer with General Mark Clark. I had a farewell supper with him and his wife Theodora on the eve of his departure for North Africa, and before I left she led me into their bedroom, where on the double bed was his gear, his helmet, side arms, high-laced boots, the surprising amount of his equipment for tomorrow.

Charlie's performance as the translator at the Anfa Conference in Casablanca resulted in his eventual transfer as the A.D.C. to General George Patton. Prior to that appointment Charlie had proved his skill in the difficult, hurried negotiations with the Resident General in Morocco, whose surrender of the French army was received literally only minutes before Casablanca was to have been demolished by our warships and bombers.

It was a happy coincidence that Charlie's best friend, Bernard S. Carter, formerly head of the Morgan Bank in Paris, was also assigned to Liaison in "Operation Torch," and after the war he wrote: "I must confess that when it was announced in Mostaganem that Charley was to become General Patton's aide, I could not help but feel certain misgivings as to whether Charlie 'could take it' — I mean physically.

"The job of aide is a grueling one — especially to a dynamo like General Patton. It means being available and on the alert at all hours with little or no moments of privacy or relaxation, which I knew Charlie needed. It means always finding the right road in a jeep traveling at full speed, and Charley was always weak on road maps. . . ."

Theodora at first shared those feelings. She knew that Charlie was susceptible to sunstroke and that Africa was hot; she knew also of his secret ambition to get back into the Air Force. But when Charlie wrote her on January 13, 1943, "My General has just made me his Assistant Deputy of Staff and says he has no intention of giving me to the Air. . . . He has been swell to me and, as a great treat, promises us all a warm summer," Theo felt the affection in those light-hearted words, and was reassured.

Charlie and Theodora were in love for life; he never looked at another, and despite the long hours and the fatigue of keeping up with "his boss," he managed to write her two full letters a week — except during the attacks. When Patton's Third Army, its whereabouts long concealed from the Germans, went into action in France in August 1944, she could guess where he was, and went with him in

86

spirit. Charlie was a vivacious writer and in his affection for Patton his words drew an intimate, living portrait.

August 8, 1944. What a week. Have been riding postilion with the General throughout practically every daylight hour. By the time you receive this, you will doubtless know that on August 1, Third Army exploded out of the Cotentin Peninsula through the Avranches corridor and since then has been going in every direction at once. The Old Man has been like one possessed, rushing back and forth up and down that incredible bottleneck, where for days and nights the spearheading Armored divisions, followed by motorized Infantry, have been moving bumper to bumper. More marching in ranks, the General occasionally darting out to haul an officer out of a ditch in which he has taken refuge from a German plane, or excoriating another for taping over the insignia on his helmet. "Inexcusable," he yells. "Do you want to give your men the idea that the enemy is dangerous?" Pushing, pulling, exhorting, cajoling, raising merry hell, he is having the time of his life. Our headquarters moves daily, in a series of one-night stands, and we are for the moment located in a tree-covered gully near Avranches.

·A few days ago, in Avranches itself, we were blocked by a hopeless snarl of trucks. The General leaped from the jeep, sprang into the abandoned umbrella-covered police box in the center of the square, and for and hour and a half directed traffic. Believe me, those trucks got going fast, and the amazed expressions on the faces of their drivers as recognition dawned were something.

We have been bombed, strafed, mortared, and shelled. The General thrives on it. Yesterday on the way back to our headquarters we were speeding along choking dust under a high blue heaven crisscrossed with the vapor contrails of our tactical planes. It was a bad stretch of road from which our bulldozers had recently pushed to either side the reeking mass of smashed half-tracks, supply trucks, ambulances, and blackened German corpses. Encompassing with a sweep of his arm the rubbled farms and bordering fields scarred with grass fires, smoldering ruins, and the swollen carcasses of stiff-legged cattle, the General half turned in his seat. "Just look at that, Codman," he shouted. "Could anything be more magnificent?" As we passed a clump of bushes, one of our concealed batteries let go with a shattering salvo. The General cupped both hands. I leaned forward to catch his words. "Compared to war, all other forms of human endeavor shrink to insignificance." His voice shook with emotion. "God, how I love it!"

And here, I believe, in the unabashed enthusiasm, more, the passionate ardor for every aspect and manifestation of his chosen medium, lies the key to General Patton's success. The A.D.C. of an Army Commander is afforded the opportunity of observing the personal approaches and techniques of scores of other commanders from battalion to the summit.

I am quite ready to believe that there may be other E.T.O. Commanders who equal our own in mere technical proficience. I have seen or heard of none, however, who can even remotely compare with General Patton in respect to his uncanny gift for sweeping men into doing things which they do not believe they are capable of doing, which they do not really want to do, which, in fact, they would not do, unless directly exposed to the personality, the genius — call it what you will — of this unique soldier who not only knows his extraordinary job, but loves it. Here in France, as in Sicily, an entire army, from corps commander to rifleman, is galvanized into action by the dynamism of one man.

And later, after Metz fortress had been taken, this picture of a relaxed dinner with Generals of the Air Force Carl Spaatz, Jimmie Doolittle and Ted Curtis, and Bruce Hopper, the historian:

"Speaking of the Ground Forces," Patton said, "why is it that our Infantry is the most unpopular and least effective of the various branches of our service?" They all kicked this around for a while and it was the General who eventually came up with the "gadget theory." "The American soldier is primarily gadget minded," he said. "Give him a tank, an airplane, a cannon, or even a truck, and he takes an immediate interest in the gadget, and because he does, he masters it, and because he masters it, he becomes, in terms of that gadget, the best damned soldier in the world. If in addition he can ride in or on the gadget he is completely happy. Unfortunately, the infantryman has no gadget other than the M-1 rifle. The M-1 rifle properly used is a marvelous weapon of destruction, but it has not enough moving parts to interest the gadget-minded American soldier. Moreover, he can't ride on it or in it and he hates walking. Hence the U.S. Infantry is at a grave disadvantage as against the gadget branches, such as the Artillery, the Engineers — even Ordnance, the S.O.S., and the Air Force. It will be the duty of future Commanders to develop a gadget which will interest the U.S. infantryman."

The letters to Theodora provided the roadmap and love story. I mean Charlie's love for her, for France, and for Patton, in his book entitled *Drive*. He intended to transpose the letters into a first-person narrative and this was well begun when he became troubled about his health. It was summer and he and Theo drove up from Gloucester for tests to be made. She telephoned me from the Massachusetts General Hospital: "We'd like to see you," she said. "Can we stop by the office on our way home?" I met them at the curb and Charlie, at the wheel, leaned across her. There were tears in her eyes. "It's cancer, Ted," he said. "We'll have to hurry with the book."

It was decided to transpose the most crucial action: "Torch" and the Anfa Conference, Sicily, France, On the Rampage, Metz, Battle of the Bulge, Across the Rhine (with the appalling visits to prison camps over-run, like Ohrdruf and the abominable Buchenwald), finally the meeting with the Russians. The letters about the interludes, such as the training in England, would stand as written. Charlie had less than a year, and *Drive*, with an introduction by his Harvard classmate John P. Marquand, and a tribute, at the close by Bernard Carter, was published after his death.

The *New York Times* has — or used to have — a practice of assigning book reviews to those who are presumed to have authoritative familiarity with the subject. Sometimes it works, sometimes it invokes jealousy or hostility. *Drive* was assigned to Captain Butcher, Eisenhower's favorite bridge partner at SHAEF. Butcher knew little about tank warfare and he was fiercely partisan about Ike, incapable of understanding the career relationship of Ike and Patton and the latter's teasing of the Supreme Commander. When the Battle of the Bulge was at its worst General Patton drew up three plans for pulling the Third Army out of its eastward attack, changing directions 90 degrees, and moving north to the relief of General Middleton. At Eisenhower's headquarters he declared this could be done in less than 70 hours and though there was disbelief ("Don't be fatuous!" was Ike's first reaction), Patton did it. As the meeting was breaking up Ike stopped and pointed to the five stars on his shoulderstrap. "Funny thing, George," he said, "every time I get promoted I get attacked." "Yes," Patton said genially, "and every time you get attacked I bail you out." That was enough for Butcher and in an angry, ignorant review he roasted the book.

A fortnight after Charlie's death I was driving down to my trout club on Cape Cod. John Marquand's quotation of the words Patton had spoken to Charlie, as they were flying home after the German surrender, came to my mind. "Codman, I wanted you to come back to Europe with me. But I've been thinking it over. You've done your duty and I think it's time you left the service and rejoined your wife. You're a gallant soldier and a gentleman — and I'll miss you like hell." The tension and sadness that underlay his last months, as Charlie and I worked together, Charlie's unconcealed grief at the death of his only son, hit me. I pulled off to the side of the road to dry my eyes.

Captain William Wister Haines, whom I met unexpectedly at General Eaker's headquarters, was a nephew of Owen Wister. But where his uncle found inspiration in a chivalrous cowhand called "The Virginian," Bill found his in danger, first the danger of a working over a "hot wire," and later, the danger faced by the crews of our heavy bombers. In 1942, as I have said, he was commissioned in our Army Air Force Intelligence, and arrived in England before the first daylight raids of our Flying Fortresses. All Air Forces were experimenting with jets and it was early in 1943 that London first got credible information that the Germans were approaching the stage of substantial production. If Göring's jets did appear in number they would raise hell with our bombers and our plans for the Invasion. It was this dread possibility which prompted the daylight raids on the ball-bearing plants at Schweinfurt and Regensburg, and on sources of fuel production, with losses — 40 Fortresses out of a division of 140 — shocking to the commander who ordered them, and, later, the Joint Chiefs in Washington. Albert Speer had dispersed his indispensable plants, deep in Germany beyond the reach of our new Mustang fighters. How long could the appalling gamble of our Forts be justified before the assembly line of German jets was crippled? Haines lived with this uncertainty, stirred by the loyalty of the crews and the punishment they were taking on their missions. At the war's end, the official estimate that 4,500 bombers — multiply that by 10 men to a Fortress — had been lost over Europe, was a record of heroism he intended to bring home to the American public.

He did so in his play *Command Decision*, which he began writing on V-J Day and finished five months after his discharge. In January of 1946, Haines sent me an early copy of the play for my comment. By the third page I was in its grip and I telephoned him that if he would transpose it into a novel, we would publish it, regardless of its fortunes on Broadway. He did this. When Jed Harris signed a contract for its theatrical production, he was furious that the book production was already scheduled, though it impinged on none of his rights.

The play contract committed Harris to a Broadway production within the usual six months. He chose to spend most of that time, and his resources, on another play that closed within a month of its opening that autumn. He was wasting prime time for a war play and by then it was apparent that he could not fulfill his contracted obligation to *Command Decision*.

The Cleveland Play House, a very capable stock company, learning of the stalemate, asked permission to produce it there for a three-week run before Christmas. These fell within the time span of Harris's control of theatrical rights. But he consented, for the obvious advantage of seeing it before an audience. He came to the Cleveland opening and again promised to put it on Broadway.

The Cleveland run proved a solid success. The novelized version was already running as a serial in the *Atlantic*. Other producers had wanted the Broadway rights when Harris got them; by the time his contract lapsed, the play looked an ever better gamble. Bill and his agent gave Harris a gratuitous extension of sufficient time for him to choose a cast and get going. But when again he failed to do so, the play rights went to Kermit Bloomgarten who, ironically, had been bidding against Harris at the outset.

Because of Harris's prolonged hesitation, the 1946 season was already lost. Bloomgarten immediately devoted himself to preparing an early production in the fall of 1947 and his efforts were capped by the brilliant choice of Paul Kelly for the lead. The play opened on October first. Paul Kelly, taut and edgy, was superb as "Brigadier General Dennis commanding the Fifth Division of Fortresses in England." Crucified and sleepless at the severity of his losses, knowing that he might be recalled because of them, he never wavers at the responsibility of sending his crews on to their murderous targets at every opening of good weather.

Command Decision was a smash hit that ran for fifty weeks on Broadway and several months on the road, Kelly not missing a single performance. In *Variety*'s annual poll of the drama critics he was voted Best Actor. Whether as a play or a novel I regard *Command Decision* as the most authentic and moving picture of the human and political conflict in our air command and of the courage of those who flew the "Forts."

Throughout the war Dr. Vannevar Bush was the head of the Office of Scientific Research and Development, an organization more resourceful and on better terms with the Executive than its opposite number in Hitler's *Reich*. A Yankee, spare and decisive, with a rasp in his voice when angered, he held the complete trust of President Roosevelt and never hesitated to enlighten Mr. Churchill.

Bush was trained as an engineer and received his doctorate in that brief period when it was conferred simultaneously by Harvard and the Massachusetts Institute of Technology. He served as a Dean of Engineering and Provost of M.I.T., then was called to Washington as President of the Carnegie Institution. He became familiar with our leading scientists and the brilliant exiles from Italy and Germany and in June 1940 he convinced FDR that a scientific agency was imperative. After Pearl Harbor, Dr. Bush enlisted 6,000 scientists under the aegis of the O.S.R.D., while his deputy, James B. Conant, on leave from Harvard, maintained our liaison with the

British. He was in close touch with the projects they were carrying on in university or industrial laboratories, careful not to interfere with those which were promising, such as the amphibious DUKW, the shark repellent that saved the lives of wounded aviators ditched in the Pacific, and the proximity fuse. But he was swift to squelch schemes that defied common sense.

There is no limit to wild ideas in a global war and one British inventor, who appeared to have the approval of the Prime Minister, came to Washington in the person of Geoffrey Pyke. His proposal, and I am now quoting from Vannevar Bush's autobiography, *Pieces of the Action*, "was for an ice island, to be called 'Habakkuk,' to float in the Atlantic as a way station for trans-atlantic planes and a home base for planes hunting submarines. . . . Churchill, in characteristic language, sent a memo to the Chiefs of Staff Committee for urgent action. . . . As the plan developed, it included diesel engines to propel the ice block, a refrigerating plant aboard to keep the ice frozen in the warm waters of the Atlantic, work shops, living quarters, etc. Submarines could knock chips off the thing with torpedoes, but presumably they could be frozen back on. I knew I was bound to hear about this confection officially."

The next thing was when Lord Mountbatten and Pyke walked into Bush's office. "Pyke told me the plan was approved and just what O.S.R.D. was now to do about it. Mountbatten looked embarrassed but not nearly enough, so I listened. Then I told Pyke, no doubt with some emphasis, that I took orders from the President of the United States and from no one else, and that ended the interview. . . . As I expected it was not long before the President brought it up. He did so in the casual way in which he usually asked me about all sorts of things, and wanted to know what I thought of the idea of an ice island. I told him, 'I think it is the bunk. If we want an island the Navy has a far better idea for one.' He never mentioned it again. He may have consulted the Navy, but I doubt it. These two short interviews probably spared this country the waste of a million man-hours of work by scientists, engineers and technicians who had much more realistic things to do."

Such was the temper of the man I visited on every trip to Washington, waiting on the bench outside his office until his secretary, Sam Galloway, would slide me in for visits that rarely lasted more than fifteen minutes. I wanted Bush's advice about the projects in the O.S.R.D., top secret then, but publishable later; I wanted the *Atlantic* to print the official history of the organization which was being written by James Phinney Baxter, on leave from the presidency of Williams College. Most of all, I wanted "Van's" autobiography. I began my quest by reprinting a single-page essay of his which had appeared pre-war in the *Technology Review*. It was entitled "The Builders," and I mildly corrected the grammar; in his retort Van asked that the fee be divided between the Carnegie Institution and M.I.T., and then went on:

I should have known that when I started an argument with you on English you would soon have me over a barrel. I rather think that the mixing of plurals and singulars may not have been mine, for I make a great many errors but not habitually this one. However, when you quote Fowler to me on the second point I am sunk, and I admit that he is right on this one as he usually is. . . .

I now know enough about German research during this war to be able to compare their performance with ours, and the results are striking. We recognize that they worked under great disadvantages when they were being bombed, but we also know that they began to gear their science for war several years before we did, and the head start is of enormous importance in such matters. The fact will ultimately appear, I believe, when the full story can be told, that in substantially every important area of war research the British and ourselves cut rings around them. Moreover, the reasons for this are beginning to be evident. They never succeeded in bringing their scientists and military men together effectively, let alone in effective partnership. They did not even bring their scientists and engineers and industrialists together as a team. . . . The area in which they excelled, that is the buzz bomb . . . , I think was a mistake from their standpoint, and the sacrifice that they made in other efforts, for example in fighter development and production, was so serious that it was by no means compensated for by the results attained. . . . Undoubtedly this program got the nod, probably from Göering and Hitler when they were frustrated in their attempts to bomb Britain, and was played as a hunch. . . .

Now this leads to an interesting and important conclusion. The most efficient way to fight a modern highly technical war is not under a continuing despotism, but rather under the temporary rigidity of controls which a democracy imposes upon itself in an emergency. By far the most effective and efficient way in which to be prepared for the fighting of a highly scientific war, and to fight it when the emergency arises, is under the democratic form of government. This is an exceedingly important lesson for this country to learn. . . .

The creation of the proximity fuse, a fuse that would fire the shell in lethal proximity to the target, was begun in Britain in 1940, and brought to perfection on our side; the fuse would save warships from the kamikaze; destroy many buzz bombs over London, and help save the Battle of the Bulge, but not until Bush had convinced the Joint Chiefs that it could be used with no fear that the enemy could devise one in under two years. His faith in its effectiveness culminated in a meeting with Admiral King. Bush recalled that "King scowled and said, 'I have agreed to meet with you, but this is a military question and it must be decided on a military basis to which you can hardly contribute.' So I told him, 'It is a combined military and technical question, and on the latter you are a babe in arms and not entitled to an opinion.' It was a good start, and the discussion went on from there — and went well." What other man in the Capital could have put it to the Admiral so succinctly?

We published Baxter's book *Scientists against Time* in 1946 and then four technical volumes, recording the achievements of the O.S.R.D., of interest to the physicists, engineers, and doctors involved but not to the public, for we lost money on three. With Bush's encouragement, however, I commissioned a series of articles, fourteen in all, by the more literate members of his team, which, under the rubric "A Scientist Looks at Tomorrow," became of progressive importance to our readers.

In our Christmas issue, 1945, Dr. V. B. Wigglesworth in his article "DDT and the Balance of Nature" warned against the unrestrained use of DDT. His warning was plain, too early and at the time unheeded: "We know far too little about the interaction of pests with their physical environment. We need to know far more about ecology and insecticides which discriminate between friend and foe." Neither the chemists nor our farmers foresaw the cumulative effect: the saturation of their fields with DDT did indeed wipe out the insects threatening their crops; after that it infested the worms and decimated the bluebirds and robins which fed thereon, and, as the rains came, it ran off into the brooks, killing the trout and suckers. When an accidental release of a vast quantity of DDT wiped out all the fish life in the Mississippi for miles below Memphis, an indignant conservationist, Rachel Carson, wrote a famous denunciation. But even as late as 1962 the science editor of *Time* dismissed her *Silent Spring* as the work of an interfering sentimentalist, and the demolition continued until at last the manufacturers and users of pesticides were forced to moderate their dosage.

A lifesaving discovery was described by Dr. Robley D. Evans in "The Medical Uses of Atomic Energy." In many laboratories during the 1930s, the atom-smashing of the physicists produced a new tool, "artificial radioactivity," which would in time be a godsend. "When the war began," wrote Dr. Evans, "many blood banks were in operation in which human blood could be stored for periods up to five days, and then transfused safely into the sick or injured." Now for the distant battlefields, Anzio or Saipan, the Armed Forces needed a blood preservative solution which could be added to freshly drawn whole blood and kept in excellent condition for a minimum of *twenty-one* days. "The sober truth is," he wrote, "that through medical advances alone, atomic energy has already saved more lives than were snuffed out at Hiroshima and Nagasaki."

The threat of an eventual holocaust was on the conscience of all those eminent men. Dr. Caryl P. Haskins, who was to succeed Bush as head of the Carnegie Institution, in a pair of papers, asked the question "Is Mankind Cohesive?" beginning in these words:

Only two great groups of animals, men and ants, indulge in highly organized mass warfare — warfare on so wide a scale that the geographic configuration of the earth becomes a factor in their operations. When the little "harvesting" ant, *Pheidole megacephala*, for instance, spread out from its original home in the equatorial deserts of the Old World on a campaign of world conquest, it soon reached Bermuda, traveling as an unbidden guest on the trading ships of man. In Bermuda its plan to exterminate the native ants would have done credit to Pizarro or Cortes. Confining itself at first to the salt-sprayed regions of the coral beaches, where any native ant would have perished, *Pheidole* built up a solid ring of occupation about the island. Then, foot by foot and year by year, it narrowed the circle, battling its way into the cedar groves and the upland swarded hills, exterminating community after community of the native ants until its particular enemy, the large but primitive *Odontomachus*, has now all but disappeared and *Pheidole* is to be found everywhere the conqueror.

. . . Human society is characterized by the most delicate, the most labile, equilibrium between a whole range of essentially contradictory characteristics. Not only is the point of balance between these opposing forces easily upset, but it varies in every group and nation of men.

. . . We have fought a war which, while it has undoubtedly failed to solve the problems of totalitarian ideology in a permanent way, has certainly laid the danger for a time. Now we are called upon to face a problem even larger and more vital, one which is even more significant in the social evolution of man. Is mankind cohesive? If so, can we evolve an entirely new level of human associative living — the world organization? This is truly the greatest evolutionary step which has faced mankind since the emergence of the modern nation.

The series concluded in March 1947 with a biological forecast, "Evolution: Past and Future," which Professor J. B. S. Haldane of

University College in London presented at the celebration of Princeton's Bicentennial. He expressed his concern at the possibility that "in the next century the human race may largely destroy itself" and then went on to a more preferable speculation, his conception of "the man of the future." But it would be fatal to think of the man of the future as one who would fit into contemporary American, British, Russian, or Chinese society, he argued, or into any society which we can even imagine today.

"If I am right he would probably be regarded as a physical, mental, and moral defective," Haldane wrote.

As an adult he would probably have great muscular skill but little muscular strength, a large head, fewer teeth than we have, and so on. He would develop very slowly, perhaps not learning to speak till 5 years of age, but continuing to learn up to maturity at the age of 40, and then living for several centuries. He would be more rational and less instinctive than we are, less subject to sexual and parental emotions, to rage on the one hand and so-called herd instinct on the other. His motivation would depend far more than ours on education. In his own society he would be a good citizen, in ours perhaps a criminal or a lunatic. He would be of high general intelligence by our standards, and most individuals would have some special aptitude developed to the degree which we call genius.

But just as, were we transported to the past, we should be unlikely to win the admiration of Sinanthropus, so, were one of these products of planned evolution brought back to our time, we should probably judge him an unpleasant individual. This thought need not distress us. We shall not meet him.

When "Van" retired he used to fish with me at my trout club on Cape Cod. One evening after a late supper as he reminisced about his skirmishes with Mr. Churchill I thought it opportune to ask for his autobiography. To my surprise he hesitated. He reminded me that Baxter's *Scientists against Time* had been published within three weeks of John Marquand's novel *Point of No Return* and had been "buried" under the advertising "we" had lavished on Marquand. It did me no good to say that Marquand was not our author but Little, Brown's, and that in any season a Marquand novel would outsell a volume of scientific history by a wide margin. Van's sparky memoir, *Pieces of the Action*, when finished in 1970, went, not to us, but to a publisher with no novelist as popular as Marquand.

CHAPTER

VI

When I was a boy Theodore Roosevelt was my hero and I grew up with the belief that a great President had to reach the people by the force of his words. With that high-pitched, carrying voice "T.R.," in those days before amplifiers, said things people remembered and kept quoting: "Speak softly and carry a big stick"; or "There is no room in this country for hyphenated Americanism." Perhaps unconsciously I tried to emulate. I was the smallest boy in my class, a runt of no use in athletics, but I found a compensation in public speaking. I learned to speak without notes or butterflies in the belly, won prizes in school and college, and for years my lecturing contributed to my editorial reach.

Woodrow Wilson, who had the intellect but not the fire, was followed by three non-speakers, Harding, Coolidge, and Hoover. It was the second Roosevelt, Franklin D., who restored the power of the presidential voice by what he said and the way he said it. On the radio his Fireside Chats had a power of revival and a confidence people badly needed and his flashes of humor drew us to him. In one of his speeches in the 1940 campaign he tossed in a reference to three Republicans who had opposed him at every turn: "Martin, Barton and Fish" (Joseph Martin, Minority Leader in the House, Bruce Barton, Congressman from Madison Avenue, and Hamilton Fish, conservative Representative from New York). It sounded as if it were an improvisation: the relish with which he pronounced the words "and Fish" brought a roar from the listeners and twice thereafter he injected the trio, as a symbol of mindless obstruction, and each time it brought down the house.

"Three times in the course of history," I once heard Alfred North

Whitehead say, to an informal gathering of Harvard students, "the relations between the ruled and the ruler were as close to perfection as human nature would permit. The first, in Athens under Pericles. The second, in Rome under Augustus, which preserved the Roman Empire for close unto three centuries. . . ." We waited, wondering what period in English history he would name as the third, "and the third is that magnificent succession in the United States of Washington, Adams, Jefferson, Madison and Monroe."

None of that "magnificent succession" needed a ghost writer, any more than did Lincoln, correcting phrases of his seven-minute Address on the train to Gettysburg. Today, when the presidential voice is broadcast to the millions in our multi-racial democracy, consultants are essential and my admiration of FDR extends to those whom he chose to help him, I mean Robert Sherwood, the dramatist, Archibald MacLeish, the poet, Harry Hopkins, that candid selfless deputy, and Samuel Rosenman, FDR's confidant since his governorship of New York.

It was clear to those who saw President Roosevelt campaign for the fourth term that he was worn thin and, however clear in mind, could not last. On an afternoon in April I was on my way to deliver an evening lecture at the Athenaeum in Summit, New Jersey, one of four strangers who shared a taxi. As we left the station the driver, in a choked voice, said, "The President is dead. It's just been on the radio." The woman beside me bowed her head and wept. It was fortunate for me that I was to have a quiet dinner with Robert Cade Wilson, an old friend, and time to shape an appropriate foreword.

In retrospect I was relieved that the President was spared the increasingly bitter confrontations with Stalin. Whether, had he lived, he could have minimized the Soviet suspicions I doubt; what is unquestionable is that not since Lincoln has a President been as deeply mourned as FDR. He hoped to live until victory was complete but knowing his fragility he had given his close friend Mr. Justice Frankfurter explicit directions about a memorial, which Felix set forth in the *Atlantic*, and the modesty of which must have surprised FDR critics.

At Manchester-by-the-Sea, on the evening of August 6, 1945, my wife and I attended a small dinner in honor of Carroll Wilson, one of Vannevar Bush's assistants, who until recently had been manager of the Manhattan Project at Los Alamos. After coffee and liqueurs we had moved out to the wide verandah, relaxing in the beauty of the moonlight on the water. There came a long distance call for Wilson and on his return he remarked quietly, "We have dropped an atomic bomb on Hiroshima with enormous destruction." "Thank God!" I exclaimed. "That ends the war." Margaret, our hostess, more gentle than I, murmured, "Oh, those poor people." I shall never forget the contrast of that peaceful night with the cryptic news of this first holocaust, so distant but soon to be imminent in our imagining.

Three days later the second bomb fell on Nagasaki. The death toll of 100,000 was 20 percent less than that at Hiroshima, but as someone pointed out, the homeless were double the population of Chicago. One of the first to recover from the repeated shock was the Emperor of Japan, who ordered his War Cabinet to surrender, which at first they were unwilling to do. A few hotheads in England argued that since we now had atomic supremacy and our armored divisions still in Europe we should confront the Soviet Union and compel them to liberate the countries they had dominated in defeating Hitler. (Had we so tried, the jungle would have been denser than what entrapped us in Vietnam.) In America, when, after a silence of three weeks Japan surrendered unconditionally, there was instant elation, followed by a brief interval of euphoria. For months to come the *Atlantic* was deluged by verses, deploring the awful future, one of the first from James Norman Hall in Tahiti, a lament summed up in his couplet:

> *You're more than a little wacky*
> *If you think it was just Nagasaki.*

It was Albert Einstein who on August 2, 1939, had warned President Roosevelt of the destructive employment of uranium, and our preparation of the bomb was authorized in fear that German scientists were already working on it. Had the Nazi scientists been first, would Hitler have blown the daylights out of Russia, then made a highwayman's holdup of Britain — and restored Edward VIII to the throne Mrs. Simpson longed for? Had Stalin been the first to possess the bomb, would he have blown the daylights out of Germany and blackmailed Turkey for the Bosporus? What President Truman did was to appoint Bernard Baruch as the American representative on the Atomic Energy Commission of the United Nations.

As the head of the War Production Board in the First World War, Baruch had earned a reputation for firm, fair decisions; President Roosevelt was fond of him and he served as a trusted go-between with Mr. Churchill. Now, with scientists Richard C. Tolman, Harold Urey, and J. Robert Oppenheimer on one side of the table, and Dean Acheson and David Lilienthal on the other, Baruch chaired a plan to establish an International Authority responsible for "1) control or

THE ELMER E. RASMUSON LIBRARY
UNIVERSITY OF ALASKA

ownership of all atomic energy dangerous to world security; 2) power to control, inspect and license all other atomic activities, and, 3) the duty of fostering the beneficial uses, the research and development of an affirmative character intended to put the Authority in the forefront of atomic knowledge." Could a more equitable formula have been devised to neutralize the bomb? Could it have been enforced? President Truman's only condition was "that we should not under any circumstances throw away our gun until we are sure the rest of the world can't arm against us."

The Russians were suspicious and obdurate; they were jealous that we had "the gun" and dead set against "inspection," which they interpreted as an invasion of their sovereignty. For six months Ambassador Gromyko boxed with Baruch while Andrei Vyshinsky vilified our intentions. At one point, Baruch tells us in his book *The Public Years*, he asked Gromyko why the American plan was not published in full in the Soviet press — "were the Soviets unwilling for their people to know exactly what we proposed? 'Oh, no,' Gromyko answered, 'it's because of a shortage of newsprint.' When I offered to provide all that was needed if they would promise full publication, Gromyko was silent." Baruch did everything possible to conciliate the Russian and in his hospitable way took Gromyko to the second Joe Louis–Billy Conn fight. As the champion pounded Conn about the ring, Gromyko leaned over and remarked, "Conn must wish he had the veto."

The Baruch Plan to control atomic energy and the Marshall Plan for the economic revival of Europe were conceived within twenty-four months, a program of generosity, horse-sense, and self-preservation. But Stalin declined to accept the conditions of either.

Dr. Albert Einstein was the initiator of our Bomb and I was curious to know what he foresaw as our next step in this impasse. I asked Raymond Swing, a reliable radio commentator, to draw him out. The statement in which they collaborated, "Einstein and the Atomic Bomb," was telephoned to my secretary and led the *Atlantic* for November 1945, three months after Hiroshima. I believe it was the first post-war appeal for a world government. The pith of the argument is in the opening paragraphs:

As long as there are sovereign nations possessing great power, war is inevitable. That statement is not an attempt to say when war will come, but only that it is sure to come. That fact was true before the atomic bomb was made. What has been changed is the destructiveness of war.

I do not believe that civilization will be wiped out in a war fought with the atomic bomb. Perhaps two thirds of the people of the earth might be killed, but enough men capable of thinking, and enough books would be left to start again, and civilization could be restored. . . .

Then Einstein took his first great leap when he proposed that the United States should immediately announce its readiness to give the secret of the bomb to a world government. (This, we may have been willing to do.) His second and longer leap was that the United States and Britain should invite the Soviet Union "to prepare and present the first draft of a constitution for the proposed World Government." (That struck me as unacceptable to all parties concerned.)

The alternative to world government was fatalistic:

"Do I fear the tyranny of a World Government?" continued Einstein. "Of course, I do. But I fear still more the coming of another war or wars. Any government is certain to be evil to some extent. But a World Government is preferable to the far greater evil of wars, particularly with their intensified destructiveness. If a World Government is not established by agreement I believe it will come in another way and in a much more dangerous form. For war or wars will end in one power's being supreme and dominating the rest of that world by its overwhelming military strength. . . ."

There were not a few idealists who believed with Einstein that we could build the foundation for world government: lawyers, like Grenville Clark of New York, Daniel Mahoney of Boston, Thomas K. Finletter, later Secretary of the Air Force, in Washington. Two of our most distinguished wounded veterans, Charles Bolte and Cord Meyer, Jr., who were members of the American delegation at the Charter meeting of the United Nations in San Francisco, became co-sponsors of the United World Federalists. But would the Soviets listen? It was a sure bet that they were at work with captured German scientists, on a bomb of their own, and in retrospect we discovered how clever they were in attracting defectors, like the British trio, Burgess, Maclean, and later, Philby. President Conant of Harvard at a private dinner in Boston estimated that our lead time was six years. He was over-optimistic.

Walter Lippmann did not accept that we or Russia or Europe were ready for the renunciation of national interest. "The renunciation of war and treaties of arbitration are . . . excellent devices for stopping wars that nobody intends to wage," he wrote.

101

I can sympathize with those who prefer the liberty of our present international anarchy to the responsibilities of an international society. I am inclined to think that a stable international order would be oppressive and unpleasant in many ways, and I am not wholly sure that I am prepared to pay the price which the establishment of peace on earth would cost. There are many advantages, especially for nations as favorably placed as the United States, in the freedom which this disorganized planet permits us.

If we prefer to retain that freedom, let us at least not deceive ourselves with the notion that we are in any fundamental sense working to abolish war. For war will not be abolished between the nations until its political equivalent has been created, until there is an international government strong enough to preserve order, and wise enough to welcome changes in that order.

We may never live to see that. We may not wish to see it. But that, and nothing less, is what international peace will cost.

The physicists who had perfected the Bomb, like the chemists who devised the poison gas in the First World War, did their duty with a mind divided: they worked to defend their nation by constructing a weapon they knew to be barbarously destructive. Their concern was relieved when neither side used the worst of the poisons they possessed. But the possibilities of nuclear weapons was limitless and no one has stated the dilemma more eloquently than Dr. J. Robert Oppenheimer, director of the atomic bomb laboratory at Los Alamos. I went out to hear him deliver the Arthur Dehon Little Lecture at the Massachusetts Institute of Technology. The place was jammed and as I listened to his grave and moving words I felt as if I were in the presence of Jeremiah. He said some unforgettable things: "Tyranny," he said,

when it gets to be absolute, or when it tends so to become, finds it impossible to continue to live with science. Even in the good ways of contemporary physics, we are reluctantly made aware of our dependence on things which lie outside our science. . . . Nowhere is this troubled sense of responsibility more acute, and surely nowhere has it been more prolix, than among those who participated in the development of atomic energy for military purposes. . . .

Despite the vision and the farseeing wisdom of our wartime heads of state, the physicists felt a peculiarly intimate responsibility for suggesting, for supporting, and in the end, in large measure, for achieving, the realization of atomic weapons. Nor can we forget that these weapons, as they were in fact used, dramatized so mercilessly the inhumanity and evil of modern war. In some sort of crude sense which no vulgarity, no humor, no over-statement can quite extinguish, the physicists have known sin; and this is a knowledge which they cannot lose.

It was that "sense of sin" which compelled Oppenheimer to oppose the development of the hydrogen bomb.

My first impression of Samuel Eliot Morison was in the lecture hall in 1919, a tall, spare Yankee, impeccably dressed, speaking in a crisp, incisive style about the Federalists, Boston, and the wealth brought back to New England by the clipper ships. Twenty years later when I came to read and cautiously edit his manuscripts, he had won distinction as a historian. Without stinting his professional duties he reserved an intellectual vitality that enabled him in the course of time to write forty-one volumes, of which we published more than half.

I have always been curious about the incidents which, often fortuitously, prepare a writer for his finest work. Morison's initial book, encouraged by Henry Adams, was about one of his own ancestors, *The Life and Letters of Harrison Gray Otis*, but his second, *The Maritime History of Massachusetts*, written with an admiration for the youthful skippers and their command of those beautiful ships which for two decades made Salem sovereign, showed where his heart lay, and has become a classic. It was published in 1921, when Sam was thirty-four. That year he was invited to Oxford, as the first Harmsworth Professor of American History. At a sherry party in his honor at Christ Church College, the wife of a don asked him how many lectures he planned to give.

"I believe I'm required to give six a term," said Morison, dryly.

"Oh," she shrilled, "I never *realized* there was so much Ameddican history for one to talk about!"

Sam did not show his irritation but if her comment was indicative of how little the educated English knew about us he would damn well give them twelve lectures, not six, and so he did with such success that he was asked to prolong his stay for three years. Ranging widely, he put together a textbook for British students of United States history, which became the basis of *The Growth of the American Republic*, published in collaboration with Henry Steele Commager, in 1942.

Back at Harvard he resumed his classwork, and at President Lowell's request, began preparing the history of Harvard, for the Tercentenary Celebration in 1936. He had written two of the projected four volumes, tracing events to 1707, then as time was waning, he edited a final volume, *The Development of Harvard and the University* by various members of the faculty. When that was done he crystallized the record — for the general reader — in a more personal, sometimes tart, single volume entitled *Three Centuries of Harvard*.

He deserved, and was granted a leave of absence, and he went to sea. He had been studying the voyages of Christopher Columbus and now, in a chartered yawl, he cruised about the Caribbean, identifying the explorer's landfalls. This was the swing point in Sam's life: it fired his ambition to *re-sail* Columbus's three voyages from Europe, to show what confidence the great Admiral had in his own navigation, and why mutiny became such a near thing after so many days in the stormy unknown. For this he needed a sailing ship of the same tonnage as the *Santa Maria*. With the help of friends, headed by Paul Hammond, he was given command of the barkentine ketch *Capitana*, and, accompanied by William Stevens's smaller ketch, *Mary Otis* — to play the part of the *Niña* — in August 1939 Morison followed Columbus's wake into what would soon be a war zone.

The "Harvard-Columbus" expedition visited Lisbon and Cadiz, then the Azores, Huelva, and Madeira, returning, as Columbus had on his third voyage, from the Canary Islands to Trinidad. There was time for further reconnaissance through the Bahamas and around Cuba. In all, Morison had sailed 10,000 miles of detective navigation, to document his research, before he began *Admiral of the Ocean Sea: The Life of Christopher Columbus*. We published it in two editions, the popular, with certain condensations, and without footnotes, as the Book-of-the-Month Club requested; the scholarly, in full and with the notes. By the time it appeared, Sam was in uniform and at sea. And, a year later, it won him a Pulitzer Prize.

Morison was fifty-four when, after Pearl Harbor, he called on Secretary of the Navy Knox to propose that he be permitted to write "a full, accurate and early record" of our naval operations. Admiral John McRae, who was then the Naval Aide to President Roosevelt, remembers FDR discussing the possibility of such an assignment and when the professor went to the White House a welcome was waiting. The President sent him on to Admiral King with the recommendation that Morison be commissioned Lieutenant Commander in the Navy Reserve, "with access to all naval activities, afloat and ashore," and no censorship.

The Admiral seemed unhappy at the prospect of having a visiting professor in the wardroom. "I don't understand this appointment. What experience have you had?" Sam modestly spoke of having retraced the three Columbus voyages. "Oh, so you're that one!" said King. It was to be a prodigious undertaking, calling for swift assimilation, incessant note-taking, sensitive interviews with commanders — and survivors — and the stamina to alternate duty at sea on combat vessels with periods ashore to check his notes with the official records and get a first draft started.

The most deadly menace in 1942 was U-boats, refueling at sea, and preying on Atlantic convoys, at a cost to us and the British of thousands of lives and hundreds of billions of dollars (the sinkings were to reach a high point of 600,000 tons a month in March 1943). It was Morison's good fortune to be ordered to temporary duty on the staff of Captain John B. Heffernan, in whose flagship U.S.S. *Buck* he sailed to Britain and back in July 1942, escorting Convoy AT-17. Heffernan was patient and a good expositor, who gave him "most valuable indoctrination in modern naval warfare and escort-of-convoy duty." In London Sam made a helpful connection with Captain A. C. Dewar, R.N., of the Historical Section of the Admiralty. On his return stateside he was shifted to the Anti-Submarine Warfare Unit in Boston, where he learned of our counter-offensive and presumably made a rough outline of volume I, *The Battle of the Atlantic*, to be filled out as time permitted.

That summer it became imperative that he form a team to help gather material — at the outset interviews with seamen who had survived torpedoing — and to keep things going when he was away. His first assistants were Ensign (later Lieutenant Commander) Henry Salomon, Jr., and Ensign Henry D. Reck, similarly promoted, with Chief Yeoman Donald Martin to do the typing. Usually in August they worked together at Morison's camp at Sawyer's Cove, Southwest Harbor, Maine. The men bunked in various cabins, gathered early in Mrs. Morison's studio, and after luncheon Sam often took them sailing; they were totally absorbed in the action they were recording; they knew where his narrative was leading and in Sam's absence might investigate a checkpoint like Bermuda, and have a draft ready for his return. Part of the problem was the change of scene as the campaigns occurred. For instance, in October Morison left for North Africa to observe and make note of "Operation Torch" and then was transported to the Pacific to witness the final triumph of our seizure of Guadalcanal. He had to keep separate and in steady focus each operation, widening the screen as further details flowed in, but the changes seemed to stimulate rather than faze him.

Morison had a brusque manner, even when dealing casually with friends. We were lunching together at the St. Botolph Club, about to finish our littleneck clams. "The derivation is amusing," I said, "clams are hard to open, so from 'clamp' you get 'clam.' "

"That isn't so," he said.

"I'm quite sure it is, Sam."

He left the table abruptly, went to the library, looked up the word in the *Oxford English Dictionary* and returned. "You're right," he said, sat down and speared the last clam.

In the early stages Sam's manner created a restraint in the wardroom. His questions could be direct and unsparing, and were not always well received, especially if there was a cloud of defeat in the engagement. Admiral Bill Halsey was one who dodged him after their first meeting. "You'll have to take care of him," he said to his aide, who, long after the event, remarked to me, "You know, there's the damnedest difference between Morison's frosty, abrupt approach and the sensitivity, the deep feeling with which he wrote about the very same engagement and the men in it, afterwards." Yes, there was.

By the war's end he had served on eleven different warships, had witnessed our amphibious landings in Morocco, Anzio, Omaha, and Okinawa; was aboard the cruiser *Brooklyn* when she was torpedoed, and on the deck of "The Mighty Mo," the battleship *Missouri*, when the articles of surrender were formally signed in Tokyo Bay. He had earned seven battle stars and, what was more, as his volumes appeared, he held the respect of the veterans in his appraisal and criticism of officers and men in our early disasters and hard-won victories.

The judgments were Sam's alone: when fatal mistakes were made in Iron Bottom Bay he named them; when Vice Admiral Clifton A. F. Sprague's desperate defense of his flattops prevailed against such odds in Leyte Gulf, Sam's praise was heartfelt. Like Thucydides he "described nothing but what I either saw myself or learned from others of whom I made the most careful and particular inquiry."

The second volume, *Operations in North African Waters*, appeared in February 1947, by which time Morison had resumed his teaching. From then until 1962 he published a sequence of fifteen volumes, a book a year. To preserve the sense of immediacy in this great chronicle he depended on the notes he had made at the time of each engagement and the eyewitness accounts gathered by himself or by his assistants, whose help he acknowledged in the preface to each volume. It was a prolonged achievement and one which gained in hindsight and fairness from his study of the official records, Japanese and German, and from the memoirs of our adversaries.

Morison called the Battle of Leyte Gulf, in the autumn of 1944, the "greatest naval battle of all time . . . seven weeks of almost continuous fighting on land, sea and in the air until Leyte was secured." It was a most controversial battle, with costly mistakes on both sides

106

and it ended forever "the battle line" of great warships with 18-inch, armor-piercing guns. As the *Monitor*, that "cheese box on a raft," ended the era of Nelson's wooden warships, so the submarines and bombers at Leyte ended the era of the dreadnoughts.

Leyte, with its maps and dramatic photographs, is my favorite of the fifteen volumes, and in its preface we see the several stages with which the author and his assistants pieced together the narrative. The preparation began at the close of the operation when Lieutenant Commander Henry Salomon, Jr., "sailed up to Leyte in Vice Admiral Wilkinson's flagship, received first impressions of the . . . battle, interviewed many participants," and, after V-J Day, went on to "Tokyo in search of Japanese material." Morison wrote his preliminary draft during the winter of 1945–1946 at the Naval War College, Newport, and presumably after his talks with Admiral Halsey and Vice Admiral Sprague, our leading commanders, between whom the blame and praise are divided. In 1950 Morison and his Japanese-speaking assistant, Roger Pineau, visited Japan for amicable discussions of the battle with three Japanese admirals, including Admiral Jisaburo Ozawa, who commanded the northern force which led Halsey astray. The final draft was resumed in 1956, with "immeasurable assistance" from Rear Admiral Bern Anderson (who "was familiar with" the Seventh Fleet), and Rear Admiral Richard W. Bates. It was Sam's magic that fourteen years after the event his account, as if written high above the ships, is so immediate, dramatic and comprehensive.

When Halsey was decoyed north by Admiral Ozawa he took with him 65 ships, including the battleships, to search for and destroy a Japanese fleet of 17, which he did. He believed from air reports that the Japanese Center Force had been put out of action, which was not so, and as the Japanese heavy cruisers and battleships emerged in daylight from San Bernardino Strait they surprised Admiral Sprague's fleet of seven "baby" flattops, three destroyers and a few "Little Wolves," the destroyer escorts. Sprague's only chance was to send the destroyers in, get every plane in the air, and maneuver his carriers out of range as the salvos of the big guns walked up on them. The Japanese shells carried dyes of yellow and purple. This is how Morison tells it:

All hands on board carriers and screen knew they had been caught cold, but they met the situation with the gay cynicism behind which the modern bluejacket hides indomitable courage. As the enemy started firing, one of the signalmen on *White Plains* remarked, "I can't read their signals but they certainly send a lot of dashes." "Yeah," retorted another, "and they are likely to be periods by the time they get here!" Anxious as the officers on the flag bridge were, they could spare a smile for the voice of Admiral Stump over TBS, trying to reassure his friend Clifton Sprague, whose nickname was "Ziggy." "Don't be alarmed, Ziggy — remember, we're back of you — don't get excited — don't do anything rash!" And as he conjured Ziggy to keep calm his voice rose in crescendo. He was indeed backing up Taffy 3, and in the finest way, with planes. The Sprague unit took the rap as far as ships were concerned, but Taffy 2 made the larger contribution of aircraft to the battle. . . .

"Wicked salvos straddled *White Plains*, and their colored geysers began to sprout among all the other carriers from projectiles loaded with dye . . . yellow and purple, the splashes had a kind of horrid beauty." Cried a seaman in *White Plains*: "They're shooting at us in technicolor!" . . .

At that moment, 0706, remarked Sprague, "the enemy was closing with disconcerting rapidity and the volume and accuracy of fire was increasing. At this point it did not appear that any of our ships could survive another five minutes of the heavy-caliber fire being received." . . .

Sprague ordered all airborne planes to concentrate on the four intrusive heavy cruisers. As his carriers were making best speed and dodging salvos, he gave them the humorous order: "Open fire with the pea-shooters when range is clear." Already some of their lone 5-inch 38s were snapping back at *Chikuma* and *Tone*. As he watched the one on *St. Lo* plug doggedly away over the stern, one old chief petty officer was heard to mutter, "They oughtta fire that thing under water — we can use a little jet propulsion right now!"

When the Japanese Admiral inexplicably broke off the action and retired, Sprague had lost his destroyers but only a single carrier, *White Plains*, and in admiration Morison dedicated this particular volume to Sprague, three years after his death.

Morison's remuneration was his Navy pay as he rose in rank from Lieutenant Commander to Rear Admiral. The royalties went to the Department of the Navy, and the series, which is still in demand, has earned in excess of half a million dollars. But there was a reprieve in the summer of 1962 when he retired from teaching and could devote his prime time to a freshly minted retrospect, *The Two-Ocean War*. Those royalties, over $75,000, went to Sam.

In its sweep and grandeur this single large volume is the quintessence of the fifteen; ample enough to dramatize all of the strategic arguments which went on between Churchill and Admiral Ernest J. King, between MacArthur and Nimitz; close enough to reveal the individual heroism, and so penetrating in disclosing the enemy's and our own errors. It is Morison at his very best, and no American historian of this century can top that. I shall quote two passages, the first of which leads to his discriminating characterization of our four greatest admirals: King, Nimitz, Spruance, and Halsey.

Admitting that King was a hard man, without humor, cordially hated by those who disagreed with him, Morison adds that "no officer on either side or in any armed service had so complete a strategic view of the war as King." Then comes the proof:

Admiral Ernest J. King was the Navy's principal architect of victory. A stern sailor of commanding presence, vast sea-knowledge, and keen strategic sense, he was so insistent on maintaining the independence of the Navy, not only from our great Ally but from the Army, that he seemed at times to be anti-British and anti-Army. Neither was true; but King's one mistaken idea was his steady opposition to "mixed groups" from different Navies in the same task force; an idea strengthened by the unfortunate experience of the ABDA command. Mixed groups were of necessity adopted on the convoy routes, with American, Canadian and even an occasional Free French or Polish destroyer in the same escort unit, and they worked well, whilst in the Pacific, ships of the Royal Australian and New Zealand Navies operated perfectly with those of the United States. . . .

We may, however, concede to Admiral King a few prejudices, for he was undoubtedly the best naval strategist and organizer in our history. His insistence on limited offensives in the Pacific to keep the Japanese off balance, his successful efforts to provide more and more escorts for convoys, his promotion of the escort carrier anti-submarine groups, his constant backing of General Marshall to produce a firm date for Operation OVERLORD from the reluctant British; his insistence on the dual approach to Japan, are but a few of the many decisions that prove his genius. King's strategy for the final defeat of Japan — the Formosa and China Coast approach, rather than the Luzon-Okinawa route — was overruled; but may well, in the long run, have been better than MacArthur's, which was adopted. King was also defeated in his many attempts to interest the Royal Navy in a Southeast Asia comeback; and in this he was right. The liberation of Malaya before the war's end would have spared the British a long battle with local Communists and would have provided at least a more orderly transfer of sovereignty in the Netherlands East Indies.

The battle of Midway, June 4, 1942, pitted Admiral Yamamoto (Japan's best), with 162 warships and auxiliaries, against Admiral Raymond A. Spruance, with a fleet of 76, of which one-third never got into the action. I pick up Morison's text as the Japanese planes were returning from their first assault on the tiny island:

109

At 0835, when the returning bombers began landing on the Japanese carriers, American birds carrying death and destruction were already winging their way from *Enterprise* and *Hornet*. Spruance had taken over from Halsey, as chief of staff, Captain Miles Browning, one of the most irascible and unstable officers ever to earn a fourth stripe, but a man with a slide-rule brain. Browning figured out that [Vice Admiral Chuichi] Nagumo would order a second strike on Midway, that he would continue steaming toward the island, and that the golden opportunity to hit his carriers would arrive when they were refueling planes for the second strike. Spruance accepted these estimates and made the tough decision to launch at 0700, when about 175 miles from the enemy's calculated position, instead of continuing for another two hours in order to diminish the distance. Spruance also decided to make this an all-out attack — a full deckload of 20 Wildcat fighters, 67 Dauntless dive-bombers and 29 Devastator torpedo-bombers — and it took an hour to get all these airborne. [Vice Admiral Frank J.] Fletcher properly decided to delay launching from *Yorktown*, in case more targets were discovered; but by 0906 his six fighters, 17 SBDs and 12 TBDs were also in the air.

Imagine, if you will, the tense, crisp briefing in the ready-room, the warming-up of planes which the devoted ground crews have been checking, arming, fueling and servicing; the ritual of the takeoff, as precise and ordered as a ballet; planes swooping in graceful curves over the ships while the group assembles. This Fourth of June was a cool, beautiful day; pilots at 19,000 feet could see all around a circle of 50 miles' radius. Only a few fluffy cumulus clouds were between them and an ocean that looked like a dish of wrinkled blue Persian porcelain. It was a long flight (and, alas, for so many brave young men, a last flight) over the superb ocean. Try to imagine how they felt at first sight of enemy flattops and their wriggling screen, with wakes like the tails of white horses; and sudden catch at their hearts when the black puffs of anti-aircraft bursts came nearer and nearer, then the dreaded Zekes of Japanese combat air patrol swooping down out of the central blue; and finally, the tight, incredibly swift attack, when a pilot forgets everything but the target so rapidly enlarging, and the desperate necessity of choosing the exact tenth of a second to release and pull out.

While these bright ministers of death were on their way, Nagumo's Striking Force continued for over an hour, as Miles Browning had calculated, to steam toward Midway. The four carriers were grouped in a boxlike formation in the center of a screen of two battleships, three cruisers and eleven destroyers. Every few minutes messages arrived from reconnaissance planes that the enemy was approaching. At 0905, just before the last of the planes returning from Midway were recovered, Nagumo ordered Striking Force to turn 90 degrees left, to course ENE, "to contact and destroy the enemy Task Force." His carriers were in

exactly the condition that Spruance and Browning hoped to find them —
planes being refueled and rearmed in feverish haste.

Now came a break for Nagumo. His change of course caused the dive-
bombers and fighters from *Hornet* to miss him altogether. *Hornet*'s
torpedo-bombers, under Lieutenant Commander John C. Waldron, sighted
his smoke and attacked without fighter cover. The result was a massacre
of all fifteen TBDs. Every single one was shot down by Zekes or anti-
aircraft fire; only one pilot survived. The torpedo squadron from *Enterprise* came in next and lost ten out of fourteen; then *Yorktown*'s which
lost all but four; and not a single hit for all this sacrifice. No wonder that
these torpedo-bombers, misnamed Devastators, were struck off the Navy's
list of combat planes.

The third torpedo attack was over by 1024, and for about one hundred
seconds the Japanese were certain they had won the Battle of Midway,
and the war. This was their high tide of victory. Then, a few seconds
before 1026, with dramatic suddenness, there came a complete reversal
of fortune, wrought by the Dauntless dive-bombers, the SBDs, the most
successful and beloved by aviators of all our carrier types during the war.
Lieutenant Commander Clarence W. McClusky, air group commander of
Enterprise, had two squadrons of SBDs under him: 37 units. He ordered
one to follow him in attacking carrier *Kaga*, while the other, under
Lieutenant W. E. Gallaher, pounced on *Akagi*, Nagumo's flagship. Their
coming in so soon after the last torpedo-bombing attack meant that the
Zekes were still close to the water after shooting down TBDs, and had no
time to climb. At 14,000 feet the American dive-bombers tipped over
and swooped screaming down for the kill. *Akagi* took a bomb which exploded in the hangar, detonating torpedo storage, then another which exploded amid planes changing their armament on the flight deck — just as
Browning had calculated. Fires swept the flagship, Admiral Nagumo and
staff transferred to cruiser *Nagara*, and the carrier was abandoned and
sunk by a destroyer's torpedo. Four bomb hits on *Kaga* killed everyone on
the bridge and set her burning from stem to stern. Abandoned by all but
a small damage-control crew, she was racked by an internal explosion that
evening, and sank hissing into a 2600-fathom deep.

The third carrier was the victim of *Yorktown*'s dive-bombers, under
Lieutenant Commander Maxwell F. Leslie, who by cutting corners managed to make up for a late start. His 17 SBDs jumped *Soryu* just as she
was turning into the wind to launch planes, and planted three half-ton
bombs in the midst of the spot. Within twenty minutes she had to be
abandoned. U.S. submarine *Nautilus*, prowling about looking for targets,
pumped three torpedoes into her, the gasoline storage exploded, whip-
sawing the carrier, and down she went in two sections.

At 1024 Japan had been on top; six minutes later, on that bright June
morning, three of her big carriers were on their flaming way to death.

At 1530 in the afternoon, at Spruance's command, the *Enterprise* launched 24 SBDs, including veterans of the morning's battle, and led by "the redoubtable [Lt. W. E.] Gallaher" they found the fourth carrier, *Hiryu,* and jumped her screen. Four hits did her in and she took down with her Rear Admiral T. Yamaguchi, "an outstanding flag officer who, it is said, would have been Yamamoto's successor had he lived."

Morison's summing up is charged with feeling:

Spruance's performance was superb. Calm, collected, decisive, yet receptive to advice; keeping in his mind the picture of widely disparate forces, yet boldly seizing every opening, Raymond A. Spruance emerged from this battle one of the greatest admirals in American naval history.

The Japanese knew very well that they were beaten. Midway thrust the war lords back on their heels, caused their ambitious plans for the conquest of Port Moresby, Fiji, New Caledonia and Samoa to be canceled, and forced on them an unexpected and unwelcome defensive role. The word went out from Imperial Headquarters that the name Midway was not to be mentioned.

Admirals Nimitz, Fletcher and Spruance are, as I write, very much alive; Captain Mitscher of *Hornet,* Captain Murray of *Enterprise* and Captain Miles Browning of the slide-rule mind have joined the threescore young aviators who met flaming death that day in reversing the verdict of battle. Think of them, reader, every Fourth of June. They and their comrades who survived changed the whole course of the Pacific War.

Admiral William F. Halsey was a kinsman of mine, and worshipped by every member of a large family. Morison's characterization seems to me balanced and fair:

Halsey, the public's favorite in the Navy, will always remain a controversial figure, but none can deny that he was a great leader; one with the true "Nelson touch." His appointment as Commander South Pacific Force at the darkest moment of the Guadalcanal campaign lifted the hearts of every officer and bluejacket. He hated the enemy with an unholy wrath, and turned that feeling into a grim determination by all hands to hit hard, again and again, and win. His proposal to step up the Leyte operation by two months was a stroke of strategic genius which undoubtedly shortened the Pacific war. Unfortunately, in his efforts to build public morale in America and Australia, Halsey did what Spruance refused to do — build up an image of himself as an exponent of Danton's famous principle, "Audacity, more audacity, always audacity." That was the real reason for his fumble in the Battle for Leyte Gulf. For his inspiring leadership in 1942–1943, his generosity to others, his capacity for choosing the right men for his staff, Halsey well earned his five stars, and his place among the Navy's immortals.

One seldom edited Sam Morison but as he and I came to an understanding I sometimes made a suggestion. In my boyhood I had spent a month each summer visiting my Navy cousins in Annapolis. It could be hot as Hades in July and for Raymond Stone, Jr., and me the two coolest retreats were the museum of ship models at the Academy and the marble sarcophagus recently erected for the body of John Paul Jones. He was one of my heroes and it was good to stand at his tomb, sucking "snowballs," cracked ice flavored with vanilla, and think of the three-and-a-half-hour desperate battle between the leaking *Bonhomme Richard* and H.M.S. *Serapis*, which Jones won. In remembrance I said to Sam that there had never been a good biography of Jones and why didn't he write one. He replied that Jones was a better man afloat than he was on shore, a mistress in every port, and very jealous of the Admiral's rank, which Congress would never grant him — besides, there wasn't enough new material about him.

But as it happened there was a trove: photostats, letters, and the availability of material about the more mysterious periods of Jones's life, a valuable collection which the Philibert sisters of Arlington, Virginia, generously placed at Sam's disposal. Although he was in the midst of completing the *Naval Operations* Sam took on Jones and I think found the change refreshing. One could feel his delight as he told how John Paul molested the British Isles in the sloop of war *Ranger* (18 guns!), taking prizes along the way, keeping the Admiralty in the dark, and capturing H.M.S. *Drake* as he blithely returned to France. After Jones's indomitable capture of the *Serapis* he was lionized in Paris. He was thirty-six and attractive, as the bust by Houdon attests; the ladies — all but the one he craved — were his for the asking. In addition to his prize money, Louis XVI presented him with a gold sword and created him Chevalier of the *Ordre du Mérite Militaire*. His intoxication with France destroyed forever the thought of settling down in America. His friendship with Benjamin Franklin and later Thomas Jefferson; his exploits in Russia when Catherine the Great commissioned him Rear Admiral, as Congress would not; his residence in Paris during the Revolution — this was the new material and Morison made the most of it. *John Paul Jones: A Sailor's Biography*, was a book club selection in 1959, and a year later when I was in England I received a cable, which according to the operator, read, "Morison wins Pulit Surprise." It was his second.

Sam Morison so disciplined his mind that he could work simultaneously on two, sometimes three, books. I have never known any author capable of such detachment with such profound results. Consider. He published *John Paul Jones* in 1959. At the same time he was completing the last two volumes of the *Naval Operations*, the final one appearing in 1962. And in 1965 came his stellar *Oxford History of the American People*, which, as he told Alden Whitman, was his favorite work of history, "my legacy to my country." The Gods had been watching and in 1963 Morison was awarded the Balzan Foundation Prize, medal, scroll and $51,000, which he and his beloved Priscilla went to Switzerland to receive. Historians are not eligible for the Nobel Prize in Literature but this, too, was recognition from Olympus.

In that magnificent succession was only one failure, the life of Commodore Matthew C. Perry, who led a squadron in the Mexican War, chased pirates, and commanded the naval expedition that opened Japan. A strict disciplinarian with a loud voice, he was nicknamed by his crew "Old Bruin." The trouble was not in the writing; the truth was the bear lived on so long — and so correctly — he became a bore.

Sam's work was divided among four publishers and each bid for his final triumph (our bid was an advance of $220,000) — *European Discovery of America: The Northern Voyages* and *The Southern Voyages* (1971 and 1974). It went to the Oxford University Press, partly because of Oxford's prestige and, perhaps subconsciously, because of that silly Englishwoman's taunt.

In September 1969, I went up to Seal Harbor to be with the Lippmanns for Walter's eightieth birthday. The morning of the twenty-third we went for one of his favorite walks in the Rockefeller woods. His legs were no longer sturdy enough to carry him to the Inner Garden, which, out of habit, Helen briskly intended to reach, so he sat resignedly on the stone wall until we completed the round.

There were forty of us for dinner, which was followed by toasts, witticisms, and poems. When the men withdrew for liqueurs I sat beside Sam. He knew without my saying how disappointed I was at not publishing his *Explorers*. "I tell you what," he said. "I intend to do a short biography of Champlain, a fine navigator and an admirable man. You shall have it." He was as good as his word, and that was my consolation prize.

CHAPTER

VII

At the conclusion of an afternoon lecture in Worcester, Esther Forbes, the novelist who introduced me, said, "Now, I have a treat for you: we're going to have cocktails with Francis Henry Taylor, director of our art museum."

The martinis were of good gin with just a drop of vermouth and our host stirred, not shook, them in a tall glass container, with rocks of ice. They were deliciously strong and I studied him with appreciation. Broad and solid, dark-eyed with a chiseled hook of a nose, he had an infectious laugh that began before he'd finish his sentence. I thought he looked like one of the Medici. Indeed, it was of Florence that he was speaking, of the art dealers there and how they would tempt an Italian prince with an audacious offer for one of his paintings and then lie in wait for the arrival of J. P. Morgan, sure that if he liked the canvas, he'd pay the price, whatever the mark-up. If this was the traffic of art it was the most irreverent and wittiest I had heard, and we had printed nothing like it in the *Atlantic*. Before we departed he had agreed to do two papers, the first on the dilemma of the modern artist and the second on decisions facing the director of an art museum in a changing world.

At the time I met him Taylor had acquired an extraordinary range of knowledge. After graduating from the University of Pennsylvania with honors in literature and the Romance languages, he went abroad, to teach English at a lycée in Chartres and to revere that great cathedral inside and out. Already an ardent Francophile, he extended his knowledge of medieval and Renaissance art by studying both the works and the financing of the great collections, in the Vatican, in Spain, and in Florence, where he became friends with Bernard Berenson. Because of his wit and candor he was, as James Plaut called him, "the *enfant terrible* of the American art world."

I was lucky to catch him when I did, brimming with life, happy with his museum and eager to write. After his first two spirited papers in the *Atlantic*, he and Pamela, his wife, dined with us and I went at him for a book. Who were our early collectors before Morgan, Frick, and Widener? What went into our first museums? We were ready to draw up a contract, but he was dubious and it took only a brief inquiry to determine that the earliest collections were a hodgepodge: sculpture, primitive portraits, a stuffed eagle, and a jar of Mrs. Chase's exceptionally large gallstones (on loan). Secondly, and even more important, no general history of collecting in the world had been written in English. So Taylor's horizon was broadened and he signed our contract for a volume dealing with the salient early and European collectors, and a following volume on the rise of collecting in America.

It was Francis's premise that the creation of art, and the collecting of it, followed the flight of gold, and that with the invention of the wheel, art began to circulate widely as it became the plunder of each new conquest. (Or change of management, as when Parliament sold off the collections of Charles I, Buckingham and Arundel.) Research for the book consumed his spare time, then in 1940 he was offered the directorship of our supreme storehouse, the Metropolitan Museum of Art, in New York City. Of course he would accept and I feared the book would be pushed aside.

I went to Worcester for an overnight visit and saw that he had enough material for six books. We spent hours deliberating over which artists to slight, in one compendious volume devoted to the history of collecting, from Rameses to the present. Before we resumed Sunday morning, I had read the pages on the Medici and their centuries of splendid sovereignty in Florence, and the French chapters on the Sun King and Madame de Pompadour, which sparkled with Taylor's light touch. But there was too much!

On my first call on Francis at the Metropolitan, I was shown to his paneled office under the eaves where he pointed with a grin to the names and tenure of his predecessors painted on the outside of the door, his the last, and beneath it, "1940–." "Rather like working," he said, "in the Old Burying Ground of Boston, with the stone carver waiting to be called."

To my relief he was still writing, but the problem of length was troubling him and I thought it would facilitate the project if it were divided in two, the first volume ending with Napoleon and the plunder he and his marshals had captured and sent back to the Louvre; the second beginning with the restoration which Wellington insisted on after Waterloo, the establishment of the great national museums in the nineteenth century and the rise of the predatory Americans. That decision became definite at the war's end, when we knew the brutal depravity of Hitler's looting.

In his scathing article for the *Atlantic*, "The Rape of Europe," Taylor revealed the order, taken from a German prisoner in Italy, which in its ruthlessness went beyond anything conceived by Napoleon's experts. It read:

Our pillage must be organized and methodical. We must take as many light-weight valuable objects as possible, such as jewels, precious metals and stones, works of art, religious treasures, books, linen, stamps, etc., so that they can be sold as easily as possible and transferred into cash deposits in safe and inviolable places. . . . This looting together with the destruction of factories and machinery and the terrors of deportation and scientific famine imposed on children and civilians should insure a speedy revenge.

Poland, being the first victim, had its cultural heritage thoroughly destroyed. In Russia, "the palace of Catherine the Great at Tsarskoe Selo was stripped, Chinese silks and tapestries torn off the walls, antique furniture and paneling shipped to Berlin. Even the inlaid floors were packed and sent away. The celebrated library of French and Russian books and manuscripts was pillaged. Peterhof was looted before it was burned and the suburbs of Leningrad were sacked. Kiev, the religious and scientific center of old Russia, was emptied of its treasures, particularly the great collections of libraries of the university and the Ukrainian Academy of Sciences."

The private collections of France, including, of course, those of the Rothschilds, were confiscated, so too the Bayeux Tapestry, which was marked for shipment to Berlin but was fortunately intercepted by General George Patton's recapture of Paris. Francis wrote before the treasures which Göring and Hitler had hidden in the salt mines came to light.

The Taste of Angels was the title Francis finally chose for the big book which, after twelve years' preparation, we published in 1948. It came as a searchlight turned on the growth of artistic appreciation and the rise and flight of gold. The narrative is documented with the intriguing finance and enlivened by the characterization of the great personages, the Medici, the Fuggers of Augsburg, the collector Popes, the court at Versailles, Christina of Sweden, Pompadour, Richelieu, and Horace Walpole, to name a few. Throughout, the reader is regaled by Taylor's penetrating judgment, and often by laughter, as when he describes the art trade in Rome under the emperor Caligula. There were many illustrations, and the author personally supervised the production of the color plates. *The Taste of Angels* was praised as an original and monumental work and Francis was pleased with the reviews.

As an expert on medieval art and a worshipper of the Renaissance, he was deeply disturbed by the change which was introduced by the abstractionists, and once his book was off his mind he spoke his mind in his article "Modern Art and the Dignity of Man." It is a provocative analysis, profound in what he says about Picasso. This is his challenge at the beginning:

Art for them [the artists] has ceased to have any moral or religious significance; they have divorced it from the area of common human experience and made it a form of private communication — when it communicates at all — whereby abstract associations of form and color convey intimacies scarcely less cryptic than those revealed on the psychoanalyst's couch. The innocent layman, visiting the national exhibitions, may be forgiven for suspecting that the chief purpose of American art is to illustrate the Kinsey Report.

And this, his appraisal of Picasso:

Picasso is at once the giant paradox and the towering genius of our day who has captured our imagination by exploiting the manic depression which has carried our generation through two world wars and is hurling us along the road to world revolution. He has caught our suicidal despair and laughed at it hysterically. Only history can determine whether Picasso, like the skeleton at the feast, is the last flowering of a civilization whose collapse amuses him, or whether there is latent in his extraordinary mobility of line and color the prophecy of a new world which is to come.

If Picasso with his uncommon gifts has shown at every turn his utter contempt for the dignity of man, one can scarcely expect much more from those lesser luminaries on both sides of the Atlantic who slavishly follow in his footsteps. Whereas it is clear that Picasso is always completely master of himself, and knows to a carefully calculated nicety what he is doing, the imitators are capable of producing only the empty forms but not the content. . . .

Those were bold words to have been uttered in 1948, and they too show how his mind was resolving the themes of his second book.

An uncertain fate hangs over the director of any museum of art, particularly if it is richly endowed. Too often the chairman of the trustees comes to believe that he or she knows best what should be done for the collection. I realized that Francis was troubled about his salary at the Metropolitan, which was surprisingly inadequate, but even more by the aggressive interference of the head of the board, which became intolerable. The freedom he had enjoyed in Worcester stood out in sunny contrast to his overburdened chafing régime in New York, and when the authorities in Worcester invited him to return, he gladly accepted.

I was happy at his decision. Once more he was within easy reach, his talk as scintillating as ever, throwing off sparks for the second volume to come. He went abroad on what proved to be his last visit to Berenson, and his account of BB's intention to bequeath his Villa I Tatti to Harvard was published in the *Atlantic* and set aside as a chapter. He wrote a brilliant profile of J. P. Morgan, the great collector he had talked about at our first meeting. But mostly the text of the sequel was in his head, or in notes when he began to suffer from gall bladder trouble. I could not believe that a constitution as robust as his was in danger. But it was. He did not live to finish that second volume.

During the First World War my predecessor increased the circulation of the *Atlantic* by 50 percent. From 1939 to mid-1946, the circulation again rose 50 percent, from 101,312 to 153,982, an increase that gave me unbounded confidence. When peace came I promised our readers three changes: "To restore the balance between literature and politics which could not be maintained during the emergency, to increase the number of short stories and to secure those essays of criticism and appraisal which made the magazine provocative and a pleasure in times past."

For the critical essays I wanted a man well read, and hungry for exceptional books, as gregarious as Clifton Fadiman and not as short-tempered with contemporary authors as Edmund Wilson. I found him in Charles Rolo. With his Oxford background, his fastidious literary palate and lively style, Charles merited a regular place in the magazine. His judgment of the new books of Evelyn Waugh, Alberto Moravia, Albert Camus, Graham Greene, André Gide, and Aldous Huxley, to name a few, related to the whole body of their work. His incisive scrutiny of the "Freudian Revolution" was so discerning, so quotable, that I was happy to have him write for us for thirteen years.

As Hemingway predicted, while the fighting went on the best short stories were by women. From Mississippi Eudora Welty sent us, I really think, the finest quartet of her galaxy — "The Worn Path," "Why I Live at the P.O.," "Powerhouse," that unforgettable portrait of a black band leader, and "Libby Is Back." In 1944 Jessamyn West broke in with her first submission. She is a Hoosier, a birthright Quaker and a graduate of Whittier College who was knocked down by tuberculosis and had to make what she calls "the horizontal approach to literature." All her tales have a Quaker quality even when she is writing about a Morgan mare named Mary with "the heart of a lion and the wings of a bird," who could win any race against a quarter-horse. "Lead Her like a Pigeon" was the title of my favorite — before she was swiped from us by the *Saturday Evening Post*. And from Ireland Mary Lavin sent a long narrative, "At Sallygap," the haunting dreams of an Irish fiddler written with that lyrical dialogue and pathos characteristic of her work. ("At Sallygap" became the title story of Mary's first book and so attracted Eudora that the three of us years later spent a happy day together at Mary's snow-white cottage beside the river Boyne in County Meath).

But the only two stories we published by a combatant were those I have already referred to, written by Lieutenant Laurence Critchell of the 101st Airborne. Yet it was predictable that when the veterans were discharged the exceptional few would be impelled to write what had been bottled up in them in uniform. I needed something larger than our modest fee of $300 to catch their immediate attention and I got it from one of my alumni, Archie Ogden, my cousin from New Jersey who had been my assistant at the Press before he left us to scout for Metro-Goldwyn-Mayer. I told him I intended to feature "Atlantic Firsts," meaning new stories by writers of promise. He said, Let us sweeten the pot: MGM will put up two prizes — in addition to your fee — for the best you get each six months, the first prize, $1,500, the second $750, and we have an option on the film rights. The prizes would be renewed for two years, and it was big money for 1946.

With such rosy prospects, when rationing ceased we bought expensive paper, increased our print order by 50,000 copies, anticipating a fresh demand on the newsstands, and sent out two million come-ons to trial subscribers, expecting our loyal advertising to pay the bill. Little did we know. At the end of the fiscal year the over-production and a shocking loss of advertising wiped out our bank account and left us deep in red. When the Danielsons bought the magazine they paid Sedgwick's price but made no deposit of capital in our account. So our narrow margin was vulnerable.

Don stated the hard truths at a directors' meeting. "Ted and I were over-confident. We failed to realize that readers stopped asking for the *Atlantic* when copies were no longer on the newsstands during the war — which explains those shocking returns. The fall-off in advertising is more serious — Buick, Chesterfield, Goodrich — were content to use our space when Uncle Sam helped to pay for their institutional ads. Now they've returned to *Time, Newsweek,* and *Look.* They're playing the numbers and we're not big enough. Our guarantee of a hundred thousand was passable in 1941; for the future we've got to produce a more attractive magazine with a minimum guarantee of two hundred thousand readers. To do that we need new capital."

Don and I cut our salaries by 20 percent and considered other economies. Charlie Morton, who had experienced the failure of the *Boston Evening Transcript* when they were about to burn their desks to heat the building, wrote me a memo:

3/12/47

Dear Ted:
A difficult period, and I don't know whether pressing these opinions on you will be helpful or burdensome. Can't help feeling an obligation to tell you how I feel about it: Can't believe that the Atlantic ought to settle for a program of contraction at this time. Institutionally, I don't believe we should be writing off the various gains of the past five years — circulation, prestige, editorial development. It's a terrific job to recapture these things once you start losing them. . . .
The terrible peculiarity of a publishing enterprise is that literally every expenditure in it can be reduced or even eliminated, and this always seems to tempt the business strategist who is trying to put the enterprise on a sound footing. Yet the minute the enterprise loses its ability to do the right thing, the profitable thing, the essential thing it is really set up to do, the thing it is celebrated for having done well, the whole scheme is headed for the boneyard. That is my deep belief, based on the most painful personal experiences. . . .

With more confidence than I felt I went down to raise the new capital in New York, remembering that J. P. Morgan had come to the rescue of the House of Harper in the 1890s. No need to name those I called on at the House of Morgan and the House of Whitney, but, in the words of my father who had gone through the wringer in the cotton business, "People were walking away." The luncheons were cordial but the hesitation plain; perhaps they suspected that an old Boston magazine designed for the intelligentsia was destined to stay small. I came back to Boston emptyhanded and for three weeks touched the lowest point in my career. In my second year as editor we paid dividends, of our solid profit throughout the war we paid 90 percent to the government (in 1944 we earned $145,000) — and now this swift reversal.

Little, Brown and Company, the long-established Boston publishers, had acquired a half-interest in Atlantic Monthly Press books in 1925, and during the nine years I edited our books I had become devoted to their president, Alfred McIntyre. Our cooperation had been profitable during the Depression, and he was not willing to see us fade. It was an enormous relief when he volunteered to purchase the Atlantic's preferred stock for $100,000 and to join our Board of Directors. Thank God, we had our seed money and the only way to go was up!

Two things cheered me while on the bottom. During the war our relations with French writers were totally ruptured. Antoine de Saint-Exupéry and Raoul de Roussy de Sales were dead, André Siegfried was old and silent. As soon as Paris was liberated I sent Monica Stirling, a young bilingual English journalist, to France, where she had spent her girlhood, and her accounts of those returning from captivity and of the incredible daring of the Resistance were moving. Now came a manuscript, unexpectedly, from Jean-Paul Sartre entitled "American Novelists in French Eyes." He began by remarking, "The greatest literary development in France between 1929 and 1939 was the discovery of Faulkner, Dos Passos, Hemingway, Caldwell, Steinbeck." Their novels, he said, "evoked a revolution similar to the one produced fifteen years earlier in Europe by the *Ulysses* of James Joyce."

It seemed to us suddenly that we had just learned something and that our literature was about to pull itself out of its old ruts. At once, for thousands of young intellectuals, the American novel took its place, together with jazz and the movies, among the best of the importations from the United States. America became for us the country of Faulkner and Dos Passos, just as it had already been the home of Louis Armstrong, King Vidor, the Blues. The large frescoes of Vidor joined with the passion and violence of *The Sound and the Fury* and *Sanctuary* to compose for us the face of the United States — a face tragic, cruel, and sublime. . . .

What fascinated us all really — petty bourgeois that we were, sons of peasants securely attached to the earth of our farms, intellectuals entrenched in Paris for life — was the constant flow of men across a whole continent, the exodus of an entire village to the orchards of California, the hopeless wanderings of the hero in *Light in August*, and of the uprooted people who drifted along at the mercy of the storms in *The 42nd*

Parallel, the dark murderous fury which sometimes swept through an entire city, the blind and criminal love in the novels of James Cain. . . . It takes some time for an influence to produce its effect, and it was during the German occupation, when the Germans forbade all printing and reprinting of American books, that we began to see in France the greatest number of works inspired by this new manner of writing. . . .

The French novel which caused the greatest furor between 1940 and 1945, *The Stranger*, by Albert Camus, a young writer who was then director of the clandestine newspaper, *Combat*, deliberately borrowed the technique of *The Sun Also Rises*. . . .

I followed Sartre's stimulus, went after Camus and got a fine story; but otherwise we drew a blank. In retrospect I was wrong to expect a burst of good writing from people so exhausted, and divided.

At home the announcement of the prizes for "Atlantic Firsts" brought forth a harvest that was to continue for years. The initial prize-winners were Cord Meyer, Jr., whose story "Waves of Darkness" was a revelation of what went through a young Marine's mind moments before he was all but fatally wounded in the assault on Guam. The second winner came from the Navy, the amusing "Night Watch" by Thomas Heggen, one of the best episodes in his later novel, *Mister Roberts*. The writers of our "Firsts" were little known at the time of submission but they form a distinguished group today: James Jones, Peter Matthiessen, Louis Auchincloss, Brian Moore, Jesse Hill Ford, Richard Yates, Harry Mark Petrakis, Edwin O'Connor, and Benjamin DeMott, to pick a conspicuous nine from some forty thousand manuscripts submitted.

Our advertising manager during the war was an old hand on Madison Avenue, a dandy in fair weather, but after V-J Day, when the agencies began saying, "Not for this year, old boy," he was ready to retire. We needed a younger, undaunted replacement and I turned to Leslie B. Crockett, Colonel in the Air Force under Lieutenant General Elwood R. Quesada, and, like many a veteran, ready to make a fresh start away from Manhattan, where formerly he had earned a sound reputation on *Business Week*. He and his wife, Kay, came to dinner and as I enlarged on our prospects, his eyes shone. As Don said, "He got religion fast." One of Crockett's first moves was to form a subsidiary corporation, selling space in *Harper's* or the *Atlantic* — or in both, with a combined circulation slightly larger than that of the *New Yorker*. Then he recruited Bill Blair and Mac Hoggson and year by year our advertising steadily became an asset.

Atlantic readers are discriminating and have to be won. Machines had been perfected to do the handwork formerly required in fulfilling and mailing subscriptions. We needed a young professional, and I got a tip from Gardner Cowles of *Look* which led to the right man. "You know Frank Herbert, who has done such a hell of a job with *Reader's Digest*? Well, his son, Frank Junior, has been trained by his old man and I'm told that he's eager to be on his own. We've been thinking of him for our organization. Might give him a try." I am grateful to Gardner for many things and especially this. Frank came to us tentatively, but, like Les, he "got religion" and steadily built up our circulation.

Throughout its early life the *Atlantic*, I repeat, had depended solely upon subscriptions: when the readers were loyal we prospered; when they were disgusted, as they were by Harriet Beecher Stowe's account of the indignities inflicted upon Lady Byron by the poet, 15,000 cancellations within three months brought us to the verge of bankruptcy. Readers had become more tolerant in my time, but we lost each year one reader in every four through death, divorce, or lack of interest. The only way to find replacements, or better, to grow, as Frank quickly demonstrated, was to offer trial subscriptions to the most responsive lists and to save time and money by placing the whole fulfillment operation in the hands of a company equipped with the New Machines.

There is the story, perhaps apocryphal, of a man named Pogue in Terre Haute who subscribed to *Time* just as the wonder machine was making its initial run. His first copy was delivered by the dozens, by the hundreds, then by truckload before it was discovered that the whiz had stuck on the letters "Pog." In our case, a costly imperfection was not discovered until after New Year's and called for endless letters of apologies. A good number of our loyalists were in the habit of giving the *Atlantic* to their friends for Christmas, in some cases as many as four or five gift subscriptions. This was a fact the machine could not digest: in too many cases *all* the gift copies went to the donor and the intended recipients each received a bill. Such miscarriages had run up into the hundreds before the readjustment could begin. When things were straightened out, Frank decided that all future gifts should be dealt with by hand.

On the scientific side I occasionally consulted Emily Flint, the librarian at the Massachusetts Institute of Technology, and received such clear-headed advice that I asked her to come to us. Em's executive ability, her skill in cutting, and her belief in the magazine qualified her to be our managing editor. It was a superb team and when I was away lecturing, Charlie Morton took charge. I sometimes wrote my column on the road, to the irritation of my friend Bennett Cerf, who called and found me gone. He said to our receptionist, "Tell Mr. Weeks that if he wasn't so damn peripatetic he'd be a better editor." Maybe. But I thanked him for christening my column, "The Peripatetic Reviewer."

The renovation of a magazine so as to attract younger readers without disturbing the loyalty of the older is a delicate operation. *Scribner's* and Henry Mencken's *American Mercury* had tried to do so and both were dead. Don Snyder was confident that with a new cover the *Atlantic* would say, "Read me!" and he consulted W. A. Dwiggins, a master of design.

Since the nineteenth century our traditional covers had been simply a table of contents in type, indistinct at five paces. In the past it had not mattered if each new issue looked just like its predecessors; the word "Atlantic" was enough. But no longer. What Don wanted was a fresh, distinctive cover with a portrait or photograph of the leading contributor in a center panel, and space below to announce the leading features. In his sample layout he devoted one cover to President Conant of Harvard, a second to Robert R. Young, the aggressive railroad magnate, and a third to T. S. Eliot.

Don placed them on his office rug and called us in. To test their pulling power, these pictorial covers were used on special editions for three cities in the Midwest, and we were elated when they outsold the newsstand draw of our table-of-contents covers in all cities of comparable size by a margin of 3 to 1 for Conant and Young, and by 5 to 1 for Eliot. That settled it. For November 1947, which would be our Ninetieth Anniversary, we prepared a special issue. The cover was a watercolor by Dwiggins of Neptune and his seahorse, riding the waves (the *Atlantic*'s colophon) and, beneath, a blue-ribbon list of contributors.

What spurred us was the sight in Dwiggins's studio of drawing boards on which were the designs for a new monthly for Henry Luce, to be called *Measure*, and intended to put us out of business. For the magazine's editor Luce had picked Willy Schlamm; the name didn't scare me but Luce's money did. For reasons undisclosed *Measure* never did emerge, but the possibility made us bolder.

We sent to press what was up to then the largest number in our history, and the diversity in those 182 pages will be seen in the con-

tributors listed in three columns beneath the Dwiggins painting. They
were:

Albert Einstein	Sir Osbert Sitwell
Robert Frost	Anne Morrow Lindbergh
Gen. George S. Patton, Jr.	N. R. Danielian
Sir Richard Livingstone	Henry James
Budd Schulberg	John P. Marquand
Rufus M. Jones	Frederick Lewis Allen
W. H. Auden	Ellery Sedgwick
Letters of Mark Twain	Sumner T. Pike
Ed. by Dixon Wecter	George Bernard Shaw
Somerset Maugham	Godfrey Blunden
Sumner Welles	

This was the aftermath of war: what I was looking for were people
in authority who were thinking of the future and others whose names
would catch the eye. Very personal were the war letters of General
George S. Patton, written to his dearest friend, his brother-in-law,
Fred Ayer, with whom I occasionally fished. Fred had told me of the
fidelity and deep feeling these letters revealed and I was touched
that Beatrice Patton let me have them so soon after the General's
death.

Sadly, "The Future of Britain" by N. R. Danielian verified what
I had seen but was unwilling to believe in that summer of 1943. (Is
there any other people on earth who could have taken such punishing
losses, of empire, of wealth, and of younger sons, with such stoicism?)

As an offset we needed a spiritual voice and the warmth of good
fiction and biography. For the first I turned to Rufus Jones, that
eloquent American Quaker, who wrote with persuasion, "What the
Modern Man Can Believe"; I asked John Marquand to let me have the
opening, very amusing, episodes of his forthcoming novel, *Point of
No Return*. And for humor we had Mark Twain. My friend Dixon
Wecter had recently been appointed literary executor of the Mark
Twain estate, and I knew that he had been editing Clemens's unpub-
lished love letters to Olivia Langdon of Elmira, New York. Mark had
seen her photograph in the possession of her brother Charles, with
whom he shared a cabin when outward bound on *The Innocents
Abroad*. When Mark returned he was introduced to Olivia at the St.
Nicholas Hotel in New York City, where the Langdons were staying.
Their first date took them to Steinway Hall to hear Dickens read from
David Copperfield. Olivia was then twenty-five, Mark ten years her
senior, and soon incurably in love.

Twice he interrupted lecture trips to court her at her home in Elmira, but both Olivia and her parents had their doubts about this breezy Westerner. At the termination of the second visit Charles was about to drive Mark to the station when the horse started suddenly, the seat broke loose, and both were pitched over backward. Mark landed on his head, "breaking my neck in eleven different places." In a state of mild concussion he was nursed by Olivia, and during the convalescence he made the promises which he renews later in his letters: "To read Mr. Beecher's Sermons over and over," and, far more difficult, to eschew alcohol and blasphemy. "Why bless your darling heart I *do* love to hear you scold! . . . It does make a deep impression. . . . But to tell the truth, I love you so well that I am capable of misbehaving, just for the pleasure of hearing you scold."

When Mr. Langdon saw that his daughter was listening to Mark's entreaties, he asked for references. Mark gave him several names including Bret Harte, editor of the *Overland Monthly*; J. Neely Johnson, Chief Justice of the Supreme Court of Nevada; and Joseph T. Goodman, proprietor of the *Daily Enterprise*, Virginia City, for whom Mark had been city editor for "three years without losing a day." But the replies had a certain hesitancy. "After reviewing these letters," says Wecter, "his prospective father-in-law gravely asked, 'Haven't you a friend in the world?' Clemens replied, 'Apparently not.' And then the shrewd old coal operator said, 'I'll be your friend, myself. Take the girl. I know you better than they do.' " Mark loved her faithfully, and for life, and predictably it was he who converted her to his skeptical philosophy, and not the other way around.

Our President, Dick Danielson, a man I revered, had come through a desperate operation (which was to grant him ten more years of life), and to cheer him I sent an advance copy of the big issue to the hospital in Philadelphia where he was recuperating. He read it from cover to cover, called it "a triumph, the best issue of an American magazine I ever read," and he studied each change we had made in the format: the typography "a delight to the eye"; the biographical streamers I wrote about each contributor ("You apply artistry to matters of apparent insignificance which a man of less integrity would push off on someone else"). Then he invoked a principle in editing so important that I read it aloud to the staff:

On the other hand perfection in detail must never ignore the *total* impact of each issue of a magazine. It is a complete book — a monthly message as to man on earth. My impression of this issue is somewhat gloomy. Let's assume that man is continually doing the wrong things and getting himself in the most awful scrapes and that his prospects for a good life are less than dim. Yet old Rufus Jones comes along and says that every once in a while mankind produces a saint and that there is something *in* man which is not of this world. That has been a recurring *Atlantic* message and it needs to be repeated and it isn't just Pollyanna. . . . I think it is inevitable in assembling an issue that each article is judged on its individual excellence and that the incidence of the assembled package of wisdom is not apparent in advance. That should be an important consideration in our editorial meetings. . . . Read the Reports and Einstein and Welles and Livingstone and Danielian and you are tempted to empty the ashcan on your head and cry what is man that Thou are mindful of him?

He was right: the overall effect was more depressing than we intended. Still, that issue did well enough on the newsstands to give us hope. But the increase in our circulation came slowly. It would take five years to reach Snyder's goal of 200,000, and for five summers he and I signed notes at the bank for loans that would carry us through the dry spell to mid-September when the incoming subscriptions refreshed our capital. You have to be confident to walk a tightrope.

In the immediate years after the bomb had fallen on Hiroshima, despite John Hersey's scarifying account of the mortal agony, many Americans lived with a feeling of exemption: *we* had the weapon; it couldn't happen here.

The U.S. Navy was more skeptical: it chose the island of Bikini, seventy-five miles due west of Eniwetok, as a laboratory in which to test the effect of two bombs on a fleet of obsolete and captured warships, manned by crews of "experimental animals" and loaded with stores and equipment. The first bomb would be dropped from a great height, the second exploded underwater at a depth of about 180 feet. Accompanying the "dead fleet" was a live fleet, carrying admirals, observers, scientists, and doctors of the Radiological Safety Section, who would stand watch with Geiger counters to make sure no one was contaminated. Among them was a young graduate of the Harvard Medical School, Dr. David J. Bradley, who had been training for six months for this mission. He kept a log of what was happening and when it was declassified two years after the test, he gave it to Charlie Morton.

The bomb from above sank a few warships, and the animal crew "will show the effect of Atom Bomb disease." As at Hiroshima the blast caused the immediate devastation. But the underwater bomb hurled up a huge mushroom of water and vapor "that climbed up to several thousand feet, then broke" and descended spewing deadly contamination everywhere, not only aboard the dead ships but the fish in the atoll, the oil flecks washed ashore, even the apparel of the workers was radioactive.

There were flashes of humor, as when a quartermaster shouted, "Hey, you guys. Get the hell off that stanchion. Can't you see you're sitting on a goddam booby trap?"

"Ah, it don't matter, Chief," kidded one of them. "I got so many of them Geigers runnin' round inside me now that you can see me all lit up at night like the Statue of Liberty."

But Operation Crossroads was abandoned in August, and most of the target fleet sunk in deep water. We published *No Place to Hide* in three parts and it became a Christmas book distributed by a book club together with General Eisenhower's *Crusade in Europe*, the one a celebration of victory, the other a warning of future peril. It was Dr. Bradley's conclusion that there is no defense against atomic weapons and that the devastating impact of a bomb and "its relatives" may affect the land and the people for centuries through the persistence of radioactivity.

One of the early editors of the *Atlantic*, the laziest, had tried the noble experiment of publishing sheet music — songs — in the magazine, and it was not a success. While I was casting about for a new approach to contemporary art, a lady came to my rescue. Agnes de Mille, whom I had never met but whose dances I had admired in *Oklahoma!* and *Carousel*, submitted a thick wad of yellow paper containing a breathtaking exaltation of Martha Graham. I had never published an artist who wrote so brilliantly, so appreciatively of a competitor. Consider this second paragraph:

Graham is one of the few people who have found an original way of communication. It is not a readaptation or personal development of the old way. It is a new way. This happens only occasionally in painting and music. It is noteworthy of Graham that in twenty years of invention she is still what she was at the beginning: the most unpredictable, the most searching, the most radical of all choreographers. Furthermore, no dancer that I can name has expanded technique to a comparable degree. She has, herself alone, given us a new system of leverage, balance, and dynamics. She is one of the great costume designers of our time, as revolutionary in the use of material as Vionnet. In point of view and subject matter, in choice of music and scenery, she cuts across all tradition. And for each new phase, there was needed a whole new style. Her idiom has shown as great a variety as Picasso's. This enormous span of achievement has covered twenty years and none of it has been easy. Some people mocked, and many turned away. The public and critics have been in turn

129

outraged, exasperated, stimulated, or adoring. No one has ever been indifferent.

Miss de Mille was due in Boston shortly for the opening of a musical for which she had choreographed the dances, so in my grateful acceptance I asked her to meet me at the Ritz for lunch on whatever day was convenient. She was there, stocky, auburn-haired, blazing blue eyes, and a becoming hat. "You see before you," she said, "a lady whose hair is full of garbage." She meant that the show was so unattractive that she had withdrawn her dances.

She talked about Graham with the love and intensity with which she had written. Yes, it was part of a book, untidy, unfinished. The manuscript was in her studio in Greenwich Village. If I could come down, perhaps we could look it over there? She was leaving the show as fast as she could pack. I went down the following week.

I remember the studio as a long room with good light and an incredible screen. The room must have been large enough for a dancer to practice and the screen large enough for a girl to change into leotards behind it. But the sides of it were covered, literally, with snapshots of Agnes and her partners, formal portraits, clippings about her performances, visual reminders of what she had been transforming into prose. This was my baptism in the world of ballet.

There was a large mound of manuscript. "Four or five articles that might do," she thought, but the immediate task was to get her approval of the cuts I had made to bring Graham down to a maximum length for the magazine. I believed I had her agreement but when she read the revision in galley proof she wrote, "I think you have worked a minor miracle, and am well pleased with the changes *except* a couple. Please, please leave in my crack about Elizabeth Arden approaching the Cross. It's the only fun in the piece and to people who know or have seen Martha it has real point." There was abundant "fun" in the piece, for example: "Ted Shawn built an Aztec ballet around her which gave her the opportunity to vent some of her ebullience. In this she had the chance, for instance, to gnaw on his leg. No one subsequently, they told me, ever did this so well." Elizabeth Arden stayed out.

In that mound of yellow papers lay the story of how Agnes fought her way into the musical theater. Her father, William de Mille, was enjoying a brief success writing comedies for Broadway when his younger brother, Cecil B., struck it rich in Hollywood, and wired him to come out. Agnes was eight when she first saw Pavlova perform; she was stunned and from that moment determined to be a dancer.

Her parents objected by sending her to U.C.L.A., where she wrote with distinction and performed in her own dances. When her parents went through a hurtful divorce it was her mother, the daughter of the economist Henry George, whose faith and savings sent Agnes to England to study under Madame Marie Rambert and to perform her comic dances at Notting Hill Gate, the other performers being the revolutionary Anthony Tudor, Sir Frederick Ashton (now the greatest choreographer in Europe), and Agnes's dancing partner, Hugh Laing. Her mother paid for the London concerts and chivied her friends into buying tickets.

"Built like a mustang," as she once described herself, making a late start in an art that should be practiced in childhood, Agnes created dances — solos — rich in comedy and as American as the flag. Rambert, her mother, and occasional applause in Europe kept her going. This was what Agnes was bringing to life with irresistible humor and no self-pity in her first book, *Dance to the Piper*. Her English training qualified her for a job with the Ballet Russe. While they were on tour in America and desperately in need of a new ballet, Agnes began teaching those tall Russians how to bend their knees like bowlegged cowhands and to dance as if they were riding. Her hour struck on the night of October 16, 1942, when in the Metropolitan Opera House she and Freddy Franklin danced the leads in her "Rodeo." She was thirty-eight, and it happened like this:

Chewing gum, squinting under a Texas hat, I turned to face what I had been preparing for the whole of my life.

This was not a great performance; we gave better later. Neither was it a great ballet. The style, as I always feared, did break. But it was the first of its kind, and the moment was quick with birth.

There was applause on my first exit. An unexpected bonus. There was applause or response on every phrase. Did the audience laugh on count eight as I had promised in July in California? They laughed, not just female titters, but real laughing with the sound of men's voices, and the laugh turned into handclapping. This happened again and again. The dancers were elated but not surprised. I had promised them laughs. The pantomime was spaced to accommodate them.

There were mishaps. At one point Kokic grew confused with his new costumes and failed to make an entrance, leaving me to improvise a love scene, without partner, alone, and exposed for sixty-four bars of music on the Met stage. Lines were crooked. Some of the girls clapped off beat. It didn't seem to matter.

The pace of the performance rushed us like a wind. The audience were roused and urging us on. Great exchanges of excitement and force and gaiety were taking place all around. The dancers rushed and whirled, grabbing the right person, because the right person was there, though unrecognizable in an unexpected dress and hair-do. And throughout the pace which was too quick for me, beyond my understanding, faster than could be savored or appreciated, was Freddie's hand, Freddie's arm, Freddie's strong back, propelling, pushing, carrying, and Freddie's feet like bullets on the wood. It was beyond endurance. It was beyond help. It was slipping away too fast, too fast. Also my collar was too tight.

"Freddie," I said at the back of the stage, "I'm fainting. Loosen my collar."

"No time, duckie. Here we go."

And as though we were blown out of the mouth of a gun, he propelled me to the footlights. We separated. Bob, bob. (Which Robert, Madame?) All the trumpets and horns threw their shafts between us. We hung on the brink. The music tore open. We rushed. We clashed. We were lifted. And all the girls had faces like stars with their hair dropping over the boys' shoulders. The great curtain fell. There was dust in my nostrils from the dusty lining of the curtain. It was over. It was done. And I had made so many foolish mistakes. So many hasty things gone wrong. Once more I had been incapable of the perfect effort. "Oh, Freddie," I said gasping, "what a stinking, lousy performance. We must rehearse like demons tomorrow!"

I looked at him wistfully but we were walking forward and we were all holding hands and bowing. A large bunch of American corn was put in my arms tied with red, white and blue ribbons. More flowers came, more flowers. The Russians did things this way. They also clapped and called out. Hadn't I stood grinding my teeth at the back of the house for years while they cheered bogus nonsense? We bowed and bowed. At the eighth bow, I looked into the pit. The fiddlers were beating their bows on their instruments. The others were standing up yelling. No one gets the union boys to do this easily. I looked at Freddie in amazement. "Freddie," I said, "this is not a claque. This is not Libidins's contriving."

"Darling, darling," said Freddie, kissing me, "this is an ovation. This is the real thing. Take it." He pushed me forward, and all the company backed away to the edge of the stage and stood there clapping.

We had twenty-two curtain calls.

Rodgers and Hammerstein were in a box, on the lookout for someone to choreograph the ballets for their new musical, *Oklahoma!* That was fortuitous. But there was nothing fortuitous about that performance or that triumph of recognition after so many defeats.

For her dances in *Oklahoma!* Agnes received $50 a week for the first four and a half years; then a half of 1 percent royalty in performances by the Theatre Guild. At that time there was no union of choreographers, nor of the dancers. This inequity called out the spirit of her grandfather Henry George, the economist who had fought the losing fight for the single tax, and Agnes did not lose: it was her drive with the support of Michael Kidd, Bob Fosse, and Danny Daniels that brought about the formation of both unions, and a fair wage for the boys and girls in rehearsal, as well as in performance.

Of the five books she wrote for us I prize *Dance to the Piper* for its unconquerable spirit, and the next book, *And Promenade Home*, for the verve of her writing and the courage with which she corrected proof when her only son, Jonathan, age four, was fighting for his life at the Children's Hospital in New York. On my Olympus Agnes is one of the brave ones.

CHAPTER

VIII

At the Harvard Commencement in June 1946, I was one of five alumni elected to "the Honorable and Reverend Board of Overseers," for a six-year term. Each mid-winter a slate of twelve or more candidates is nominated from the alumni of the College and the Graduate Schools and, recently, from the alumnae of Radcliffe. The entire electorate of 150,200 is canvassed in the spring, and the results are announced Commencement afternoon.

In 1637, the first Board of Overseers, six ministers and six magistrates, was appointed by the General Court "to take order for a colledge in Newetowne" (Cambridge), but shortly, its interference so irritated President Dunster that in 1650 he obtained a new charter from the Court, placing control in the hands of the President and Treasurer and five Fellows. It is this self-perpetuating body, long known as "the Corporation," which actually runs the University. The Overseers have become the sounding board of the alumni: they retain the right to veto decisions of the Corporation, which they very rarely exercise; they maintain their tradition of interference by grumbling, and if the grumble is loud enough, action may be modified or stopped. Example: in 1921 A. Lawrence Lowell, the last of Harvard's autocratic presidents, in his strolls about the University, observed that there were an increasing number of Jewish students. Lowell's proposal that a quota of 15 percent be set for the College deeply disturbed both governing boards, and I like to think it was the Overseers who called on Lowell's predecessor, the eighty-year-old Charles William Eliot, to intercede, which he did, and the motion was squashed, though not before the rumor had reached the press and infuriated many eminent alumni.

I had admired President James Bryant Conant from a distance before I came to watch him in action. A graduate of the Roxbury Latin School, he had been a brilliant, precocious student of chemistry and had risen to be head of that department before the Corporation, searching for Lowell's successor, discovered that this scientist had critical and innovative ideas about the future of Harvard. Oddly, it was Conant's extensive study of Cromwell's Rebellion and of Oxford and Cambridge in the seventeenth century which arrested the first member of the Corporation who came to test his qualification. His reference to "a self-denying ordinance" knocked in the eye the likely possibility that the Corporation might choose one of its own members for the presidency, and Conant followed this by pointing out that Lowell's infatuation with the tutorial system had resulted in the appointment of professors of mediocre merit. When he said that the standards for promotion were not high enough to suit him, the Corporation listened, and ultimately elected him.

President Conant's greatest innovation was the National Scholarships, and they changed the character of the College. The awards were exceptionally large in the Depression and at the outset, in 1936–1937, were given only to students from the old Northwest Territory, Minnesota, Wisconsin, Michigan, Illinois, Indiana, and Ohio. "The essence of the plan," as Conant says in his firm, candid autobiography, *My Several Lives*, "is, of course, to increase Harvard's representation in the very places where it is weak." The winners, that first year, came from ten private schools, but twenty-one came from *public high schools*, and this emphasis on the high schools, as the scholarships were extended to the Far West and the South, unquestionably raised the standard of undergraduate scholarship while making Harvard more democratic. The addition of those scholars was not at the expense of candidates from the private schools in the East. Prior to Conant one-third of Harvard College students were commuters. When the tuition was as little as $400 one would live at home, in Roxbury or Cambridge, and commute. As tuition rose and residence in the Harvard Houses was required, the number of commuters dwindled.

I was proud that Conant in 1940 was the first university president to speak out strongly for "The Committee to Defend America by Aiding the Allies." I felt he was right, even before Pearl Harbor, to ask for a leave of absence, and to organize with Roger Adams the National Defense Research Council. In 1941, as Van Bush's deputy, he flew to England to pledge cooperation with the British scientists, and then served as the connecting rod between Los Alamos and Washington. As the tide turned against Hitler, he wrote for us an article describing the man of ideas he hoped would speak out as America emerged from the war economy. The title was "Wanted: American Radicals." It led our issue for May 1943, and the force of his argument for a classless society is suggested in two paragraphs. The first:

No one needs to be told that the American radical will be a fanatic believer in equality. Yet it will be a peculiar North American brand of doctrine. For example, he will be quite willing in times of peace to let net salaries and earnings sail way above the $25,000 mark. He believes in equality of opportunity, not equality of rewards; but, on the other hand, he will be lusty in wielding the axe against the root of inherited privilege. To prevent the growth of a caste system, which he abhors, he will be resolute in his demands to confiscate (by constitutional methods) all property once a generation. He will demand really effective inheritance and gift taxes and the breaking up of trust funds and estates. And this point cannot be lightly pushed aside, for it is the kernel of his philosophy.

I believed that both Jefferson and Emerson would have approved of those words. But I was severely rebuked by alumni who were thinking of the University's endowment, and who did not take seriously this paragraph in Conant's conclusion:

Such in brief is my specification for a genus *Americanus*, whose voice I do not hear. The reader will undoubtedly derive the impression that I am sympathetic in my own personal views with the hypothetical gentleman I have just portrayed. That is true. But I should like to make it clear that I am arguing for his introduction into the American scene not because I believe all his aims should be achieved, but because I believe his type of thinking would prove a most beneficial leaven. I urge the need of the American radical not because I wish to give a blanket endorsement to his views, but because I see the necessity for reinvigorating a neglected aspect of our historical pattern of development.

The Overseers meet in Cambridge six times a year in the large central room of University Hall, a room filled with portraits and busts, and, in Eliot's day, still big enough to hold the entire faculty. Meetings are conducted by the president of the Overseers, seated at a table with the president of the University beside him, ready to elucidate each point on the agenda. As I watched President Conant the impression grew that we confronted a New England Puritan, incisive, ascetic, determined to have his way but with a keener sense of humor than is usually found in such a make-up. He put his proposals with a half-smile and, to mix my metaphor, the smile often had a bite to it. He was quick to sense opposition and when he did the long line of his jaw tightened. He had Cromwell's love of battle and, as he said, surprisingly, in his autobiography, "My tendency to expect the worst when dealing with other people may well be traced to a prolonged self-inflicted dose of British seventeenth-century history."

Early in my first year, before I was accustomed to speak out, my daughter received a letter from a boy she had been fond of at Shady Hill, a big oarsman from an old Yale family who had gone through his long service in the P.T. boats dreaming of what a relief it would be to get out of uniform and into New Haven. Now he was there and he wrote her with dismay: four of them, crowded into two small rooms, the dreary food, the difficulty of getting access to the required reading list, and worst of all, being taught by instructors younger and greener than they — what the hell had happened to the place? I knew conditions in Cambridge were quite as exasperating and it occurred to me to read the letter aloud, not divulging the name. So when the formal business had transpired, I rose and asked permission to read a letter from an undergraduate I believed was known to several present. As I quoted the drab details I could see Conant begin to fidget. In conclusion I said, "It is small consolation for me to add that this letter was written in New Haven, since I am sure similar . . ."

The president broke in, "Mr. Weeks, I surely don't need to remind you that we are not accountable for our cousin's shortcomings!"

There was a roar of laughter and then in the pause that followed Mike Farley, a Boston lawyer, with a famous dead-pan expression, stood up. "Mr. President, I should like to make a motion. It seems to me that those Overseers residing at a distance, say in Chicago, or San Francisco, must sometimes wonder if it is really worth the trouble to come all that way, spend the morning approving faculty appointments, eat an over-hearty lunch, and then fly home. I move that something be done to make the Overseers' meetings *more interesting*."

The motion was passed unanimously, with grins, and as might be expected, Messrs. Farley and Weeks were appointed a committee of two to recommend in what way the meetings could be "of more interest." Which we did: first, we asked that instead of there being only a single 48-hour meeting in Cambridge, traditionally in the spring, that there be a second, in the fall, at a time when we could meet department heads and attend lectures on subjects that appealed to us. Second, that we be permitted to lunch informally with the undergraduates in the various Houses, one Overseer to a table. Thirdly, that articulate spokesmen tell us of the exciting developments and teachers in the Humanities and in new areas such as Social Science (I still remember Archibald MacLeish's glowing account of the English Department). And, finally, that we be taken to see the outlying provinces of the University, such as the Harvard Forest in Petersham and the Arnold Arboretum.

For Commencement and other formal occasions an Overseer dons a cutaway and high silk hat as befitting his place in the academic procession. I had not worn either for some time and as we assembled at 9 A.M. for a brief session before the exercises, I took an early shower, toweled off and then, unclad, stood before my wife's pier glass in our bedroom, seeing how I looked in my high hat. I had forgotten that the curtains had been taken down for the summer and that I must have been plainly visible to anyone curious enough to peek from their back windows on West Cedar Street. My best wedding cravat was well tied and I was putting on the long-tailed coat when the doorbell rang. In my finery I stepped down to answer it and there was a policeman.

"Good morning, sir. There's been a complaint. Someone exposing himself by the window. Stark naked. Would you have any idea who it might be?"

"I haven't the foggiest idea, sergeant. What an oddball. Sorry."

Normally the meetings in University Hall on Commencement morning last less than forty minutes, but at this one on June 5, 1948, Conant sought the approval of a new professor in Economics, J. Kenneth Galbraith, and it was clear from the start that there was to be some interference. A split had developed in that department between the conventional, the "Taussig economists," and the disciples of John Maynard Keynes. Galbraith was a Keynesian, and our conservative members, George Whitney of J. P. Morgan, Clarence Randall of Inland Steel, Sinclair Weeks, and others, wanted none of him. But Conant was very positive that we needed this man; I had the feeling that he'd go to the stake for him. Arguments flew back and forth until the Harvard Choir, directed under our windows, let go with a full-blast rehearsal of the Harvard Hymn. Further exchange being inaudible, the appointment was held over till the fall.

We all trooped across the Yard, where the procession was forming, and I spied, just entering the gate, a martial figure in unfamiliar mufti, General George C. Marshall, come to receive an Honorary

Degree; he was unattended so I introduced myself and found his escort.

Traditionally, what is remembered of Commencement is spoken in the afternoon. General Marshall was the most revered figure in Washington and what he said became the genesis of the Marshall Plan. It came to the listeners in a brief paragraph of altruistic generalities which the General, with Truman's approval, had tacked on before leaving Washington, and few present — not including President Conant or myself — fully grasped its meaning. On the tenth anniversary of Marshall's great pledge Harvard bestowed an honorary degree on Barbara Jackson and she was asked to deliver the address on Commencement afternoon. Geoffrey Crowther had come over for the occasion and he and I sat together, *in loco parentis*, as that lovely figure who knew so well the needs of Africa appealed for America's aid to the Third World, speaking from the heart with eloquence that brought 14,000 people to their feet.

Every member of the Governing Boards feels the expectation as he dons the starched shirt and cutaway and smooths his high hat; the excitement grows as in the academic procession he passes through the ranks of the seniors on the way to the platform to face the thousands of students, parents and the pretties. It goes up another notch at the Chief Marshal's spread for recipients of the honorary degrees, with the traditional salmon salad and champagne, and reaches the climax at 2 P.M. when, grouped about the President on the lower steps of Widener Library, we take the salute of the classes returning for reunion, led by the oldest living graduate, and are stirred by a loyalty good to feel.

The question of Galbraith's appointment came up at the first meeting of the Overseers in the fall. The Corporation had approved it and Conant clearly wanted no interference from us. I had never met the Canadian-born economist, but during the summer I queried friends in Washington who were familiar with his war work, and their letters, particularly those from Walter Lippmann and Herbert Elliston of the *Washington Post*, and others were positive endorsements. After the expected objections from George Whitney, Clarence Randall, Charles Cabot, and Sinclair Weeks — "Galbraith would upset the balance in the department" — I spoke in the affirmative and read my letters, which must have affected the uncommitted, for the vote was 24 to 6 in Galbraith's favor. That duty accomplished, I forgot him. It never occurred to me that he could write until he had given the word "affluent" his own coinage. That's the kind of thing that wakes one up at two in the morning.

Each member of the Board is assigned to "oversee" one or more departments of the University and to file an annual report on their condition. In addition he serves as chairman of a Visiting Committee, composed of eminent authorities, not necessarily with Harvard affiliations, who survey a department from the outside, and who meet in Boston and Cambridge at least once a year to concert their findings. My first and most difficult assignment was the Arnold Arboretum, an enclosure of trees and flowering shrubs in Jamaica Plain of which by deed of trust the University was the caretaker. If Harvard was found negligent, the Arboretum would revert to the City of Boston.

Charles Sprague Sargent had been director of the Arboretum for fifty-four years, and it was he who made it internationally known: the park grew from 125 to 265 acres less manicured but not much less renowned than Kew Gardens; a modern herbarium was built and a most valuable library of nearly 50,000 volumes and 22,000 photographs made it a center for research. On Sargent's death in 1927 a memorial fund of a million dollars had been added to its endowment. Then came the Depression, two destructive hurricanes, and the shortage of manpower throughout the war, leaving an urgent need for restoration. The time had come when it was necessary to renovate some of the old collections and to initiate new, extensive plantings.

I did not appreciate this nor did I appreciate the rivalry for funds between the botanists in the Arboretum and the biologists in Cambridge. During Conant's absence two distinguished biologists, Drs. Irving W. Bailey and Paul Mangelsdorf, had compiled a report which the president on his return recommended to the Overseers, saying that "for once I find the biologists in complete agreement." It seemed to me that its main plea was for a new building in Cambridge, and with the others I voted for its adoption.

The Visiting Committee of the Arboretum was composed of twenty-two members, including Henry F. du Pont, Childs Frick, John Ames, Godfrey Cabot, Mrs. Grenville Clark, Mrs. George Agassiz, Mrs. Frank Crowninshield, Mrs. Delano McKelvey, some wealthy, each expert in horticulture. I do not have a green thumb, and while I worship trees, I knew I was out of my depth at the luncheon I arranged for the group at the Harvard Club of Boston. But I did not anticipate their united cold front. The following week I called up Mrs. McKelvey and invited myself to tea. I know she liked fly-fishing, and after a few words about Kennebago I took the plunge.

"What went wrong at our luncheon? Why were you all so set against me?" I asked.

"There was nothing personal," she replied. "But you must have read the Bailey-Mangelsdorf Report. Don't you realize what it threatens to do to the Arboretum? Many of us on the Committee helped to raise the fund in memory of Charles Sargent. Now, apparently with the president's approval, we're told that Harvard proposes to break up Sargent's priceless library and to spend the money we gave, not to revive the Arboretum but for a new building in Cambridge. It's outrageous!"

As I questioned other members of the Visiting Committee, I was convinced that this was a tempest larger than a teapot. I warned my classmate, Keith Kane, who was a member of the Corporation and the president's assistant in public relations, that these people were really up in arms. Grenville Clark, also on the Corporation, at his wife's persuasion, had changed his vote; so did I in my report to the Overseers, and Conant dubbed us "two-vote men." But the attitude which prevailed was, in the words of one cynic on the Corporation, "Why shouldn't we skin that fat cat?" The Visiting Committee engaged two capable lawyers, Mike Farley and Robert G. Dodge, to resist the Report, and the conflict dragged on for years. The University finally compromised: Sargent's library was left intact and the memorial part of the Arboretum endowment was not spent on bricks and mortar.

I recall this episode not because I like to criticize my alma mater, to whom I owe so much. Had Conant not been distracted by the war his prudence might have restrained the biologists. At the time I speak of, the University had already divested itself of two "outlying provinces" for which there were no longer sufficient academic interest or funds — the Bussey Institute had been closed and the Gray Herbarium gone to seed. In today's pinching economy other endowed institutions will have to divest themselves of provinces they can no longer afford, and will do so, I hope, without infuriating donors whose intent deserves respect.

The remainder of my term was more peaceful. In addition to the Arboretum I was assigned to the Harvard University Press and my favorite, the English Department. When I was an undergraduate it had been the most distinguished English faculty in the world; George Lyman Kittredge, John Livingston Lowes, Dean Le Baron R. Briggs, Bliss Perry, and Fred Norris Robinson as a galaxy had only one defect — they all reached retirement at about the same time. The tragic deaths of F. O. Matthiessen and Theodore Spencer and the tactless release of Bernard de Voto slowed the rebuilding, but thanks to the brilliant teaching and scholarship of Walter Jackson Bate, Harry Levin, and Robert Fitzgerald a recovery has been achieved.

We Overseers were taken, as I hoped we would be, to the Harvard Forest, and on the long bus ride back I sat beside Conant having one of the happiest, candid talks I can recall. He spoke of his dislike of the annual Honorary Degrees, of how he wished they could be reserved for very special occasions, or done away with altogether. I asked him about the ever-tightening testing for entrance to the College, for which he and his aides, Bill Bender and Henry Chauncy, were responsible — was there no way to make some accommodation for the slow starters (I was one), a boy, exceptional perhaps in only one subject, but not in the I.Q.? Weren't we turning down too many sons of sons of Harvard? The Puritan's answer was "No."

In my lecturing, spring and fall, I traveled an average of 15,000 miles in America and was constantly being informed. I went to many colleges and universities, in time to over 135 campuses; occasionally I found a contributor in the faculty and always a core of students who aspired to write. At the University of Minnesota, for instance, I delivered a mid-morning talk of forty-five minutes to several thousand in the Convocation Hall; the question period came after lunch for the few hundred particularly interested in publishing. Or at Saint Olaf College, also in Minnesota, the most musical of all our smaller institutions, it was an evening affair, introduced by the president, the faculty and students peppering me afterward.

Quite often I was entertained by members of the English Department; sometimes they gave me pointers about the magazine, sometimes about themselves. I spoke at Columbia University a week after Gertrude Stein and they could not forget her. "I really think," said one young assistant, "she is the most impressive woman we've ever had here!" "Oh, come on, Tom," said the skeptic, "she looked as if she'd been shipwrecked and had come ashore in the captain's clothes."

I returned frequently to those universities which were blest with exceptional teachers of composition. At the University of Pittsburgh, where I became a trustee, Edwin L. Peterson was, to my knowledge, the first to demonstrate good writing in his enormous, popular class in freshman English. Above him was a large screen on which was amplified whatever was on Ed's lectern — a student's theme or the photostat of a page by Hemingway or Steinbeck. As he spoke "Pete" would underscore the text to emphasize the strength or weakness of an adverb, or to ask for the substitution of another word. He made his people aware of the excitement of words. At the University of Michigan Roy Cowden was venerated as Dean Briggs had been at Harvard in my time. He was the first to administer the Avery Hopwood Awards. Hopwood, a former student at Ann Arbor, had made a fortune as a popular playwright before he was drowned in Lake Geneva. He left the whole of his fortune to Michigan, to stimulate the writing of plays, poetry, and fiction. Under Cowden's coaching and that of his assistants (one of them Katherine Anne Porter, guest lecturer in 1953–1954), the Hopwood winners began to publish books which eventually filled a large bookcase in Roy's study. In the South at the University of Alabama I visited the classes of Hudson Strode, who had skill in stimulating short story writers, a couple of whom we published.

There were others, like Wallace Stegner of Stanford, and Charles Fenton of Yale whose promise was cut short by his tragic death. The point I am making is that partly because it was known that the *Atlantic* was not above considering both faculty and undergraduate writing, and partly because of my presence, the magazine began to appear in many classrooms; eventually as many as 40,000 subscriptions became "required reading" (and years later, when the curse of that word "required" rubbed off, not a few graduates subscribed).

Emerson found lecturing arduous and so did I. What is bracing is the extraordinary beauty of our country and the exciting difference in the local problems, which inform a lecturer who listens and which he would never know about if he stayed home. "We're so short of water that we're mining for it," said the president of the University of Arizona. "In the San Joaquin Valley it's a question of whether they can continue to grow more vegetables *or* more people," and he explained the struggle for the Colorado River. A commencement address in Ohio led me to a weekend at Malabar Farm, where I commissioned four articles about the experiments with which Louis Bromfield had revitalized his once-abandoned farm. The Allegheny Conference, which had cleaned and renovated Pittsburgh, invited me to a luncheon at the Duquesne Club, where Leland Hazard explained why the Mellons were investing seventy million in the upgrading of the University of Pittsburgh and became a friend and indispensable contributor. For twenty years I spoke in Richmond, Virginia, as master of ceremonies at the annual Book and Authors Dinner, and the friends I made there promoted me to a very dear affiliation on the Board of Colonial Williamsburg.

Next to John Mason Brown, who was tops, I suppose I was the

143

most cheerful lecturer on the circuit. Early in our doldrums I received my first request to speak at Chautauqua. Originally a tent colony, founded by Bishop John Vincent to improve the teaching in Sunday schools, it became nationally known when visited by General Grant. Ever since it has been celebrated for its emphasis on faith, good music, and the arts. The response to my talks in that vast amphitheater buoyed my confidence, and it has warmed my heart to be called back, summer after summer.

Pomona College, during the administration of President E. Wilson Lyon, was one of my points of recall on the Pacific Coast. Before my lecture there in 1954 the president said, "We have a remarkable boy in the freshman class, a Hindu who is blind. I've asked him to be in my office after your talk. . . ." Such was my introduction to Ved Mehta. I think my very first impression of Ved was of the confidence with which he moved despite his loss of sight. He told me he was beginning an autobiography — he was then eighteen. I asked if I could see it, and in the two following summers when he thumbed his way across the continent to attend the Harvard Summer School I learned of his turbulent youth.

At the age of four meningitis had destroyed his sight. His father, an English-trained doctor, had lost everything but courage when his family was driven from the Vale of Kashmir during the Partition. At twelve Ved, aware that schooling in India could take him no farther, pleaded to be taught Braille. Privately, he typed, in stuttering English, an application for admission to a score of American institutions. The only one to accept him was the Arkansas School for the Blind, where, in his words, he was "a donkey in the world of horses." At Little Rock, he took his English in stride as he was taught how to use his "facial vision" in navigating the city streets, to hold the head high so as to walk more surely in a straight line, to tell by sound and by his feet when he was approaching a curb, to listen for the traffic to stop, never to run across a street, to sense by the wind on his cheek or the oncoming tread how to avoid other pedestrians and, as his perception increased, how to orient himself in a crowded drugstore. He would be sent on errands and tracked by his instructor, who would check his performance.

While Ved was studying at Harvard he made frequent trips to our office to go over his manuscript with my assistant, Nancy Reynolds. He came in by subway and only once did I see him fall. He was late for lunch and I had gone down to our steps to await him. I saw him in the distance but he had no way of knowing — nor I — that the pavement across the Commonwealth Avenue Mall had been dug up

144

and that on the inner side of the curb, there was a deep depression, into which he pitched. He brushed himself off, turned back to the Ritz-Carlton to wash up, and then imperturbably skirted the pit to our meeting.

California is, I believe, the only state to make a yearly grant to blind undergraduates of $1,000 to pay for the reading aloud of essential texts. At Pomona Ved developed his wonderful capacity to absorb what he heard. We published his indomitable book, *Face to Face* — I found the title in First Corinthians — the year after his graduation but I did not realize until later how troubled he was by the reference to his blindness in the blurb and advertising — he did not wish to be judged with pity, and forbade any such allusion thereafter.

During his graduate study at Balliol College I took him to call on John Masefield. In the college I was touched by the affection the English students showed for him, but neither his tutor nor I realized how far Ved had gone in his thoughtful study of contemporary English historians and philosophers, and that he would be publishing his appreciation of both as he turned thirty. It was William Shawn, the editor of the *New Yorker*, who nurtured Mehta, giving him financial security and the encouragement to interpret the West to the East and India to the world.

CHAPTER

IX

James Hilton was the first author I knew who acknowledged the intimidating effect of the atomic bomb. Hilton had become a best seller in 1934 with a sentimental story about his schoolmaster father, *Good-bye, Mr. Chips*, and had sustained his popularity with light novels, as entertaining in film as in print. In 1950 we were lunching together in Hollywood to discuss the manuscript he was working on. "It's giving me a hard time," he said, "I've made three starts and at about page one hundred twenty up through the typewriting come the words 'So what?' It's impossible to find the confidence I used to have." I did not take him seriously, thinking it a temporary block; he did succeed in finishing that novel but it was far below his best.

Like Hilton, Geoffrey Household wrote a short novel, *Rogue Male*, which we published in the *Atlantic* before the war. *Rogue Male* was perfectly timed: the story of an English aristocrat and big game hunter who sets out to stalk the dictator of an European great power and has the target in his telescopic sight when he is overpowered by the bodyguard. Tortured and given up for dead, he survives, evades pursuit, and escapes to England, where he outwits the foreign agents in London and holes up in a Dorset cave, planning to try again. The dictator was, of course, Hitler, the escape was thrilling, and the book was a sensation in London as with us. But before it was published Geoffrey had volunteered, been trained for Special Intelligence, and had left England not to return for five and a half years.

Household has persevered successfully in his writing because he has the mind of an adventurer. He is a compulsive traveler with the gift of tongues. Were he not an honorable man he might have become a rather terrifying criminal. After taking a First in English Literature at Oxford, he left home to become a confidential secretary in the Bank of Rumania. In Bucharest his salary enabled him, as he says in his autobiography, to enjoy "women, wine, food" and to develop "a quite unexpected facility for modern languages." Three years in the Balkans and then he took to the road, selling bananas in Spain with Bilbao as his base and acquiring "a passionate love of all things Spanish." After a brief sojourn in New York in 1930, he was once more on the road, selling printers' ink throughout Europe and South America, three years of hard travel, with an occasional interval for a short story. "My beginnings as a professional writer stemmed from your acceptance of 'The Salvation of Pisco Gabar' and the financing of my post-war novel," he told me.

The War Office was unaware of his literary ability, and he kept it so, not wanting to be tied down to a desk. In 1939 he wrote me, "Captain is my rank. But Major would be more suited to my bald head and many infirmities, and I should like to finish the war as one. [He did.] Meanwhile I enjoy the particular game I am playing. It's not dangerous and yet fascinating. I shall return to my desk and my craft regretfully but with a mass of material and characters. . . . We're in for a long job I think. At least the only thing likely to shorten the war would be revolution within Germany, and I don't see it coming yet."

With his knowledge of Rumania, he was sent on a mission to Bucharest; one of a handful of agents planning to dynamite the Ploesti oil refineries before the Nazis seized them. When their cover was blown by the French he was posted to Greece and given a command in the disastrous campaign which ended on the beaches of the Peloponnese. There he managed to extract his men, "nearly naked but reasonably unashamed." For the rest of the war he was immersed in Intelligence in Syria, Palestine, and Iraq.

The curtain lifted in February 1945, when Geoffrey was posted home with a month's leave. "I've no ambition to govern Germans . . . and of course, there's plenty to write. I propose to start with a few short stories and then to attempt a full-scale picaresque novel of the Middle East which won't have much bloodshed in it but will, I hope, catch the spirit and tell the story of the million men who were exiled for four years between Cairo and Tehran.

"You have heard, I suspect, of my Korda contract. I think I wrote you about it. . . . [Alexander Korda was then the monarch of British films.] I have to work for him for twelve weeks in the year in return for which he pays me enough to keep me very comfortable for the rest of the year. This comes in very handy as I picked up a new wife and two babies in the M.E. and we all have expensive tastes. . . ."

English rationing was still enforced and I remembered how severe it was. We ordered a monthly shipment from Denmark of ham, butter, lard, and sugar, which brought an exclamation of gratitude and an amusing footnote about his writing: "The novel is flowing at last. This is simply and solely due to the importation, at long last, of cheap red wine. I either wouldn't admit to myself or had honestly forgotten that I could not write without a glass of wine to release the imagination. Two glasses make the writing facile and bad; one is just right; none at all and I just stare at the paper."

As Geoffrey's novel about the Levant, *Arabesque*, neared completion he invited my wife, Fritzy, and me to spend the Easter weekend of 1949 with them at their house on the Dorset moors. For twelve years our correspondence had built up a friendship (though we had yet to meet) sustained by my delight in his short stories and the triumph of *Rogue Male*. As rationing was still on I contributed a prime roast of beef and a porterhouse steak, which were flown over from Canada and arrived on Good Friday.

Geoffrey's photos had not done him justice: the finely shaped head and the eyes, thoughtful or vivacious; the clipped moustache was a relic of the war and so too the air of command. He had rented an old schoolhouse, rambling and spacious, with his father, a former teacher, settled in one wing. Ilona, his war bride, was a fair-haired Hungarian. I was amused by her accent and her contralto laugh. I soon observed that she was as competent as she was lovely — she drove the car, protected Geoffrey's workroom from the children, her meals were delectable, and her "Now, Geoffrey!" when he let go one of his wild predictions was the neatest of punctures.

He had arranged some fishing for me, and our first afternoon he and I and his little son, Nyulsi ("Little Rabbit" in Hungarian), walked across meadows to a neighbor's narrow chalk brook, where I cast the wrong places and never stirred a trout. As we filed home, the little boy in the lead, I heard his piping voice, "Mr. Weeks must be a very poor fisherman not to get even one!" "Hush, boy!" Easter was overcast with a boisterous north wind and cold, and now I was to fish the river Piddle, a wider chalk stream well cared for by Sir Ernest Debenham, whose son had been at Magdalen with Geoff. We paid our respects to the white-haired octogenarian, who was stretched out on a couch with a view of the ruffled water. "Use nothing but a March Brown," he said. "Place it in the center of the stream, and you should have some sport." In the cutting wind, Nyulsi, in short

Helen and Walter Lippmann in their woods at Southwest Harbor, Maine
(COURTESY OF MRS. GEORGE PORTER)

Nora Waln, London 1941, "the fourteenth year of our partnership as editor and author"

John Masefield at Oxford

Geoffrey Crowther, editor of the Economist, 1943 (COURTESY OF THE ECON◖

Dame Edith Sitwell

Ralph McGill (PORTRAIT BY
ROBERT TEMPLETON)

*Dr. Vannevar Bush in his
laboratory at the Massachusetts
Institute of Technology*
(PORTRAIT BY EUGENE
MONTGOMERY)

Samuel Eliot Morison on the cover of the October 1960 Atlantic
(JAMES AVATI)

Francis Henry Taylor in the
Worcester (Massachusetts)
Art Museum, 1940
(KARSH, OTTAWA)

Edward Weeks, Charles Morton, and Charles Rolo beneath the portrait of the Atlantic's first editor, James Russell Lowell

(Below) THE ATLANTIC: *Donald B. Snyder, Publisher; Frank Herbert, Circulation Manager; the Editor; Leslie B. Crockett, Advertising Manager* (LENSCRAFT PHOTOS, INC.)

Barbara Ward Jackson (COURTESY OF THE ECONOMIST)

gnes de Mille at the time when she was ancing the lead in Rodeo, *1942* (ANGUS C BEAN)

Joan Bright Astley, author of The Inner Circle (NICK BARLOW)

Dylan Thomas

*Fred and Portland Allen and the
editor at the Book and Author
Dinner in Richmond, Virginia,
May 1955*

Kathryn Hulme, author of The Wild Place *and* The Nun's Story (SENDA OF KAUAI)

A full editorial meeting, 1957. To E.W.'s right Emily Flint; her assistant, Louise Desaulniers; Penelope Greenough, manuscript reader; Priscilla Merritt, assistant copyeditor; Phoebe Lou Adams half turned, talking to Peter Davison. To Davison's right: Donald Snyder, publisher; Daniel Thompson, a reader; Curtis Cate, Paris correspondent; Nancy Reynolds, assistant editor of the Press; Charlie Morton and, behind Morton, Virginia Albee and a visitor (FAY FOTO SERVICE, BOSTON)

Edwin O'Connor, after the success of The Last Hurrah (HANS NAMUTH)

(Below): Harold Ross and Edwa Weeks, recipients of honorary degrees at Dartmouth College, Hanover, New Hampshire, 1950

Catherine Drinker Bowen at the boathouse on Eastern Point, Gloucester, Massachusetts

Emily Flint and E. W. autographing Jubilee: 100 Years of the Atlantic *at the Book Store on Chestnut Street, Boston* (FAY FOTO SERVICE, BOSTON)

George F. Kennan in his library at Princeton (CONSTANCE GOODMAN)

My three companions at a round-table discussion in the Soviet Union: From lower right, Arthur Schlesinger, Jr., with glasses and bow tie, Alfred Kazin and Paddy Chayefsky

Peter Ustinov and E. W. at dinner party following Ustinov's address to the General Court of Massachusetts

Joseph Wambaugh, at the publication of The New Centurions

James Alan McPherson, winner of Pulitzer Prize in Fiction, 1978 (TANIA D'AVIGNON)

pants and bare knees, and Geoffrey, shivering under a blackthorn, watched. But not for long. My fly hardly touched the water when there was a trout after it. In an hour I had my limit of six, enough for supper — and a two-pounder for Sir Ernest.

What worried Geoffrey, as we sat talking, was the danger of being "typed." "Your tact is superb, Ted! But I know perfectly well that I am in grave danger of being considered by the public — apart from my short stories — as a mere thriller writer. And that means I'll never be allowed any other kind of fiction."

I objected that as far as I'd read in *Arabesque* he had British and French security officers, Christians and Moslem Arabs, a Rumanian cabaret artist, the Palestine police, and a heroine, half-French, half-English. Who else had such characters at his fingertips?

"Perhaps," said Geoffrey, "but I remember how disappointed I used to be myself when John Buchan wrote anything which wasn't sheer action."

That exchange took place nearly thirty-three years ago. In that span Household has written nineteen novels. He has never lost his command of suspense — his novel *Watcher in the Shadows* is almost as frightening as *Rogue Male* — but in diversity of theme, in the unforgettable people who spring to life in his stories, and in his capture of the beauty of England, particularly Devon, Dorset, and Somerset, he has created the almost perfect balance and relief from terror. Few writers have been given such a discerning appraisal of their work as L. E. Sissman, the poet, wrote for the *New Yorker*, May 1, 1971. Sissman dismissed Household's misgivings of long ago. "His interests and abilities are a little too broad and generous for him to have become merely a talented novelist of suspense, and while we read Household for his tension, we enjoy perhaps more his elaborations and observations by the way. He combines Defoe's humanity and morality of the free-born Englishman with Stevenson's subtle sense of human psychology; he shares both writers' love of adventure and of the exotic locale." The critic then picks out four novels, "whose pertinence and literary merit transcend their classification as novels of adventure or suspense: 'Rogue Male' (1939), 'Fellow Passenger' (1955), 'Watcher in the Shadows' (1960), and 'Thing to Love' (1963)."

It was an admirable choice as the four books display the extraordinary range of Household's subjects: *Rogue Male*, the symbolic duel between British aristocracy and the Nazi; *Fellow Passenger*, the best of Geoffrey's comedies; *Thing To Love*, a Czech army officer in command of an armored division in a Latin-American republic and adored by his men, fully aware he is the final support of a disreputable dictator against rebels (whose policy he admires), and *Watcher in the Shadows,* in which a French officer hunts to death in the Cotswolds a supposed war criminal, not realizing he was a double agent.

I think the pressure of the bomb periodically compelled Geoffrey to search for a better way for man to govern than by rearming for a holocaust. This theme appears awkwardly in the novel he wrote after demobilization; it would reappear and was always difficult to handle. I reproached him for overstressing anarchism in a novel he was writing in 1949. This was his answer:

[November 29, 1949]

Dorchester, Dorset
My dear Ted:

. . . I am an artist, not a politician. I present to you a man who believes that western democracy is merely a temporary answer to the twin evils of communism and fascism. He is the narrator, and my business is to keep him in his part. I also present to you three aspects of anarchism, constructive, destructive and neutral. That does not mean that I sympathise with anarchism any more than the actor who plays Othello must sympathise with murder. But, if you are to be entertained, I must not sympathise any less. . . .

The restoration of London was accomplished with unbelievable speed. One of the first streets to recover its beauty was St. James's.

Max Beerbohm recalls being shown by his friend Laurence Binyon, then Keeper of Prints in the British Museum, "a very ancient little water-colour drawing. The foreground of it was a rather steep grassy slope. At the foot of the slope stood a single building, which I at once recognised as St. James's Palace. Beyond the Palace were stretches of green meadows; and far away there was just one building — the Abbey of Westminster. And I thought how pained the artist would have been if he had foreseen the coming of St. James's Street. . . . Yet I could not find it in my heart to deplore the making of that steep little street, destined to be so full of character and history."

Three hundred and fifty years have passed since that artist did his drawing, and we who tread the "grassy slope" today see it as the capital of man's taste. Here are the famous clubs: at the top of the slope, White's with its wager book of reckless bets in the eighteenth century and its legends of the three-bottle men; Boodle's, with the most lovely façade; the massive stone solemnity of the Conservative

Club; and Pratt's, in a small cul-de-sac off St. James's, with its scarlet and black interior and its preposterous stuffed fish in glass tanks, a mockery of the stuffed salmon elsewhere — Pratt's was once the farthest limit for an officer of the Guards on duty at the Palace, and here one waits, as he did, sipping sherry while the chop or Dover sole is grilled.

This is a man's street. He may be shopping for hats at James Lock and Co., who have made the best since Rufus King was our minister to the Court of St. James's. Lock's made them for Mr. King as they did for Lord Nelson, and the shop has the same appearance and the same civility as when they were served. Close beside Lock's the tempting wines of Berry Brothers draw one into their shadowy establishment. Their wine cellars run under St. James's and were especially reinforced to resist the weight of the heavy gilt coaches bringing Charles II back to the throne. Below Berrys' look for Pickering Place, where the bucks from White's once used to duel and where Emma and Horatio Nelson once had a hideaway. And just around the corner is Hardy's Ltd., where an angler seeks his flies and advice about the best streams in the Isles.

As I read my diary of the visits in the 1940s to 1950s I realize, alas, how much more good and thoughtful writing was then available, than now.

At five Fritzy and I went for tea to Lady Sybil Colefax where we found T. S. Eliot, Thornton Wilder and Rose Macaulay. Thornton who will spend next year at Harvard, had been visiting Max Beerbohm; he told me Max had resuscitated and polished for the *Atlantic*, an essay on George Moore which he had first begun to write in 1912, said it was a beauty. . . .

T. S. Eliot and John Hayward with whom he shares an apartment, came to Sunday lunch. Eliot pushed John, who is crippled, in a wheelchair from Chelsea to Flemings on Half Moon Street. Eliot will write for us about his plays. . . .

At Oxford dined with Isaiah Berlin and Lord David Cecil at New College. Isaiah in wonderful form and we spent an hour sunning ourselves in the Fellows' garden while he discussed not one but the three books he is preparing to write, one of them, "The History of Ideas in Europe, 1789–1807," sounds as if it would certainly have source material in it for us. . . . Spent that night in student's room as warm as an icebox. . . .

Large, stiffish lunch party at Edith Sitwell's club. 18 guests, Arthur Waley who did the superb translations from the Chinese; Roy Campbell the poet, Sacheverell, Edith's scholarly younger brother. Fritzy sat next to T. S. Eliot: I overheard her say, "My husband likes people but I like places," and they were off.

151

At the *Economist* I went to Geoffrey Crowther for advice; to Barbara Ward for her contributions. Our friendship began to ripen in 1947, when she was so exhilarated by the Marshall Plan. She was swift to perceive its possibilities and proud of us for doing the unprecedented, and it was in this mood that I saw her at a huge cocktail party given by Thomas and Gretchen Finletter. Tom had come to London to direct Marshall Aid to Britain and Gay, his wife, had just finished a very entertaining book for our Press. Barbara waved at me and we had a few moments together as I dated her for a luncheon. Then I rejoined our hostess. Barbara meantime had become the center of a British square of masculinity. "There she stands," said Gay, "looking like something out of Botticelli — and she knows more about pig iron than any woman in the kingdom."

We lunched at the Ivy and did not discuss pig iron. In conversation Barbara's animation was charming. She had a high regard for President Truman and was delighted that I thought he might defeat Governor Dewey. She spoke of Stalin's intransigence and quoted a jibe of Churchill's that made me grin. "I think," said Winston, "that Mr. Stalin believes — and he is quite right in believing — that Britain and America will behave like perfect gentlemen to the end." Pause. "Whereas, were I in office, he would not be so sure. . . ."

She was, as I knew, an ardent Anglo-Catholic, and uppermost was her desire to write an essay to be called "Christianity and Human Rights." I commissioned it for our Christmas issue, in which I liked to have a paper of religious conviction. This was the first of the many Barbara wrote for us in the years to come and as I sent it to press I wondered, ruefully, why it was so much less eloquent than Barbara speaking. There was a good deal about divorce, which she discussed in a severe but troubled way. Two years later I knew the explanation. Barbara, at the age of thirty-three, was finally, deeply in love with Robert Jackson — in time to be Sir Robert — who had distinguished himself in the war and who had a wife and family in Australia.

A radiance came into her writing after Robert received his divorce and the Church sanctioned their marriage. I asked her to be ready to write for us, as the struggle between Tory capitalism and Labour's socialism intensified and particularly when an election seemed imminent. This pleased her, and the two early articles she did, "Decide or Drift" (February 1949) and "Deadlocked in Britain" (May 1950), were widely quoted.

She lived with the conflict between Communism and the free world ever in her thoughts and rearming was not the only way she urged democracy to bestir itself. Her manuscripts were eagerly awaited by our staff, and I can think of no writer who accepted our suggestions and criticism with better grace. Lester Markel was at this time the autocratic editor of the *New York Times Magazine*. He, too, admired Barbara and as he worked on a far shorter wavelength than I, he occasionally and at the last minute would invite her to do a short piece about the British, which took some of the icing off the longer article I had commissioned months earlier. So, before one simmering crisis I told Barbara I wanted the exclusive rights to what she was writing, and she agreed. As the date drew near, Markel went into his act and Barbara explained our arrangement. He telephoned me Saturday evening and got me out of my seat at the Boston Symphony. "You mean to tell me you have the exclusive rights of Miss Ward's opinion?" In this case, I said, that was correct. "Well, I'll be god-damned!" And there was a loud click.

It was said that Robert Jackson aspired to be a governor of the Bank of England. The government instead sent him as an advisor and evaluator to Ghana, which was acutely in transition, and of course Barbara went with him. The Jacksons were soon confronted with difficulty, for Nkruma had attracted another English consultant, a Socialist of extreme views who undercut Jackson at every turn. The infighting proved a nervous strain; what sustained Barbara was Nkruma's request that she write for his young men training for civil service an explanation of the constructive things which had been achieved under colonialism. This was the origin of her strong and clarifying book *Five Ideas That Changed the World*, a reassuring book, for Barbara to write and for the Ghanians to read.

Barbara was a superb speaker; her clear voice and fine eyes could hold any audience, her remarks scintillating as she built up her argument, without notes. I helped to arrange lectures for her at Wellesley and Smith colleges, President Dickey of Dartmouth had her open his course for seniors on "The Great Issues," and wherever she went there was a demand for her return. So between her journeys with Robert she planned to fit in an annual visit with the Weeks family on Beacon Hill. Every one of us looked forward to her coming, and at small dinners we introduced her to those I knew she would en-joy — Arthur and Marian Schlesinger, then the Galbraiths, and at one fortuitous buffet which outgrew our dining room, Adlai Stevenson, just back from Taiwan, Adlai Junior (at the Harvard Law School) and his fiancée, the Hamish Hamiltons from London, and

Archibald and Ada MacLeish. The Rhine wine was conducive and Adlai's description of his reception by Chiang Kai-shek and of a clandestine visit by an insurgent general, were engrossing.

As the party broke up I overheard Ada inviting Barbara to Cambridge the next morning to sing duets. So after Sunday breakfast I sat listening as Barbara did a little rehearsing at the piano. Then in perfect Cockney she began singing Eliza Doolittle's opening lyric in *My Fair Lady* — "Wouldn't It Be Loverly." When she finished she turned to me. "You see," she said, "it's simply not strong enough. I intended to study music at Oxford and it was only after I learned the truth that I turned to economics."

In their new office the *Economist* had a private dining room, and here at lunch Geoffrey Crowther introduced me to "our Defence Correspondent, Miss Joan Bright," a tall, dark-haired young woman with hazel eyes. Physical attraction is sometimes instantaneous. "But why," I wondered, "such a young woman in that job?" There were just the three of us at our table and I listened as Miss Bright reported to her chief, with indignation, what she had seen in Poland; she had returned from Warsaw, where the fear and hatred of the Germans burned deep. The Nazi occupation, she said, was responsible for the disappearance of six million Poles; during the Insurrection of 1944, *in eight weeks*, 200,000 citizens of Warsaw were buried under their homes, hunted, shot, or hanged in the streets — a ghastly preface for the homecoming of those released from the slave-labor camps in Germany. Then she described the Soviet-selected administration, in which were able, dominant Jews who had been trained in Moscow. It was a very impressive recital. I could see why Geoffrey admired her.

Two nights later she dined with me at the Savoy, and as we talked and danced, there began an understanding as dear to me as any in my life. Joan found me an English secretary, chose the plays we enjoyed together, and agreed to write *Atlantic* Reports on the places about which she was informed, beginning with Vienna.

It was piquant that a woman as beguiling as Joan should sidestep matrimony until she was thirty-nine, and, on her own, rise to a position of trust and authority among warriors. She was the third of five sisters, and in her proficient way she became at twenty a secretary at the British Legation in Mexico City. It was not a demanding job; she lived with an uncle, the weekends at Acapulco and the occasional visits to the United States gave her a very active social life and an understanding of Americans that would come in handy.

Mexico City was a far distance from the dark clouds over Europe. A stranger from London, a much older man, wise and generous, told her she was wasting her time, and volunteered to pay her fare back to England. It was sound advice and she took it.

Back in England Joan's ability did not go wanting. From the British Consul in Munich, whom she had known in Mexico, came an invitation from Mr. and Mrs. Rudolf Hess to live in their Berlin home and teach English to the family. She declined. But in the autumn of 1938 she was interviewed by a brisk colonel at the War Office, who warned her of the tortures awaiting her if caught by the Germans, and then had her sign the Official Secrets Act, as a prelude to her military career.

Joan's mother used to call her "nervy," hard to manage, but now it was her discretion as much as her efficiency which qualified her for the top-secret section in Military Intelligence, known as "irregular warfare" or "MI(R)." "I am sorry," said Lieutenant Colonel Ian Jacob, when she sought a permanent appointment in the Ministry of Defence. "We don't employ women here as private secretaries; we draw officers from the Army and Navy, but I will send your name around." That was an encrusted tradition which her mentor, General Ismay, bypassed. Churchill had suggested that a Special Information Center be set up in the War Cabinet Offices so that British Commanders home on leave could familiarize themselves with the plans developing in other sectors. Joan, with three girls to help, was to keep the Center open round the clock. To it were delivered two hundred files of telegrams, minutes, reports, letters and comments, along with comfortable armchairs; there would be eight hundred files by the end of the war. This library made her two rooms a haven for men like General Wavell, Admiral Ramsey, and Sir Alexander Hardinge, Private Secretary to the King. The days were gone when women could not be entrusted with dangerous information.

Joan's next step came after Pearl Harbor. It became imperative that Churchill and Roosevelt, their Chiefs of Staff, and scientific advisors should confer, secretly, for the Atlantic Charter meeting and later in 1943 in Washington, twice at Quebec, and Cairo, and then, with Stalin, at Tehran, Yalta, and Potsdam. Joan, now nearing thirty-three, was appointed "an administrative officer for the British delegation," served as an aide to Commander Knott, R.N., and flew on ahead to make the arrangements. There were secretaries, of course, but Joan took full charge at Moscow, Yalta, and Potsdam. Call her housekeeper, chaperone, consultant on liquor supplies and sleeping pills, hostess, and a popular partner at the dances as victory came in sight. All the British secretariat admired General George C. Marshall and before one party formed a pool to go to the girl, if any, whom the General invited to dance. Joan won. (When the Conferences were over she returned to "the Files.")

In 1946 while in Bermuda Joan wrote up her notes. She allowed me to read them early in our friendship: they were fascinating — the long flights, the humor with which she coped with the unexpected, her admiration for those driven, brilliant men, with their differences. Had it been published in the late 1940s it would have made quite a packet. But no inducement could persuade her to let me — or anyone else — print it then. She had no intention of commercializing on the confidence reposed in her. She told me that she was at work on two regimental histories, of the Ninth Lancers (tanks) and the Northumberland Hussars (no tanks), and would be ready for assignments when they were finished. I provided her with a new portable typewriter and she chose subjects as diverse as East Africa, Finland, Sweden, and the Arab refugees. On my English visits, after her marriage to Philip Astley, she found time to be my advisor, hostess, and, occasional chauffeur. I encouraged their son Richard to take a year at Dartmouth after Eton, and when she came over to see him in one of our coldest winters she cheered and comforted my dear Fritzy, who was mortally ill. But not until 1971 did she finish and release her war memoir, *The Inner Circle*, which I published, with the regret that so many of the seniors who would have valued it earlier were dead.

During the centuries of acquisition Britain produced travelers who went abroad not to grasp but to identify. The breed, such as Charles Montagu Doughty of Arabia, T. E. Lawrence, and Freya Stark, were endowed with iron constitutions and disarming curiosity, and their juniors are still exploring remote parts of the Commonwealth to learn and protect. Among my English contributors are a handful who were so inspired: H. M. Tomlinson, author of *The Sea and the Jungle*, Barbara Ward, Joan Bright Astley, Geoffrey Household the novelist, and my dearest friend in Parliament, Sir Frederic M. Bennett.

At the end of his seven years in the British Army (1939–1945), Freddy and his bride, Marion, went on a honeymoon, Capetown to Cairo to Calais, 13,000 miles, in a Ford Mercury, to see and understand much of what is now the Third World. Freddy's legal mind defies authoritarianism; he was a guest of the Greek government in 1947 and 1949, to observe the Communist infiltration there and the children's refugee camps; in 1956 the Masai, the Kipsis, and the Baluhya and Wakamba asked him to help them in writing a constitution for Kenya; they conferred with him in London for six weeks, and the constitution has stood the test. His sympathy for the million and more Poles who became British subjects after the war led him to fund the building of the Memorial Obelisk in London in memory of the thousands of Polish officers slain at Stalin's order in the Katyn Forest. In his thirty years in Parliament he has risen to be the British leader in the twenty-two-nation Council of Europe, one of its senior Vice Presidents, and Chairman of the Political Committee of the seven-nation Western European Union (Defense) Assembly, within NATO, and an always warmly welcomed observer in Turkey, Jordan, Pakistan, and China. I marvel that he keeps up such a pace. During the Parliamentary recesses I have enjoyed happy visits with Freddy and "Mouse" at their country house in Wales where, amid his flocks of peacocks and jungle fowl, we have farmed out amicably, not always in agreement, my American and his British hopes of keeping the peace.

Every periodical that values style has to establish its rules of grammar, which it expects its contributors to follow. One aims at consistency: it won't do to have an English writer spelling "honour" on one page and an American spelling it "honor" on the next. When Henry Mencken was preparing to publish the *American Mercury*, he wrote my predecessor, Ellery Sedgwick, saying that the *Atlantic* always looked "clean and well edited" and did we have a style sheet? We sent him a copy of *Text, Type and Style*, in which our former head copyeditor, George B. Ives, defined the *Atlantic* usage such as the proper distinction in the use of "that" and "which," the obligation of having a pronoun agree with its antecedent (which Van Wyck Brooks violated time and again), the desirability of *not* splitting the infinitive, etcetera. Some writers object to being copyedited. Edith Wharton objected strenuously and we let her have her idiosyncrasies. Hemingway, aware of our preference not to print four-letter obscenities, deliberately used "shit" in the two stories he wrote for our Centennial issue and we let it stand. The word "nigger" had been unacceptable as long as I can remember, but if a black writer uses it we do not question him.

A lecture trip took me to the Pacific Coast shortly before the banquet at which the Oscars are awarded, and the press was full of the usual ballyhoo and speculation. It occurred to me to invite Raymond Chandler, the very popular mystery story writer, to do an article for us on what the Oscars stood for, and I expected it would be irreverent. Four of his novels, including *The Big Sleep* and *Farewell, My Lovely*, had been made into successful films, and he was a member of the Academy of Motion Picture Arts and Sciences. His manuscript reached Boston as I was about to leave for England, and every one of us rejoiced at his characterization of Hollywood.

He began with an appraisal of the motion picture:

The motion picture is *not* a transplanted literary or dramatic art, any more than it is a plastic art. It has elements of all these, but in its essential structure it is much closer to music, in the sense that its finest effects can be independent of precise meaning, that its transitions can be more eloquent than its high-lit scenes, and that its dissolves and camera movements, which cannot be censored, are often far more emotionally effective than its plots, which can. Not only is the motion picture an art, but it is the one entirely new art that has been evolved on this planet for hundreds of years. It is the only art at which we of this generation have any possible chance to greatly excel . . .

But, he added, the "making of a fine motion picture is like painting 'The Laughing Cavalier' in Macy's basement, with a floorwalker to mix your colors for you." He deplored the splurging cost and "the hypercritical bluenose censorship" which handicapped our films in competition with the French and Italian, and then he reviewed "the annual tribal dance," the Oscars:

If the actors and actresses like the silly show, and I'm not sure at all the best of them do, they at least know how to look elegant in a strong light, and how to make with the wide-eyed and oh, so humble little speeches as if they believed them. If the big producers like it, and I'm quite sure they do because it contains the only ingredients they really understand — promotion values and the additional grosses that go with them — the producers at least know what they are fighting for. But if the quiet, earnest, and slightly cynical people who really make motion pictures like it, and I'm quite sure they don't, well, after all, it comes only once a year, and it's no worse than a lot of the sleazy vaudeville they have to push out of the way to get their work done.

I wrote Chandler of our delight, told him we thought that "Oscar Night in Hollywood" was preferable to a trick title, and that John Groth had been commissioned to paint a sardonic cover for our March issue. His manuscript was turned over to the copyeditor but I neglected to warn her, before I flew to London, not to tamper with Chandler's prose. This was a mistake.

On top of the correspondence that had accumulated during my fortnight abroad, my secretary, Kay Ellis, had placed Chandler's glorious remonstrance:

La Jolla, California
January 18th, 1947

Dear Mr. Weeks:

I'm afraid you've thrown me for a loss. I thought Juju Worship in Hollywood was a perfectly good title. . . . I've thought of various titles such as Bank Night in Hollywood, Sutter's Last Stand, The Golden Peepshow, All it Needs is Elephants, The Hot Shot Handicap, Where Vaudeville Went When it Died, and rot like that. But nothing that smacks you in the kisser. By the way, would you convey my compliments to the purist who reads your proofs and tell him or her that I write in a sort of brokendown patois which is something like the way a Swiss waiter talks, and that when I split an infinite, God damn it, I split it so it will stay split, and when I interrupt the velvety smoothness of my more or less literate syntax with a few sudden words of barroom vernacular, this is done with the eyes wide open and the mind relaxed but attentive. The method may not be perfect, but it is all I have. I think your proofreader is kindly attempting to steady me on my feet, but much as I appreciate the solicitude, I am really able to steer a fairly clear course, provided I get both sidewalks and the street between.

If I think of anything, I'll wire you.

Kindest regards,
Raymond Chandler

Beginning with his first contribution, "The Simple Art of Murder," in December 1944, Ray Chandler wrote for us until his death in 1958, and his letters to me are endearing. I wish there were twice as many, I wish I had been quicker to take his hints. He was lonely, and in the winter of 1957, being fed up with Hollywood, he went to London, which he loved. He was well received, so well that he reproached me: "The only trouble with you is that you can't spare enough money for people like me. In England, poor England, I was offered £450 for a short story up to 10,000 words about Marlowe." While in London he wrote some poems, one of which, over the protest of my poetry expert, I accepted, the poignant recollection of an old love.

Ray added: "Also I have been trying to learn the English language, which is superficially like ours, but very very different in its implications. Ours, when not too professorial, is creative, imaginative, free and even rather wild. Something like the English of Elizabeth's time. English is almost a Mandarin Language, but it is beginning to loosen up and I think I might possibly do something with it, since I am beginning to feel that I have done about all I can do with the mystery story. One gets into a feeling of tired routine. The public, apparently, wants the same thing forever. But a writer gets awfully tired of his tricks, or I hope he does — certainly I do."

And then in June 1957, I received this funny, touching revelation:

Dear Mr. Weeks:

Instead of my writing critically about Hollywood, would it interest you to have me describe some of my more humorous experiences, such as, for example, the time I was loaned out to MGM and there was no couch in my office? I had brought my own secretary from Paramount, and made that part of the deal. The Producer told me that Mannix, the Studio Manager, had decided there should be no couches in writers' offices, because they spend too much time on them and not always alone. I sent my secretary down to the car for a couple of steamer rugs, spread them out on the floor, and lay down on them. The Producer rushed to the telephone and called Mannix and said, "My God, I've got a horizontal writer here." The next day, there was a couch in my office, but the atmosphere of the Thalberg Building (known around MGM as The Iron Lung) depressed me.

I told my Producer, a very nice fellow, that I had rather work at home. He told me that Mannix did not allow writers to work at home. I said with my usual impudence, "I'll work at home, I think — if at all." And they let me do it.

Another thing amusing to me at least was that after I had handed in a batch of script to the Producer and he had looked it over, he would say, not quite on the edge of tears but rather close, "Can't we keep some of the book? Isn't it one of your books we bought? Isn't that why you're here?"

"I'm sick of it, George. It's so much easier to write new stuff."

"For God's sake," he said, "this is supposed to be an adaptation of something we bought from you. And you keep on writing entirely different scenes. They are all right in their way, but how do I explain to the front office that a writer who was hired to do the screenplay of his own story pays almost no attention to it?"

He was not angry — only troubled.

"I guess it's not my kind of story," I said, "or not any longer. When a writer breaks his heart to do a job and does it as well as he can, he just doesn't want to do it all over again and worse."

"But we bought the damn thing."

"Yes, but to me the point is that I am stale on it. Perhaps some other writer could do a much better job — naturally leaving out any line of dialogue that might have any possibility of making what else he did look like a dead carnation. After all, these boys are trying to exist. They are not vicious as a rule, but in order to exist when they take over a screenplay, they have to make it *their* screenplay."

"I don't like it lousy," the Producer said sadly.

"You're a producer, George. You surely must know by now that there are not twenty writers in Hollywood who can write, in the sense we are talking about. Many do good honest jobs, but . . . !"

Has a writer ever disclosed more honestly the grind of converting one's book into a screenplay? All he needed was my encouragement to shape this for the magazine. Why didn't I wire him the green light, as in times past? I was thick in the preparation of our Centennial issue — for which it would have been ideal — but I hesitated.

CHAPTER

X

In questions of faith the *Atlantic* has never feared to be unortho-dox. We were founded when the battlesmoke over Darwinism was still in the air. From the first, Unitarians were strong in our councils, but they too could be put to the test just as I intended to devote a future issue to the Catholic Church in America, for the magazine was fundamentally non-sectarian. The release of the bombs in 1945 was more shocking than any previous assault on organized religion for it raised the question, Does man have the faith and the moral strength to prevent atomic destruction?

The writer who despaired over this was W. T. Stace, an English-man trained in British civil service, now teaching philosophy at Princeton. His essay "Man Against Darkness" declared that ever since Galileo and Newton the universe had lost its purpose, that man was governed by blind forces, and that God and religion were dead. His argument was shocking and remorseless. The gist of it was in these words:

Religion could survive the discoveries that the sun, not the earth, is the center; that men are descended from simian ancestors; that the earth is hundreds of millions of years old. These discoveries may render out of date some of the details of older theological dogmas, may force their restatement in new intellectual frameworks. But they do not touch the essence of the religious vision itself, which is the faith that there is plan and purpose in the world, that the world is a moral order, that in the end all things are for the best. This faith may express itself through many different intellectual dogmas, those of Christianity, of Hinduism, of Islam. All and any of these intellectual dogmas may be destroyed without destroying the essential religious spirit. But that spirit cannot survive destruction of belief in a plan and purpose of the world, for that is the very heart of it. Religion can get on with any sort of astronomy, geology, biology, physics. But it cannot get on with a purposeless and meaningless universe.

If the scheme of things is purposeless and meaningless, then the life of man is purposeless and meaningless, too. Everything is futile, all effort is in the end worthless. A man may, of course, still pursue disconnected ends, money, fame, art, science, and may gain pleasure from them. But his life is hollow at the center. Hence the dissatisfied, disillusioned, restless spirit of modern man.

The effect of such despair on the readers was to make them reconsider what they believed, and why — and they did so, in many lengthy letters and more than a dozen articles of reaffirmation. Clare Boothe Luce was so aroused that she wrote a small book in reply. "We thought you were very courageous to have printed Stace," she told me when she came up to speak at Boston College. "Henry was not sure he would have done so."

We chose four statements, for a symposium in reply to Professor Stace, led by Canon Bernard Iddings Bell, an Episcopalian, Consultant in Higher Education at the University of Chicago. Under the title "Is It Really That Dark?" he spoke for the humanist:

The humanist rarely stops at humanism, unless his career is cut off by early death. He either goes on from humanism into theism and so finds in God the meaning of things and people, including himself, or else he joins Dr. Stace and his non-mystical friends and shivers in hopelessness. Dr. Stace hates the humanist as thoroughly as he does the theist. Both to his mind are obscurantists and cowards.

In the Middle Ages people discovered purpose chiefly through theistic mysticism; in the Renaissance, for the most part through humanistic mysticism. We twentieth-century people increasingly neglect all mysticism, along with creativity and a glad acceptance of nature, and rely instead too entirely on inductive science, which reveals no purpose. But the purpose is still there, discoverable. The trouble is that we refuse to use the techniques that reveal it.

The controversy and self-searching burned for months. The strongest refutation of Professor Stace was written by Theodore M. Greene, Professor of Philosophy and Master of Silliman College in Yale University. His article "Man Out of Darkness" (April 1949) denied that religion had lost its power:

Not only has organized Christianity lost no ground during the last decades; it is actually increasing its following in this country, in England, and in some portions of Europe. More people are going to church with, in many cases, a deeper sense of spiritual need. Theological seminaries are crowded with students who are, on the whole, abler than their pre-war predecessors, yet seminaries are unable to satisfy the demand of churches for more clergy. Missionary activity is increasing in scope and improving in quality. Christianity is more widely spread geographically and more deeply rooted among more peoples than it has ever been. The Christian ecumenical movement is making rapid strides: through it Christians are coming together on a world-wide scale as never before. . . .

No less significant is the renewed interest of college students in a faith to live by. Most of these eager inquirers are largely ignorant of the Bible, Christian doctrine, and the Christian tradition. Many of them are highly critical of Christian orthodoxy and traditionalism and are indignant at what they (often justly) regard as self-righteousness, wishful thinking, and cant in organized religion. Few are properly equipped to grapple intelligently with the basic problems of religious faith in our secular society. But they are neither complacent nor dogmatic; they are deeply troubled and sincerely anxious to find whatever light and strength religion can provide. In short, the "spirit of religion" is a vital force in their lives.

Years later it was rumored that Dr. Stace had recanted and become a convert to Roman Catholicism, but at the time his argument, premised in part, as he acknowledged, on the writing of Alfred North Whitehead, expressed the bleak pessimism brought on by the Bikini tests.

On September 23, 1949, President Truman announced that the Soviet Union had successfully tested an atomic bomb. It would be difficult to measure the extent of the shock that swept America. For a time there were those, I among them, who walked about as if we wore a small bomb like a derby on the back of the head — how soon would the autumn loveliness of the Public Garden be destroyed? There was a flurry to reactivate Civil Defense, and bomb shelters were built in backyards. A flashlight, canned goods, and a pail of sand were closeted close to the cellar in town houses. Roger Babson of the Babson Institute in Wellesley proclaimed that Wellesley was a safer place to live since it was beyond the perimeter of a direct hit on Boston.

Apprehension was perhaps more acute among scientists who were faced with the inevitable decision: should they proceed with the testing of the hydrogen bomb? Dr. J. Robert Oppenheimer was firmly opposed to the overkill of the hydrogen monster and Conant and Van Bush sided with him. But if the Soviets went ahead, what other deterrent had we? While the argument went on Dr. Bush had second thoughts, which he expressed in this address, then off the record:

Clearly the picture which I have presented of our side is far from bright. We have come to a crossroads and even in action, complete passivity, or dogged pursuit of the road on which we are traveling is nevertheless a grave decision . . . which only history will reveal in its true light. Such a decision was made when it was decided not to admit Russia to the atomic bomb development during the war. It was a natural decision and a conservative decision but it may very well have been the step which has led to the atomic bomb race. If we look back upon it now, we can see that we would have lost very little and could have gained much if the opposite course had been taken. . . .

Now that the Russians have the bomb in their hands to study, they will almost of necessity follow through the same line of thought that we have traveled. The atomic bomb is probably the only weapon which can defeat them. We are both in the same boat, except that they have more immediate experience of what it means to be at the receiving end of a total war. . . .

It is clear that any settlement which we may attempt with the Soviets cannot be on the basis of atomic energy alone. Our concentration on this field originally was based on the feeling that if an accord could be reached in this question other problems would fall into place. The march of events has changed this situation. An agreement with the Russians must include all arms and not be confined even to the general question of weapons of mass destruction. Russian land armies and submarines involve our European commitments, and must be included in any general settlement. Our strategic air force and distant air bases are aimed at the heart of Russian life. . . .

Can we trust the Russians to honor treaties, settlements and agreements? More experienced men than I have said no. This is a common experience with great nations. The term perfidious Albion was once applied to the British with honesty and fervor. No great nation will continue indefinitely an arrangement which it regards as unfavorable. Whatever arrangements are made they must be of real advantage to both sides and we must look to intelligent self interest to keep them workable.

We may not be able to trust the Russians, but can we afford not to, at least to an important degree? We must always remember that they are asking themselves the same question because our power is hardly inferior to their own and is a formidable sight from across the oceans.

Many people will perhaps be disappointed because no practical proposals are suggested in this address. That is a task for statesmanship, but statesmen will not and cannot undertake the task unless they are fully supported by the people. Many attitudes will have to be changed and not all on the other side before the cold war can be called off. We will have to make concessions which will be disagreeable to many and alarming to some. A real and urgent will for peace must arise in the country. Only then can the statesman proceed with confidence.

The advent of a new poet, whose lines defy convention as they excite the imagination, occurs very rarely in any editor's régime. It occurred to us in 1947 when at the suggestion of Edith Sitwell, I wrote to Dylan Thomas inviting him to send us one of his new lyrics. In reply came a letter of two sentences in minuscule handwriting, enclosing a long poem:

The Manor
Witney
Oxfordshire
22nd, August 1947

Dear Mr. Weeks,

Thank you very much for your letter asking me to contribute to the Ninetieth Anniversary Number of The Atlantic.

Here is a new poem.

Yours faithfully,
Dylan Thomas

"In Country Sleep" was unquestionably poetry; it made the other verses in the office look flat. But what did it mean? I deferred to Phoebe-Lou Adams, our most respected judge, and this was her analysis:

On reading this for the seventh time, I believe Thomas is describing the progress of the human spirit from primitive folk lore, to paganism, to a comfortable Christianity, and beyond that to mysticism. The earlier progress is largely voluntary, mysticism is largely involuntary, a species of possession. The second section of the poem attempts first to describe mystical experience, and then to defend it as a valid communion with an outside power rather than the rather repulsive hysteria which it sometimes appears, to the rational mind, to be. I would hate to be called into court to prove this theory, line by line, and I'm sure our readers will deluge us with questions on this one, but it is first class poetry.

We accepted the poem gratefully, paid Thomas the same fee we had paid Whittier for "Snow Bound," and we asked for more. This time the response was unprecedented: he said he would send us another when he had a poem that was good enough. The normal reaction for a poet is to dig down into his trunk if nothing new is available. *Atlantic* readers were not as keen as we for another; as PLA predicted, they reproached us for printing the incomprehensible.

A year and a half later Thomas submitted "In the White Giant's Thigh" — and he would never send us a better. This is a celebration of the life force linking man and nature, too long to be quoted in full, but its pulse and the beauty of the imagery are conveyed in these opening lines:

> *Through throats where many rivers meet, the curlews cry,*
> *Under the conceiving moon, on the high chalk hill,*
> *And there this night I walk in the white giant's thigh*
> *Where barren as boulders women lie longing still*
>
> *To labor and love though they lay down long ago.*
>
> *Through throats where many rivers meet, the women pray,*
> *Pleading in the waded bay for the seed to flow*
> *Though the names on their weed grown stones are rained away,*
>
> *And alone in the night's eternal, curving act*
> *They yearn with tongues of curlews for the unconceived*
> *And immemorial sons of the cudgeling, hacked*
>
> *Hill. Who once in gooseskin winter loved all ice leaved*
> *In the courters' lanes, or twined in the ox roasting sun*
> *In the wains tonned so high that the wisps of the hay*
> *Clung to the pitching clouds, or gay with anyone*
> *Young as they in the after milking moonlight lay*
>
> *Under the lighted shapes of faith and their moonshade*
> *Petticoats galed high, or shy with the rough riding boys,*
> *Now clasp me to their grains in the gigantic glade,*
>
> *Who once, green countries since, were a hedgerow of joys.*

This was the most distinctive English poetry since T. S. Eliot; we accepted it with elation — and a larger fee — and were to publish two more before his death.

Dylan Thomas could be ironic and very funny. An English editor had asked him to describe the steps which help to establish a popular poet. Thomas (who had been struggling for recognition since 1930) gave us his answer in a short article, "How to Be a Poet." His first example is a man "dropped into Civil Service at an early age," who attempts to escape from red tape by writing a poem.

It is, of course, about Nature; it confesses a wish to escape from humdrum routine and embraces the unsophisticated life of the farm laborer; he desires, though without scandal, to wake up with the birds; he expresses the opinion that a plowshare, not a pen, best fits his little strength; a decorous pantheist, he is one with the rill, the rhyming mill, the rosy-bottomed milkmaid, the russet-cheeked rat-catcher, swains, swine, pipits, pippins. You can smell the country in his poems, the fields, the flowers, the armpits of Triptolemus, the barns, the byres, the hay, and, most of all, the corn. The poem is published. A single lyrical extract from the beginning must suffice: —

> *The roaring street is hushed!*
> *Hushed, do I say?*
> *The wing of a bird has brushed*
> *Time's cobwebs away.*
> *Still, still as death, the air*
> *Over the gray stones!*
> *And over the gray thoroughfare*
> *I hear — sweet tones! —*
> *A blackbird open its bill,*
> *— A blackbird, aye! —*
> *And sing its liquid fill*
> *From the London sky.*

A little time after the publication of the poem, he is nodded to in the corridor by "Hotchkiss of Inland Revenue, himself a week-ending poet with two slim volumes to his credit, half an inch in the Poets' Who's Who or the Newbolt Calendar. . . ."

Neither Thomas nor his wife, Caitlin, was provident; by the time his books, lectures, and broadcasts over BBC produced a sustaining income he had become a hard and self-punishing drinker. The lecture trips to America earned money but were a wracking stimulant. He appeared to be tipsy before he went on the platform, yet the readings were eloquently delivered. But afterwards he completed the intoxication that killed him. It was a pitiful waste.

My friend, James R. Killian, president of the Massachusetts Institute of Technology, telephoned me in early June 1952 to say that Lewis Douglas, who was to have delivered their Commencement address, had laryngitis, was speechless — and could I possibly fill in? I was fond of both men, and I said I'd be happy to try. As I had less than forty hours to prepare I asked if I could have a quick meeting with the head of his History Department. The Institute had recently discontinued its formal courses in English and was grading students on the ability with which they wrote their papers in Modern History.

This was a new experiment; I was sure there must have been some unexpected results and that such humor at the outset would help the audience forget their disappointment at not hearing Douglas.

The night before Commencement at M.I.T. the speaker has the pleasure of dining with the president and members of the Corporation. I was seated beside the genial, towering David Shepard, then vice president of the Standard Oil Company of New Jersey. We discovered an affinity in fly-fishing and he described his favorite stream, the White River in Colorado. I went on to ask how he recruited young executives of promise. He said there had been three stages in the oil business. In the early days in Pennsylvania and Oklahoma, the leaders were self-made, the rugged enterprising men in the field whose technical skill was limited to using a divining rod and who had a back strong enough to fire an oil still. After the pioneers the openings were pre-empted by engineers with a scientific education and initiative. Then came a gradual change in recruitment. In a recent year, he said, his company and its affiliates hired 990 college graduates, exactly one-third of whom held non-technical degrees. This surprised me, and he explained that at a conservative estimate their full-time executives devoted more than half of their working hours to problems of human relations rather than those of a technical or economic nature.

At the reception which followed Commencement Shepard promised to write for us. His article "Management in Search of Men" (March 1956) was a stimulant such as we seldom received from industrialists and was clearly written by Dave himself. And so by my "casting my bread upon the waters" my wife and I, two summers later, were invited by Dave and his wife, Kay, to a fishing holiday on the White River.

Clarence Randall, the president of Inland Steel, was a second executive who wrote with invigoration, candor, and humor — and no help from a public relations officer. Clarence's career was a prime example of the value of a liberal arts degree. Class of 1912 at Harvard, clubmate of Robert Benchley and Joseph Kennedy, he graduated from the Harvard Law School and began practice in Chicago. After a suit in the Ishpeming Peninsula in Michigan, which he prosecuted successfully for Inland, the management began to rely on him and his good judgment. Eventually his capacity with people moved him, without technical training, into the top spot.

He turned to me with an article the *Cornell Business Review* had invited and declined — on the difficulty in finding men who would *continue* to make the hard decisions. I took it, encouraged him to go on; helped him bring out his statesmanlike philosophy of business and had published three of his books when President Eisenhower called him to Washington as an aide and troubleshooter. Clarence continued to write for us; he, Charles H. Percy, and I formed a friendly trio at one summer session of the Aspen Institute. I became very fond of him, especially his candor in handling touchy subjects: "Can We Invest in Turkey?" (November 1953) and "South Africa Needs Time" (May 1963).

Leland Hazard of Pittsburgh was my third jewel of executives — and the most quizzical. Of Kansas City, originally, where in the Depression he was appointed receiver in bankruptcy for a firm owing the largest debt to Pittsburgh Plate Glass. When he paid it off dollar for dollar, in gratefulness the glass company decided they wanted him exclusively as their attorney. A wag said that "Pittsburgh was just large enough for one Leland Hazard." He was into everything: the Allegheny Conference; the guiding spirit of Radio Station WQED; and when television came it was Leland who strongly backed and raised the funds for Martha Graham's dances (as he financed my five TV programs on "Writers of Today" over WGBH, Boston). He was deeply involved in education, as was his wife, Mary, and both of them collected modern art — when the Pittsburgh Museum was hesitant to accept a Calder mobile, Leland had it hung in the Pittsburgh airport. For us he wrote two of the most reasonable articles on management-labor relations the *Atlantic* has published, "Inflation and Strikes" (February 1958) and "Strikes and People" (December 1966).

I searched but could never find the like of these three amid the leaders of Labor. "What *is* the *Atlantic*?" asked Walter Reuther, after reading my request for an article when the UAW was in the midst of a strike, as I recall, against Chevrolet. I asked for a "statesmanlike article." I question if he ever wrote a word of it; it was an impersonal, slanted diatribe, probably by his P.R.O., which I paid for as promised but refused to print. I had no better luck elsewhere.

CHAPTER

XI

Ralph McGill was the spearpoint of a group of Southern journalists, each conspicuous in the fight for civil rights for the negro. His allies were Mark Ethridge, editor of the *Louisville Courier-Journal*, Virginius Dabney of the *Richmond News-Leader*, and Jonathan Daniels of the *Raleigh News and Observer*. Among the more persecuted were Hodding Carter in Greenville, Mississippi, who was denounced by the state legislature, under relentless pressure of the White Citizens Council, and so often threatened with physical violence that he carried a pistol. In Little Rock, Arkansas, Harry Ashmore was victimized by the same threats, the same hostility, and he finally moved to the West Coast to stop the punishment of his newspaper, the *Arkansas Gazette*.

McGill was the chief target of abuse. Atlanta, with its infusion of industries from the North and West, had become the capital of the New South. McGill's paper, the *Atlanta Constitution*, had grown to be one of the great newspapers of the nation. Ralph rarely turned down a speaking engagement and he applied the pressure constantly in his editorials and his column, "One Word More," which came to be syndicated in 300 papers, and which he wrote seven days a week for thirty years. Accordingly, in the South, he was blamed, personally, for what happened following the decision the Supreme Court handed down on May 17, 1954, declaring segregation in the nation's schools to be unconstitutional. This was "Rastus" McGill's doing, so the Georgia rednecks believed, and their attacks on him intensified. It would take a brave man to tackle McGill physically, for he had gained in weight and strength since the days he played guard for Vanderbilt (at 154 pounds) so the retaliation was anonymous: telephone calls abusing his ailing wife or young son, and, at night, louts in cars shouting obscenities, dumping garbage on the lawn or burning crosses, and peppering the mailbox with a shotgun. "Atlanta," Ralph said, "is too busy to hate." In this he was over-optimistic.

McGill's forebears were Scots, Irish, and Welsh country folk in east Tennessee, never owning slaves — which caused his critics to call him "a carpetbag Southerner" — but which also accounted for the flavor of what he wrote. His column was homely, humorous, compassionate, sometimes furious. As a sickly child he had spent many days in his grandmother's kitchen and when he wrote about country ham with red-eye gravy and cornbread, or fried mush with syrup, you could taste it. When he thought about the family mule, this is what he remembered.

There is something of a mystery about the mule. He is a hybrid, "without pride in ancestry or hope of posterity," but he has sense like a man. The horse is a silly fool which will run back into a burning barn because it is a symbol of safety. A mule will break down a door to get out.

A horse will work until he breaks down. A mule has sense enough to stop when he is tired and refuse to budge until he feels like it. And those whose daily lives have been shared with a mule know that the mule listens and understands. And though the city dwellers will scoff, such men get back an answer from the mule.

Welsh sentiment flowered into his three columns about Christmas — for the twenty-third, Christmas Eve, and the Day itself — which were written for his five-year-old son and so well-liked that they were reprinted unchanged, year after year. Whether he touched on politics, civil rights, poker, or a favorite foxhound he was read by those who derided him, even by politicians like Eugene Talmadge. In his wrath, as he told how the Klan had caused a negro church to cancel its Easter service because white ministers were invited to attend, his words hit hard:

The Klan is antichurch and it always has been, despite its cynical and depraved use of the cross. Men who set it in flames violate every Christian concept. The Klan is un-American and always has been, despite its use of the flag, and its hypocritical protests.

The Klan is not powerful in Georgia or the South. It is powerful only in communities where law enforcement isn't willing to kick it in the teeth . . . where the people are uselessly afraid of a few small-souled, evil wretches.

McGill was in London when the Supreme Court delivered its decision and the news was relayed to him at midnight by his friend Eugene Patterson of the United Press. "I'm surprised it was unanimous" was Ralph's comment. He lay awake till dawn reviewing the slow painful progress since 1896 when an earlier Court had endorsed those deceptive words, "separate but equal." He anticipated the resistance of Southern governors to desegregation, and his article "The Angry South" explained to *Atlantic* readers how deep-seated was this defiance:

A region, like a nation or a man, is a product of its history and traditional environment. Deep in the instincts of many Southerners is a fear of what might happen "when the children all drink out of the same bucket." Many of these people are entirely sincere when they say that nonsegregation means a "mongrelized" race. They will die before they agree, they say. And they mean it. . . . "Tell them we will die rather than yield" is a somewhat common statement. "Don't they know there will be violence?"

In October 1958, the temple, seat of Atlanta's biggest Jewish congregation, was bombed. McGill's editorial, entitled "A Church, a School," began:

Dynamite in great quantity ripped a beautiful temple of worship in Atlanta. It followed hard on the heels of a like destruction of a handsome high school at Clinton, Tennessee. The same rabid mad-dog minds were, without question, behind both. They were also the source of previous bombings in Florida, Alabama, and South Carolina. . . .
Let us face the facts. This is a harvest. It is the crop of things sown. It is the harvest of defiance of courts and the encouragement of citizens to defy law on the part of many Southern politicians. . . . It is not possible to preach lawlessness and restrict it. . . .

For that denunciation — it was written in twenty minutes — and the one that followed, Ralph was awarded a Pulitzer Prize in the spring of 1959.

On a visit to Atlanta, Peter Davison, then the associate editor of Atlantic books, reinforced my urging for McGill to do a book: as Peter suggested, it should be a blend of his autobiography, the evils of racism, disfranchisement, educational and economic peonage, and the changes for which he had pleaded. Ralph wrote that he was deeply appreciative "and beset by doubts and fears," but they were resolved after a skull session in Boston. This was not to be a collection of articles; it was to begin affectionately with his boyhood, his grounding in the Southern tradition, his years at Vanderbilt, the sports writing and travel which preceded his outreach in Atlanta, where he came to know the black leaders and to entertain them in his home.

The book became possessive, one chapter emerging from a visit to Ghana where he interviewed the famous black protester, W. E. B. DuBois, another blocked out on the long flights as he accompanied Vice President Nixon to the Soviet Union. The writing quickened in June 1961, when President Pusey of Harvard conferred on McGill the honorary degree of Doctor of Laws with a citation that brought 12,000 to their feet. "In a troubled time his steady voice of reason champions a New South." It was slowed by the fatal illness of his wife, Mary Elizabeth (the night of her death a shot was fired through Ralph's window), and by a plaintive warning from McGill's dedicated secretary, Grace Lundy, asking for an extension of the delivery date. "I can tell Mr. McGill is getting very tired." When *The South and the Southerner* was at last off the press it won the Atlantic Non-Fiction prize of $5,000. It is true and searching and compassionate. When I wrote him I said, "No award I have ever had a hand in has given me more pleasure than this."

One reviewer praised it as "perhaps the most valuable Southern contribution to our American literature in our century." The *New Yorker*, more measured, said, "He uses a quasi-autobiographical, quasi-reporting method instead of merely arguing, and the result is that he teaches rather than preaches." Supercilious liberals who had not been through the heat criticized McGill for not joining the Freedom marches, unaware than the *Atlanta Constitution*, involved in libel suits provoked by McGill, had forbidden him to go. Others, "holier than thou," believed he had not gone far enough and questioned his conviction that it would take time and force before integration could approach reality. How mistaken they were we know from the deep defiance of integration even in northern cities like Boston.

After Ralph's death, my friend Oscar Handlin, the historian, reviewing McGill's career, wrote:

Our last meeting was, I think, in November, 1967. I had been to the meeting of the Southern Historical Association with Mary [Handlin]; and we had a long leisurely lunch with Ralph and his wife at his club. We covered a whole range of subjects — personal, political, race and Vietnam. I was not surprised, but gratified, to discover how close our agreement was on every issue on which we touched. I remember the bitterness with which he spoke of certain dualistically liberal journalists whose dogmatism undermined their sense of responsibility and of crafts-manship. These observations were touched off by attitudes toward Vietnam expressed by the *Times* and the *Globe*, among others. They encompassed a more general set of attitudes that he feared would destroy American liberalism.

In retrospect, I think that he was depressingly foresighted.

In understanding the man, I always came back to an earlier conversation in which he talked about his boyhood and mentioned the middle names he did not use in his writing. It seems to me significant that he grew up in the kind of Southern family, the father of which named his son Ralph Waldo Emerson. In Ralph's work, one could see the influence of a genuine moral commitment which had close affinities to New England transcendentalism — optimistic and grounded on the faith in human progress, hardheaded, realistic and bounded by the knowledge of what could be done. He was an individualist, in the true sense of the word — one who was guided by his own appraisal of what was right and what was wrong and willing to stand up for it. He was always subject to attack, and not only by conservatives. I remember that the year *The South and the Southerner* appeared, I voted to award it a certain prize, on the jury of which I served. I found myself in a minority, not so much because of the opposition of conservatives, but because of the hostility of liberals which went back to what seemed to me an obscure difference of opinion, in which Ralph had been guided by his own views rather than following the conventional liberal line. I then learned something about the intolerance of many liberals. I also learned something about the independence and conscientiousness of Ralph McGill.

Had it not been for what Ralph taught me I doubt if it would have occurred to me to publish in full the letter which Martin Luther King wrote from prison. I believe the *Atlantic* was the only magazine to do so.

In 1943 when the nation was devoting every resource to the defeat of Hitler, the president of Tuskegee Institute in Alabama, Frederick Douglas Patterson, sat brooding about the survival of the private colleges for negroes. All were running deficits, costs were spiraling and the gifts which had once closed the gap were not forthcoming. He wrote an open letter to his fellow presidents urging them "to pool their small monies and make a united appeal to the national conscience." Shortly, twenty-seven of the accredited four-year colleges (responsible for educating 85 percent of the negroes in professional careers) had agreed to an equitable division of such a fund if the money could be raised.

John D. Rockefeller, Jr., quietly took hold. He invited representatives to our major cities to dine with him in the Rainbow Room of Rockefeller Center; to represent Boston he chose public-spirited Mike Kelleher, and Mike asked me to come along as his deputy. In that beautiful setting high above Manhattan, Mr. Rockefeller introduced us to Fred Patterson, who was to head up the new fund, and as Fred described the origin of those twenty-seven colleges, what was needed to keep them solvent, and the struggle his black students went through even to get to college, the cause was won. We knew Patterson was the ideal leader and the money would come.

Our initial quota for Boston was $50,000 and we fell short by $4,000. Midway in our second year Mike died suddenly of a heart attack and, in sorrow, I took over, first as local chairman, later as master of ceremonies in Washington or wherever the annual convention might call, still later, when the Fund brought that very able money-raiser John Bradbury to Boston, as advisor to the New England campaign.

During my thirty years with the United Negro College Fund, I was learning. In the beginning we had the banker Ralph Lowell as our treasurer, and other sprigs of the old Abolitionist roots, Miss Harriet Curtis and Judge and Mrs. Lawrence Brooks, who blew the bugle and never missed a meeting. I learned that friends like Joe Spang, the president of Gillette, would give individually but that it would take time before we got the big corporate gifts. I expected that when Ralph McGill spoke at our annual meeting it would open Northern pocketbooks. The black community in Boston took heart and I realized what it meant to them and to uninformed whites when we had presidents like Dr. Albert Manley of Spelman or President Jerome H. ("Brud") Holland of Hampton Institute to tell us of their institutions. When men as persuasive as William Andres and William Bullen, both of Dartmouth, held the chairmanship for two years or longer, we would go over the top. On my lecture trips I managed to visit a number of the colleges and at Talladega, a coed fell in step with me after my talk and said, "But you made no mention of lynching. Don't you realize how we still fear that horror?" No, to me lynching was as unthinkable as the ancient torture of being drawn and quartered.

The United Negro College Fund has become a major calling since that slim beginning in 1943. In 1954 we gave a luncheon at the National Press Club in Washington to which we invited members of Congress and their wives. There were thirty-four tables with a president of a negro college the host at each. Harriet Sampson sang for us and when President Eisenhower entered at the close of the meal we planned to have the famous Hampton Choir greet him with "The Battle Hymn of the Republic," but their bus did not arrive until the building was surrounded by the Secret Service and the singers in their robes were passed through only in the nick of time. The President took his seat on the dais, and before I introduced him I told him that our Executive Committee that morning had reported corporate gifts of $4,000,000 for new buildings on our campuses. That surprising generosity added to the spontaneity of his remarks.

In Boston our annual meetings were held on Sunday afternoons and in the mid-winter of 1956 we chose a Sunday when Senator John F. Kennedy would be in town. I asked him if he could possibly give us a short address as the climax of our program. "Well," he said, "I'm doing four other talks that day. What time do you want me?" "Five-thirty," I said. "I'll be there without fail. But you'll have to start without me." M.I.T. had just completed the new Kresge Auditorium, and President Killian generously offered it to us. We filled it and the program went like this: Invocation by Howard Thurman, the chaplain of Boston University; songs — and encores — by Roland Hayes. The treasurer reported that New England's contribution for the past year was $750.00. Then it was my turn to hold the audience until JFK arrived. I told them he was on his way and then I asked our negro candidates for graduate degrees, men and women who were studying at Harvard Medical School and the School of Public Health, at Tufts Dental School, at Boston University, and Suffolk Law School, to rise and face the audience. They filled the first two rows and it had taken time to find them. But they were our living proof of what the UNCF stood for, and the applause was a tribute to their advance. And as the graduate students were settling down I heard the approaching sirens, and my anxiety was over. Kennedy entered, eager and smiling, and when that large audience, more black than white, had quieted he said what he felt in those short, thrusting sentences.

After the benediction everyone wanted to shake his hand, beginning with the graduate students, and it was six when I escorted him back to the limousine. "It mustn't be easy to raise money for your fund," he said. "It isn't," I replied, "though it's easier now than when we began." "Put me down for a thousand," he said, as we parted. He remembered us again that spring; his book, *Profiles in Courage*, was awarded the Pulitzer Prize and he endorsed that check to the UNCF.

I encouraged my friend DeWitt Wallace, founder and editor of the *Reader's Digest*, to put up prizes of $1,000 each for the best short story, poem, and essay written by students at the United Negro Colleges, and was happy that one of them was won by the most talented black to write for the *Atlantic*. With his prize money James Alan McPherson entered the Harvard Law School, and before he had his LL.D. we were publishing the first of the short stories which would bring him the Pulitzer Prize in Fiction in 1978. More of James later. There are forty-one accredited colleges today in the United Negro College Fund. Boston's quota for the year ahead, as I write, is $250,000 and for the country as a whole, $20 million.

CHAPTER

XII

As we turned into 1950 the Republicans had been in the minority for eighteen years. At their lowest ebb in 1936 Henry Cabot Lodge, Jr., was the sole Republican freshman to be elected to the Senate. I much admire "Cabot," as his friends call him. He reminds me that early in his campaign we stood beside each other in the stag line at a Myopia dance. I asked how the campaign was going. "I'm not aware of any great demand," he said with a laugh. "I demand!" I replied. So did a plurality of 140,000 others in his defeat of James Michael Curley. He was reelected in 1942, sent to Africa accompanying the initial shipment of American tanks for the British 8th Army, and then resigned his seat to serve in France and Germany. Now in his third term I believed he could arouse his party from its dragging conservatism and we featured his article "Modernize the G.O.P." on the cover and in first place, March 1950.

Party platforms are often a featherbed of generalities. Cabot was specific under every subhead. He began with taxes: "Republicans should support a change in the law relative to the taxation of corporations doing a business of less than one million dollars so that they could file their returns as a partnership. Practically all the activities of venture capital start as small businesses. This would provide a powerful lift for the little man with a bright idea. . . ."

Under old age, the group tragically described "as too old to work, too young to die," he proposed "an increase to be financed by raising the payroll tax by not more than one percent so that an old couple would receive an average benefit of between $90 and $100 instead of the average $40 in the present law. . . ."

Under civil rights he demanded

1. Eliminate the poll tax.
2. Make lynching a federal offense.
3. End racial segregation in the armed services.
4. Eliminate segregation in housing projects or in educational aid projects financed by the federal government.

I have selected these examples from an extensive, vital program which was reprinted by the hundreds of thousands and which explains why Lodge was so persuasive in securing the nomination of General Eisenhower two years after his proclamation.

While Lodge's words aroused the G.O.P., my wife and I prepared to fly to London in April. I needed her help with the English manuscripts, and after a fortnight of reading we would have an Italian holiday with Sir Osbert and Edith Sitwell at "Montefugoni," on the outskirts of Florence.

In London an editor entertains or is being entertained at luncheon, 1:00 to 2:30 (go light on the wine), at tea, 4:30 P.M., at drinks, 6:00 (the gin is excellent), supper at 7:00 if going on to the theater, or at a black-tie dinner party at 8:00. I delight in English dishes, the turbot Lord Nelson loved, or Dover sole, mutton, brisket, and the boiled potatoes, but never mind the sprouts. But the diet is more starchy than ours and I feel puffier by the day. I awake at sunrise, tossing with ideas. By Friday, to use an expression of my boyhood, I am "ready to bust a gut." English breakfast coffee tastes as if it were boiled in a Plantagenet coffin, and is no self-starter.

My consultant under these conditions was for a number of years, Mr. Beauchamp (pronounced "Beecham"), the knowledgeable clerk at Hardy's Ltd., on Pall Mall. Hardy's keep a famous day-book, reporting the state of the fishing on the good streams throughout the British Isles and on Mr. Beauchamp's advice, come Friday afternoon, I would be on my way to Leckford Abbas, beside the River Test in Hampshire, to cast a fly, rest my eyes, eat simply — and sleep!

The Test is the best medicine in the world for an angler, and on one visit I caught two respectable fish. I telephoned Isaiah Berlin — this was before his knighthood — whom I was planning to see on Monday at Oxford.

"Isaiah," I said, "do you like trout?"

"Yes, in principle, in principle. . . ."

"The hell with principle. I've just caught two good ones in the Test and I'll bring them over."

Isaiah's ascent was accelerated by the war. In the summer of 1940 the idea was to send him to Moscow as Press Attaché, but Berlin was stopped in his tracks in Washington and recalled, accompanying

Lord Lothian on that fine diplomat's last return to London. Isaiah's next appointment was a stepping-stone: back he came to America as an official in the newly created British Information Services, to dole out information (one did not like to call it "propaganda"). Operating first in New York, then in a widening circle in Washington, Isaiah got on famously. In his Oxford accent he speaks with a rapidity, three times as fast as the average, and since he is aware of this, he repeats himself so that his meaning shall not be missed. He is one of the most perspicacious of men, the Erasmus of our time.

Berlin's first draft of a thing called the *Weekly Political Telegram*, corrected or added to by other hands, became of increasing interest to the Foreign Office, the Cabinet, and to the P.M. when he read it. So it was that this brilliant young don, a teacher of philosophy, with a special interest in nineteenth-century political ideas, became a thermometer of Anglo-American relations. In his rounds he had ample time to study President Roosevelt and to evaluate his own Prime Minister, whom he had never met. The portraits he drew of them and their contrast in leadership he framed in a perceptive essay which the *Atlantic* published in September 1949, under the title "Mr. Churchill."

Toward the end of the war, Mrs. Churchill heard that Irving Berlin was in London, and wished the P.M. to thank him for his generosity to some wartime fund of which, I think, she was in charge. Winston, recalling an "I. Berlin" for whose information he occasionally felt grateful, suggested a quiet lunch at 10 Downing Street, for the three of them. The composer naturally accepted and found himself surprised, but somewhat baffled by the intense interrogation to which he was subjected about American politics, whether Roosevelt was likely to be reelected, etcetera. In the end, when he could not get any replies to his political inquiries, Churchill said in desperation, "Mr. Berlin, when do you think the European war is going to end?" To which Berlin replied: "Sir, I shall never forget this moment. When I go back to my own country I shall tell my children and my children's children that in the spring of 1944 the Prime Minister of Great Britain asked *me* when the European war was going to end!" At this point Winston firmly broke up the lunch and marched out.

When Mrs. Churchill explained the mistake, the P.M. was delighted and told the cabinet that afternoon, and someone told Alexander Korda, who was sharing an apartment in the Savoy with Irving Berlin, and thus the confusion was relished, forgiven, and the other "I. Berlin" duly thanked.

In 1949 Isaiah came over to teach for a year at Harvard, a happy appointment. Early in the autumn the undergraduates invited him to be the speaker of honor at the annual spring banquet of the Signet, Harvard's literary club. He was pleased to accept and forgot about it until the April date was closing in; then he came to me in distress. "What shall I say, what shall I say, what shall I say? I must be brief, brief, and amusing. . . ." Well, in the course of one Oxford evening I had listened to him explain why the Soviet Union was better understood if it was conceived of as a particularly brutal kind of British public school with a martinet headmaster: "You must be rugged with the boys. Keep them cold, keep them cold, cold; feed them poorly; punish them repeatedly; the fear of the Lord, etc. . . ." Marxism, he went on, was rather like religion in the old-fashioned public schools, officially accepted but seldom taken seriously, except by boys who were thought rather priggish! Politics was like sex at such schools — if mentioned it led to punishment, if practiced, to expulsion. This came to mind. "You'll have to take it slow," I said, "and repeat every point, twice, because their laughter will drown you out." "You really think so?" "I'm certain." Of course I was right: he had them rocking in their chairs.

John Masefield had been in the hospital seriously ill since my last visit, and Mrs. Masefield answered my telephone call. "Oh, he's very much better," she said. "He wants you to come right down. But mind, the doctor says, no more than an hour." When Fritzy and I drove out to Abingdon for tea on Tuesday afternoon we found the poet seated in a big chair in his library, thinner, but the countenance as ruddy, the voice as deep as I remembered. On the desk beside him was a solid chunk of wood. "It's from a Spanish galleon, a treasure ship, sunk off the isle of Mull. The Duke of Argyll has been trying to raise it but the current is too treacherous. The divers sent it to me. Spanish walnut. See how it's ingrained by the sea."

As his wife served tea John talked about the Armada. "They came up with the wind at their back, a massive fleet of 140 ships, the transports in the middle. A fearful sight. Indeed, if the Duke of Parma had joined them with his troops, they might have landed, for our fleet could not get out of the harbor. . . . There might have been more Spanish blood in England than there is today.

"But they were led by the young, inexperienced Duke of Medina Sidonia, who was hamstrung by rigid instructions from Philip II. While they stood offshore, waiting for the Duke of Parma, the wind shifted from the southwest to west, to northwest, and now it was at our backs.

"Soldiers manned the Spanish galleons. Hawkins, who built the British fleet, was the first to have his ships manned by sailors, steered and fought by sailors, and the soldiers manned the guns. Our ships were smaller and lower and much more maneuverable: they wove in and out and as the galleons rolled in the heavy sea, our guns hit below the waterline and their guns tore through our rigging. It was like our Spitfires against Göring's bombers. The Spaniards fought well the first days, but then, bedeviled by headwinds, the fatal decision was taken to break off and to sail northeast along a strange and hostile coast. They could not return as they had come. It was disaster, weevils in the food, water running low, defeat in their hearts, and the wind driving them toward the rocks. Only some forty ships returned home. The King of Spain bowed his head in grief and prayer — he thanked God that he had enough men and power to launch a second Armada — but it never came." He ruminated as he spoke and there were pauses and sidelights such as "One of the admirals survived, but he could not face his king. He returned to his village, took to his bed, turned his face to the wall and died in disgrace."

In the semi-sleep of illness the mind reaches back into the past. Masefield had retraced his boyhood, recalling the people and episodes which had beckoned him into a life of storytelling and it was this he was eager to write about when his strength returned. "My grandfather," he said, "had a friend who knew Keats, Leigh Hunt, and Hazlitt, and I like to think the friend took him to see them." When, a year later, I prepared to publish his two-part serial, *The Joy of Storytelling*, I sent him a proof of the cover our artist (a landlubber) had painted of John, with his white thatch, silhouetted against a clipper, all sails set. Back it came, with the foresails correctly spaced and outlined in red ink.

I visited him on each of my annual trips until his death. He became my tutor in ancient Britain, lending or giving me books from his library: once when we were discussing the Roman conquest and the fear that deepened when the legions were withdrawn, he remarked that historians had no idea of how large the settlements were until aerial photography revealed the outlines — "Here," he said, "Collingwood is the best man on that," and turning to his bookshelf, found the volume and inscribed it to me. The poems he sent me no longer had the fire of his youth, but in their resonance and clarity they held, as did his prose, the vigor of England's past. He had been the Poet Laureate for so long that the editors in London had forgotten that he had anything new to say.

My closest England publishers were Robert Lusty, the head of

Hutchinson's, and Sir William Collins, both of whom published books of mine, Hamish Hamilton and his partner, Roger Machell, who had done the English editions of Walter Lippmann, Agnes de Mille, and other Atlantic authors, and John Murray, the sixth of that name to preside over that historic monument of a publisher's nineteenth-century establishment on Albemarle Street.

On our last evening we dined with Jock Murray and Diana in their gem of a home high on Hampstead Heath where the spires of London are clearly to be seen from the lawn beneath their plane tree. Their eldest — quite beautiful — daughter was then studying in Florence, and when they told me she had been seeing Bernard Berenson at I Tatti I said that I too would be calling on him and asked Diana what kind of a gift would appeal to him. "We always bring him a canister of Earl Grey tea," she said. "Oh, but I can't get one here on a Sunday night," I said. "Would you by chance have an unopened one I could pay you for?" "Bad luck," she said. "We've just opened a new one and must have used two inches of it." "Oh, that's no difficulty," I said. "You could just stuff the bottom of it with tissue paper, and he'd never know the difference!" "Shame on you!" she said, not quite sure whether I was serious. "No," I said, "I'll buy four neckties in Paris tomorrow and make him choose the three he likes best." Which I did — and Berenson had a hard time deciding.

As things worked out, our flight to Rome landed us at the airport in mid-afternoon and we had only a full morning the next day in which to see what we wanted before boarding the train for Florence. Personally I was not too disappointed, for Rome was greatly over-crowded, with pilgrims everywhere, and the streets noisy until nearly midnight. At 7:00 A.M. I became the typical American tourist. Leaving our packed bags with the hotel porter, we took a taxi to St. Peter's, where I acquired two tickets for a complete tour, and a young, intelligent-looking guide. "Now," I said. "Listen. We wish to go directly to the Sistine Chapel. We want to get there before the tourists crowd in, and we don't have time to see anything on the way." This went against his grain and he expostulated, but by taking shortcuts he did precisely what I asked for and for nearly half an hour we had nearly a private view of that glorious chapel, tilting our heads backward, the better to appreciate the frescoes on the ceiling. There was a boarded alleyway leading into the chapel and out, and as we started to leave a swarm of pilgrims came streaming in. "Now" I told our guide. "To the exit."

Busloads of tourists were disgorging as we slipped into our taxi and were driven to the Convent of the Blue Nuns, where we were shown into the "cell" or, to be more accurate, the very spacious apartment, occupied by George Santayana. I had been serializing his book *Persons and Places*, in the *Atlantic*, and in my last letter I had explained that I was coming to Rome and would be glad to tell him the latest news of Boston. He was more robust than I expected, those dark luminous eyes beautifying his expression. He was indeed curious about Cambridge and the Back Bay, which he had last seen in 1908. His questions about Guy Murchie and Governor "Cam" Forbes of the Philippines reminded me that they were two of the renowned athletes who admired him during his teaching at Harvard. He asked me what Boston thought of his novel, *The Last Puritan*, and I gave a respectful reply. I said it surprised me to hear the amount of nostalgia he seemed to have for New England. "I want to know how much it's changed," he said. He spoke of Mrs. Jack Gardner and Gretchen Warren the poet, and at some length about Walter Lippmann, his student in whom he took the most pride. After about an hour we excused ourselves, saying that I did not want to tire him and that we would soon be on our way to Florence, where we would be visiting Sir Osbert and Edith Sitwell. Thanks to a stalwart porter we caught our train with four minutes to spare.

In Sir Osbert's second volume, *The Scarlet Tree*, we were given the sardonic characterization of his father, Sir George Sitwell: his intense devotion to the family's lineage, his imagined ill health ("Sir George is the hero of his bed," as Henry Moat, his canny butler, put it), and the vast sums he expended on his gardens and the artificial lake he dredged at "Renishaw." Here was the first account of "Montefugoni," that enormous castle on the outskirts of Florence for the purchase of which Sir George used his children's inheritance.

My dear Osbert: You will be interested to hear that I am buying in your name the castle, and I do hope that you will prove worthy of what I am trying to do for you and will not pursue that miserable course of extravagance that has already once ruined the family. . . . Such an economy for now we can produce our own wine and champagne.

Actually, it did produce wine and olive oil and, after their mother's death it also provided Sir George with his favorite sanctuary. When the old man died in Switzerland in 1943, Osbert, who inherited the title and the extensive properties at "Renishaw," discovered that his father had set up "Montefugoni" as an Italian company: what profit remained after the sale of olive oil and the vintage was to pay for Osbert's, Sacheverell's, and Edith's visits, long in good years, short in bad. A priceless butler, Luigi, was in charge, and with his wife did the scrumptious cooking.

In the Florence station we were met by the Sitwells' driver, in what proved to be a rented car; he spoke English, and as we drove I arranged to hire it for our sightseeing in the days ahead.

"Montefugoni" in times of stress had been inhabited by as many as three hundred persons. During the recent Nazi occupation, part of it, shut off by a locked gate marked "Verboten," had safeguarded many treasures of the Uffizi Gallery, which the Germans evidently were too busy to disturb. The entrance was superb rococo. The high-ceilinged rooms on the ground floor opened on a broad terrace, which descended through the grove of olive trees to the brook at the foot of the valley. For his comfort Sir George had installed central heating for the master's suite on the second floor, and as the weather was sharp and windy Fritzy and I were installed directly above on the third floor, where traces of warmth wafted up into our bedroom, though not into the stone-cold bath.

From the evidence, our rooms had not been occupied since the fighting: the drawers of the large bureau were lined with German newspapers of the summer of 1944. In the top drawer, lying on the German newsprint, was a small white page, ripped from a pocket-book, and recording in an English hand "Today's casualties," and beneath, the names of four privates, a corporal, and a sergeant, a reminder for the company commander of letters to be written home. I gave it to Osbert when we came down to lunch.

We were a family party, Osbert and his friend David Horner, Edith and the Weekses. Each meal was preceded by "mezzo-mezzo," a delicious blend of the dry and sweet Sitwell vermouth; and the Italian meals, delectable and, at lunch, so ample as to demand a siesta, were flavored by the "Montefugoni" white and red wine, which, as Sir George predicted, were indeed in demand in the restaurants of Florence. I told Osbert that I had the car for the mornings so that we could explore the beauty of Florence and of towns like San Gimignano, under his guidance, and this was an experience as rich as that in Rome had been rapid, for he showed us what he loved and told us why. As we passed, the Italians who recognized him would murmur, "Milord Inglese," as they must have done for Lord Byron. Osbert knew Florence as well as he knew London and he responded to Fritzy's appreciation. ("My husband likes people but I like places," as she had remarked to T. S. Eliot.) It was true, I cared more for the human scenes on the famous bronze doors of the Baptistry, and the tomb of the Medici, and Michelangelo's "David," than for the architecture. And we moved at such a pace that I imposed one ground rule: after an hour of sightseeing I should be allowed fifteen minutes for a cup of espresso or a bite of pastry.

At afternoon tea back at the castle we discussed literary projects. Osbert had completed four volumes of his autobiography, *Left Hand, Right Hand,* which had won him renown and royalties far greater than his early work. A fifth volume, portraits of the artists Claud Lovat Fraser and Walter Sickert, and other men of talent he admired, was in the works. He was contemplating a sixth, which for reasons of discretion was not to appear until fifty years after his death. He was eager for me to reprint his most colorful travel book, *Escape with Me,* which he had written about imperial China while in Peking in 1939. The first edition had barely sold 2,000 copies in America, and diplomatically I reserved the decision until *Noble Essences* had made its run.

Edith, who gloried in Osbert's success, had promised I should have her new books of prose (Vanguard Press had published her poetry in the United States from the start and I respected their claim). Beginning in early girlhood Edith had filled notebooks with quotations from poets she admired, together with her emotional response and criticism. There were now over sixty such books, more pungent and appreciative as she herself became a poet, and I suggested that she select her favorite passages to form a volume of more than academic appeal. I knew that both Osbert and Edith were on close terms with the Royal Family, and had been advising Princess Elizabeth in her reading. (Were Masefield to die, Britain for the first time might have a woman Laureate.)

On the third day of our stay a telegram came from Evelyn Waugh saying he was making a pilgrimage and could he spend Thursday night at the castle. He was welcomed, and the night before he arrived Edith speculated about his manners. "He always begins by scolding," she said. "Who will it be this time?" "I shall be the guilty one," said David Horner. "He knows I am a Catholic and that I have not been on the pilgrimage."

Evelyn made his appearance at noon. This was his first sight of "Montefugoni" and he stood for a moment, transfixed, at the entrance. He and I had lunched together in the past and I introduced him to Fritzy as we all moved indoors. On the large table in the drawing room, where we were about to be served with "mezzo-mezzo," lay the four volumes of Osbert's autobiography in the English edition.

As luck would have it, Waugh picked up volume II, which had been profusely illustrated with wash drawings by Richard Plumer, an artist Osbert had befriended.

"Oh, Osbert, how could you?" Evelyn cried, his thumb pinning down one of the overblown pictures. "These dreadful drawings!" Suddenly the youth who had studied art at the Slade before he began to write came to the surface. Expostulation was not enough. Book in hand, he led us from point to point comparing each drawing — to its detriment — with the architectural reality. This was not the usual guided tour. When the last picture was dismissed, we returned some-what subdued for our drinks. Evelyn had had his scold, and as we went into luncheon his jollity returned.

I was the first to awaken from the afternoon siesta. Fritzy was still snoozing, so I dressed and made my way quietly down to the terrace where I sat until I heard a nightingale begin to cluck in the trees bordering the brook. I stole down to hear more. The first bird was answered and I froze, listening, until, glancing back I saw a figure descending the terrace. It was Evelyn and as he approached I could see he was distressed. "My dear Weeks," he said, "I am embarrassed about that tirade of mine. I hope you don't think that any of my criti-cism was directed against Osbert's prose. He has written a monument to the past such as none of us could have done. It was those dreadful pictures which put me off. . . . Do forgive me."

The incident seemed forgotten by dinner and laughter began build-ing up as Evelyn elaborated on his latest "bulletin" from Billy Butlin's Camp. Butlin, a born organizer, had set up a series of camps where city workers, clerks, typists, nurses, teachers, at last released from five grim years of war rations could enjoy the country food and country air for a few pounds a week — provided they did not object to Big Brother's vigilant anti-sexual discipline. "The bugler wakes you for setting up exercises at dawn. Long walks or gardening in the a.m. If a couple is seen pairing off, 'Come now, let's go for a good run. . . .'" "Why don't you and Osbert," I said to Evelyn, "share a cabin there for a week and write me what it's like?" Edith ducked her head, convulsed in laughter at the prospect. So was I, as "the tentmates" began to plan what they would bring with them to defy the routine.

We were serenaded by the village band on our last evening. "I believe they are all Communists," said Osbert, "but always glad to see us here." It was sad to have to fly back to London and the stack of manuscripts that had to be read in haste before returning home.

* * *

Walter Lippmann had taken a four months' leave of absence from his column and in September he and Helen came for a weekend with Fritzy and me in Beverly Farms. They were on their way to Lenox, Massachusetts, where he would spend the autumn working on a new book — the beginning of his *Essays in the Public Philosophy* — and the temporary freedom was tempting them both to consider the termination of his column, "Today and Tomorrow."

There is no more beautiful spot in New England than the Berkshires in the fall, and Helen wrote Fritzy asking her to keep on the lookout for a nice comfortable house with two or three acres and good trees, about an hour or so from Cambridge. Walter had told me that if he retired he would want to be in touch with the Widener Library, and while he had no desire for full professorial rank, he might be willing to conduct a seminar at Harvard for graduate students in government, or perhaps philosophy. It seemed to me an attractive prospect, and I told him I'd raise the possibility with the president. In my letter to Conant I began with Walter's decision to terminate his contract with the Herald Tribune syndicate, his desire to live within reach of Cambridge, and his wonder "if he could be of any use." "He is not thinking of an assignment in full professorial rank but rather as a tutor and research fellow who might conduct a seminar for graduate students in Government and perhaps be of service to the Society of Fellows." The president's reply burst that bubble:

Harvard University
Office of the President

October 8, 1951

Dear Ted:

I have canvassed the suggestion in your letter about Walter Lippmann with one or two discreet people here in Cambridge. The reaction is as I expected. We have no position which pays a salary which would be open to Mr. Lippmann. Of course, I'm not sure from your letter that he wants a regular position. You will understand, as a former Overseer, though he may well not since it's some years since he was in contact with the University, that a university position ought to be one which involves a good deal of hard work. It would be unfortunate for the morale of the entire staff if even distinguished people were sort of to retire to a life of leisure in University Chairs! In fact, I'm a bit amused with the way in which people who have had a busy life elsewhere, be they Mr. Lippmann or Mr. Lilienthal, feel that academic surroundings would be a nice place to be a professor, which to their minds means, often, taking life pretty easy. As a matter of fact, the life of a professor is a very strenuous one as Archibald MacLeish will tell you at the drop of a hat.

189

I see no reason why Mr. Lippmann might not carry out his ambitions with a trial run, so to speak. Why doesn't he come and live in either Boston or Cambridge and see if the University would gave him an opportunity to present his views to students on a purely non-salary basis. . . .

So Walter's taste "of being an Englishman of letters in the midst of amiable people," as Helen put it, came to an end before the snow was deep. I think Conant underestimated Walter's willingness to work, yet in retrospect, I am sure his suspicion was correct; I doubt if Walter or Helen would have been happy during the long winters in New England. Walter's influential role in the Capital, the stimulus of his trips to Europe, and Helen's eager participation in each, were not so easily dismissed. Even in Washington's present ugly mood.

In the space of five years American public opinion had swung angrily against our former ally, the Soviet Union. Many veterans had returned from the war questioning the Kremlin's intent, and the Russian take-over of Poland, Jan Masaryk's suicide in Czechoslovakia — did he jump or was he pushed? — and the fact that Russia possessed the Bomb hardened our suspicion of Communists. The accusation of Alger Hiss, the defection of the British spies Burgess and Maclean, provided the impetus for Senator Joseph McCarthy's political persecution of the State Department, the Army, and suspected citizens. From the accusation of being a Communist it was a short step to "guilt by association." People became genuinely fearful; they lived with the question "We or they?" and their misgivings deepened as the Senator destroyed the careers of loyal, intelligent men on the China desk in the State Department whom Secretary Dulles would not defend. Despite his outrage President Eisenhower was advised not to show his contempt for McCarthy when speaking in Milwaukee and not to contradict when General George C. Marshall was branded a "traitor."

Senator McCarthy's reign of terror went on until 1954 and it was a deplorable period of national distrust. What halted it was the exposure of the Senator on television and his self-destruction under the probing of two honorable men. The first was Edward R. Murrow. In preparing his interrogation of McCarthy for the CBS program "See It Now," Ed and his assistant, Fred Friendly, used film clips and sound tapes of McCarthy to portray a legislator who was relying on insinuations and his congressional immunity. The accusation that there were "fifty-seven card-carrying Communists in the State Department" was not a half-truth; it was poisonous nonsense — and he never named them. After denouncing the Democrats with being "soft" on Communism, McCarthy over-reached himself (a month before Murrow went on the air) by referring to "twenty years of treason" and then the all-embracing assertion that "those who wear the label of Democrat wear the same historic betrayal."

Murrow's program should be rerun for those who never heard it, as Jack Gould reminded us in the *Los Angeles Times*, on its twenty-fifth anniversary. There sits McCarthy, with his young, whispering assistants, Cohn and Shine, there sounds his shrill giggle as he makes his intentional slip of the tongue against Adlai Stevenson, "Strangely, Alger — I mean Adlai. . . ." Murrow's courageous, unanswerable summing up is what each of us should remember, particularly these three paragraphs:

No one familiar with the history of this country can deny that congressional committees are useful. It is necessary to investigate before legislating, but the line between investigating and persecuting is a very fine one, and the junior senator from Wisconsin has stepped over it repeatedly. . . .

This is not the time for men who oppose Sen. McCarthy's methods to keep silent, nor for those who approve. We can deny our heritage and our history, but we cannot escape responsibility for the result.

The actions of the junior senator from Wisconsin have caused alarm and dismay amongst our allies abroad and given considerable comfort to our enemies. And whose fault is that? Not really his, he didn't create the situation of fear, he merely exploited it, and rather successfully. Cassius was right. The fault, dear Brutus, is not in our stars, but in ourselves.

A fortnight after that confrontation McCarthy began his examination of the Army, thirty-six days of televised inquisition, in the course of which a Boston lawyer, Joseph Nye Welch, stripped the Senator naked before millions with his soft-spoken "Senator, do you really believe that?" We owe a debt to those two, Ed Murrow and lawyer Welch, who revealed the demagogue for what he was.

But how severely he had shaken our faith in our system was expressed at the time by Judge Learned Hand, who, at a banquet in Washington, cried out: "My friends, will you not agree that any society which begins to be doubtful of itself, in which one man looks at another and says, 'He may be a traitor,' in which that spirit has disappeared which says, 'I will not accept that; I will not believe that; I will demand proof; I will not say of my brother that he may be a traitor; but I will say produce what you have, I will judge it fairly and if he is, he shall pay the penalty, but I will not take it on rumor,

I will not take it on hearsay. I will remember that what has brought us from savagery is a loyalty to truth, and truth cannot emerge unless it is subjected to the utmost scrutiny.' Will you not agree that a society which has lost sight of *that* cannot survive?"

I quoted that in my lectures while the Senate was making up its mind to censure McCarthy, for that great judge had rightly perceived that the mere suspicion of Communism was being injected as a poison in our veins. The interrogation of those suspected of being "security risks" dragged on for years. The brilliant scientist J. Robert Oppenheimer was so labeled, and when the Senate refused to approve Philip Jessup of Time, Inc., as a United Nations delegate, the swing man on the committee, Senator Alexander Smith of New Jersey, declared his disbelief in all the charges against Jessup but voted against him because he was "controversial"!

As a liberal editor I came under fire from the sycophant journals which echoed McCarthy's charges. *Counter-Attack*, long since deceased, blasted me because as Chairman of the Peabody Awards I had presented a medal and citation for the best news coverage of the year to ABC, some of whose commentators they distrusted. A second sheet reminded its readers that in 1945 I had published two articles, "Getting Democracy in Poland" and "Bor's Uprising," by Anna Louise Strong. I had indeed. She wrote well and it seemed to me of interest to hear what a correspondent with the Red Armies had to say and that our readers would make allowance for her bias. In 1930 she had written a series about the Soviet Union for Mr. Sedgwick and that year had married a Russian Communist. Her account of the brutality and treachery suffered by the partisans in Poland was not in the least reassuring of any "democracy" in that enslaved state but my mistake was in not stating and repeating in our biographical note that Miss Strong's husband was a member of the Party. For this the accusing sheet — I think it was the *New Leader* — dubbed me "the Red Brahmin of Beacon Hill."

Part of the nuisance in such nonsense was the effort of the FBI to run such suspicions to earth. One of the agents, circulating in Boston to check my record, called on Father Francis Lally, Cardinal Cushing's trusted lieutenant and incidentally my friend. After some preliminaries he was asked to describe me — was I a dangerous influence? "Well, no," said Father Lally, as he told me later, "I'd call him a pillar of the community."

CHAPTER

XIII

At a luncheon post-war three close friends, New Englanders of Irish descent, were contemplating their future. "I'm going to run for Congress," said Torbert McDonald, former football captain and star halfback at Harvard College, then studying at the Law School. "If I make it, a few years in Washington will help my law practice. How about you, Eddie?" Edwin O'Connor, a graduate of Notre Dame, now a freelance writer, was equally positive. "As soon as I can get the time," he said, "I'm going to write a novel about Boston." They turned to the third. "I'm going into politics," said John F. Kennedy; "what else can I do?"

Boston elected its first Irish mayor in 1884; others followed, including JFK's grandfather, John F. Fitzgerald, first elected in 1905, and again in 1910. From that day to this politics in Massachusetts has become a tribal occupation. The Irish rule the Massachusetts State House and Boston City Hall; they converted the Commonwealth into a one-party state, and if in a wave of revulsion a Republican is elected Governor or Senator, he cannot be re-elected without the support of the Boston Irish.

Fred Allen was one of my idols years before he became one of our authors. I saw him first in musical comedy when he came before the curtain, without props, and in that gravelly voice and his look of mild incredulity, eased into what *Variety* called "the brightest talk ever heard in vaudeville." When Lana Turner in a sweater was our pin-up girl, Fred remarked, "You can't get any more out of a sweater than you put into it." He said of a faded actor, "The professor was a retired magician who had eaten his rabbit in the early days of his retirement." He described Arthur Godfrey, the TV entertainer, as "the man with the barefoot voice." I was sure he could write a book and I wanted to publish it. My pursuit began in 1941 at the annual luncheon for the winners of the Peabody Awards in Radio. As chairman of the judges I conferred a medal on Fred for having produced "the finest comedy of the year." He accepted it with the same mild look of incredulity.

At a dinner party in New York I sat next to Fred's attractive wife, Portland Hoffa. I told her that for the Weeks family Sunday evening was reserved for "Allen's Alley." There never had been a program as funny. Fred's characters we saw in mind: Senator Beauregard Claghorn, who spoke with the bombast of Texas; Titus Moody, the Vermonter; Ajax Cassidy, a boyo Irishman; and Mrs. Nussbaum, with her Yiddish poems for every occasion.

I told Portland that she was the perfect foil, as indeed she was. Her voice, which in real life is charming, sounded on the air, as Fred said, "like that of an E-flat Frankenstein monster." One of the glories of radio was the captivating intonations of the voice, and as Fred led her on with his "And . . . ?" "And so?" her ingenuous lines became incredibly funny. "How much of the show does he write?" I asked. All of it, she replied; his writers, Herman Wouk and Howard Armbruster, help but Fred revises. "Someday," I said, "Fred will write a glorious book, beginning with his start in vaudeville." She agreed, but Jack Goodman of Simon & Schuster was ahead of me, and anyway, as long as Fred was on the air he would *never* have time for a book. Well, there was no hurry, and I went back to Boston to learn more about him.

His real name was John Florence Sullivan and he was born in Cambridge, Massachusetts, May 31, 1894. His father was a bookbinder, fond of the bottle, his mother died when Fred was three, and he was brought up by her sister, "Aunt Lizzie," to whom he was devoted. He attended the Boston High School of Commerce, and on his fourteenth birthday his father took Fred to the Boston Public Library, where he signed on as a "runner" for sixty cents a night. As he learned his way around the stacks he chanced on a book on the origin and development of comedy; it fascinated him and he began to collect jokes. At home he was teaching himself to juggle tennis balls and tin plates (much later, pointing to a scar on his nose, he said, "One I missed"). At the Christmas show Fred's juggling and comic patter convulsed the library employees, and a pretty girl remarked as he was packing up his props, "You're crazy to keep on working here in the library. You ought to go on the stage!"

At seventeen Fred broke into vaudeville, as a juggler on "Amateurs' Night" for $1.00 and carfare home. The managers liked him, and under the show name of "Freddy St. James" he played the small New England theaters for $25 a week ($4 of it sent home to Aunt Liz). As he could keep only four balls in the air when an expert could handle eleven, Fred billed himself as "the World's Worst Juggler" — and carried on a line of patter making fun of his mistakes and whatever was absurd in the world.

In 1916 a contract took him to Australia, where the war compelled him to vary and add sympathy to his lines: not too much fluff when he was being listened to by people whose men were in the trenches, or dead. His billing ran on for eleven months; he did not have a close friend in the country and, as he wrote in his autobiography, *Much Ado about Me*, he schooled himself:

I spent all my spare time reading. I went through Shakespeare, Artemus Ward, Bill Nye, Eli Perkins, Josh Billings, and the works of all the current British and American humorists. All the English humor magazines were new to me. I discovered *Punch, Tit-bits, London Opinion. Answers, Pearson's Weekly*, and the others. I bought every joke book I could find in the different cities. When I had an original idea I wrote it down and filed it away.

I was able to write new versions of old jokes to use in my act. I learned that any joke or story can be told in many forms. . . . Before I left Brisbane I resolved that, with the time I had to study as I played the Fuller circuit, I would try to improve my act, my jokes, and my writing.

More mature on his return to the United States, he needed a new name for a higher salary. As "Fred Allen" he was given top booking at the Palace Theatre on Broadway, and then, as vaudeville faded, Fred's voice and wit on radio gave heart to American households during the Depression and the Second World War. In his formats, "Town Hall Tonight" and "Allen's Alley," there were jokes but, increasingly, more satire as he commented on Gromyko or a bestselling novel, or the New York World's Fair. He was an omnivorous reader of newspapers; for his remarks he used material that did not come from Hollywood, his humor was original and brought him the largest, most loyal audience in radio.

I had never lost hope that Fred would write for us. After Jack Goodman's sudden death, no one at S&S seemed interested, and when I again approached Portland she said to wait: negotiations were under way to produce "Allen's Alley" on television. Privately, I believe Fred himself was dubious whether that superb cast would be as irresistible in plain view. It was at this point that Fred's high blood pressure, the result of those eighteen years of close-timed performances, became alarming; the doctor put him on a strict diet and ruled out cigars, salt, alcohol, and television.

In 1951 I learned that Fred's agent had died, and that among his effects were bound copies of all of Allen's radio scripts, all eighteen years of them. The *Atlantic* bought the set and I asked Edwin O'Connor to drive down to New York with me to meet Fred and pick up the books.

Eddie, tall, handsome, and sunny, a big man, light on his feet, was the *Atlantic*'s daily visitor, and everyone on the staff loved him. He was living nearby in a furnished room, living on $50 a week as the radio critic of the *Boston Herald*, and devoting early morning hours to writing a novel which we expected to publish. Toward noon he'd wander in, to joke with Charlie Morton, pause at my door with his slogan, "Keep working; keep singing, America," accompanied by a little tap dance, and go on to charm the girls. I knew he needed money and that he was perfectly qualified to read Fred's scripts professionally and pick out the best. I wanted Fred to intersperse the comedy with what went on behind the scene, such as his feuds with his different sponsors, and their advertising agents ("that idiotic Yale quarterback, Jack LeRoy"), his happy acquisition of Portland (one of three daughters of a theatrical family, each named for the town she was born in), his running gags with Jack Benny, and those rare performances when things went completely out of control. I proposed this on our drive to New York and Eddie agreed to collaborate.

Portland had been baking a cake and we sniffed its fragrance as we were shown into Fred's "office," in their apartment on Sixth Avenue. Eddie and Fred had never met before and I was impressed as they looked at each other: Fred, courteous and reserved; Eddie with admiration. Fred had been typing a letter to Commissioner Long of Massachusetts, with whom, he told us, year in, year out, he carried on a losing argument against having to pay taxes in the Bay State. This led Eddie, who was a wonderful mimic, to sail off into a parody of what Mayor James Michael Curley would have said about the matter, in his unctuous voice: "Surely, my dear man, you would not begrudge our fair state a small return for the schooling and inspiration which have led to your triumphant career!" Fred listened with amazement and suddenly, like a stone through a window, his deadpan was shattered into laughter. "That is very, very funny!" he exclaimed and their friendship had begun.

Eddie and I drove down several times as the book was written; he and Fred would go over Ed's selections and Fred would ruminate aloud about the inserts, then we'd go out to lunch at the nearby Longchamps, Fred making a wry face at his unsalted chicken and lettuce, and both men ganging up on me at the close. In my youth Mother had taught us that it was polite "to leave the last bit for Mr. Manners" and sometimes I still did. I don't know why I ever told this to Eddie but now if I left a bit of meat on my chop bone, Fred would remark casually, "Mr. Manners will have quite a mouthful today, eh, Eddie?"

When we had finished, we accompanied Fred to his bank before we parted. Always to the bank. "What do you think he does in there, Eddie?" "Well, I'll tell you what I think," said Ed. "He asks for his bank balance and adds to it whatever he's depositing. One of his dearest friends was Jack Donahue, the tap dancer, who kept on performing after the doctor had warned him it might be fatal. Jack died penniless. Fred means to be sure Porty is well cared for." (And she was).

Fred's first book, *Treadmill to Oblivion*, came into print as happily as the friendship that encouraged it. The radio industry had never before been scrutinized so intelligently or so amusingly by one of its star performers. What Fred brought out so well was that radio listeners were induced by the sound effects and the character of the voices to use their imagination as they never did in front of the television screen. Radio at its best was an art which depended neither on violence nor on throwing custard pie in someone's face. And nothing in television has ever been quite like Fred's performance with the English falconer, Captain Knight, and his trained eagle, Ramshaw. This is how it began:

CAPTAIN: I think Ramshaw would prefer to fly without the script.
ALLEN: He'll ad lib, eh? Well, I'm not telling Ramshaw how to run his business, Captain. It's up to you.
CAPTAIN: Very well. I shall have Mr. Ramshaw fly around the stage and land back on that bandstand. Ready, Ramshaw? Go!
(Bird flies around stage and lands.)

"That was the way it was supposed to be," Fred wrote.

In the empty studio, Mr. Ramshaw took off from the Captain's wrist, spread his wings, flew a few feet and grounded himself on top of the bandstand. We tried it several times at rehearsal. Things went smoothly. Mr. Ramshaw even appeared to be enjoying himself.

That night, as the program progressed, everything was fine until

Captain Knight read his line, "I shall have Mr. Ramshaw fly around the stage and land back on that bandstand. Ready, Ramshaw? Go!"

And Ramshaw went. He took off from the Captain's wrist gracefully but when he got aloft the glare from the brass instruments in the orchestra (the orchestra had not been at rehearsal) apparently confused him. He couldn't seem to locate the bandstand. He started flying around the studio, his talons clawing the air ad lib. Women were shrieking, afraid that Ramshaw would light on their heads and descalp them. Captain Knight augumented the bedlam by rushing around the studio shouting pertinent instructions in his British accent to the eagle, who was busy wheeling over the audience giving an impression of a buzzard in a moment of indecision. As though he wanted to get as far away from the turmoil as possible, Ramshaw perched on top of a high column up near the ceiling. The imbroglio caused him to forget even the cruder points of etiquette. Mr. Ramshaw gave visual evidence that he was obviously not a house-broken eagle. The visual evidence fortunately just missed the shoulder of a student who had come down from Fordham University to advise me that I had won a popularity poll at the school. He was sitting on the stage after having presented me with a plaque earlier in the show.

As the audience laughed and shouted, the program carried on. Captain Knight was remonstrating with the eagle and advising him to come down from his lofty haven. In one pocket the Captain carried a few chickenheads for emergencies and to sustain Mr. Ramshaw during the day. As he pleaded with the eagle the Captain started to wave a chickenhead as a sort of grisly reward if Ramshaw would abandon his prank and return to captivity. Chaos was in bloom — the Captain with his British hullaballoo, the audience screaming with laughter, the women squealing with fright. Jokes were told, songs were sung, commercials were read. Nothing was heard.

The program went off the air on a note of sustained pandemonium. The Captain dispatched a lackey to procure a large raw steak. Apparently Mr. Ramshaw was myopic. From his lofty perch he couldn't recognize the tidbit, the chickenhead, in the Captain's waving hand. The king-sized steak, however, he did identify. Mr. Ramshaw flew back to the Captain's wrist and his supper. . . .

Treadmill to Oblivion has two dedications. The first is to Portland:

> *Who stayed in a closet until*
> *I finished writing this book*

and the second:

> *Ed O'Connor, who has the memory*
> *of an elephant, helped me with this tome.*

*Ted Weeks, who has the energy
of a beaver, also helped.
It proves that with an elephant's memory,
a beaver's energy and two friends,
a radio actor can write a book.*

Shortly after *Treadmill* was published, by pre-arrangement, Fred
and I walked down to the Boston Public Library to present an auto-
graphed copy to the librarian, Milton Lord. Photographers from *Life*
were also in the lobby, and after they had taken their shots we were
shown to the director's office, where spread out on a table were the
leather-bound ledgers showing how much — at most $3.50 — Johnny
Sullivan had been paid week by week from 1904 to 1908. Then we
went into a room nearby where, waiting to greet him, was a small
group of aged veterans who had been on the staff when Johnny was
their delivery boy. As we entered, Fred said to me in an undertone,
"I feel as if it were Judgment Day."

Treadmill broke all records for a book on radio, and in the spring
Fred and Portland went down with me to Richmond, Virginia, for
the Book and Authors' Dinner, sponsored by the Junior League and
Miller & Rhoads. It is an annual affair attended by nearly a thousand,
and after Douglas Southall Freeman retired I became the m.c. It
is the most auspicious send-off for any author in the South.

Fred, one of the five writers who were to speak, admitted on the
flight down that he had no idea of what to talk about, but during the
preliminary festivities, the luncheon, and the cocktail party on the
lawn of the Valentine Museum, he naturally heard a good deal about
Virginians and their ancestry. I called on him last, sure that he would
be amusing. He began by paying a compliment to me which, as I remember, went something like this: "Thank you, Mr. Weeks. Ladies
and Gentlemen: I feel I should begin by telling you how generously
my Boston publishers have supported my book. I know it is hard to
believe but during the first week of publication they had two men circulating in Grand Central Terminal, each carrying a copy of *Treadmill* under his arm. In addition Mr. Weeks has brought Portland
and me to this happy occasion. I had heard of your Virginia hospitality but had never been privileged to enjoy it until today. Some of
you have spoken to me about your famous ancestors, and I thought
it might be of interest if I told you about mine. My family lived on
the wrong side of the tracks in Boston and my grandfather held a
grudge against the New York, New Haven, and Hartford Railroad.
Night after night grandfather would go out and lie down on the

tracks. Year after year he grew shorter and shorter. . . ." In that dry voice, Fred kept on improvising; the audience rocked and the laughter spilled over into the reception afterward where, as his doctor had ordered, he took not a single drink.

Fred, in his prime, found it difficult to relax on vacation: he liked to read but he did not play games, and summer bathing in Bermuda he said was "like swimming in warm sarsaparilla." During the heat of July, when "the Alley" was not on the air, he could usually be found in Old Orchard, Maine, caddying for his nephew. He was working on the very last pages of his autobiography, *Much Ado about Me,* when his heart failed. His second book is alive with his zest, his wit, his love for Portland and his foster mother, Aunt Liz, who, on one of the few times she saw him perform, was surprised and indignant that people should be laughing so heartily at her boy. Surely he wasn't "the worst juggler in the world."

Democracy did not come to Poland, not as Anna Louise Strong had anticipated in our columns, not in any form. Of all the peoples engorged by the Soviet Union the Poles were the most abused; first, when they were overwhelmed by the Nazis and then when Warsaw was "liberated" by the Red Army. The execution of thousands of officers in the Katyn Forest, presumably at Stalin's order, buried those who might have led a dissociation such as Tito's, and the emasculation of the Polish Government in Exile, on its return from London, finished immediate hope of moderate opposition.

There remained at large two groups of exiled Poles: first the warriors, veterans of the Polish Division, and the Navy and the fighter pilots who had flown with the Royal Air Force, many of whom — one million and more — as the future became clearer, chose to remain in England. It was about them that Martha Gellhorn wrote in her story of heartbreak, "Weekend in Grimsby." Martha, young and beautiful, began her career as a war correspondent in Spain, where she fell in love with and married Ernest Hemingway; she finished it in Europe, attached to "a regiment of lovely, goofy Poles." Her story, set in a small English seaport, years after the fighting ended, was a picture of the Poles, valiant in an adaptation one could not forget. After its publication we sent Martha to Poland and in her article "Home of the Brave" (March 1959) she stressed with what difficulty the young were living under the yoke.

The larger, more helpless deposit were the Poles the Nazis had deported as slave labor within the Reich. There was no mercy in that uprooting: families were broken, wives separated from husbands,

Jews and resisters sent to concentration camps. General Lucius Clay estimated that four million of the slave laborers from all the conquered countries were uncovered by the Allied Armies and repatriated by rail, highway, and air by July 31, 1945 (the Russian prisoners of war, some of them, slashed their wrists rather than go back). That left over two million "human debris," spread deeper in Germany, to be sorted out, resuscitated, reunited with their families, if possible, by small teams of UNNRA — but then resettled, where? It was this compassionate, sometimes comic, rescue operation which Kathryn Hulme described in her book *The Wild Place.*

Kate was born in San Francisco before the earthquake and from her grandfather, a saltwater skipper and captain of the *Great Republic*, she inherited her capability. She stands five-feet-four, is sturdy and decisive as she speaks in her deep voice. During the war she donned the nineteen pounds of horsehide "leathers" of an electric-arc welder and worked in the Kaiser shipyard. The call to the United Nations came while she was welding. In July 1945, she was in France, one of a twelve-man team being readied to run a D.P. (Displaced Person) camp in Germany. "Wildflecken" — the "Wild Place" — high in the Bavarian Alps, to which she was sent, had been the secret S.S. training center for the ski troops destined for Russia. Within its perimeter were sixty blockhouses accommodating three hundred and fifty persons each; fifteen kitchens, and five hospitals. Here when her team of twelve arrived were twenty thousand Poles and a maternity ward where another forty-five babies were expected that month.

Kate was second-in-command, her French boss, Pierre, "as full of emotions as a Paris taxicab driver and not ashamed of a single one." Her aides were a Polish countess, released from Dachau, who was a dependable judge of social complications, "Chouka," a Belgian nurse who administered the hospitals, and Ignaz, a former pilot in the Polish Air Force, who became her driver and man-of-all-trades. Her immediate problems were whether to grant another travel permit to a Polish Boy Scout who had tracked down his mother in Coburg and a brother and sister also in the French Zone and was eager to go to Munich, where someone had seen his father. Or what to do about the flour pilfered steadily from the bakery by those who distilled it into vodka. Or how to placate the German farmers whose cows and pigs left footprints in the snow up to the camp fence but not a trace thereafter. The emotional, never-ending predicament was how soon to dispatch the repatriates, twenty-five to a cattle car, Polish red and white flags flying, slogans chalked on the wall, five days by rail, to a Poland she hoped would be as free as promised.

Kate came to be mayor of this strange community, which, as trains bringing new thousands came to the sidings, grew to be as large as Laramie, Wyoming. Word was seeping back that Poland was no longer free but a prison to be avoided. So there loomed up the agonizing questions of where else these people could settle — and how large was the quota for the United States? It took five years of Kate's administration before that camp was emptied.

One of the rewards in publishing is to see promise in a manuscript which other editors have missed. Ten years before Kate Hulme came to "Wildflecken" Knopf had published a book of hers and, loyally, the first draft of *The Wild Place* was shown to a young reader for Knopf. Back it came, with a note saying that the subject matter, alas, was not in the Knopf tradition and he regretted. . . . Then a reader for Simon & Schuster had a look, with the same disappointment. But in 1952 we in Boston gave Kate the Atlantic Non-Fiction Prize of $5,000, and the book justified our confidence.

There was an unexpected sequel. "Chouka," the Belgian nurse, whom Kate first suspected of not being strong enough for the job, was not only tireless but had the poise and sympathy of one long disciplined in medical care. She was the daughter of a famous Belgian doctor; she had entered a nursing order and for twenty years had served in a mission in the Belgian Congo before the symptoms of tuberculosis led to her being recalled to the mother house. The war broke into her calm; she could not subdue her abhorrence of the Germans. She participated, against the rule, in helping American flyers to escape, and, rather than endanger the convent, asked the archbishop to release her from her vows. This was done, her dowry was returned to her, and as an ex-nun she offered her services to UNNRA.

At the "Wild Place" she became an inspiration to Kate, and it was with her urging that Kate became a convert to Catholicism. When the camp was closed they returned to America together. "Chouka" became superintendent of nurses at a hospital in Los Angeles and Kate began the most difficult book she would ever write, *The Nun's Story*. This exchange between us shows her travail and our response to Kate's accomplishment.

April 22, 1955. KH to EW:

. . . It doesn't breathe yet, Ted, but I continue to beat it on the buttocks. C. S. Forester (at the party) said "How lucky you are to have

202

another book started, before this one comes out. Then you won't give a thought to the critics, you'll be so *in* the new book!" But he doesn't know what a schizophrenic I am. I'm living the two lives right now — the written book and the unwritten one. Haunted. Even my dogs look at me as if they were seeing a witch on a broomstick.

. . . Next time you write me, be stern, give me a little hell. Your kind words always undo me.

October 3, 1955. EW to KH:

You have written a deeply impressive story and I am proud of you. I like Sister Luke and I admire her for her dedication, her integrity and her resourcefulness. You have taken me inside her heart and brain as she moves up from novice to full admission in the Order; you make me feel as a religious must feel; you make me respect her superiors — what good people are the Superior General and Mother Mathilde; most of all you make me realize what Sister Luke gave up when she left the convent. Your chapters on Africa are the heart of the book; the spirit of Schweitzer walks through them and when at the end Sister Luke makes her touching departure in her compartment banked with flowers with the little ebony statue in her lap our love for her reaches its high point.

October 8, 1955. KH to EW:

. . . Those last three chapters are the real chore. I cannot make out if you consider them anticlimax in toto, or just in their theatricality. Actually, I never did end this story on the line of dialogue I longed to use. Because, I could not carry the in-the-world history of the ex-nun that far. A long time later, when she was adjusted to the world and had found her place in it, my nun realized that she would always be a nun, that although she had unlearned the nun's way of walking and looking downward, she could never completely undo the inner formation and once she said to me (when telling how she tried to inject a little charity into her nurses who treated patients like a number) "Isn't it strange, the whole nun comes back."

The whole nun comes back. I saw that as the final line of my story. I saw it even as the title. It was the idea I wanted to leave with the reader. Once a nun, always a nun. It's my defeat that I could not find a way. . . .

Always when reading a manuscript I hope to publish I keep jotting down comments, suggestions for revisions interspersed with praise of what I like. This became more exacting than usual with *The Nun's Story* for my criticism was supplemented with a scrutiny by my Catholic copyeditor, Louise Desaulniers. These excerpts from the two of us explain why Kate began calling me "Simon Legree."

PAGE 2   "St. Bernadette's water" should be "in the Lourdes water" or "in Our Lady of Lourdes water." LD

PAGE 6   Could the renunciation of Jean be more deeply felt? What does he look like? Make Jean tell us. EW [Jean was the suitor "Chouka" had rejected before she entered the order.]

PAGE 42   The simile "shed like combat time" is inappropriate; this is taking place in a time of peace with little thought to the military. EW

PAGE 49   I doubt if you can see the dimensions of a thing before it has grown. Cut "the dimensions of" . . . EW

PAGE 165   The operation is magnificent — were no masks worn? And her first exploration without gloves? EW

PAGE 168   "the hopeful green of Advent" is wrong. In Advent the purple vestments are worn. Green is worn during the long Pentecostal season which runs from Pentecost Sunday in May through to the First Sunday of Advent in late November. LD

PAGE 205   The reference to the early Greek music of the Paschal time Kyriale seems a bit wrong. The Kyrie is of course the only part of the Mass that is of Greek origin, but the Kyriale contains the whole chant of the ordinary of the Mass, and most of this is Gregorian. LD

PAGE 219   What a heavenly tree top! Strong, good writing. . . . EW

John P. Marquand was one of the judges of the Book-of-the-Month Club who approved of *The Nun's Story*, and the first paragraph of his report placed the book in its proper perspective: "It was only after I had finished *The Nun's Story* in proof that I learned that in all its essentials it is based on truth, that a Sister Luke is actually alive today who truly passed through the adventures so delicately and beautifully narrated by Miss Kathryn Hulme. This fact surprised me more than it might most readers, because as a writer I have discovered that truth nearly always fits awkwardly into the artistic demands of fiction whereas *The Nun's Story* from first to last reads like a magnificently constructed novel, whose moments of drama arrive exactly when they should and whose final climax has a breath-taking emotional intensity. Indeed. *The Nun's Story* is such a literary achievement that this balance between fact and fiction becomes nothing more than an academic matter, for a better account of a dedicated life and search for spiritual values through a disciplinarian existence and the clash of this discipline with human emotion has very seldom been written." Spoken truly, for it was the "emotional intensity" of Kate's portrayal of Sister Luke that made the book so memorable in hard covers, in paperback, and in Audrey Hepburn's exquisite interpretation in the film.

At our editorial meetings Charlie Morton would bring up the subject of illustrations in color. The discussion went something like this. Weeks: "What would you begin with?" Morton: "Alastair Cooke on the great English country houses." "O.K., and after that?" There would be a pause followed by suggestions of the Grand Canyon or Alaska, which stranded us in the *National Geographic*'s domain. Curtis Cate, a youthful new member of the staff, had the most original idea. Curtis had been brought up in France and was bilingual. "How about the French Impressionists?" he asked. "Both for the cover and a portfolio inside." I could see that. "How much would it cost?" "Plenty," said our publisher, Don Snyder.

Our solution came straight out of the blue, and unsolicited. James Laughlin, the founder and editor of *New Directions*, received a grant from the Ford Foundation for a plan to improve international understanding. He proposed that "Intercultural Publications," under his direction, be subsidized to publish a series of quarterlies in Europe, made up of the best material drawn from contemporary American magazines. His request was granted, and from 1952 to 1955, *Perspectives* circulated at a nominal price in Britain and, in translation, in France, Germany, and Italy.

Then Laughlin conceived a more difficult series of supplements, containing essays, stories, articles, and poems that would be freshly commissioned in countries with whose culture most Americans were unfamiliar. The problem, of course, was to translate and circulate them in the United States. When the Foundation approved, Laughlin came to me: would the *Atlantic* accept these foreign supplements as an addition to a regular issue? They would average 40,000 words, contain at least 4 pages of illustrations in color, and need an editor in each country to select the writers and translators. I would have veto power over contributions or translations below our standard — and a grant of $245,000. He thought it would take six months to get each supplement in print.

My staff realized that this would be an extra burden, especially for the copyeditors — but were just as eager as I to begin. "That'll solve our color problem," said Charlie Morton. The first country was India and we immediately ran into sensitivity. I wrote Harvey Breit, the editor in India, that I had commissioned an article by Nirad C.

Chaudhuri, a critic as independent as Elmer Davis, and shortly came a stiff note from Madame Pandit stating that under no circumstances would she or Nehru appear in the same issue "with that man." Which meant that we should publish Chaudhuri before or after the Indian Supplement. We anticipated there would be difficulty in translating the poetry but were surprised that we had to contend with a subsoil of hatred. In the supplement on Indonesia, whether the subject were their early history, their dances, or the density of population, by the third or fourth paragraph a tirade burst forth against the Dutch. I had to set the ground rule that tirades against colonialism be restricted to no more than two articles.

For the ensuing twelve years we published twenty-one Foreign Supplements, the first ten financed by the Grant, the last eleven on our own. There was natural curiosity about those countries where Americans had given their lives — Italy, Germany, Japan, France, and Red China. Laughlin edited three of the best, "Japan," "Germany," and "Burma." "Africa Below the Sahara," edited by William Polk, had the most striking cover, and "Italy," edited by Thomas Mann's daughter, Elisabeth Borghese, was the most beautiful, and "Red China" was the most difficult since the borders of the country were closed. Its editors, Tillman and Peggy Durdin, longtime correspondents for the *New York Times* in Hong Kong, had become skilled in gathering material from usually inaccessible sources.

The Supplements attracted seasoned travelers; the single-copy sale jumped; from the start we printed a reserve of 5,000 copies yet those about the "unfamiliar" countries vanished in six months. We were learning to use color effectively. Most important, we learned that as much as 50 percent of the *Atlantic*'s content can be devoted to an authoritative discussion of a single topic — if it is well written. And they noticeably added variety to our covers.

Our photographic covers had unquestionably attracted readers on the newsstands, so we took the bolder step by commissioning portraits in watercolor or oil. When we used a known artist like Gardiner Cox of Boston or Tom Lea of Texas, or James Avati, with subjects like Robert Frost, Hemingway, or Sam Morison, success was guaranteed, but if we gambled on a commercial illustrator the result was sometimes ridiculed by my daughter, Sara, an artist in her own right, and my son, Ted, who is Curator at the Birmingham Museum of Fine Arts. The smiling countenance of Clarence Randall posed against the blazing hearth of Inland Steel they dubbed "Shadrach, Meshach and Abednego." A romantic rendition of Robert Louis Stevenson bearded, lonely on Samoa, with Polynesians in the background, brought from Charlie Morton the irreverent "Jesus Christ on a toot!" It was Carlton Lake, art correspondent of the *Christian Science Monitor* in Paris, who improved my choice. He had collaborated with Picasso's mistress, Françoise Gilot, in writing her widely read *Life with Picasso*, and our serial had for its cover Picasso's blue, vaselike portrait of her. Carlton's subsequent papers on Marc Chagall, Henry Moore, Alberto Giacometti, each produced a stunning cover as did his suggestion that Hemingway might permit us to reproduce Mirò's exquisite painting "The Farm." An editor can be his own art department if he doesn't err too often.

The most distinguished of our prize novels was *The Last Hurrah* by Edwin O'Connor. I have already told how beloved Eddie was by our staff; it remains to tell of the struggle that preceded the writing of his famous book. He entered Notre Dame intending to study in the School of Journalism. Professor Frank O'Malley, the teacher who was to make all the difference, said dryly, "You can learn all you need to know about journalism in six months. English literature takes a little longer." Eddie responded to that advice, and his reading was enriched by his conferences with O'Malley. On his graduation in 1939 he became a radio announcer on the Yankee Network and was soon writing and producing radio shows. He had a pleasing voice and as he trained himself to write for the ear he became not only a mimic but a master of dialogue.

During the war Eddie served as an Information Officer in the Coast Guard. Soon after his discharge he decided to freelance, supplementing his savings as a radio and TV columnist on a Boston newspaper. He sold his first short story to us in 1947 and was finishing a short novel, *The Oracle*, a satire on a commentator who is a heel, when he began the collaboration with Fred Allen. *The Oracle*, published by Harper's, earned just enough for a visit to Dublin, his favorite city next to Boston. When the royalties were gone he returned to his furnished room on Marlborough Street. There his loyal landlady heard him calling one midnight, found him coughing blood from an ulcer that had hemorrhaged, and he was rushed by ambulance to City Hospital. Roderick MacLeish, who was reading manuscripts for us, heard the news on the early broadcast and I remember his appealing to the staff to give their blood for the urgent transfusions; actually Eddie received Extreme Unction and transfusions at the same time.

His strength came back slowly. He was permitted no cigarettes or alcohol in the future, and Eddie knew he was vulnerable. In the long nights he began to perceive the promise of a novel. During the New Deal the power of patronage had shifted from city hall to Washington, and bosses like Mayor Hague of Jersey City and Boss Crump of Tennessee were losing their grip. Here in Boston was the most colorful of them all, James Michael Curley, who had served five terms as mayor, twice as governor, and briefly in Congress before a short sentence in a federal penitentiary — during which he was re-elected — spotted his record. The rumors of his corruption often had color: it was said that his daughter's trousseau was ultimately paid for by Jordan Marsh after the bill was disregarded and that the cost of her wedding reception was borne by the Copley Plaza for the same reason. On balance were Curley's occasional acts of benevolence, as when he converted the Frog Pond in the Boston Common into a paved wading pool for kids from the North End during the hot months. And no one could deny his charm as a speaker. For the celebration of the Boston Tercentenary, which took place on the Common, an Oxford historian, the Honorable H. A. L. Fisher, was imported to give the address, but Mayor Curley's opening remarks were so appropriate and well spoken (in seventeen minutes) that they put the long-winded don in the shade.

Eddie's novel *The Last Hurrah* is about the career of Frank Skeffington (Curley), who, after forty years in politics, involving him in bitter rivalry with the banks and the opposition press, is making his last run for the mayoralty against a man he derides as "a six-foot hunk of talking putty." It is a leisurely story, alive with the Boston Irish and pointed up by superb scenes — the dance at the Ninth Ward Democratic Club, Skeffington's attendance at a wake, the intensity of Election Night, and the farewell to his Praetorian Guard. The action, as Esther Shiverick Yntema, one of our editors, said, "is sustained by the talk — the various, garrulous, vituperative, sentimental, funny, bombastic Irish talk." The names are apt as any in Dickens: "Ditto" Boland, Skeffington's yes-man, the piano player "Fats" Citronella, "Timsy" Coughlin, "Jumbo Kim" Kilcullen, and the madcap of them all, "Charlie" Hennessey. Listen to him as he taunts his friend "Mother" Garvey.

Charlie examined him critically. "There's a big vein twitching away at the side of your head," he observed. "By the left temple. That could be a bad sign, my dear man. The blood pressure could be up very high, it goes with your age. I tell you what to do: never mind the doctors. Buy yourself a little kit and take your own pressure, that's the thing. Just strap it around your arm and pump it up, and whenever you feel yourself throbbing away like a motorboat tell yourself to calm down. Say prayers, suck on a Life Saver, take a warm bath: anything to keep the pressure under control, my dear man. Otherwise a man your age could pop like a balloon some fine day. Or there's a new drug out the Hindus discovered over in India: they make it out of a poison plant. I read about it the other day. One pill a day and you're in slow motion. I'll get the name of it for you tomorrow."

"Never mind the big veins in my head!" Garvey shouted. "Never mind my blood pressure! I didn't come here for that. For the love of God keep to the point, and the point is this: *Will you or won't you help us to lick that thievin' scoundrel who's gettin' rich on the city and on us all? Will you or won't you, Charlie?*"

"Sense, sense, sense!" Charlie said reprovingly. "Talk nothing but sense, my dear man! I'm surprised at a man like you paying attention to nut rumors! Frank Skeffington a rich man: oh, marvelous! And all nonsense! The man's not rich. He has no money, no money at all. It's all legend. He's stolen millions, but it's gone, all gone, easy come, easy go, like slush down a manhole in March! Frank doesn't even want to be rich; he *has* to get rid of the money. It's a common psychological type, my dear man. You read about it all the time in the medical journals. He spends like the King of Armenia and he's the softest touch in the city. There's not a bum in town that doesn't park on his doorstep in the morning and whine, 'Help! Help! I'm a dying man!' Now you or I, my dear man, would call the cops and let him die a decent death in a prison, but Frank is always there with the ten-spot. Oh, good-hearted! You have to say that for him. A crook and no culture, never reads a book in spite of what people think, but a grand heart. When he dies he won't have a quarter and the family won't even be able to pay for a casket. I'll have to bury him myself. I'll have to call up the telephone company and say, 'Good morning! This is Charles F. Hennessey. Have you got an old booth about eight feet long and two feet wide that you're not using today? I want to bury the mayor!' Oh, marvellous!"

Jim Curley took the book's success as a personal triumph. When O'Connor was asked to speak at the University of New Hampshire Curley sat prominently in a front row and at the end of the lecture, Eddie was autographing copies at one end of the hall and Curley at the other.

Life ran a feature story, comparing Skeffington with the Mayor, with photographs of Curley at various stages of his career and, after a decent interval, a deputy called on *Life*'s editor to ask if a mistake had been made: His Honor had not yet received his share of the fee. Amends were made, I have been told, to the tune of $10,000.

In advance of publication Eddie had warned us that he would not accept any offers for serialization. He did not want the book cut. But when *The Last Hurrah* had climbed to the top of the best-seller list, he received a telephone call from Kenneth Wilson, the editor of Reader's Digest Condensed Books, offering $85,000 for the right to publish a shortened version. O'Connor's first impulse was to turn it down, but before he did so he telephoned his friend Edmund Wilson, at Wellfleet. The conversation went like this:

"Edmund, this is Eddie. You remember I said I was not going to let anyone cut *The Last Hurrah?* Well, the *Reader's Digest* has just telephoned; they want to make it one of their Condensed Books."

"How much will they pay?"

"Eighty-five thousand."

"Of course you must take it." Pause. "Eddie, do you think they would be interested in my book on the Dead Sea Scrolls?"

After seven years in a furnished room Eddie could afford to move to a spacious apartment overlooking the Common, and to plan a summer visit to Dublin with Fred and Portland Allen. The foreign rights were being sold, and in India Nehru praised *The Last Hurrah* as "the best political novel ever written." It should have been awarded the Pulitzer Prize.

O'Connor was determined never to repeat. There was a five-year interim, during which he was happily married, before his next serious novel, *The Edge of Sadness*, appeared. It is a plaintive portrait of a priest who, having recovered from alcohol, was retrieving his duty in a drab parish — a thoughtful and touching story, worthy of the Pulitzer Prize, which O'Connor now received. But, alas, the temptation to write plays that had taken hold after the filming of *The Last Hurrah* diverted Eddie's mind and ended only in disappointment. Before his sudden death he had begun writing *The Cardinal*, which was to have been a broad, sympathetic story of Catholic society. Would that that dear, talented man had been granted five more years!

CHAPTER

XIV

On my return from Italy in June 1950, Harold Ross, the editor of the *New Yorker*, and I were awarded honorary degrees at the Dartmouth Commencement. Among the other recipients were Judge Harold Medina, who had just concluded the nine months' trial of a group of Communists charged and convicted of violating the Smith Act; Wallace Harrison, the eminent architect, and George Kennan, who delivered an impressive address. The details are as bright in memory as that June day which marked the beginning of my fellowship with President John Dickey.

An undergraduate member of "The Green Key" was assigned to meet each recipient, to ensure his comfort (and punctuality), and mine was waiting for Fritzy and me at the Hanover Inn, attended to our bags and was parking the car when Ross and his daughter arrived. His escort did the necessary and when they departed the four of us settled down for a nightcap. I was always fascinated by Ross's appearance: the deep lines about his mouth, those inquisitive, bright eyes, and his wiry, bottlebrush hair.

Saturday morning the exercises were held out of doors, in the Bema, and Ross and I were seated side by side on the dais, glancing through the program, when he remarked, "It says here you'll get an 'LL.D.,' but I'm to be a 'Doctor of Humane Letters.' Means I'm a kinder man."

"The hell it does," I exclaimed. "You turned me down for my first job!" (Actually he had. He was editing the *American Legion Monthly*; told me he was raising money to start a new magazine and would have nothing to offer for six months.) At that moment the president called his name, Ross squashed the mortarboard on his head, and stood up.

To me the academic procession with the new hood on one's shoulders is a self-conscious affair. During the winter when my only exercise is chopping wood, I put on six or seven pounds and during the spring when I am fishing in heavy underwear and high rubber waders I lose this and more, with the result that my cotton drawers begin to hang loose. Sitting under a hot June sun, in a blue serge suit, topped by cap and gown, can be a steam bath, and by the end of a Commencement if my drawers have slid down to my knees, I am hobbled, and in public there's just no way to hitch the damn things up. I cannot recall how often I have had to hobble back to the divesting room.

At Hanover, the festivities conclude with a reception at the president's house, and he and I were standing beside his wife's beautiful display of African violets in the living room when he said, "I'd like you to go fishing with me in the Dartmouth Grant. Commencement for us is a two-week affair, the first for the seniors and their parents, the second for the alumni and reunions. When it's all done I go north for three or four days on the Dead Diamond River, which still holds wild trout. Do you think you could make it?" I made it for the next sixteen years.

At the time Dartmouth was founded the State of New Hampshire, short of money, made two donations, the first of a township, ultimately converted into cash, the second, the Grant, a forest of 37,000 acres, nine miles under the Canadian border, lying within the embrace of the Diamond River. At Hell's Gate the river divides, the Swift Diamond swings to the west, the Dead, with its slower flow and deeper pools, to the east. They reunite to form a splendid gorge and between them lies the forest which the college has husbanded to this day. At the southern end, within sound of the gorge, is the Management Center, where the forester and fire warden are on duty and where the president brings his guests. We cook for ourselves — that is, John, or young John, did — and the rest of us boil the water and wash up. In addition to the canoe, which we strap on the car top at Hanover, are Mrs. Dickey's contributions: steak, hamburg, cherry pie, brownies, and plenty of eggs, just in case a sudden rain muddies the water — or the trout are not as hungry as we are.

There were two almost as regular as I, Sidney Hayward, secretary of the college, and Dexter Keezer, former president of Reed College and then on the staff of McGraw-Hill. At other times came Jim Conant, Arthur Harrar of the Rockefeller Foundation, David McCord, and Sinclair Weeks, whom I unluckily dunked.

The president brought his canoe and in the shed at the Center hung an aged Oldtown canoe whose bow seat had lost its wicker and was hard on the haunch. After breakfast John in the four-wheel-drive would launch the first couple with sandwiches, ten miles upstream, at Hell's Gate, and the second at "the Farm," the midpoint. He insisted that he preferred to wade the deep pools at the "Top of the Falls" and with those long legs of his he was one of the few who could do it. Meanwhile we shorter mortals would be footing through the unblemished stream, using the canoe only when the water was too deep. In its winding course the Dead Diamond creates a series of half-moon beaches, with trout in the pools at the head and the tail, and under the bank midway. The riffles of the canoe put them down, so we'd shove it securely into the brush and the foremost angler hugged the shore before he began casting the head pool. The sandy beach might show the print of a deer and otter, sometimes the skeleton of a trout eaten on the spot, but no trace of man and never a beer can at the bottom of that clear water. The lower boat would reach camp at dusk, at 5:30 John would pick up the Hell Gate couple, and the fish we lost would grow in the telling.

Evenings, as the damp clothes were drying by the fire and the bottle passed, we talked about education and Canada, a country about which Dickey is a specialist. John had come up to Dartmouth from Iowa in 1925; had worked his way through the Harvard Law School as a night guard at the Charles Street Jail, and left his law firm to serve in the State Department under Secretaries Hull, Byrnes, and Dean Acheson, with a distinction that caught the attention of the Dartmouth trustees. There was no search committee. When Nelson Rockefeller, who was on the Board and knew that Hopkins had made up his mind to retire, said, "How about John Dickey?" "Why," replied Hopkins, "that's the fellow I want, too."

At the very first meeting with the trustees, Dickey showed the judgment and firmness that marked his whole administration. Plans were under way for the erection of a large auditorium in the last available opening on the historic green and white campus. It was a sensitive matter as it was intended to be a memorial to his widely beloved predecessor, but John courageously requested that the building be deferred until he had more time to study it. He was convinced that an auditorium on the scale contemplated would seldom be used. What he envisioned was the Greek agora, the commingling of work and pleasure, to be named the Hopkins Center; with sound-proof rooms for musicians, a studio for those eager to paint, and galleries in which to hang an exhibition, with two theaters, large and small, *and* an auditorium holding nine hundred — but all in a visible relationship, and to be built by "Wally" Harrison. He got it, not without opposition, and Hopkins Center has proved an inspiration to the students and to outlanders within a radius of fifty miles, the first step in the transformation of what was once called "a woodsy college" into what Dartmouth is today.

Dickey's September welcome to the undergraduates, never more than 1,500 words, written with the freshmen in mind, was an invitation to maturity: colloquial, sensible, and cordial. (The twenty-five of them and a selection of John's commencement citations have been collected by Edward C. Latham in a book entitled *The Dartmouth Experience.*) In 1946, for the seniors, President Dickey inaugurated the Great Issues Course; to Hanover for the weekend he invited national figures, like John McCloy, Assistant Secretary of War under Stimson, or a physician like Dr. Alan Gregg, or an eloquent woman like Barbara Ward. On the Thursday before their arrival Dickey set up a preparatory session, outlining the speaker's career. Monday evening the guest spoke for an hour, then the seniors went their way to discuss what they found provocative. Tuesday morning at 9:00 they reassembled to ask their questions. In the case of Dr. Gregg, he was still fielding questions at noon. This course went on every week through the college year and attendance was compulsory. The stimulus was such that in various forms the Great Issues Course was soon adopted in other institutions. There were two immediate reactions: the *Chicago Tribune*, with its venom against the New Deal, ran a series of articles under the headlines "New Dealism Forced on Dartmouth," "Seniors Forced to Listen to Propaganda," "Dickey a Drum Beater for Utopia." The second was a grant of $75,000 from the Carnegie Corporation for the new course.

Dickey placed great emphasis on the teacher-scholar relationship. Every member of the faculty teaches — including the president — and he attracted to Dartmouth those who loved to do so: John Kemeny (John Dickey's successor), the mathematician, from Princeton, Walter Stockmeyer from M.I.T., Arthur Wilson, the Diderot scholar, from Oxford. He continued his building program by picking Pier Luigi Nervi, the Italian architect, who designed a vast, open field house of poured concrete, as serviceable for track and baseball as for Commencement, if the weather be foul. Nervi built a second, for hockey and basketball, but with acoustics that do justice to a symphony orchestra.

In a leading article Dickey wrote for the *Atlantic* in April 1955, "Conscience and the Undergraduate," he discussed the twin objectives which any liberal arts college like Dartmouth should aim for — competence and conscience. This was his opening:

The American male at the peak of his physical powers and appetites, driving a hundred and sixty big white horses across the scenes of an increasingly open society, with weekend money in his pocket and with little prior exposure to trouble and tragedy, personifies an "accident going out to happen." He is not always a college undergraduate, and not all undergraduates are trouble-prone, but I am sure that any close observer of the campus will agree that there is no more vulnerable human combination than an undergraduate.

Conscience was the more elusive factor and what he intended the reader to understand was the trust which he, the president, reposed in his most responsible undergraduates:

During the past ten years I have watched our post-war undergraduates face up to problems of conscience in passing hard disciplinary judgments on fellow students, in taking their own measure on the issues of racial discrimination and the honor system, and in meeting the easy-to-duck challenges of such things as the campus community chest, the needs of DP students, and the unadvertised troubles of some hard-pressed North countryman in the outlying community. It is no false bravery to say that having watched both his doing of these things and his contagion for trouble, I am prepared to take my chances with the kind of world the undergraduate creates when he works at it.

And he does work at it. It is a common thing for our undergraduate committee handling the investigation and recommendations on disciplinary cases to sit into the early morning hours of the night. There is no duty on a modern campus more distasteful to an undergraduate than sitting in judgment of the shortcomings of his peers. He is keenly aware that "but for the grace of God, there go I" and he probably still retains a strong trace of the American schoolboy's loyalty to the group as against the authority of the school. And yet I have never known an outgoing undergraduate judiciary chairman whose capacity for both compassion and just judgment was not admired, indeed envied, by students and faculty alike.

Recently this committee sat until 2 A.M., considering whether to recommend the dismissal from college of a boy who had gotten himself into trouble. It was a hard case all around, and it was only after an independent investigation, a hearing of the boy, and lengthy deliberation that the committee finally decided the interests of the college required dismissal of the student. Before he went to bed that night the undergraduate chairman on his own initiative called on the boy's parents at the Inn to report the decision and to give them the kind of explanation he would

215

have wanted his parents to get if he were being dismissed. This is more than responsibility; this is conscience.

Tall John Dickey, with his barrel chest, stentorian voice, and broad smile, striding through the snow and the years, became in my judgment the most innovative college president in America.

President Eisenhower received his Dartmouth honorary degree in 1953, discarded his prepared speech and talked about "the burning of the books." A year later he came to New Hampshire to visit Sinclair Weeks and to speak in the three northerly states. I was fishing in the Grant with John and Sid Hayward when word came that the President would like to stop off for luncheon on his way to Maine. Members of the Dartmouth Outing Club came on the run, to dig a pit and cook overnight the baked beans for the press and camp followers; we three anglers accumulated forty-two trout, and old Sam Brungot, the fire warden, with a worm, derricked from his secret hole a beautiful trout of just under three pounds for the President. There is a telephone at the Gate House which guards the road into the Grant, and shortly after we heard that the caravan of cars had passed, an eagle from his nest on the high ledge across the valley launched into flight and, curious about the long centipede below, rode the air current toward us. As the President's car drew up and Ike stepped out, John said, "Mr. President, there's an American eagle right overhead, come to greet you."

I admired the way President Conant conducted himself in the Senate hearings leading to his confirmation in 1953 as High Commissioner. Anyone wishing to be reminded of the patience and integrity with which he stood up to the tricky insinuations of Senator Joseph McCarthy should read pages 567 to 574 of Conant's *My Several Lives*. My admiration went up another notch when after his four successful years in Bonn he returned to the United States and, with no thought of retirement, rolled up his sleeves for a prolonged survey of an American comprehensive high school.

In the first year of exploration Conant and his team examined over a hundred of those most highly recommended, for the most part schools located in small cities where a single high school accommodated all the youth. Conant himself visited fifty-nine of them, and the findings in his book, *The American High School Today*, provoked controversy, appearing as it did when Sputnik had made us wonder if and why we were slipping. In an earlier, much quoted address, at the University of Virginia, Conant had unequivocably supported the public school in preference to the private school in these resounding words:

The greater the proportion of our youth who attend independent schools, the greater the threat to our democratic unity. Therefore, to use taxpayers' money to assist such a move is, for me, to suggest that American society use its own hands to destroy itself.

This conviction was reaffirmed in the new book, together with the recommendation that the number of high schools could be drastically reduced by collaboration within a district, and that the public school, not the parochial school (Catholic, Lutheran, or Jewish), should be the recipient of tax money. Such truths, strongly stated, challenged professors of education and proponents of the private school, and Conant became their common target. His second report, *Slums and Suburbs*, examined the ghetto schools, those with heavy enrollment of blacks, and I need quote only one of its concluding observations:

Social dynamite is building up in our large cities in the form of un-employed out-of-school youth, especially in the Negro slums. We need accurate and frank information neighborhood by neighborhood.
Employment opportunities in the large cities must be promptly opened on a nondiscriminatory basis. Because of the attitude of management and labor this can be done only through the use of federal funds.

The warning was slightly premature. The dynamite did not begin to explode until 1966.

Conant was again the butt of criticism because of his positive belief that negro schools could be upgraded and his negative statements about busing. While he was defending himself from the darts of angry parents and teachers, and before he plunged into his third investigation, *The Education of American Teachers*, he and I went fishing with our mutual friend John Dickey. On our way to the Dartmouth Grant we paused at Berlin, New Hampshire, to pick up the game warden, a robust Irishman who was introduced to Conant as he squeezed into the front seat. "President Conant," he said, "I've just finished your book" (I could see Jim hunch his shoulders for what was coming), "and I believe every word of it! I'm a Catholic but here in this town of ours two out of every five kids go to the parochial schools — and that's no way to get the best we need in our public schools!"

That was a June when the Dead Diamond yielded some of its good trout and one evening after Jim and I had finished the dishes I told

217

Conant that I wanted to do a series on the best high schools, large, small, and different. "You talk to my deputy, Eugene Youngert," he said. "He's a Vermonter; served for eighteen years as superintendent of Oak Park–River Forest High School in Illinois: he'll tell you what a community must do to support a *good* school.

Mr. Youngert's article was the curtain-raiser, "What Makes a School Good" ("a community willing to pay, willing to serve on the school board, and determined to work in harmony with the superintendent"). Then we began the series with the schools in Newton, Massachusetts. (The most experimental — a basic course in college math — attention to those with reading difficulty — special course on computers — a three-year sequence on development of Western Man.) Our next choice was the non-graded high school at Melbourne, Florida, close to the missile test center at Cape Canaveral ("Bright students advance as fast as they are able; achievement rather than grade promotion"). The third, Allentown High School in Pennsylvania ("Educating for Industry: a remarkably balanced program for vocational, technical and academic studies"). Then came "Education the Year Round," an evaluation of the Dunbar Vocational School in Chicago with its offering of vocational skills in an underprivileged area, 90 percent black, 10 percent white.

We were soon deluged with readers' requests. "Don't overlook Bucks County!" "I hope we're going to hear about East High School in Denver?" (Yes, it was coming). In the fifth we published the case for the junior high, selecting the Nathan Eckstein School in Seattle. By then I had nominations enough for two years and was wondering when we could stop.

In came a call from Corning, New York, from a vice president in charge of the Corning Glasswork Foundation.

"How many of those good schools are you planning to write about?"

"At the moment," I said, "we're copyediting one on the high school in Green River, Wyoming. Very small, but for three generations it's ranked in the top ten in the teaching of physics. Why do you ask?"

"Well, we have offices in a number of cities and we're planning to send the school superintendent in each place to have a look at those schools which the *Atlantic* has been praising." This was surprising approval. We extended the series to nine articles, ending with "Challenging the Gifted," by Alexander Taffel, a glowing appreciation of the Bronx High School of Science, established in New York City in

1938, "to identify boys and girls of high potential in science and mathematics."

I was in Washington shortly after Sputnik went up, and at a small dinner party I introduced James and Mrs. Reston to the Caryl Haskinses. Caryl had succeeded Dr. Vannevar Bush as president of the Carnegie Institution. "Dr. Haskins," asked Scotty, "how long do you think it will take us to catch up?"

"It won't happen overnight," Caryl replied. "Too often in education we've been willing to settle for competence rather than excellence."

An eccentricity, long regarded as a family joke, or by over-anxious mothers as a symptom of a retarded child, has at last begun to receive serious corrections. I am referring to the inability of some boys to spell, to read, and, in aggravated cases, to write. This came home to me in 1949 when Dr. J. Roswell Gallagher sent us a striking article entitled "Can't Spell — Can't Read," based on his experience as school doctor at Phillips Andover Academy. Ros had received a Carnegie Grant to explore the problem then troubling some forty-two boys at that famous school. Reading is an arbitrary discipline. The Chinese read up and down the page; we normally read across the page from left to right, but for the boys Dr. Gallagher was studying, bright in other respects, and many left-handed, it was normal to attempt to read from right to left, and in writing to reverse their lettering.

I was embarrassed to recall the Halloween when young Ted (who threw left-handed) and I were hollowing out a pumpkin. "Now carve your name," I said. Ted took the knife in his left hand and cut, right to left, ᗡƎT. I recalled how my Grandfather Suydam could not help reversing even so simple a statement as grace before Sunday dinner, while his daughters, my mother one of them, bowed over in laughter. ("Lantify, O Sword," he would begin.)

Dr. Gallagher continued to write for us and I asked if he could possibly include Ted in one of his day-long tests. He did, and his report was emphatic. "Your boy is really handicapped and must have special teaching. If it wasn't so late in the spring I'd say take him out immediately — before he gets any more inferiority!"

Dr. Gallagher and Dr. Edwin M. Cole of the Massachusetts General Hospital were at the time two of the few specialists on dyslexia in the East and its prevalence went unrecognized in most private and all public schools. We know today that on an average one boy in ten is afflicted — the incidence among girls is less — and that schools and teachers are striving to cope with the problem with special, slow instruction, "one on one." I was conducting a radio program, "Editor at Home," on Sundays over ABC when young Ted was transferred to Proctor Academy in New Hampshire (where he was successfully prepared for Haverford College, and ultimately a master's degree), and I devoted two of my talks to dyslexia, citing the mistakes and the reversals it causes in writing and reading. It took me weeks to answer the letters from worried parents, enclosing samples of their children's writing and asking where could they go for help. (To complete our saga I inherited dyslexia lightly, Ted more seriously, and my namesake, young Edward, more severely than either of us.)

Dudley Cloud, one of my editorial assistants, came to me from Harvard, where he had been working with freshmen whose reversals and inept writing were reported by different instructors throughout the year. Dudley, formerly an able teacher at the Loomis Institute, was so familiar with the symptoms of dyslexia that he said to the dean, "If you'll let me see the entrance examination papers I can spot in advance those seventy or more who are dyslexic and help to straighten them out at the very beginning of freshman year." It is consoling that young people who are bright and articulate — but can't write or spell or read like the rest of us — are receiving remedial help to pass their way into college and the appreciation of books; it is pitiful that so many hundreds of thousands who still go undetected are puzzled by, or simply shun, books for the rest of their lives.

I love competition. At tennis I was a moderate second-rater, but I never missed the chance to see the Davis Cup matches, especially when Bill Tilden, in his prime, stood off the Three Musketeers from France: Henri Cochet, René LaCoste, and Jean Borotra. Tilden could not write as well as his doubles partner, George Lott, who in his *Atlantic* paper "Tight Spots in Tennis" drew a striking picture of "Big Bill" in action. I went after articulate athletes. In baseball I wanted the catcher, who can control his team. Birdie Tebbets and Moe Berg, both of the Boston Red Sox, wrote for me, and Berg's article "Catchers and Pitchers" is true "inside" baseball. Moe was tall, good-looking, a superb linguist, Phi Beta Kappa at Princeton, who, after his playing days were over, served Nelson Rockefeller in Latin America. When he was in Boston we went to Fenway Park together, Moe putting a finger to his lips and shaking his head if someone in the dugout spotted him.

Allen Jackson, an All-American guard who had twice played for the University of Michigan in the Rose Bowl, strongly criticized the pressure athletes in the Big Ten are subjected to in his "Too Much Football." And long before his appointment to the Supreme Court, Byron ("Whizzer") White was a member of the Pittsburgh Steelers, and I used all my blandishment trying to persuade him to do an article. I called on him at the Hotel Manger in Boston. His team-mate, a big hulk, slept soundly on the other bed throughout our talk. "How did you get your nickname?" I asked. "Oh, in college. I'd stay back under the punts," he told me. "As the ends came down I'd try to split them, taking the ball on the run. First time I tried it under lights in Pittsburgh the ball hit me on the nose." I wanted him to write on "football: pro and con," but he was not to be persuaded.

I was always happy to get down to Texas, where I looked forward to a round of golf at Fort Worth. Dear friends, Hallie and Bob Hardwicke, put me on the trail of the Texas writers they admired: J. Frank Dobie, the last link with the great ranches, Roy Bedichek, who saved the whooping cranes, and Tom Lea, who wrote and illustrated for us his fine narrative *The Brave Bulls*. I have always had a soft spot for O. Henry's stories about the "Gentle Grifter," written while the author was serving time he did not deserve, and the remembrance kept me looking for a loquacious Texan with a five-gallon hat and high humor.

I found him in Dillon Anderson, but he did not conform to type. Dillon was a dark, very handsome, sophisticated lawyer, a wizard at cards, and brimming with *joie de vivre*. During the war he was promoted to colonel in G-5 in the Middle East, where his expertise in petroleum diplomacy was rewarded with the Legion of Merit. In 1952 his activity for the election of President Eisenhower brought him frequently to Washington (he became Secretary of the National Security Council, 1955 to 1956), and his wife unknowingly became my ally. Because he had flown so much in Asia Minor, she made him promise that henceforth he would travel by train, and so it was in the Pullman compartment on the long haul to and from Houston that he wrote the "I and Claudie" stories which delighted our readers. The "I" in the stories is Clint Hightower, a born grifter, as cocky as he is susceptible; Claudie, his partner, is a big lummox who sings with "a country bass," charms the girls, and is smarter than Clint believes. Their adventures, as they go "chowsing around [in a trailer] from pillar to post, never latching on to a good thing," were redolent of the country food, the good nature, the plains and lingo of the Southwest. My only problem was to keep "I and Claudie" from monopolizing half an issue; in the telling the narratives were as outsize as the Lone Star State, and when I had to cut there were groans from Dillon.

In December 1954, after publishing two volumes of "I and Claudie," Dillon began a new series with "Portrait of a Poker Player." Without his law practice Dillon could have made — and did make — quite a pile at gin rummy and poker at table stakes. But in this piece the bully at the table is Billingsley (a likeness of one of his dear friends, Richard F. Burns), and one of the victims is Anderson, who describes the play in dry, gullible terms. Poker rarely figured in the *Atlantic*'s past, but for those who love it, as I do, this is the best, the toughest short description ever in our print. I quote from the episode: "Billingsley will draw two cards to a flush." They are playing draw poker with openers:

Say there have been three hands passed, swelling the pot to a sizable amount. Thereupon the hand, let us assume, is opened by a pair of aces. A pair of deuces calls, matched by another caller holding a straight, open at both ends. Billingsley swoops down, raises the bet the full size of the pot, and explains piously that he is doing it merely to give a little protection to the opener. Stark terror grips all the players, but Billingsley usually gets two or three customers. Honest draws are made by the others, but Billingsley, looking as contented as Walter P. Chrysler might contemplating the Chrysler Building, says that two cards will do for him. After the draw he bets the first installment on a Jaguar and launches on his campaign speech. He insists that he hasn't a damn thing. He wants to know whether we are mice or men to let him "bull the game" like that. He will even stand up in his address and call for a pitcher and a glass of water — which, of course, no one brings him.

In this particular act he will frequently go off into the next room while the rest of the players sweat. Then he will come back and, pretending to assume that nobody will call, will start dragging in the chips. Hart says he would have called him, but he didn't catch, and Hart really would have. (Hart is positively the originator of that deathless morning-after quotation, so current these days, "I lost my shirt, Mother dear, but I kept the game honest.")

Beads of perspiration pop out of the pair of aces, the openers, since the draw has produced another little pair. Similar beads cover the pair of deuces, now joined by a third. The straight is busted and flown. Finally Billingsley drags down the pot with no callers and shows his hand: three miscellaneous hearts and two orphans that look as if they belonged in a used pinochle deck. He announces in a loud tone that he would rather have three hearts in this game than three aces in any other game he ever played in. Also he sometimes laughs boisterously at this juncture and asks if there are any pitch players in the crowd.

The whole thing is simple. The two times that I called him on this particular play — once in 1938, just before I sold my car, and again last week — he wasn't using exactly the same technique that I have described. The first time he really had a big pair and a kicker; then he caught two to match the latter on the draw — a cat hop, so called, to a full house. Last week he had filled his flush. But you get the general idea anyhow, and I have the satisfaction of knowing that Billingsley wasn't bluffing either time. Successful bluffing, I have said a thousand times — and I say it again here — is a thing that can't be allowed in a well-ordered game.

As many a woman has done before her, Catherine Drinker Bowen began to write after her first marriage ("seven of them happy years, five in desperation") had gone on the rocks. Like her older brother, Henry Drinker, she had a passion for music. She had studied the violin at the Juilliard School, and it was natural that her first papers, which I edited in the mid-1930s, were about musicians. Her father, an eminent engineer, had been president of Lehigh University, and after the divorce Kitty, with her son and daughter, took refuge with her aging parents, who were living in retirement at Haverford, Pennsylvania. She began earning egg money, writing pleasant personal essays about amateurs like herself who would rather play string quartets than eat. We published them in a modest volume entitled *Friends and Fiddlers*, little suspecting it would unlock a door. On the strength of "the Fiddlers" she was commissioned to do a biographical portrait, *Beloved Friend*, the letters of wealthy Madame von Meck to the man she adored but never met, Tchaikovsky. Published by Random House, it became a book club selection and the royalties liberated Kitty. In 1936 she traveled to Moscow to complete the research for a third book about musicians: *Free Artist*, the story of Anton and Nicholas Rubinstein. But American readers were not interested in the brothers Rubinstein; the failure brought her to a hard decision, and when she turned away from music she came to us.

Kitty descended from a long line of Philadelphia Quakers. Her great-great-grandfather, Henry Drinker, refused to take sides in the Revolution and was packed off with other eminent members of his sect for six months' imprisonment in York. Whereupon his wife, Elizabeth, led a delegation of wives by cart to Valley Forge to appeal to General Washington, who wisely referred them to Congress, and the peace-determined Quakers were released. This feminine perseverance Kitty inherited. She was the youngest of six, and in her *Family Portrait*, she writes, "Four brothers, older than I, inhabited a world that I could never enter and about which — I know it now — I was possessed of an unremitting curiosity from the age of eight. . . . Always, in real life, my brothers were teaching me, they looked down from their heights and pulled me along. "Go forward, Katz, with that right skate. Don't just slide, *push out*! Get your whole body into it. . . ."

That explains why each of Kitty's finest biographies, beginning with *Yankee from Olympus*, the life of Justice Oliver Wendell Holmes, is devoted to a man's world and to the distinction he brought to it. There is an additional reason why she never chose to write about a woman. Kitty's older sister, Ernesta, was incomparably beautiful, whereas Kitty, with her strong Drinker jaw and her dominant nose, was plain, her beauty living in her eyes. Aunt Cecilia Beaux would paint several portraits of Ernesta, never one of Kitty. (Had she lived longer the artist could not have missed the distinction which the younger sister acquired in maturity.) Kitty early realized that her sphere of action would have to be different from Ernesta's.

The "hard decision" I have referred to was this: in the turbulence of 1939 Kitty was eager to write about the famous American she most admired, the late Justice Oliver Wendell Holmes. But could a woman trained to play the violin acquire sufficient knowledge of the law to do so? Her oldest brother, Henry, himself a distinguished lawyer, counsel for the Pennsylvania Railroad, was dubious. But the dean of the University of Pennsylvania Law School was more encouraging. He guided her reading of the sources and was impressed by her power to assimilate.

She made repeated visits to Boston to interview the Wendells, Olivers, Jacksons, Holmeses: "solid people" she called them, "sound and adventurous," bound together by family ties like those in Philadelphia. Their recollections mirrored the intimacy of "Wendell's" friendships at Harvard, his recuperation after being thrice wounded in the years 1861 to 1863, the diffidence he felt toward his exuberant father, the little doctor and popular poet, Oliver Wendell Holmes, Sr., and Wendell's slow-fire devotion to Fanny Dixwell, whom he married.

Her reading notes at the back of *Yankee from Olympus* supported the verity and warmth of her text. Here is how she saw the home on Beacon Street in which Wendell was brought up:

In 1941, before the Holmeses' house at 296 Beacon Street was dismantled, I visited it and had tea in Dr. Holmes's library, by courtesy of Mr. and Mrs. Edward Jackson Holmes. Stepping in the front door, I was instantly back in the nineties. Over the banister hung the portrait of Abiel Holmes, handsome with brown eyes and flowing curly hair. Upstairs in the library the books, the statuettes, the carpet and fringed lampshades, the Spy cartoon on the wall, breathed of the Doctor. Mr. Edward Holmes crossed the room and opened a door. On its inner side hung a small mirror, just level with my chest — (I am not tall). Dr. Holmes had hung that mirror. It was just the right height for him to brush his hair.

Here is how Wendell and his father witnessed the beginning of the Great Fire:

On November 9, 1872, Dr. Holmes heard the fire bells. From his Beacon Street windows he saw a column of light down by Boylston and Tremont Street. He and Wendell went out together. It was the beginning of the great fire that raged for two days, destroying millions of dollars' worth of property. Writing Motley, the doctor quotes Wendell's remark to the effect that huge buildings crumbled and came down without a sound, like feather beds.

And again:

Bishop Lawrence (1850–1942) gave me my best scenes of the household both on Charles and Beacon Streets. "Pitter patter all the time in that library," the Bishop said. "Melia Holmes (Wendell's sister) was the only person in Boston who could out-talk Phillips Brooks. People used to say Wendell put a *but* after every sentence so he could go on talking. But he had a romantic quality the others lacked."

There were innumerable Boston interviews in Holmes's circle; others with eleven of his law clerks, his coachman, his many admirers in the Capital.

Early in her research Kitty was granted permission to consult Justice Holmes's letters, four hundred of which were in the keeping of the Massachusetts Historical Society. But the executors, John Palfrey and Felix Frankfurter, were troubled at the thought of a *woman* writing such a book. When they realized that she was writing an interpretative rather than an academic biography, they pulled the rug out from under her, denying her permission to quote directly from the unpublished Letters. This might have deterred a lesser character; it forced Kitty to find corroboration of what she knew from other sources, and she did. In her exasperation she turned to an old friend, Barbara Rex, who became her advisor on every page of *Yankee* and every book she wrote thereafter. Kitty, of course, could not be denied access to Holmes's *Speeches* and *Collected Legal Papers*, which were in print, together with Shriver's edition of the Massachusetts opinions, the *Holmes–Pollock Letters* edited by Mark deW. Howe, *The Constitutional Doctrines of Justice Holmes* by Dorsey Richardson, and Francis Biddle's *Mr. Justice Holmes.*

In all the editions of *Yankee from Olympus* appears this description of her method:

This book is a picture and a translation, an attempt to bring Justice Holmes out of legal terms into human terms. All my search for material and all my selection of material were based on this conception.

The statements and conversations of the main characters came from published records, records in manuscript or the word-of-mouth testimony of people who knew the Holmes family. I have never distorted these statements or changed their meaning, although in quoted material I have occasionally shifted the sentence sequence. But I have often embellished them, deliberately and with purpose. In a portrait, authenticity is not achieved by names and dates, but needs something further. When it seemed especially necessary to engage the reader's attention for something Justice Holmes was going to say — or the doctor, or Uncle John or Fanny Dixwell — I invented the chairs in which they sat, the window out of which they looked as they spoke. For instance, when Wendell Holmes was ten, I had him lean against a tree and suck a blade of grass while his Uncle John told a story about Caesar Augustus. But I knew the tree was there, beside the Gambrel-roofed House, because I had seen a picture of it, and I knew that Uncle John had told that story not once but many times.

We selected four installments of *Yankee from Olympus* for the *Atlantic* and Kitty was insistent that her account of the *Northern Securities* case and the *Lochner* case be printed in full. "I have tried to write the cases as a journalist would write them, sitting in the courtroom, who gives the primary facts, then something of the case's impact upon the country at the moment. To this, as biographer, I add something of Holmes's own feelings and the feelings of persons concerned in our story, such as Theodore Roosevelt."

Kitty was in New York when she heard that the Book-of-the-Month Club were to distribute 300,000 copies of *Yankee from Olympus* to their subscribers. In exuberance she wrote me:

February 19, 1944

Dear Ted:

Saw Harold Ober [her literary agent] in New York who says that Book Club is printing 300,000. News drove me hog wild. I went out and bought fur coat, suits, gloves, at a very fancy place where I sat in a panelled room and a black girl brought me lunch for nothing. Woke up today absolutely appalled and stuffed the fur coat in a box under the bed.

Would 300,000 books in a line reach from Beach Haven to City Hall, Philadelphia? There is something a little mathematical.

Hastily,
Kitty

There was more to come. The book was selected for the Armed Services Edition in 1944, and no telling how many men in uniform read it. John Lindsay (the Mayor-to-be of New York) was one of them who wrote the author that her book had opened up a whole new horizon for him. At home Joseph Henry Jackson, the best critic on the Pacific Coast, published his review in the *San Francisco Chronicle* under the headline "A Book to Know America By." In hard covers our edition went through 27 printings, followed by 11 editions in paperback. Kitty spoke to the American public, who responded to her interpretation.

Throughout the triumphant reception of *Yankee from Olympus* Kitty could hear the muttering of the professorial historians who objected to her method, especially to that word "embellished," which to them meant "improvising": that is, a departure from the known fact. It is a fact that Fanny, Mrs. Holmes, was very witty, and to prove it Kitty described a call which Mrs. Arthur Hill made on Mrs. Holmes, before the move to Washington. "Mary," said Mrs. Holmes, *getting up and moving to her friend,* "look at me! How can I go to Washington — I, who look like an abandoned farm in Maine?" Mrs. Hill had never forgotten that despairing remark, but it was the active description I have italicized which the professors objected to. How did Mrs. Bowen know? Wasn't she inventing?

Kitty had forced her way through the underbrush of law and was absorbed in understanding how our most distinguished judge of the twentieth century formed his decisions, and with what force he expressed them. Law was the mainspring of our Republic, and for her next subject she chose John Adams, the young lawyer, whose initiative and boldness were so decisive in our break with Britain. In retrospect she told me: "I only wrote this book so I could find out where John Adams got all those notions about how to write constitutions, in 1774, when the various colonies kept writing and asking him, 'You say we mustn't declare independence till we have each written our state constitutions.' Well, how do people write constitutions?"

She followed John Adams up to the age of thirty-seven, after he had composed the constitution for Massachusetts and was preparing for the Constitutional Convention of 1776 in Philadelphia, where he spoke with such vigor, and with rare diplomacy, that the Convention passed over the expectant John Hancock to nominate a Virginian, George Washington, to command the Army at Cambridge. This book meant a jump backward of two centuries, to a total dependence on documents, to a familiarity with the Adams houses in Quincy, Massachusetts, the books young John consulted, and, for warmth, the letters to and from his devoted wife, Abigail. Once again there was a male obstacle, the deaf and crotchety Henry Adams (nephew of Henry the Writer), guardian of the then unpublished Adams Papers, who exclaimed, "Mrs. Bowen, I wish I had never laid eyes on you!"

She used her same "method"; she "embellished" the scenes in Philadelphia with a vividness that made the professors sputter, and the lawyers, less snobbish than the academicians, did not give a damn: they respected her and invited her to speak at their meetings.

I remember our struggle to find a suitable title. "Johnny Yankee" was thought to be an eye-catcher, but when the Book-of-the-Month Club telephoned their acceptance they wished to call it *John Adams and the American Revolution*, which was Kitty's preference in the first place.

By now well-wishers — and rival publishers — were bombarding her with new subjects: Jane Addams, Edna St. Vincent Millay, John Marshall, Roger Taney, old Judge Sewall of Massachusetts. But she took her time and what she wrote in her workbook was:

(Coke)?
Milton?
Cromwell?
I. Newton?

Kitty let the decision simmer while she enjoyed herself writing the essays which compose her *Adventures of a Biographer*, from which I have been quoting. Two of them had their inception as lectures, for she was an admirable speaker, wearing the new sables

John Adams had provided for her. In one of her essays, "The Company of Scholars," she recalled the impatience that welled up in her at an academic convention as she sat listening to professors "trying to take the heat out of history while I sit here trying to put it in." Afterward, she controlled her temper when a young instructor, having asked how many copies of *Yankee* had been sold, whistled and remarked, with unconscious arrogance, "Someday I'm going to take a year off and write a popular book." I doubt if the smart aleck ever did. Kitty's lead time for a full-length biography was three years.

She chose Sir Edward Coke because to her he "was English law personified." It was his duty as Queen Elizabeth's Attorney General to try and condemn Sir Walter Raleigh and then the Earl of Essex. After their executions, when he was seventy, Chief Justice Coke's turn came to be sent to the Tower. But King James ultimately was compelled to set him free "because he had become an oracle amongst the people." Coke, in 1628, was author of the great *Petition of Right* (which became a model for our Revolutionary petitions); he had the audacity to set the law above the throne, whence came the title of her book, *The Lion and the Throne*. She said, "I wrote it almost inevitably, after Holmes and Adams. For me it's like ABC backwards. It's the principles of our kind of government, told through the life story of three men, and told backwards in a sort of natural progression. Each man built on the work of the others."

Twelve years after her struggle and triumph with *Yankee*, Kitty was invited to speak at the theater of the Folger Library in Washington. When the lecture was announced Justice Frankfurter asked if he might introduce her. This came as a surprise, as little had passed between them since that day when he told her to her face that his blood ran cold at the thought of her writing about Holmes's great cases. What now transpired is best described in *Adventures of a Biographer*:

Justice Frankfurter got up, stood forward to the footlights and with immense vigor announced that I had written some eight books — he had sent to the Congressional Library for them and had read all but one. That one he still thought better not to read. He had done what he could to prevent my writing it. Mrs. Bowen, he said, would confirm that statement. The Justice turned, looked piercingly at me where I sat on the platform, grinned, and returned to the business at hand. There were people, he went on, who worked better under difficulty, and I was one of them. "I stand here," he told the audience, "I stand here to make amends." He went on to use the word apology, but he need not have used it. What he said that night I shall always remember; it touched me closer than his strictures

229

ever had. And after the battle, need the disputants prove the blows? A duel is a duel and keeps fighters on their toes, where fighters should be.

In every biography she had written there had been situations or persons who had tried to block her. My editing began with her *John Adams* when I joined Barbara Rex as one of her "seconds." In winter I would enjoy overnight visits in the charming home she had made for her second husband, McKean Downs, in Haverford, Pennsylvania. In summer I saw her more frequently in her workshop on the shore of Gloucester Harbor. It was a small boathouse, once part of her aunt Cecilia Beaux's estate on Eastern Point, and a short drive from my cottage in Beverly Farms. There sometimes on the porch, or if windy, within, we would lunch on cold ham and avocado salad, talking books, to the sound of the water lapping beneath.

The Philadelphia Award, a gift of Curtis Bok, is the highest honor the City of Philadelphia confers, annually, on one of its citizens. In 1957 the rumor spread that it was to go to a lawyer, perhaps to a Drinker. Why, to Henry, of course, for his leadership in law and music. But no, when the announcement was made, it went to his youngest sister, Catherine. That year she also received a National Book Award and at each reception one could admire her fine carriage and her air of distinction.

Early in her preparation for *Yankee*, to clarify her understanding of the Constitution, Kitty read Max Farrand's *Records of the Federal Convention*, four volumes of the speeches, as reported by the delegates, who were arguing about that great charter in Philadelphia during the sultry summer of 1787. Now in her maturity, a patriotic desire drove her to recapture the excitement, the hard-drawn compromise and the idealism of that achievement. It was a stubborn subject, snarled up by economic theorists, and long taken for granted by most Americans. She sought the professional advice of two expert historians, Julian Boyd and the dedicated Quaker John H. Powell, and both responded. *Miracle at Philadelphia* was her last major work, and in his appraisal of the final draft Mr. Powell says this to Kitty:

There is in this book an unusually adult spirit. That may seem a strange thing for me to say; what I mean is, that books on the Convention have usually not been adult, they have been partisan. And every historian knows the immaturity of the partisan. They have treated Delegates as if they were not whole personalities, wholly engaged; they have not let us see them as men. How you have achieved this, is the result of your

230

artistry. And I think it is, insofar as I know the literature, the most wholesome, the most realistic book on these men, that has appeared.

For the Federal Convention is astonishing most of all for its idealism. Only an immature scholar, could ever consider these men as motivated by less than a genuine and mounting concern for the welfare of the whole people. To think of them as special pleaders, for special interests, is unrealistic and — from the evidence — false.

The idealism certainly is here. Even (I hope) the idealism of Justice Yates and Mayor Lancing; certainly the idealism of the drunken Martin, happily the idealism of the thoughtful and courageous Doctor McHenry. . . . And of course, the patient idealism of Madison, the strong steadiness of General Washington, the imaginative flights of that Phaeton, Hamilton.

Gertrude Stein once remarked that "it is the business of an artist to be exciting." In her books Kitty Bowen has demonstrated that it is also the business of a biographer. I am proud of *Miracle at Philadelphia*, proud of its superb portraits and its power to inform; proud, too, that it is dedicated to me.

When she came up for her last summer in the Gloucester boathouse, she was writing about a Philadelphian, herself defying cancer, determined to finish, by dictation in the hospital if necessary, as it was, her *Scenes in the Life of Benjamin Franklin*. In our day when American ideals often seem blurred it is good to remember a woman as brave, gifted, and as patriotic as Kitty.

CHAPTER

XV

When a senior citizen reaches his hundredth birthday, reporters question him on what precautions he took for longevity. Very few magazines ever live that long. In England, *Punch* and *Blackwood's* are two that did, although the latter has recently folded. As our rival, *Harper's*, approached its centennial in 1950, Frederick Lewis Allen, the editor, and his able assistants, Russell Lynes and Eric Larrabee, decided to reprint in one commemorative issue the best things *Harper's* had published in the past. This compelled us to find an alternative: we determined to bring together in November 1957 the work of the most distinguished *living* writers, a declaration which, were it found in a cornerstone opened in A.D. 2057, would tell survivors what we were like. It would be more expensive than mothballs.

We began sixteen months ahead of time by compiling lists of the writers we wanted. The staff was unanimous on the big names we knew would be hard to get. It was my job to keep in mind "the mix." Every magazine editor is aware — some less keenly than others — of how much depends upon his mix, by which I mean the way he plans his table of contents. It is simple arithmetic that if you lead with a thoughtful but heavy article of ten pages on foreign policy, it should not be followed by another "think piece" of eight pages. The success of a normal issue will often depend on the first three contributions, and it is human nature to be attracted by dialogue rather than solid columns of black type.

The abolition of slavery was the issue which pressed on the New England conscience when Lowell sent our first issues to press in 1857, and a century later, the obedience and slavery imposed by Communism was an abomination in American eyes. An article on Russia's Imperial Design should clearly be one of our first three. Edward Crankshaw wrote it.

I believe that the most original American editor of my lifetime was Harold Ross of the *New Yorker*. An article that would capture Ross's character, and his way of doing things, must be up front, and I thought that E. B. White could do it to perfection. But after a week of deliberation he declined, perhaps because it came too close to what was sacrosanct. James Thurber? Charlie Morton spoke up, "I know him. Let me go down to Connecticut and urge him." It was Charlie's greatest coup. We had to keep after these most desired pieces to make sure they would reach us in time. Two weeks before the delivery date Thurber telephoned, "Charlie," he said, "this article on Ross is running too long; I think there'll have to be two." "Great," said Charlie. "Send up the first — and keep going!"

The final paragraphs of Thurber's first paper I, who never knew either man intimately, find touching:

I became one of the trio about whom he [Ross] fretted and fussed continually — the others were Andy White and Wolcott Gibbs. His admiration of good executive editors, except in the case of William Shawn, never carried with it the deep affection he had for productive writers. His warmth was genuine, but always carefully covered over by gruffness or snarl or a semblance of deep disapproval. Once, and only once, he took White and Gibbs and me to lunch at the Algonquin, with all the fret and fuss of a mother hen trying to get her chicks across a main thoroughfare. Later, back at the office, I heard him saying to someone on the phone, "I just came from lunch with three writers who couldn't have got back to the office alone."

Our illnesses, or moods, or periods of unproductivity were a constant source of worry to him. He visited me several times when I was in a hospital undergoing a series of eye operations in 1940 and 1941. On one of these visits, just before he left he came over to the bed and snarled, "Goddam it, Thurber, I worry about you and England." England was at that time going through the German blitz. As my blindness increased, so did his concern. One noon he stopped at a table in the Algonquin lobby where I was having a single cocktail with some friends before lunch. That afternoon he told White or Gibbs, "Thurber's over at the Algonquin lacing 'em in. He's the only *drinking* blind man I know."

He wouldn't go to the theater the night *The Male Animal* opened in January, 1940, but he wouldn't go to bed, either, until he had read the reviews, which fortunately were favorable. Then he began telephoning around town until, at a quarter of two in the morning, he reached me at Bleeck's. I went to the phone. The editor of the *New Yorker* began every phone conversation by announcing "Ross," a monosyllable into which he was able to pack the sound and sign of all his worries and anxieties. His loud voice seemed to fill the receiver to overflowing. "Well, God bless you, Thurber," he said warmly, and then came the old familiar snarl: "Now, goddam it, maybe you can get something written for the magazine," and he hung up, but I can still hear him over the years, loud and snarling, fond and comforting.

After the appearance of the first article, Thurber and his wife, Helen, went down for a short stay at the Algonquin in New York. The telephone never stopped ringing; when they went out on the town they were overwhelmed by old friends and former contributors, congratulating and confiding what they remembered. Thurber kept going; Charlie repeatedly went to Connecticut to stoke the furnace and the ten installments which we printed consecutively of *The Years with Ross* were unquestionably the most successful serial in the magazine's history.

For every reason we had to have a story by Ernest Hemingway, sentimentally because back in 1927 the *Atlantic* had published his powerful "Fifty Grand," his first long story to appear in the United States. He remembered this — and perhaps the $400 we paid for it — when he agreed to contribute. Five months before the delivery date I asked Phoebe-Lou Adams how she'd like to fly down to Havana. "Stay as long as it's necessary to get his promise," I said. "And be sure to wear that big hat with the red poppy on it." She arrived to find that he was off on a fishing trip. A fortnight passed before he returned; then she was invited to tea at the Finca, and tea it was, little cakes and literary conversation until Hemingway blasted our foreign policy and discovered she shared his unenthusiastic view of President Eisenhower and Mr. Dulles. "Those old men," he said, "will be laying out their arthritis and their cancers on Peace Tables where everybody else knows the United States is out of business." Period. "Have a drink!" The drink turned into a view of the grounds and Hemingway's writing tower, where at every window a cat peered out. After cocktails and dinner, good talk continued, punctuated by cats climbing up the screened door. Ping, ping, ping-thump! There was an army of them and they were not admitted.

The deal was settled and eventually we received, not one story but two, with this reminder:

When Miss Adams was down she told me you could only pay $1,000 for a story. But, she told me the *Atlantic* would very much like to have two stories. The price for the two stories to you for this special number because the *Atlantic* published "Fifty Grand" so long ago is $2,000. It is embarrassing to me to have to tell you how much of a financial sacrifice it is for me to give you the stories at this price. . . . It was a pleasure to take the monetary loss in what I regard as something worth doing.

Very truly yours,
Ernest Hemingway.

(We sent him a check for $2,500, and in a later letter I urged him to go to the Soviet Union, where he was so highly regarded, and told him that I thought his presence might persuade them to pay royalties to those American writers whom they translate and publish.)
He replied:

. . . I read with great interest what you wrote in the Atlantic about your trip to the Soviet Union. Am glad that they like what I write there. Mikoyan came out here to the finca to bring me a collected edition of my writing that they had published and we had a very pleasant talk. Katchaturian, the composer, was also out and we have seen several other Russians who were here with their Exhibition. I did not talk about royalties with Mikoyan since he was a guest in our house but some of the other Russians assured me that they were going to pay royalties sooner or later to American writers they had published. I told them that I wanted no preferential treatment and suggested that they pay a proportion of the royalties owed to all American writers. In this case I would be happy to accept my share if other American writers were also paid their shares.

The damned work I have piled up makes it impossible to figure on a trip to Russia now although I may have to go to Europe to check various things in these two pieces of work I am finishing. But it would be wonderful to go there sometime to shoot and fish and I have always looked forward to it. Now, with the news of the shooting down of the U2 plane and what that may lead to we better all be prepared to be guilty by association if Nixon comes in. You went over there and I had actual Russians here in the house. Only Miss Phoebe Adams will be safe, and maybe she won't be because she was here at this same finca although at a different time and she works in the office with you. . . .

Our Paris correspondent, Curtis Cate, flew to Copenhagen to see Isak Dinesen at her country house on the Baltic coast, found that she was working on a new set of tales, and persuaded her to send me a beauty. Curtis also called on the exile Czeslaw Milosz in Paris, who proposed to write an essay, "Joseph Conrad in Polish Eyes"; it was a tragic revelation of Conrad's parents' passionate patriotism and its effect on their only son — written twenty-three years before Milosz was awarded the Nobel Prize.

Of the four poets in the issue, Robert Frost chose a subject singularly American, "Kitty Hawk," forever memorialized by the Wright brothers:

> *We are not the kind*
> *To stay too confined. . . .*
> *Don't discount our powers. . . .*

It is a long poem, and in Peter Davison's words, "it summons in prophetic terms the history and force of man's inspired wrestle with nature over the centuries past and in the years ahead."

Most poignant was "The War Orphans" by Edith Sitwell, written after seeing a photograph of Korean children asleep in the snow. And most ironic, this poem by Phyllis McGinley:

A LITTLE NIGHT MUSIC

> *It seems vainglorious and proud*
> *Of Atom-man to boast so loud*
> *His prowess homicidal*
> *When one remembers how for years,*
> *With their rude stones and humble spears,*
> *Our sires, at wiping out their peers,*
> *Were almost never idle.*
>
> *Despite his under-fissioned art*
> *The Hittite made a splendid start*
> *Toward smiting lesser nations;*
> *While Tamerlane, it's widely known,*
> *Without a bomb to call his own*
> *Destroyed whole populations.*
>
> *Nor did the ancient Persian need*
> *Uranium to kill his Mede,*
> *The Viking earl, his foeman.*
> *The Greeks got excellent results*
> *With swords and engined catapults.*
> *A chariot served the Roman.*
>
> *Mere cannon garnered quite a yield*
> *On Waterloo's tempestuous field.*
> *At Hastings and at Flodden*
> *Stout countrymen, with just a bow*
> *And arrow, laid their thousands low.*
> *And Gettysburg was sodden.*

> *Though doubtless now our shrewd machines*
> *Can blow the world to smithereens*
>   *More tidily and so on,*
> *Let's give our ancestors their due.*
> *Their ways were coarse, their weapons few.*
> *But ah! how wonderously they slew*
>   *With what they had to go on.*

There were essays by Dr. Carl Jung, James B. Conant, Max Beerbohm, Reinhold Niebuhr, and Edwin Way Teale, twenty-nine contributions in all, mounted in a typographical format with color by that master artist designer Gyorgy Kepes. It was the most distinctive issue in our history and the first to carry the *Atlantic* to a sale of over 350,000 copies. For the contents we paid $20,000.

Hemingway's words about "those old men," Mr. Eisenhower and Dulles, "at the Peace Talks . . . where everybody else knows the United States is out of business" are not easily forgotten; not in 1957 when they were spoken, not today when men who have retired from high posts in our government are wondering, "Can we make it?" It would be hard to find two more dedicated Americans than General Eisenhower and John Foster Dulles as they assumed office. What went wrong?

Eisenhower was chosen by General Marshall for his diplomatic ability to firm up and, when necessary, conciliate his joint command of British veterans and confident, impulsive Americans, and he held the loyalty of both. Informally Ike spoke with compelling charm. For more thoughtful occasions he was what John McCloy called "a yellow-pad man," writing out on yellow pads in longhand what was in his mind and heart. At war's end he so wrote the Guildhall address he delivered in London, clearly the most moving testament to Anglo-American unity ever uttered.

Such clarity deserted him at the Wednesday morning press conferences during his presidency. He seldom declined to answer a question even if it was obvious that he had not been sufficiently briefed and knew little about the issue. James R. Reston, Washington correspondent of the *New York Times*, once said to me: "The American public will never realize how far the press has gone to protect the President at our conferences. Of course, he's been briefed. But when asked a loaded question, a tough one, he'll flush with anger and then submerge in a jumble of words and platitudes. I stop writing. At last, when I hear him say, 'But this I do believe . . .' I know he is coming to the surface and I pay attention." This submergence, this confusion, was especially costly when civil rights were the issue, as they so often were during his two terms.

President Eisenhower's instincts were right even if he lacked the words to express them in what I have called "the presidential voice." But because he depended so much on the chain of command he was at times misled by his subordinates. Ike's instinct told him not to condone Senator McCarthy at their meeting in Milwaukee, but his political advisors persuaded him to give the appearance of endorsement. Was there no one in the National Security Council astute enough to ground the U-2 spy flights months before the summit meeting with Khrushchev in Paris? Why didn't the General himself dismiss the half-baked scheme for the "liberation" of Cuba instead of passing on the mess to Kennedy? Even as I ask these questions I remember how charming Ike was at the "trout luncheon" in the Dartmouth Grant, and with what conviction he gave us his farewell warning against "the military-industrial complex."

Had John Foster Dulles possessed the objectivity of Henry Stimson, he would have been a better Secretary of State. But he was a zealot, a cold, righteous one, indulging his own convictions, believing they must be right for the country. He lost the confidence of our allies, he destroyed Anthony Eden, and in Asia, handing out mutual defense pacts to whatever weakling asked, he pieced together that paper tiger, SEATO, and tied us inevitably into the disaster in Vietnam. Yes, this is hindsight, but it is not hindsight to ask why a man of such moral indignation did not have the political courage to support those career officers in State whom he must have known were not guilty of McCarthy's charges. The scars and timidity he left behind him in the State Department were still there when Ed Murrow went down to serve in it in 1961.

The more you do, the more you find to do. While we were preparing our Centennial issue, my decisive managing editor, Emily Flint, and I, on weekends, were scrutinizing the one hundred million words which had appeared in the magazine in the past. We both went through the years of Abolition, the Civil War, and carpetbaggers. I asked Em, very sensitive about women's prerogatives, to take the years 1870 to 1900, when our editors seemed surprised that women could do anything right but multiply. We shared the twentieth century. It became obvious that the *Atlantic* was most vital when the country was aroused, but at its second best when, under Thomas

Bailey Aldrich, editor and country were complacent. For one six months' period Aldrich could find no other poet worthy of publication but himself.

To avoid the weary trudge of chronology we arranged the selections under subjects which were of recurring interest to all nine editors, with the advantage that we could place the writers of the 1860s side by side with those of the 1940s. It may be sacrilegious to think of cutting Emerson and Thoreau, but when they were too long-winded we did. We did not cut short stories or poetry. Such became *Jubilee: One Hundred Years of the Atlantic,* a volume of 740 pages, chosen as a special premium of the Book-of-the-Month Club. As I wrote the introduction and some 20,000 notes of identification, the royalties were amicably divided: 60 percent to Weeks, 40 percent to Flint.

We naturally began with the subject "One Nation Indivisible," in which Lincoln predominated, and ended with "A Divided World," in which Theodore Roosevelt, Walter Hines Page, Woodrow Wilson, Brooks Adams, William James, Alfred North Whitehead, Albert Einstein, and Walter Lippmann, writing at the conclusion of national crises, spoke their warnings about the future. I quote briefly from three of the writers who struck us as particularly relevant.

Brooks Adams, in 1903, in his survey of Empire, of which ours was then the baby, concludes:

The tale of Rome is threadbare; that of England is still new. If our people would know the price which Great Britain is now paying for defeats a century old, they may learn . . . in the report of the Inspector General of Recruiting on the degeneracy of the British army.

Alfred North Whitehead, in 1939, after scrutinizing the dissatisfaction of the Arabs in Palestine:

Any fusion of Jewish and Arab interests must be produced by the Jews and Arabs themselves. This primary objective of statesmanship seems to have been largely overlooked by the Jewish controlling agencies. It would not be fair to the mass of emigrants from Central Europe to expect from them any insight into the complications of Syrian life, but the controlling agencies in England and the United States might have been asked to show some grasp of the essential objectives.

Unfortunately in public utterances, whatever may have been done behind the scenes, there has predominated the demand that Great Britain should force upon Palestine an unrestricted Jewish domination. In one instance there was even a suggestion that the Jewish agencies should refuse to attend any conference to which dissentient Arabs were to be admitted.

This attitude, if maintained, is signing the death warrant of the Jewish home in Palestine — perhaps not today, but in the near future. In the region of large political affairs, the test of success is twofold — namely, survival power and compromise.

No one perceived the early results of our "melting pot" more accurately than my cousin Dr. Alice Hamilton. A graduate of Bryn Mawr who had taken her M.D. at the University of Michigan, she then became the junior partner of Jane Addams at Hull House in Chicago. Her clinic in that famous settlement house drew her into industrial medicine. When at my urging she was writing her autobiography, *Exploring the Dangerous Trades*, I asked her which of the many bloodstreams in our multiracial society were the swiftest to be "Americanized." Her summing up, so true to her spirit, appeared in our group entitled "The City."

The Greeks moved fastest. They were single-minded in their pursuit of business; they came to our classes long enough to get a working knowledge of English, but they wasted no time over unpractical subjects. The Jews came next, for though they too were good in business, even then they had a wide range of other interests and some of them were dreamy idealists. Bohemians soon took the upper jobs in industry; Italians and Poles were slower to reach prosperity, but they too climbed up.

The only exceptions I ever met were a few Irish families which were wrecked by drink and went steadily down from bad to worse. An Irish policeman once said to me, "There's nothing better than a good Irishman and there's nothing worse than a bad one." It is true. Among the Irish I met in the slums were poets and artists. They had the manners and the charm of old aristocracy — and they could sink to lower depths than any other immigrants. I wonder if those two things go together — that to be capable of the highest carries with it a capacity to fall the lowest. Certainly among the Irish wrecks from drink were some of the warmest, most generous, and most lovable people I have known.

CHAPTER

XVI

Détente with the Soviet Union reached a peak in the summer of 1959. Never since have we and they had such an opportunity to inspect, admire, and criticize each other. The stage was set by Khrushchev in a speech in which he repudiated the tyranny of Stalin; inside Russia it created incredible relief and an expectation of better living conditions, and outwardly a lessening of hostility. Vice President Nixon's visit to Moscow early in 1959 opened the door for Khrushchev's visit to the United States that fall. Meanwhile plans for the American Exhibition in Sokolniki Park, Moscow, were in a final stage: everything we were to display — our books about Russia, our outboards, our fashions, automobiles, paintings, everything characteristically American — had been approved by the Soviet censors and were on the way. In addition, there was to be "a cultural exchange" of doctors, artists, writers, and scientists; the Americans to arrive in the spring and summer of 1959, the Soviet delegations to come to us some months later.

I was very pleased to be chosen by the State Department as one of the four to represent American authors and editors. The others were Arthur M. Schlesinger, Jr., biographer of FDR, Professor of History at Harvard, and a friendly contributor to the *Atlantic*; Alfred Kazin, whose literary essays and autobiography we featured, and Paddy Chayefsky, the playwright, whom I did not know. His popular film *Marty* was to be shown in two hundred Soviet theaters while we were there. Carl Sandburg with his guitar would pay a short visit, and Leonard Bernstein was to conduct the New York Philharmonic in a series of concerts.

Our passports with Dutch and Russian visas would be delivered

241

by a courier before our flight to Moscow via Amsterdam on August first. We were each told to bring seventy pounds of books (and, for me, copies of the *Atlantic*) to present to the writers' unions. I asked permission to carry my flyrod and some flies for Mikhail Sholokhov, the novelist, with whom I hoped to fish on the Don. The only caution was to be careful when eating chicken Kiev, a delicacy stuffed with seasoned butter. Cleaning establishments were non-existent.

At the Soviet Embassy, the Cultural Attaché, an intelligent woman with flawless English, said we would be the guests of the writers' unions in Moscow, Leningrad, Kiev, and probably Tashkent: there would be round-table discussions and visits to authors in their dachas, summer homes, informally, at tea or for supper. She suggested we prepare a list of those writers we hoped to talk to.

My staff thought highly of my going: it might enable me to scout Soviet writers for a Russian supplement. I asked what they'd like me to bring back to them; only one, Phoebe Adams, spoke up: "a fur hat." I took my inoculations, packed books and magazines, attended a farewell cocktail party — and twenty-four hours before departure Washington telephoned that our Russian visas had not yet arrived. Alfred, Paddy, and I agreed that we'd fly anyway and pick up our visas at the Soviet Embassy in The Hague. Schlesinger decided to follow later.

The supper on the KLM flight, with a pleasant wine, was a relief after the pandemonium of Idlewild Airport, and the three of us took stock. I always enjoy Kazin, so hearty in his admiration, so contemptuous of what he disapproves. Paddy, a generation younger, was stocky, vital, and impulsive. Both regarded the Soviet delay as a deliberate snub. Perhaps it was; Alfred's parents were from White Russia, Paddy's from the Ukraine. Paddy, privileged to take colored films of our expedition, was carrying a movie camera.

At The Hague our Second Secretary, John Glidden Day, escorted us to the Soviet Embassy; he explained our predicament to an impassive Slav, who unlocked the safe, withdrew a huge ledger and puzzled over the hand-written instructions of what to do for "American Specialists" in need of visas. He seemed perplexed that we had traveled this far without them, but promised to telephone when they arrived.

I did not mind marking time a little in Holland. The weather was perfect, the restaurants excellent, the museums with their exquisite Rembrandts and Vermeers a joy. Alfred was eager to see the War Memorial in Rotterdam, which Lewis Mumford had praised in the *New Yorker*. Although the Dutch had proclaimed it an "open city" the Nazis had bombed to death the old town and its inhabitants. This the Dutch had rebuilt with low-level apartments and shops of gaily colored material, interspersed with touching little reminders, in modern sculpture (mother leading child who is covering her eyes in fear). Looming against the sky were the two memorials of metal, both designed by Russian exiles, one geometric, the other a towering figure in anguish, hands upraised, lips in outcry, an unutterable protest against brutality. We visited the Rembrandt House and Rijksmuseum in Amsterdam, returning for a very pleasant cocktail party with our Chargé d'Affaires, Herbert Fales, and his charming wife. Alone I went to little Delft to see the convent-fortress, the Prinsenhof, in which William of Orange had raised the rebellion against Philip II. (But we should have been in Russia!) On the sixth day, in a rage, Alfred and Paddy flew to London. Three hours later our visas arrived and I wired them to return.

They caught up lost sleep for much of the flight in the clean Soviet jet, waking in time for us to begin our separate lists of the Russians we hoped to meet. Each list began with "Boris Pasternak," who we heard was under house arrest. The Russians revere him as a poet; *Dr. Zhivago* was his only novel, and in Soviet eyes his fiction is minor compared to that of Mikhail Sholokhov (*And Quiet Flows the Don*). Had the Nobel Prize been divided between Pasternak and Sholokhov, it might have been more difficult to refuse.

To meet us at the Moscow Airport were Morris Rotherberg, Second Secretary of our Embassy, four members of the Writers' Union, headed by Alexei Surkov, the former president, and Frieda Lourie, the first of our several translators, fluent, dark-eyed and eager. Thunderheads burst into a torrent as we crossed the bridge leading to Red Square and gave us a dramatic first sight of the Kremlin walls, the golden onion domes and crosses of St. Basil's Cathedral, and Lenin's Tomb. There was a rainbow, perhaps a good omen, as we drew up before the Sovietskaya, reserved for VIPs and by far the best hotel in Russia. It was built above and around the Gar, that pre-Revolutionary restaurant, described by Bruce Lockhart in *British Agents*, where Rasputin once used to entertain. Perhaps it was my seniority which entitled me to such a suite: vestibule, large living room with a serving table covered with a white cloth, bedroom with twin beds, a dressing room with pier glass and closets, and a bathroom for hot tub or shower.

We dined in the Gar at 10:15, Frieda helping us to order not only dinner but breakfast for the following morning. Our table was reserved for us by the small American flag as a centerpiece. So, I noticed were other tables for other nationals, East Germans, Chinese, and other Asiatics. Russian couples danced between the tables, the men in shirt-sleeves, the women in cotton prints, to the deafening jazz of an orchestra on the stage. There was one strikingly handsome Russian pair, the girl a lovely brunette with blue embroidery at the throat and on the sleeves of her white blouse. At midnight we left for a ride on the Metro to Red Square. It is the most immaculate and ornate subway I have ever seen: a very deep escalator leading to a platform of marble, inlaid and gilded, with crystal chandeliers overhead. As if to say: we who for centuries have gazed from a distance into noble interiors shall now put them to everyday use. The Square, with its immensely wide avenues, was impressive in the moonlight. On the lower step of the reviewing stand sat an American student answering in Russian the questions of a cluster of Muscovites.

After deep sleep our first duty was to attend the annual Exhibition of Economic Achievement of the sixteen Republics, a multi-colossal state fair of the best produce in the USSR. Crowds were pouring in, by train, bus, army truck, and in farm trucks with boards for seats — Frieda said there would be 200,000 by noon. Small fry were fishing for carp in the artificial lake; we joined their elders and were shown through Butter, Tobacco, Flowers, Atomic Energy (pictures of atomic powered ice-breakers and the isotopes for medical use). Paddy, suffering visibly from indigestion, wilted, and was taxied back to the hotel. Alfred and I plugged on, peering into building after building, some of Asiatic design, until we reached the fountains, the mammoth statue of Lenin — and a taxi at last. Yes, a prodigious display, of which the people were obviously proud.

After lunch I was preparing to nap when I discovered that I had been wired for sound: there on the carpet of my living room lay a 2-foot strip of thin, bright wire, presumably knocked loose by the powerful Katinka while cleaning. I laid it on the serving table where I was to place other shreds in days to come. Each time, they were removed. That evening before we went to see a puppet show, I ordered chicken Kiev, speared it incautiously, and a dark liquid spurted over my lapel. I mopped it with water, and before retiring, explained the disaster by repeating "Chicken Kiev" to the iron matron who presided over our floor. Next morning the coat was returned, spotless.

This was our day of official welcome. A car provided by the Writers' Union drove us to our Embassy, where Ambassador "Tommy" Thompson gave us friendly advice. Then with our gifts we went to the headquarters of the Moscow Writers' Union. As we en-

tered the drive I had a picture not unlike that of a Southern planta-
tion, white columns at the entrance, poppies in the grass plot before
the door, and in the turn-around the brooding, seated figure of
Tolstoy, the only statue of him in Moscow.

Our meeting was presided over by Alexei Surkov, which surprised
me as "Mr. K" had removed him from the presidency. But then and
in all meetings thereafter he was present as a watchful commissar
and our closest touch with the Politburo. Some thirty writers faced
us across a green baize-covered table and two interpreters were at
our backs. Our books and magazines were presented and, as a greet-
ing seemed expected, I spoke, hoping to point up topics of interest
before we approached the sensitive controversy over royalties. I mentioned the disappearance of American stories in dialect: "The Negro,
the Irish (who are the bosses of Boston), the Germans, Italians, the
Island Greeks, the Poles, the Armenians, and many others, have been
blending their talent into one evolving language which is American.
This movement, which I believe has its parallel in your country . . ."

Surkov was having none of that. "The Soviet Union is producing
literature in sixty languages!" he asserted. Kazin remembers my
saying, "Golly!" — a word I never use, but there was no hiding my
incredulity. Alfred, in his memoir *New York Jew*, goes on, "Now
Surkov is wearing me out as his mighty voice, his great Russian wind
instrument of a voice, fills the room with literary statistics." Such
was the formal beginning of our "exchange." Our critical questions
occasionally brought a flush: a Russian would retaliate with something equally disparaging and indignantly each side would try to
score points.

Finally, Surkov, glancing at the list of those we wished to see,
each headed by Pasternak, remarked, "Between Pasternak and ourselves there is a peaceful coexistence." Before the meeting ended
we were told that the car and driver would be at our disposal throughout our stay in Moscow, and that we were each to receive 300 rubles
"for presents."

We learned several things as those round-tables continued. We
learned how over-confident the Russians were of their knowledge of
contemporary American writers. Hemingway they revere and have
admirably translated; they put him at the top, followed by Erskine
Caldwell (one of the few to whom they do pay a royalty), Arthur
Miller, and Lillian Hellman. They alluded to Theodore Dreiser, who
in his dotage had written love letters to Stalin and a last book, *Tragic
America*, of Communist vaporings. Kazin ironically corrected them.
"He was 'ga-ga' at the end," Alfred said, and launched into one of

his swift, salty interpretations, asking, incidentally, if they had any novel of William Faulkner's in translation, or of Saul Bellow, or Thornton Wilder, J. D. Salinger, or Norman Mailer? "No."

When Schlesinger joined us his queries, even jocular, were hard-nosed. "Why, at breakfast must Gospodin Weeks be obliged to read a copy of *Pravda* in translation instead of the Paris edition of the *Herald Tribune*, which we cannot buy here? Anyone can buy a copy of *Pravda* in Washington." Pause, a reproachful look: did we expect them to litter up their bookstores with all those half-naked women which they saw on the newsstands in New York City?

We learned how sensitive they were to our questions — why did they not pay royalties to foreign authors, even Hemingway? — and our queries about the prescribed formula for "Socialist Realism" — that novelists and poets should celebrate "a positive hero," should avoid any criticism that reflects unfavorably on the authority, and be puritanical in writing of sex. As always happened both sides were more candid after the round-table dissention broke up. While we were eating grapes, a poet who had boasted of receiving 40,000 letters in response to his long patriotic poem drew me aside. "Try to understand our relations with our readers," he said. "During the early years [of the Revolution] it was imperative that we reach and sustain them. This was imperative during the War. Later there will be time for latitude and experiments." (But how much "later"?)

We lunched with Henry Shapiro, the calm, wise correspondent for the United Press in Moscow for over twenty-five years. The Soviets respected him, respected his marriage to a beautiful Russian, and were in no hurry to see him go. Present were his attractive daughter, who had studied at Barnard, and Marshall Shulman of Harvard. Sholokhov was a friend of Shapiro's and when in town would stop by for some "American vodka" (bourbon). "I doubt," Henry said to me, "if they'll let you fish with him on the Don. There's a good deal of poverty, and still some resistance, there. If he comes to Moscow I'll let you know." And it was through Henry that we received a caution from Pasternak: please not to press our request; it would be denied and might lead to his further humiliation. He appreciated our interest.

Henry told us of Khrushchev's speech before the annual Congress of Soviet Writers, lasting two and a half hours, how he had asked for more lively books, protesting that the crop of contemporary novels was so dull he had had to stick pins in himself to keep awake. Henry said that when "Mr. K" mentioned the famous poet Anna Akhmatova by name, she fainted — Stalin having exiled her son because of his mother's defiance — and was revived to hear "K" praise her work. And that he had insisted on the publication of Solzhenitsyn's *One Day in the Life of Ivan Denisovich*, which had previously been prohibited. Paddy was on his high horse, baiting the pretty daughter about the freedom she must have enjoyed at Barnard. She took it well and did not conceal her divided affection for New York and Moscow.

Our visits to distinguished writers in their homes were relaxed and enjoyable. A translator accompanied us and, in Moscow, the ever-present Surkov. (I could never be sure whether he was watch-dogging us or our host.) Protocol took us first to the dacha of Konstantin Fedin, an airy summer house in a lovely grove of white birch. It was in keeping with "K's" liberalization that Fedin should have replaced the censorious Surkov as president of the Union of Soviet Writers. In voice and appearance he was a gentle man: as he served tea he mentioned his pleasure in bird-watching, and, with our schedule in mind, he spoke of Tolstoy, wished to be sure we had set aside one day to visit Yasnaya Polyana in Tula, Tolstoy's country house, even though it was a very long drive. He reminded us that 1960 would mark the fiftieth anniversary of Tolstoy's death. I liked Fedin's rumination: that Tolstoy seems to be saying to his heroes — show me your attitude toward death . . . not one of his beloved heroes, Rostov, Volkonsky, Kutuzov, Natasha, Tushin, or Pierre, is made to die a pitiful, unworthy death. Fedin's essay on Tolstoy was the first I commissioned for our Russian issue.

The aging Samuil Marshak received us in an apartment walled with books. He was of Robert Frost's vintage, his career bridging the years between Czarist Russia and Khrushchev. Gorky heard his youthful poems at a reading in 1904 when Chaliapin and Glazunov, the composer, were also present; later, when Marshak became ill with tuberculosis Gorky sent him to convalesce in Yalta; and on recovery in 1911, to London to learn English. Marshak's teacher was a Scot, and while in England Marshak translated Blake, Wordsworth, and, more improbable, Burns. His translation of Burns's poems in Russian had now sold over 700,000 copies, which in addition to his own poetry had made Marshak wealthy. Naturally what I wanted from him was a profile of Maxim Gorky — and the manuscript reached me in Boston shortly before Marshak's death.

One late afternoon as I was freshening for dinner I glanced out my window to see in the wing opposite and on my level a striking-looking brunette in white, framed in her casement and gazing steadily at me. It had happened before. Was she merely curious, as I was, or a plant? How, with that impassive dragon seated by the elevators, was I to know? I never did.

That evening Alfred, Paddy, Frieda, and I went to the Popov Circus, an altogether glorious performance. At twenty-seven Popov was an irresistable clown, blond, innocent-eyed, witty and credulous. All the action centered in a single ring, with none of the distraction of Ringling's. The animal acts, the glossy trained bear, the tigers swimming in their tank were of surprising effect; and always the inquiring Popov tripping in and out. Beside me was a blond twelve-year-old boy, dissolved in tears of laughter. His mirth gave us a double-take. During the intermission I bought a large slab of sweet chocolate which I presented to him. Mother grateful — but "only one piece now."

It was at Leningrad that we encountered the first deliberate hostility. We left at midnight on the Black Arrow, a train so overcrowded that Alfred and Paddy shared one compartment; the female interpreter, whom I shall call "A," and I in the compartment adjoining. Nothing unusual about this in the Soviet Union and despite the boys' sly innuendoes as they passed our open door, "A" took it as a matter of course. She was the most interesting of our translators, married — her husband a physicist — well read, and reserved. To meet us came the Secretary of the Leningrad Union, an Armenian, who confided to "A" as we walked down the platform that he despised Americans and would do as little as possible to entertain us. He was as good as his word, for that afternoon at what we thought was to be a welcome he had us driven out to a Writers' Home — for retired hacks, translators, aging authors of children's books — of whom a languid eight were rounded up to receive our gifts and exchange "civility." The home was on what had once been the Finnish seacoast and on the way back "A," incensed by the Armenian's rudeness, told us what he had said. "To hell with the Writers' Union!" said Paddy. "Let's see what I can do at the Leningrad Film Studio."

He did plenty. "A" got us an early appointment — "No more than thirty minutes, please" — with the director, Yuri Nikolayev, and, despite the crowded waiting room, Paddy charmed that forthright, attractive man for the remainder of the morning. A Kirghiz ballet was on location and on our way to the set the dancers sped by us in the corridor, the girls beautiful in their exotic costumes. "One of the nice things about our profession," Paddy said to Nikolayev, "are the people we have to work with." The Russian paused, listening to the translation, then burst into a roar of laughter. He had us ensconced on what might have been a throne, and in the rehearsal the boys with their swords and spears, the girls with their beauty all but devoured us in their ballet. Back in the director's office, Paddy played his ace: in the course of the next two days would it be possible for an assistant to show us reels of those pictures which had made Nikolayev's reputation? "You mean you'll come back both morning and afternoon?" "Yes — and might the director or producer of each film be presented to us briefly?" Nikolayev nodded with pride.

It was a blessed deliverance from the repulsive Armenian. We began with three reels of *Eugene Onegin*, in color, with music by the Leningrad Symphony. What a masterpiece! — the costuming superb, the exciting duel in the snow, the interiors the real interiors of the old palaces. Then to a projection room with a wide screen, where we saw the great actor Cherkasov play the lead in *Don Quixote* — never shown in the United States — and I invited the director of that film, Grigory Kozintsev, to do an article for us on the making of Russian movies. We saw the sets and rehearsal of Chekhov's "The Lady with the Dog"; two ballets, parts of *The Woman Who Tamed the Tigers* and too much of *The Last Inch*, a tearjerker at which Paddy hooted. (It seemed to me the Russians weep more readily than we do at the theater, but the few plays we attended were war plays, touching scars still livid.) As we took our farewell of Nikolayev, Paddy expressed our gratitude, smiling as he asked: "What happens if the Bosses disapprove of a new film?" With a broad grin the Russian drew his forefinger across his throat. No, I thought to myself, you're too valuable.

Alfred had his happiest exploration at the Hermitage, the admirable art gallery adjoining the Winter Palace. The French Impressionist — Degas, Cézanne, Monet — and Picasso paintings purchased prior to the Revolution had rarely been exhibited but were out of storage, to his delight. And at any hour the beauty of Leningrad drew us out in our car to the Nevsky Prospekt, where elders in white blouses, Chekhov characters, were drinking tea. This sad, wonderfully designed, dilapidated old capital with its bridges, canals, and pastel palaces had lost one quarter of its inhabitants in the German siege and its side streets were still pitted with shell holes. Some shrines were restored, Peter's little hut, where he lived while the marshes were being drained, the restored exterior of the exquisite seaside Peterhof, which the Germans had demolished, and the grisly cells in the Fortress of Peter and Paul, each identified by photos of former inmates. One doubts if Leningrad ever again would be a seat of power.

We returned to Moscow, no longer VIPs, as we were consigned

to ordinary rooms at the Ukrainia, a vast, colorless hotel whose elevators seemed permanently stuck on different floors. Arthur Schlesinger arrived, and the four of us were driven out to watch how the Russians were reacting to the American Exhibition in Sokolniki Park. It is a large park, which now was crowded with viewers and long lines patiently waiting their turn. We arrived just as the Fashion Show was being announced by the director, Vera Zerina, an attractive designer from New York, a Russian-speaking Pole with a Manhattan sense of humor. From the platform before the dressing rooms ran a long serpentine promenade at eye level and packed around it were some two to three thousand men and women, laughing at the director's jokes until suddenly stilled by the entrance of the models in gay sport clothes. They acted in pantomime, donning rain gear as an imaginary thunderstorm threatened (all the while the speaker described materials and prices), and dashing indoors to reappear as a wedding party and later in business or evening dress. The whole performance with its brief intermissions ran to about forty-five minutes. I fell for the chic Zerina, as did the Russians, some of whom locked arms to hold their place for a repeat performance.

Beside the fashion promenade, originally there had been four small booths for complimentary hair-dos. But in the opening week, when admission to the Exhibition was limited to the highest Party officials, every woman wanted one, and what with the crowding and exasperation, in the name of peace the hair-do parlors vanished.

In the small lake were skiffs with American outboards, tethered to a stake with yards of rope. Father would take the kids aboard, pull the starter and go the limit, turn about and try again. The new models of our cars were not the imposing gas-guzzlers but the smaller and lighter — light enough for five Russians to lift while one crawled beneath to look at the underside.

The selection of American books about Russia reached back to the elder George Kennan's classic on Siberia, and included biography, economic studies, volumes of literary and critical essays. After they had been winnowed by the Soviet censors the books were listed by our librarians and replacement copies of what they thought might be provocative — and possibly stolen — were shipped to our Embassy. They were right: certain titles had to be replaced in the exhibit; the most popular volume was the Sears, Roebuck catalogue, and this was replaced daily.

But it was the display of modern American painting and sculpture which produced the most intense and fascinating "exchange" in the entire Exhibition. During the early years of the Revolution, the Communist Party had denounced abstract art as "decadent," "bourgeois," and "uncultured," had forbidden its exhibition, and driven into exile Wassily Kandinsky, Marc Chagall, Naum Gabo, and his brother, Antoine Pevsner. It was to be expected that *Isvestia* would come down hard on such works in our display, and so did *Pravda*. Actually they were in a minority, since the selections were made by a jury of art historians to show *what had been going on in all aspects of American painting and sculpture* since the Russians had cut themselves off from the West.

We had two Curators. Mrs. Edith Halpert made a crucial decision: she installed the eighteenth- and nineteenth-century paintings on the ground floor of the Glass Pavilion, where the Stuarts, the Copleys, and the Winslow Homers were so understandable that the Russians termed them "the Eisenhower art." The contemporary art, including the more abstract, she placed in the galleries on the second floor, and, anticipating their attraction, she managed to procure metal barriers for protection from the crowds of viewers.

It fell to the second curator, Mr. Richard McLanathan, who took charge after the opening, to elucidate the meaning of what was shown in the galleries. "The paintings and sculpture," he wrote later, "provided the most obvious demonstration of freedom of expression and of choice in America, and the very strangeness to the Russians of some of the more abstract art merely served to emphasize this further. The galleries became a common meeting ground for Russians and Americans to discuss not only art but also many other aspects of American and Russian life."

McLanathan wrote for *all* the works of art explanatory labels which, translated into Russian, were photographically enlarged so as to be read from a distance. He prepared an explanation of the entire exhibit which was recorded in Russian on tape and broadcast in the gallery areas and indoors and out. Both he and Mrs. Halpert instructed our young Russian-speaking guides in the basic facts of modern art so they could answer the questions of viewers who habitually locked arms to hold their place before a puzzling picture. For instance, they would stand arguing before Jack Levine's painting "The Homecoming," depicting a cadaverous general, with many decorations, at a banquet, seated beside a fawning woman and his aides. The general is reaching for a stalk of celery. "What is the meaning?" they would ask one of our young undergraduate guides. "Non-war," she would reply. Light breaks, followed by grins, nodding of heads. "*Da, da.*" Then, "What became of the artist?" "He is painting as usual." "Isn't this the painting that President Eisenhower didn't like, and some woman publicly criticized his taste? What happened to her?" "She came to Moscow as the first curator of this exhibition."

From one to three o'clock every day the galleries were open only to artists, museum personnel, teachers, and advanced art students and to them our larger, handsome catalogues were distributed. When word of this got about, 90 percent of the throng suddenly styled themselves "artists." Since all Soviet citizens must carry their credentials, the Soviet guards good-naturedly screened out the imposters. For the professional audience McLanathan did a 30-minute gallery guidance, and it became so popular that he had frequently to repeat it. As the numbers kept rising he called on visiting American art experts to help with the elucidation, and, diplomatically, he used English-speaking Soviets to interpret.

There were genuine artists among the Russian visitors, though not all were members of the Artists' Union, because, as one expressed it, he "didn't want to paint nothing but politics." Despite the almost constant presence of secret police, a number were able to show our curators photographs of their work, including several who later participated in exhibitions which were broken up by the KGB with bulldozers and firehoses. "Since the opinion of an informed Westerner meant much to them," McLanathan recalled, "we acknowledged the commendable quality of most of the work, and the outstanding level achieved by a few of these courageous men and women, dedicated to continuing a vital native Russian creative tradition."

Numbers tell their story. In previous American exhibitions abroad it was estimated that between 200,000 and 400,000 came to view our art. In Moscow the number of viewers rose to over 1,000,000 — and the daily problem was to keep them moving!

Pasternak, as I have said, was beyond our reach; nor was I permitted to fish with Sholokhov, or meet him. (The flies I brought with me I ultimately gave to him in Washington when he came in Khrushchev's party.) Alfred and I did, however, enjoy a lively meeting with Aleksandr Tvardovski and the editorial staff of *Novy Mir*, a meeting, as my diary records, which was frank and informative. I liked Tvardovski, a poet, handsome, broad-shouldered, with fine blue eyes. He and Konstantin Simonov have alternated in editing the literary *Novy Mir*, a monthly, well printed, well illustrated, and of 250 large pages — so spacious that it can run long poems and serialize a novel in two issues. It has a huge circulation — and no advertising to worry about! As the editor of an old, struggling independent, I could only look upon this fat, state-supported beauty with envy.

I distributed six copies of the *Atlantic*, and the staff were commenting on its make-up as Surkov walked in, but he did not disturb our professional exchange. I explained that our larger issues were of a 64-page form plus a 32 and a 16 (less than half the size of *Novy Mir*) and that our editions were larger in the autumn than in summer. They asked about "my Publisher," meaning Proprietor, and were amused when I explained our owner's connection with the Deering plow and tractor. I said we read everything offered to us, 50,000 manuscripts or more a year; they said theirs came "by gravitation," about a quarter of that number; their fees ranged from 3,000 to 4,000 rubles for each 22 pages of type. I said our top fee was $1,000 for a contribution of 8 or 9 of our pages, and we paid more for a serial. I mentioned that our managing editor was a woman — we called her our "hatchet-woman" — who was theirs? When I acted out the translation they laughed and pointed to one they called "the pusher." The question of freedom-to-print-what took us to thin ice; I knew Tvardovski was daring to the point of being reprimanded. Perhaps this explained the alternation of editors.

Russian hospitality begins traditionally with vodka and it will conclude hours later — depending on the capacity of the guests — with vodka. When the four of us accompanied by our interpreter arrived at the Moscow apartment of Konstantin Simonov at five o'clock on a Sunday afternoon, we were greeted by our host and his wife and ushered straightaway into the dining room where at one glance we could see that our work was cut out for us. The long table at which we were seated was covered with appetizers: smoked fish, sunflower seeds, pickled herring, thin black bread, salted cucumber and tomatoes, and caviar with the blinis Madame Simonov soon rustled up. The centerpiece was a tall carafe of white vodka; at my end of the table was a second carafe of pink vodka flavored by the currants at the bottom, and at the opposite end was a third carafe flavored by cherries. "Get down to business," said our host.

Simonov was dressed casually in his old Air Force tunic. He had been a Soviet lion ever since he wrote his heroic novel of the siege of Stalingrad, *Days and Nights*, which, in translation, had been a selection of our Book-of-the-Month Club. His good looks, his close-cropped hair, merry eyes, and a dash of Byron made him quite irresistible. During the war he had fallen in love with the wife of Russia's foremost ace, and when the airman was killed he married the widow, wrote a play about their affair, cast her in the leading role, and was rewarded by having his play produced in two hundred theaters throughout the Soviet Union. His zest and audacity sparked the conversation and as the toasts drew down the vodka, the cold dishes were succeeded by delicious servings of borscht, lamb spitted with peppers, huge bowls of rice, the golden melons and black grapes of Turkestan. You can imagine that we warmed toward each other. The carafes were replenished and when we arose from that table shortly before midnight, we were less steady than when we arrived.

Our delegation had been trying to make up its mind whether to take the long trip to Georgia and the Black Sea or whether to fly the 2,300 miles to Tashkent and Samarkand. Simonov in his enthusiasm decided for us. "Tashkent, by all means!" he said. "That's where I have my dacha. The Uzbeks are marvelous people, straight out of the Middle Ages, and their fruit and lamb are the best in Asia. They were famous warriors under Tamerlane but the fighting has long been bred out of them and they never fired a shot in the war. They are people of the earth, and you'll enjoy them. As for you," he said, pointing to me, "I shall tell my friend Hamid to take you fishing for the blue trout of the Pamir."

The Russians are hero worshippers and they treasure the personal links with the past. One of Lenin's early edicts forbade so far as it could the looting of the great estates. The ancestral costumes preserved enrich the Bolshoi. Many churches have been closed, but the finest of the ikons one sees in the Kremlin have been skillfully cleaned. There is a magnificence and glitter in the museum of the Czars on whose parquet one treads in overshoes of felt, but the Czarina's court gowns and the living quarters of the last Nicholas do not breathe. Occasionally there is a touch of make-believe. On our visit we climbed the outer stairs to the tiny bedroom of Ivan the Terrible. "This is his bed," said the quite lovely blonde who was our guide. It was so narrow and new it might have come from Sears, Roebuck. "Oh, come on!" I exclaimed. "Ivan was big and he loved the girls. What happened to his real bed?" She blushed at my teasing. "It was burned by Napoleon," she said.

What did breathe was Tchaikovsky's home at Klin, a thoughtful renovation, his personal belongings so casually arranged — the unfinished sheet of music on the piano rack, his white kid gloves, cloak, and opera hat in his dressing room, the whole setting as if he had stepped out shortly before we arrived.

The Germans were deliberately vindictive in desecrating such shrines — perhaps scholars had mapped them out in advance. All that remained of Chekhov's dacha was a shell-shattered gatepost bearing the enameled number of his address. The best-preserved memorial is Yasnaya Polyana, Tolstoy's country estate, from which the Soviets had removed the books, paintings, and all personal belongings before its capture. The Germans used the house as a barracks, smashed things up, and applied the torch in their hurried retreat, but members of the historic section saved it and no scars show.

Yasnaya Polyana is 140 kilometers from Moscow, a distance Tolstoy once walked, pack on his back. The road, rough and high-crowned, was, I suspect, little different from what we jolted over. We encountered a succession of the gray-green army trucks, heavily laden and each forcing us into the ditch; after three hours of this we approached Podolsk, the last large town before the overgrown German trenches. I remarked on the number of television masts on the roofs. "No one has a good word for it," said Yuri, our young male interpreter, "but everyone wants a set." "Same with us," said Alfred. Thereafter, the little villages were of rude cabins, rebuilt of peeled logs. We halted in a small square and Alfred inquired the way to a lavatory. "Find a tree," said the village cop.

So, after our brief picnic in a meadow, we came at last to Tolstoy's beech woods and orchards, drove past the duck pond, farm huts, and stables to the white frame house with its vine-covered verandah, where Tolstoy was born and which was his home for sixty-five of his eighty-two years. (The more grandiose mansion of his grandfather had been sold to cover Tolstoy's gambling debts, and no longer survives.)

We were received by Valentin Bulgakov, Tolstoy's last living secretary — "reverential" was the word I used in my diary — in his seventies, clear in memory and with fluent English. (In 1909 one of Tolstoy's banned works had been seized in the mail; the then-secretary was blamed, and Bulgakov, then in his twenties, filled the vacancy.) After a pause in Tolstoy's experimental school we entered the home, a museum with love. On the verandah table were the samovar and tea tray; within the library, the Edison phonograph and primitive Remington (his wife did the endless typing), the boot Tolstoy had been stitching before he took that last walk to the railway station, the crutch and wheelchair for his fading strength, the desk where he wrote *War and Peace*, and on the wall a framed copy of William Lloyd Garrison's handwritten letter, ending, "Freedom for each, for all, forever!" In his bedroom on pegs hung his white blouses and wide-brimmed hat. Next door was the room of his favorite daughter, its walls covered with her paintings of the family and the place. I kept wondering if the religious fervor which once filled the Russian churches had been transferred to shrines like this.

The sun was setting as we walked through the birch woods to Tolstoy's grave. I said to Bulgakov how happy Ambassador Kennan had been to find him there. His face lit up — "That great scholar," he murmured. He went on to recall vividly Tolstoy's final break with his wife, Sonia, and the angry despair with which he strode away from Yasnaya Polyana for the last time. He was speaking of Tolstoy's illness when we came before a turf-covered mound in a silver glade, no marker but the fresh cut flowers on top and beyond, a beautiful vista through the birch forest toward the setting sun. After such a turbulent career it was the most tranquil grave for that great writer, and I wondered if Tolstoy had actually envisioned it in his youth, when he and his brother went searching for "the green stick."

Altogether different was Paddy's visit to his mother's birthplace in the Ukraine. He had expressed his wish to do so at our first meeting in Moscow and repeatedly thereafter; to us it seemed a perfectly natural desire but not to the Soviets. The matter was deferred until we arrived at Kiev, capital of the Ukraine, when he was within range. Then the battle of wills became hot. It appeared that the birthplace, the name of which we had mistranslated as "the village of the sounding drum" was in a desolation, long held by the Germans and one from which virtually all able men and women had been conscripted for slave labor in the Reich. Paddy's family sentiment was opposed by Moscow's determination not to expose such poverty.

While we were shopping — I for two fur hats and embroidered blouses and scarfs — Paddy forced a showdown: he reserved a night flight to Holland and had our interpreter notify Moscow at 8 A.M. that unless a car and driver called for him that morning he would cut short his stay and explain why to the American press. The Union capitulated but sent no car until 11:45 — still hoping to dishearten him — and the drive to the birthplace took five hours. Paddy was the first American the villagers had seen; none of his relatives had survived, but one old man recalled Paddy's uncle and grandfather. He was beginning to take pictures when — before ten minutes were up — the interpreter and the driver hustled him back into the car for the long way home. In darkness Russians drive by "dims," switching to bright only if the road is clear; at the approach of another vehicle (those ever-present trucks), they slow to 20 and pull off to the ditch. Six hours of this can be torture, and when they reached the Kiev airport the last flight to Moscow had departed. But Paddy, exhausted, had accomplished his mission.

Our journey of 2,300 miles from Moscow to the Uzbek Republic took us to the medieval, peaceful part of the Soviet Union. There were two incidents in the long flight. My flyrod in its metal case escaped me and rolled down the aisle, causing confusion — what was this thing the Americanski was carrying? Then, during our stop at Sverdlovsk, a large mining center where we had tea in the airport, Paddy was approached by a Russian who asked for a cigarette. Paddy held out an open pack and was about to light a match. But the miner, who'd been drinking, was accepting no favor: he produced a 10-ruble note, and when Paddy shook his head, tore it to pieces and tossed them into our ashtray. The miner's mate retrieved the scraps, the drunk was hustled out of the bar, and a fellow passenger apologized to us through our interpreter.

For centuries the Uzbeks had suffered invasions, first by the Arabs, next by the Mongols; they rose to their might under Timur (Tamerlane), then, after lapsing into four centuries of tribal rivalry, became a Russian "protectorate," and were forcibly possessed in 1864. Unlike the Afghans, they have accepted their fate, becoming a pastoral, non-militant part of the Soviet Union. Our meeting with their writers was pleasantly relaxed and the Union Secretary, Hamid, had made reservations for us to attend a folk opera, performed in the open Saturday night. And he promised to pick me up before dawn Sunday for the mountain drive in his jeep in search of "the blue trout."

Tashkent, the capital, was part ancient, part new. Our hotel was half-finished, our rooms smelt of fresh plaster, and the opposite wing was only a skeleton. But the "old town" where we spent the first morning was as it had been for centuries: one-story dwellings of adobe facing the market, so alive with people bargaining between the tables heaped with grapes, peaches, and melons. I bought a fisherman's straw hat of Uzbek weave and the boys chose embroidered Uzbek skullcaps.

The throngs were too preoccupied to be distracted by Paddy, who was sighting his movie camera at this colorful bazaar in the baking sunlight. All the while our guide kept apologizing — it was very soon to be torn down and, he assured us, modernized, and did not believe me when I expressed regret.

Moscow had waited until now to show us a farm cooperative, and we saw one of the best. The chairman, a stocky, obviously competent Uzbek farmer, had 1,900 hectares under cultivation: he conducted us through the cotton fields, then to the orchards, and finally to the grape arbors, where in the shadow of one of the tallest a table was spread for our luncheon. It began with a hot, steaming vegetable soup and the dry crisp pancake bread; then, shish-kebab, pilaf, a fortified cold white wine and toasts, vodka and toasts, melons, purple and white grapes, watermelon and more toasts. All of us, including the chairman, were perspiring under the dry, brilliant sunlight as there seemed no end to the delicious fruit. Paddy took some movies of the feast and then unsteadily we swayed our way back to the car and gave our thanks.

On the drive to Tashkent we paused in a village square at the sight of an aged couple, right out of the Old Testament, the prophet, bent, bearded, and blind, being led by his wife, who must surely have been in her late seventies. Alfred sprang from the car and, speaking to them in Hebrew, brought forth a lamentation of persecution which the interpreter did his utmost to quell. In that pitiable encounter it seemed to me Alfred had confirmed his worst suspicions just as Paddy had angrily confirmed his on the exhausting drive to his mother's birthplace. It was a pity as they both had spoken with genuine expectation on our flight from Holland.

Saturday afternoon came a message from Moscow, canceling my drive to the trout streams. "Tell him the water is too low." My companions refused to do so. "The poor devil's been carrying that rod everywhere," said Alfred. "No, Yuri, you've got to do it," and, perspiring in his embarrassment, Yuri did. (I still wonder why Authority forbade my going.) Hamid, I believe, was as disappointed as I. He invited us to a dinner party at his home but told me to bring my rod. We arrived at six o'clock and the vodka toasts were followed by a delicious mutton broth. Then Hamid asked me to put together my rod, which I did on the porch, every move watched by his eleven-year-old son.

Through the outskirts of Tashkent runs a narrow café-au-lait stream, which ends in a cement-faced cascade emptying into a tossing, muddy pool. Having seen the color of the water, I tied on a silver-bodied red and white fly. A procession formed, the eleven-year-old at the head, proudly carrying the flyrod, followed by the rest of our party and curious neighbors who joined along the way. On the hill-top facing the cascade, rugs and a tea-service had been placed. Steps had been cut for me down to the pool. There I cast, while from above jibes drifted down. "Hamid says, why not use a worm?" If there were fish in that brown water I never touched one. When tea was finished, we retraced our march and, leaving the rod on the porch for the boy to examine, I took my place beside Hamid for the resumption of dinner. His final toast was: "To Mr. Weeks, who today has caught nothing but friends!"

At the end of August Alfred and Paddy flew home; our last official function with them was to pay our respects to Lenin's tomb (no longer shared by Stalin). Arthur Schlesinger and I stayed on to see the opening performance at the Bolshoi. It is usually the opera by Glinka which glorifies the uprising, led by Ivan Sussanin, that liberated Greater Russia from Polish domination. It is deeply felt patriotism, magnificent in the massed chorus, sardonic in the ballet, which is a mockery of the Polish court, heroic as Ivan Sussanin rides on stage on his white stallion. Every seat was filled, and the effect on the audience was intoxicating.

I had requested a last favor: to attend the opening of the Gorky Institute, the small, elect college for Soviet writers. Frieda, our interpreter, came with me. I was received by the director, with visible distrust. Beside him sat a more kindly-looking professor of poetry. To my questions they explained that the enrollment was limited to 400 students, selected from the sixteen republics. The youngest in the entering class was twenty-one, the oldest, a former pilot of thirty-four. All had done their military training, worked in forestry, factory, or on the land, publishing their manuscripts in the journals of their trade. Those judged the most promising could attend the Institute for five years; they would become fluent in Russian, and if they lived up to their promise (and respected the canons of "Socialist Realism," which the director did not say but I must), they would return to their native republics to contribute to its literature and be published by the state.

I asked what happened if a student's work fell below expectation? Oh, said the director, other students were being instructed by correspondence courses, and one of the ablest would replace the failure. At this point the professor suggested I might like to attend the first meeting with his new students, and the director, eager to get rid of me, approved.

"There'll be eighteen in the class," said the professor, as we moved down the corridor. "I'm going to ask each to read one of his poems and explain its meaning. They will be very nervous — more so in your presence." So we entered a room of intent, open-collared — it was still warm in Moscow — young writers. Frieda and I sat off to one side. I could sense the humor in his welcome and the smiling reference to me. Then beginning at his left the professor called on a tall Estonian to recite one of his poems in his native language, and explain in Russian what it meant. Next were a couple of Georgians, then a more sophisticated student from Moscow, then a Mongol, and an Uzbek, until all were heard. Most of them read, the paper trembling.

Frieda would whisper the theme. One who had worked in the mines compared the darkness of the pits to the darkness in his life when his father had been killed in the defense of Kiev; the pilot spoke of the exhilaration of flying amidst the parapets of white clouds; more than one dreaded the threat of atomic disaster. They were eager, clean-looking and serious. Often I recognized the ballad form — and, in the diversity of tongues, I realized why the translator is more highly respected than with us.

Afterwards I tried to fit the pieces together. They would become familiar with Russian but would be expected to go on writing in their native tongue. They would be drilled in Marxist dialectic, and imbued with the four canons of "Socialist Realism." First, to write about "a positive hero" — who leads, who excels in his calling, and who will suffer any sacrifice for Mother Russia. Second, to respect the physical attraction of sex, but not to describe it voluptuously. Third, to be critical of personal inefficiency or corruption, as found, say, in the slovenly chairman of a cooperative farm. But never criticize the Politburo. Finally, if one cannot contrive a happy ending, leave the possibility of hope, of dignity, of heroism in death.

At what I think was our last round-table meeting in Moscow Arthur Schlesinger asked the hardest question. "How does it feel to have to write under thought-control?" Several of the Russians flushed in angry resentment but it was the veteran novelist Leonid Leonov, winner of the Lenin Award, the Soviet equivalent of the Nobel Prize in Literature, who replied in even tones. "It is not easy. Three times in my career my work has been questioned: in 1921 when in my first novel I described the corrupt underground in our Revolution, again in the 1930s when a story of mine was not approved, and, thirdly, when a play of mine could not be produced until after Stalin's death." I wondered if an American novelist, under suspicion during the McCarthy purge, would have answered as honestly.

I returned to Boston having commissioned twenty-one contributions for an issue on the arts in the Soviet Union. With the exception of a poem by Mayakovsky it was all contemporary; half the contents were written in response to my suggestions, the rest selected from *Novy*

Mir or recent Russian books. All the writers I had come to admire were included: Sholokhov, Pasternak, Marshak, Leonov, Fedin, Kataev, Simonov, Margarita Aliger. In his short poem "To My Critics" (translated, as were all the poems, by Babette Deutsch and Avrahm Yarmolinsky), Aleksandr Tvardovski expressed what I believed this talented group had at heart.

> *Teach me, would you, my critics, give me a facile*
> *Lesson: yes, according to you*
> *I must be deaf, blind, shape my verses*
> *By what I may and what I may not do.*
>
> *But forgive me if I foresee a future*
> *Hour, oh, not near, when you'll hector me,*
> *You yourselves, questioning, insisting:*
> *Poet, where were you? What was it you did see?*

That special issue appeared in June 1960, and on the newsstands was the most successful of the year.

The purpose of the "exchange," as I understood, was to admire talent, to look below the surface and compare what we saw with what we knew was below the surface at home, and to reach out for understanding. The Soviet writers are as dedicated, and as desirous of being recognized as ours and they have the skill to express themselves despite the restrictions of Socialist Realism.

The youth, whom I watched on Sunday picnics, on boat trips, on planes and the subway, carried books or were reading. I think books, on the average, mean more to them than to us, and TV (because of scarcity) means less. At Kiev on a bench overlooking the Dnieper, I talked to a soldier on leave who was deep in Stendhal's *Red and the Black*. Despite the daily dosage of the anti-American press I rarely felt hostility. In the picnic grounds below the Peterhof is a fun-place, a patch of small rocks, concealing a waterspout. One is dared to cross it and on a false step will be doused from the ankles up. Paddy attempted to dance across and was well sprinkled, to the laughter of onlookers. He dried off as we were served tea, and I remember the naval officer with gold stripes who caught my eye as he passed our table: he smiled, drew his forefinger across his throat, shook his head emphatically, and waved farewell. It is my impression that the Russian people like us, envy our freedom, and dread war as much as we. How much they are infected by the antagonism of the Kremlin I cannot guess.

CHAPTER

XVII

The United States in the 1960s was a confused, half-sick society. Vietnam was taking its toll of those who fought, those who fled to Canada and Scandinavia, and those who crowded into our colleges. (The deferment of college students from the draft was a shameful act.) The smoking of marijuana had begun to infect the high schools. More than half of all hospital beds in the United States were occupied by the mentally ill. The demonstrations at Berkeley and Harvard, the hippies lounging on the Boston Common, the homosexuals on Beacon Hill, the drug addicts, the grimy, overnight "revival" at Woodstock, New York, left no doubt about the demoralization of our youth.

In three issues between 1961 and 1964 the *Atlantic* went out to confront the neurotic problems with which so many were afflicted. The first, for July 1961, with a striking cover, a scarlet and white overlay of Freud's head, announced "A Special Supplement on Psychiatry in American Life." In 51 pages of text eight contributors, half of them doctors, examined the effect of the Freudian revolution on medicine, writing, religion, art, children, and morals. It was a well-mixed concentration, it was timely, and our offer to send an annotated list of books selected by Charles Rolo, to those who wished to know more, accounted for a record sale of over 91,000 copies on the newsstands.

More critical of Freud's obsession with sex was Dr. C. G. Jung's two-part reminiscences, which began in November 1962. Jung was Freud's most brilliant pupil, and now at the age of eighty-three he recounted what had brought them together, and their progressive differences.

Early in the war the son of a friend of mine suffered a nervous breakdown; he was taken to a conservative Boston psychiatrist, who, after a single examination, pronounced, "Your boy is schizophrenic. The case is hopeless." In the twenty years after that withering pronouncement analysis and treatment had become more diversified and successful. This advance was the provocative theme of the *Atlantic* for July 1964, bearing on the cover the words "Disturbed Americans — A Special Supplement on Mental Health." I am grateful to the seven who wrote with such clarification and hope. In the opening article, "The Meaning of Mental Illness," the historian Donald Fleming of Harvard drew this important distinction: "As a physician, Freud dealt chiefly with neurotics, who still had strong links with reality and some prospect of functioning successfully in the marketplace; and as both a physican and a theorist, he felt little confidence in grappling with the problems of people over fifty. . . . By contrast, Jung had a rich experience of institutionalized psychotics, more or less permanently cut off from reality; and a high proportion of his private practice was older people."

Dr. Wilder Penfield, that enlightened director of the Montreal Neurological Institute of McGill University, wrote "The Uncommitted Cortex; The Child's Changing Brain." And Dr. James A. Paulsen, psychiatrist-in-chief of the Student Health Service at Stanford University, explained why one out of every nine students in our colleges was so emotionally disturbed as to need medical leave, hospitalization, or extensive and intensive psychiatric treatment.

Dr. Robert Coles, a child psychiatrist whose reputation is now international, explored the problems of psychiatrists and the poor.

And Dr. William Sargant, comparing psychiatric treatment here and in England, remonstrated with the Freudians in America in these words before describing the progress in England:

One of the greatest tragedies and strengths of a Freudian analysis seems to be that it can completely brainwash even the most intelligent doctors, as well as many of their patients, into believing that Freudian dogma holds the only key to the real understanding of mental illness. In England, for instance, we have had a very active Freudian school for more than forty years, but there are only about 250 Freudian analysts who practice this method alone, compared with 2500 other psychiatrists who are fully prepared to use and combine all methods likely to help any individual patient. It has generally been found over the years that psychoanalysis is a poor weapon to treat most forms of mental and even neurotic illness.

Freud found this in World War I, and it became more and more obvious in World War II, when it was necessary to get a soldier well and back to duty or discharge him as one of psychiatry's treatment failures. Psychoanalysis and methods deriving from it have, in fact, proved able to help only a very small portion indeed of the thousands and thousands of mentally ill patients in Britain and elsewhere. And one has only to go today into the mental hospitals of the United States to see the total failure of Freudian methods.

Freud himself, when he came to England in his eighties, was still vainly insisting to his followers — some of whom had gone mad, he thought — that his methods were useful only in a limited number of cases of hysteria and obsessive neurosis. . . .

Such vigorous criticism of Freud's American disciples and their infatuation with the couch left readers very curious about the alternative treatments. Electric shock, which does relieve the suffering of the schizophrenic and which, Dr. Sargant said, had restored those in England suffering from deep depression "in a matter of weeks," has been used more judiciously in America. The anti-depressant drugs, originally discovered by Americans, have proved remarkably helpful to a large number of patients with milder depressions and help basically good personalities to get well quickly. And the lobotomy operation for the chronically mentally ill has been modified without loss of effectiveness under the name of cingulotomy. I doubt if any American practitioner could have drawn as effective a comparison as Dr. Sargant did, and his challenge increased the attraction to this issue. The single-copy sale came to over 86,000.

James Thurber received twenty rejection slips before he appeared in the *New Yorker*, which is to say that a turn-down may be disheartening but is rarely a stoppage. In 1958 I rejected a short story by an unknown in Chicago; it had come close to our liking, and I explained in my letter where we felt it failed. The moment he received the letter Jesse Hill Ford resigned from his well-paying public relations job, packed his wife, children, and St. Bernard into the family car, and drove south to his in-laws in Humboldt, Tennessee. Dr. Davis, his wife's father, had a large practice and a generous heart. He believed in Jesse and was willing to back him until that story, or a new one, was accepted.

It is difficult to exaggerate the freshness, the exuberant, laughable characterization in "The Surest Thing in Show Business," Ford's new story, which appealed to all of us. It won the prize as an *Atlantic* "First." It paid off his gamble, was read aloud to anyone within reach of the doctor, and set Jesse on his course as a professional writer. The story I had rejected became the genesis of his first novel, and I promised to reserve space for him as long as he maintained his pristine quality. In his soundproof room apart from the children, Jesse wrote nineteen stories for the *Atlantic* in the ensuing decade.

He was born in Nashville, Tennessee, grew up with a fever for fishing and hunting, a warm-hearted romantic whose years at Vanderbilt gave him ballast. Having earned his freedom, with the help of his wife, who was teaching, he made friends in Humboldt, found a big capable black cook, and openly expressed his sympathy for the blacks during the freedom marches.

I had happy visits to Humboldt and before one of them I learned that I was to be captured in a pageant by Confederate cavalry in uniform. Accordingly, I packed my belongings in a disreputable-looking carpetbag which the girls concocted for me in the office, and it was a sensation when the mayor and Jesse met me at the airport. . . . There were bleachers for the spectators, a Confederate general in full dress, the high school band played "Dixie," field pieces fired away, and a prisoner I became. After a sufficient period in Andersonville, I was released. We all trooped in for coffee and doughnuts and I was presented with a saber once used by a trooper of General Nathan Bedford Forrest, which with my carpetbag I carried home.

It is the curse of a fiction writer in a small community that neighbors fancy they see themselves in his stories. I tried to dissuade some of them from thinking that this was so, but resentment was in the air when Jesse published his big novel, *The Liberation of Lord Byron Jones.* In it a black has the courage to defend his wife against the advances of a corrupt white lawyer. It was a selection of the Book-of-the-Month Club, widely read, and made into a vivid movie.

Then disaster hit as arbitrarily as lightning. The good doctor died, Jesse's younger son, a star halfback in high school, was ganged up on by the black members of the squad. In a mistaken effort to shield him, Jesse was involved in the fatal shooting of a black, charged with murder, and finally exonerated after a haunting trial. It would be years before his spring could run clear again. This would have silenced a lesser writer, but Jesse has persisted.

The Oxford Book of English Verse, edited by Sir Arthur Quiller-Couch, was a distraction in the Ambulance Section I served in during World War I. The copy belonged to Harry Crosby, was kept out of the mud and read by several of us in our many months in France. I pleased "Q" by telling him so at his evening seminar on Aristotle's *Poetics,* which I attended at Cambridge in 1922. He had completed that anthology in 1904 and it must have earned him a small fortune; what I did not tell him was that it had two noticeable flaws: there were too many minor poets (some doubtless his friends) of the late nineteenth century, and it neglected Americans.

Now, half a century after "Q" made his selection, I was wondering whether to authorize an up-to-date anthology that would do better justice to both British and American poets. Archibald MacLeish was teaching at Harvard, and I sought his advice: would he be interested and would he want an English partner? It was worth doing, he said, a colossal job, but only one should make the selection — and it was not for him. I kept the project on the back of the stove, and after we had published Edith Sitwell's *Poet's Notebook* and shortly before she became a Dame of the British Empire, when she and Sir Osbert were dining with me at the St. Regis in New York City I asked if she would do it. She burst into tears: it was what she had been longing to do for years!

The contract was signed in 1952, without either of us realizing how long an undertaking it would be. Of necessity it would be a larger volume than the *Oxford Book* and I felt it would be helpful if our poetry editor, Phoebe-Lou Adams, would give me her opinion, negative or positive, of the Americans selected in earlier anthologies that I might pass on to Edith. Adams began with the sacred cows, the first "Thanatopsis" by William Cullen Bryant:

A Wordsworthian imitation, which he later polished up cannily, this thing, under the name of "Thanatopsis," became a veritable wheelhorse of 19th century American education. People still live who were in their youth compelled to memorize all of its 82 lines. The bulk of his work which I'll wager nobody but me has read in the last fifty years, is bad beyond belief. This old whited sepulchre was one of the worst poets that ever operated without being suppressed as a public nuisance. *We can make history by ignoring Bryant, and we should.*

Sidney Lanier seems to have survived because he wrote fruity, saccharine verse in elaborate stanzas that never quite come off properly, and he died relatively young. Three generations of editors have hoped, wistfully, to pass him off as the local Keats. We might as well give up. "The Marshes of Glynn," always reprinted, is much his best. No.

Henry David Thoreau, primarily a prose writer. The collectors who include him stick to his work which suggests either his friend Emerson or an economical version of Bryant . . . a good deal of other poetry, cranky, irregular, sometimes awkward but more interesting because it suggests that Thoreau was groping for what Emily Dickinson later achieved. He didn't find it.

Edgar Allan Poe. The total of his work is surprisingly small and the sentimental trifles confected to amuse pretty ladies surprisingly large. Yet he must be included, for he's the first American poet with an unquestionably individual voice.

John Greenleaf Whittier. "Snowbound," his best poem, is a long affair — must be over 700 lines. It's always printed in full, but we could be bold and stop with 212 lines, where there's a natural break following a lot of attractive northern farm detail and a lapse into religious nostalgia which, in fact, states the whole point of the poem.

We knew Edith honored Walt Whitman and Emily Dickinson, but early in the twentieth century were borderline cases like Edwin Arlington Robinson, who had been awarded three Pulitzer Prizes by conservative juries that had refused to recognize Amy Lowell, Ezra Pound, and T. S. Eliot. Miss Adams wrote:

Robinson was much given to long, involved poems in which he explored psychology and the subtleties of love, turning these things around and pawing them over with delicate persistence, until they crumbled like the wings of a dead butterfly . . . vivid but inconclusive character sketches were Robinson's best trick. He described people in such a way that one seems to know all about them, and yet one knows nothing about them at all.

I was glad to have such an irreverent and thorough consultant as the work progressed. Then I realized we were accumulating over 3,000 pages! Cuts were essential.

John Pearson, in his biography *The Sitwells*, refers to *The Atlantic Book of British and American Poetry* as Edith's "most onerous anthology." Indeed it was at times "onerous" for all involved. Edith's Notebooks, the source of her prefaces to the major poets, had been written too often with a soft lead pencil, so that in the recopying there were literally hundreds of misspellings, and omissions, which had to be caught in proof. Repeatedly the question arose as to which edition of the poet we were to follow. I marveled at the enduring patience of our head copyeditor, Mary Rackliffe.

Early in the undertaking, in the course of their second lecture trip, Edith and Sir Osbert spent Christmas holidays with us in Boston. The old tradition of open house on Christmas Eve was still observed, and Beacon Hill was candle-lit and snow-covered when our friends trooped in to talk to Edith, seated at one end of our big room, and to Osbert, by the fire with a bottle of Château Mouton Rothschild nearby. The first visitors arrived at 9 o'clock, the last at 2 A.M.

267

Later that week I introduced the Sitwells to a packed audience in Jordan Hall. There were many undergraduates present, and such a response to the poems they read that they were called back for encores. I had anticipated this and warned Osbert to be ready to read passages in *Left Hand, Right Hand.* As they came backstage after the final ovation, Edith with tears in her eyes said, "When I remember the jeers and catcalls at my first performance of 'Façade...'"

The anthology, ever growing, began to approach finality after six years but not until certain worldly considerations were agreed to, viz. this paragraph in her letter to me of February 5, 1958:

I am sending your notes to you with remarks in red ink, as that seems the clearest way of doing it. I didn't know Ciardi's work, and am certainly impressed by it. Let us keep 2 Ciardi poems. I agree about Robinson Jeffers. I don't, actually, know why he writes poetry! But I suppose we had better keep *Hurt Hawks.* But let us be merciful as we are strong, and leave it at that. Let us put in Amy Lowell's *Lilacs* but away with the brocade one. I don't like Elinor Wylie. Still, I suppose we had better have those two short poems. . . . Leonard Clark is the Yorkshire Post Poetry critic (the Y.P. is very influential) and is one of the four principal Government inspectors of Schools. He is a firm supporter of mine. I think his poetry tame but worthy in a way. I think we had better keep him. I think Sacheverell's *Battle of the Centaurs* wonderfully beautiful, and think we must keep it. If we don't put one poem by José García Villa in, we shall have his death on our conscience. I agree about William Plomer. I do think we must keep in Arthur Waley, as he has brought quite a new world into poetry. I am still worried to death about the Spenser. I suppose it would unhinge the whole technical side of the book, wouldn't it, if we put in the wonderful passages about Sea Monsters that I enclose. I don't wish to drive anyone to madness, but if it would be possible, I should be so grateful.

At first Edith refused to have any of her poems included, as witness this volley of cables in March:

March 20   Please delete my poems writing explain also about photographs. Edith

March 20   Regretfully withdraw your poems also without regret the Filipino. He is not good enough we all feel that David Jones has too much space finally please ask Eliot if he approves omitting all his notes about Wasteland. Ted

March 21   Technically impossible cut David Jones impossible delete him as would be insulting stop situation with Eliot delicate think notes necessary am deleting 58 bad quatrains Fitzgerald thus giving space for Eliot notes Oliver Wendell Holmes an absolute horror must we have him it is shaming. Edith

March 24   Holmes coming out but Thoreau imperative and Wylie not offensive. Shall we reproduce Eliot notes as printed in book or will you send revised. Ted

March 24   Regret Wendell Holmes and Thoreau utterly frightful must ask you delete them also Elinor Wylie these poems disgrace book please replace Villas poems also notes Wasteland. Edith.

I insisted that five of her poems must be printed at the close, and they were. And in a letter to me a year later came these forgiving lines:

We are now getting along grandly.

The early galleys were very difficult, naturally, being in such old spelling. But we are now racing along.

Perhaps it is not for me to say so, but I really think it is a heavenly anthology. I wish we had had more Spenser — but there one is.

I am going to be crowned Queen of the May next Wednesday at an enormous luncheon party given by Messrs. Foyle (of the giant bookshop) who are giving me the Poetry Prize of the year. The Home Secretary is to "pay me a tribute," and others also. And will the faces of the Grub Street journalists who have insulted me be red!!! In the evening I am going to be televised.

How much I am enjoying reading through the poems in the anthology. For beauty the book does, I think, beat any other anthology ever compiled.

May I say how overwhelmed I and my two secretaries are at the astonishing learning and helpfulness of the lady [our top copyeditor, Mary Rackliffe] or gentleman who is responsible for the queries, corrections, etc. Will you please convey to him or her my immense gratitude.

My love to you and Fritzy.

Dame Edith had agreed to autograph 5,000 sheets, to be tipped into premium copies, after which it was up to me to explain to booksellers why I believed her vast selection of 181 poets (855 poems) was unique. I pointed out that she had discarded a number of Victorians together with lesser writers of the eighteenth century, now turned to wood, and in the space so gained she accorded John Donne, Andrew Marvell, and Christopher Smart a more comprehensive presentation than any previous collection. In her choice of ballads and of the early religious poems antedating Chaucer, she had brought to light beauties rarely if ever in each other's company. Shakespeare commands the central space. Her prefaces to his work and to the 31 other poets make an illuminating appreciation of what follows. She included the beautiful translations by Arthur Waley, T. S. Eliot, and Robert Lowell, and, finally, this is the first single volume to set the best of the moderns in Britain and America in generous comparison. Louis Untermeyer wrote me that "the first 800 pages are as nearly perfect as any survey of six centuries could be"; it was her whimsical choice among the moderns that he objected to. In London Cyril Connolly's review in the Sunday *Times* was the most searching. "In Dame Edith," he wrote, "we have a living major poet whose judgment we can trust and who combines the sensibility of our time with a professional understanding of what poets have been trying to do. She cannot be duped or imposed upon by what is either sincere and clumsy or brilliant and frivolous." He regretted the omission of John Betjeman and of Laurence Binyon's "Burning of the Leaves" as I regretted the omission of Richard Wilbur. But he concluded that this was "one of the two most important anthologies of our time," the other being the five-volume compilation by Norman Holmes Pearson and W. H. Auden.

Our American edition went into a sixth printing, and the English edition published by Victor Gollancz was a success. Edith's royalties were larger than those of any of her previous books, a happy conclusion to our long "onerous struggle."

The beauty of Peter Ustinov's career is that he has done so many different things and done them all so well. One must read his autobiography, *Dear Me*, to unravel his antecedents, but the chief bloodline is Russian. Peter's grandfather was a rich eccentric, with a large estate, including mines in Siberia. In his youth, as an officer in the Guards, he was expected to take two vows on New Year's Day, one to the Czar, the other to the patriarch of the Russian Orthodox Church. Because he had fallen in love with the daughter of a Baptist, the young artistocrat did pledge his allegiance to the "Little Father" but declined to take the religious vow. For this he was exiled. With his Baptist bride and carrying his inheritance in rubles in a suitcase, he left Russia for good, and took up residence in Württemberg. There Peter's father was born. The old man, tiring of Württemberg and the Baptist, carried what remained of his fortune to Jaffa, Palestine, and ultimately married an Armenian.

Peter's father was educated in Germany, fought for the Kaiser and at the end of the First World War, with a reporter's credentials, went to Leningrad to see what remained of the Ustinovs, met an attractive young artist who was happy to escape, and after their marriage Peter was born in London. This prologue helps to explain Peter's multi-racial understanding and his gift for languages.

He is also an incredible mimic. As a pudgy boy he did not collect automobiles. He *was* one. When he walked the paths of Green Park, the grinding of his gears and his horn frightened pedestrians out of his way. If you have heard his record, "The Grand Prix au Rock," in which he is all the racing cars, as well as the idiotic English commentator describing the race, you will appreciate how that came to be.

In our office Phoebe-Lou Adams, meditating on the newly reported moon shots, sent me a memo: "Why not ask Peter Ustinov to write a short story about who lands on the Moon?" *Variety* had stated that Ustinov was closing *Romanoff and Juliet* for the summer but would take it on the road in the fall. I located him at the Algonquin.

"I want you to write a short story for us during the holiday."

"But I have never written a short story. What about?"

"Well, suppose we and the Russians land on the moon within an hour of each other. What do they do to the moon — and each other?"

"Oh, a fantasy. . . . Well, I'll try. When do you want it?"

"September eight."

An hour later his agent is on the telephone.

"I understand you've commissioned Peter to write a short story. What do you propose to pay?" Pause. "If he enjoys doing it, and it's good, he may do several."

"I'll tell you what," I said. "I'll guarantee $10,000 and if he does more than six we'll renegotiate."

"Okay."

The summer went by, and the first week in September, and no manuscript. In answer to my cable came a reply from Paris. "Story 50,000 words airmailed." This had me worried until it arrived and I found the operator had added an extra zero.

Peter had taken my dim suggestion and turned it into a battle royal at 10 Downing Street in which the inventor of a man-carrying rocket has been circumvented by the War Office in the person of General Toplett, "a soldier with a face like a whiskered walnut." In the presence of the inventor the general is explaining to the prime minister his plan "to land light air-borne forces as near the perimeter of the crater as possible, and to advance from there in four colums until we reach the green line here." "It's revolting!" cries the inventor. "I didn't evolve a man-carrying moon rocket in order to see it subjected to the kind of thought which has made such a mess of our planet!" The comedy goes on from there.

A month later came a second story, "A Place in the Shade," a spoof with sly digs at Hemingway, which produced these comments from our staff:

Beautifully written, amusing spoof of bullfighting and Spain. Simply stuffed with witty trifles. CWM

Marvellous bull fight in which everything goes wrong. I love every word of it, including the poet, who is needed as part of the guff against which the mayor — a really splendid invention, that mayor — ultimately revolts. PLA

Wonderful. The funniest Ustinov yet. I had to close the door of my office to avoid disturbing people while I read it. I have an especially soft place in my heart for The Wolf of the Sahara. I do think, however, that a little cutting here and there will be a help. There are so *many* characters. PHD

I howled: I think it keeps you guessing all the way and that its ribbing not only of the Spanish but the tourists — everyone — is very funny. You take this versatile guy as he comes and pray for more. EAW

But the third, "Add a Dash of Pity," for all its comedy, is a narrative of powerful irony. It is told, post-war, by an English military historian who is trying to get the truth about an action in Italy, involving heavy casualties, from a cautious, self-serving English general, from the brave brigadier whom he courtmartialed, and from their German opponent, General Schwantz. The characterization is superb; every part is a good one — including the wives — and why it has not been produced on television I cannot imagine. It became the title story of a collection for, as the agent predicted, Peter wrote eight for us, one a month, longhand, usually seated on the john to get away from the telephone, in hotel after hotel, while *Romanoff and Juliet* was on the road.

There is a postscript to *Add a Dash of Pity*. When Admiral Nimitz was being pressed to write his memoirs, he shook his head. "I've been thinking about it," he said, "but then I read a story by Peter Ustinov, called 'Add a Dash of Pity,' and I decided no."

We went on to publish Peter's plays, a volume of his drawings, a second book of short stories, and two novels. Each of the latter was begun, then interrupted for months while he completed first *Spartacus* and then *Topkapi*. Interruptions are not good for the emotional development of a novel.

By the time Peter had turned fifty, I had a better appreciation of his versatility. He gives the liveliest interviews of anyone in the theater and his flashes are so quick and amusing that one is tempted to think of him as a comedian unaware that there is a serious strength in his make-up. I believed this underlying strength would be appreciated in his autobiography. But it was too rich a subject to be sandwiched between films and plays. To do him justice it had to be written straight through. I knew he could draft a play in three weeks; this would take longer. When he came to Boston to address the General Court on the subject of state aid for the performing arts, I was listening, and we dined together that evening. "Well, that might be possible," he said in answer to my suggestion, "but I'll make no promises."

Then fate came to my assistance: Peter pulled a ligament and for a time could not perform. Being stationary, he began to write of his parents, his mother, an artist whom he adored; his father, who loved to show off, and of their curious rivalry. He wrote of his misery as a fat boy in a British public school, and of the comedy of his years as a private in the Army when he was doing his first one-act plays and taunting the psychiatrists who were examining him for promotion. Then with peace the pace quickens: we see his amazing versatility as an actor, director, playwright, musician, and in his serious pages his service for UNICEF; his concern for the Russians, and his abomination of war which inspired his later plays — all this in *Dear Me*.

CHAPTER

XVIII

On the morning of my departure from Moscow, as I said farewell before Arthur and I boarded the plane, two elders from the Writers' Union drew me apart and in a friendly manner presented me with a small gold trinket in the form of initials. No explanation was possible and as our flight was just announced I never learned its significance, nor ever shall since it was later stolen, together with my Phi Beta Kappa key and other keepsakes, in Boston.

The following year, 1960, I entertained two delegations of Soviet writers, five in each party, accompanied by courier-translators from the State Department. As the leader of each group was a Russian I admired, we were soon on terms of easygoing informality. The first arrived in leaden February and I began by inviting them to an editorial meeting in my office. We sat down two deep around the long table with Leonid Leonov, the novelist, on my right. In my welcome I presented each with a copy of our supplement "The Arts in the Soviet Union" together with a check for $300, in recompense for the 300 rubles we had been given in Moscow. Then Emily Flint and I described the April issue, which was on press. In it were three articles denouncing the abuses of our National Parks, the most incisive by Paul Brooks, "The Pressures of Numbers," which I quoted. The protection of our natural resources, I explained, had become a serious problem. Leonov held up his hand. "With us too," he exclaimed. "The novel I am working on is about the reckless waste in our forests. . . ."

I took them to the exhibition of Andrew Wyeth's paintings at the Massachusetts Institute of Technology. The delineation of the rustic New England scene clearly appealed to them. They had come to Boston after visits to Los Angeles and Chicago, which had confirmed the prejudices of the woman writer in the group about our addiction to violence. She was a stern-faced blonde who had not unbent. The Institute has a small, impressive chapel of brick designed by Eero Saarinen, without windows, the lighting reflected from moats of water. I had telephoned to ask if the organist could be playing Bach at the time of our entrance and except for him we had the building to ourselves. The blonde was transported. "This," she cried, beating her bosom with her fists, "is a highly intellectual building!"

We went to lunch at the Old Union Oyster House, sawdust on the ground floor, small booths, much as it was when Louis-Philippe, in exile, was lodging in the attic. I had reserved the large center table on the second floor, where we were watched with curiosity by other diners. Before the broiled live lobsters were served came the ceremony of tying on the large white bibs, bearing the red stencil of a lobster in the center. They followed our lead as we cracked the claws and dug out the meat; I had ordered two extra for seconds and after the last tidbits were gone they proceeded to fold the bibs with such care that I asked the head waiter for packets of four for them to take back to their families.

Leonov declined to attend the cocktail party which Arthur Schlesinger had arranged at Harvard — he still resented Arthur's baiting questions. "Would you like to go shopping instead?" "Yes," he said, "for a radio." So, on our way to Cambridge we took him and a courier to the Radio Shack. Days later when the time came to put them aboard their train for Washington there was the big block of a radio, console size, stoutly roped for travel. "But, Leonov," I said, "why so big?" The translator was at his side. "All my life," said Leonov, "I have written with music. When I was young my wife and I had one room in an apartment we shared with nine others, including children. To shut out the sounds I wrote with the radio playing. Now I want the best." We could hear the train approaching. He seized both hands to thank me. "Never forget," he said, "how much we are in awe of you!"

The second party arrived in the autumn when the foliage was turning. For the first evening my wife, Fritzy, and I arranged a cocktail party at home, with several of our Russian-speaking friends, Edmund and Elena Wilson, George Kennan, and Ernest J. Simmons, the biographer of Tolstoy, to ease the conversation. We need not have worried. The leader of the delegation was Konstantin Simonov, the Soviet ace, editor, and writer who had been so hospitable in Moscow and who now presented me with a gift, a pair of silver-mounted drinking horns. "In Russia," he said, as he handed them to me, "it is customary that one be filled with vodka — or whiskey — and that you and I share its contents. Which half do you prefer?" "The second," I said. The horn held a surprising amount of bourbon. Simonov drank the top off without a quiver. When I had to come up for air before I finished there was a roar of laughter — and the conversation began.

Helenka, the woman in this delegation, and I had liked each other in Russia, and her English was perfect. As her eye roved she asked, "Why so many, many sets on your shelves? Must you read everything of an author?" "Oh, no," I protested. "I've inherited them from my grandparents; in their day it was fashionable to buy an author complete — even if you only read one or two. The only set I've ever finished was Kipling's."

I wanted them to meet Robert Frost. Kathleen Morrison had smoothed the way; Robert was genial and teasing. He read his shorter poems, pausing at each stanza. A special translator Kay had invited could reproduce the imagery and the feeling with a skill that touched the Russians. They could not have enough of him, and the dialogue went on for three hours.

The weather was glorious. In two cars we drove to Marblehead and on another day to Lincoln and Concord. The roadside maples were ablaze as we passed the white farmhouses and I heard Simonov exclaim, in Russian. "What did he say?" I asked the courier. "This would be a not bad place to live."

Fritzy's sister-in-law, Mary Elizabeth Watriss, lived in Concord, deep in the woods, and I had asked if she and her husband, Freddy, would mind my bringing four or five Russians in for tea. She understood me to say "fifteen" and luckily prepared a mountain of sandwiches and cupcakes. It was her young son, Jimmy, my godson, who minded. When our two cars drew up at "Hurricane House" she was charmingly surprised, Jimmy sullen. The ten visitors were ravenous. There were refills of tea, as cakes and sandwiches vanished, and then Freddy suggested drinks. *"Da! Da!"* until finally Mary Lib said, "Now, Jimmy, will you show our guests your trains," and he came to life. In the basement Fred on spacious tables had laid out an electric railroad with two trains, passenger and freight, stations, bridges, tunnels, signals, headlights — with dual controls. The Russians were fascinated and they took turns running the Boston & Concord Railroad until it was time to depart.

In 1961 President Kennedy appointed George Kennan Ambassador to Yugoslavia. That spring the Nobel Prize for Literature was awarded to Ivo Andric for his trilogy *The Bridge Across the Drina.* The Serbian novelist resided in Belgrade, and the coincidence was inviting. We had published nothing from the satellites, of which the Yugoslavs were the most audacious and some said the freest. I decided to fly over and, with Kennan's help, gather material for a supplement about the new nation which Marshal Tito had welded together.

The Yugoslavs are among the toughest fighters in Europe which they proved under Tito's leadership in World War II as they held down twenty-two Nazi divisions while they eliminated the monarchy and the conservative faction under General Michaelovitch. Traditionally their native pride and their rivalry made them uneasy pawns for Russia and Austria. But Tito compelled them to a new purpose, to throw out the Germans, and then, with Cromwellian firmness, to withdraw from Stalin's embrace. This was the first broad crack to appear in the Soviet monolith and there is a puritan disdain in Djilas's *Conversations with Stalin* as he depicts the break, the overbearing boasts of the Russians, and their drunkenness.

The Ambassador had kindly sent a car to the Belgrade airport. The Second Secretary who greeted me was luckily of my height, as my suitcase had flown on to Constantinople, and for forty-eight hours I borrowed his shirts and pajamas. My room at the Hotel Metropole was well heated but the bathtub presented a problem. Attached to the faucet, like a long metal snake, was a hand shower, with a perforated head. I tried unsuccessfully to detach it but I am not good with gadgets. "All right, you fill the tub then!" but as I leaned down and turned it on the snake sprang up at me, drenching my only suit with hot water.

Things went more cheerfully thereafter. The next afternoon at the Embassy I was introduced to a number of writers; Kennan made my mission clear and the Ministry of Information stacked my room with novels, books about Yugoslavia's new industry, and books on art profusely illustrated, the text by the ranking critic, Oto Bihalji-Merin. He spoke no English, but his good wife did, and the three of us spent hours together. Six months in the United States on a Ford Grant had cured his antagonism toward Americans; he knew the work of every Yugoslav artist of consequence, set up studio appointments, and helped me in the sensitive choice of what to reproduce. I was astonished by the variety of the art: in Belgrade, the Imagists and Abstract Expressionists who regularly exhibit in Paris; in Zagreb the modern primitives who paint on glass, and in the museum the stunning nudes, carved in wood by Ivan Mestrovic; the medieval frescoes from the thirteenth-century monasteries in Serbia and Macedonia. I was tempted to buy more than I could afford. I began with lithographs, splurged on a lovely springtime oil by Vyaclvic and wondered how I could get a copy of one of the frescoes, painted on plaster (and very heavy), home.

With the Russians recently in mind comparisons were inevitable. The artists are free to paint and to exhibit what and where they please; they are talented and they sell in Paris. There is a native humor in the folk dancing, a dash and vividness such as I never glimpsed in Russia. And, as Mrs. Kennan explained, every gesture and costume has its meaning. In the afternoon Belgrade traffic was shut off from prominent boulevards; couples strolled or relaxed at the sidewalk cafés; the newsstands were busy and one *could* buy the Paris edition of the *Herald Tribune*. The men are taller and darker than the Muscovites, the women handsome, and I heard more laughter.

Ivo Andric, as was appropriate for a Nobel laureate, had an apartment in the former royal palace in Belgrade. His novels and short stories had won him the prize, and with a courtesy reminiscent of his youth in Vienna, he agreed to let me have a new story. The Yugoslav writer I could not get to was Milovan Djilas, once one of Tito's closest confidants, perhaps his successor. A Montenegrin, born in 1911, Djilas as a young lawyer first went to prison for leading demonstrations against the monarchy. While serving a three-year term he learned to speak Russian, which during the war enabled him to lead three missions to the Soviet Union seeking arms. He naturally resented the malicious taunts Stalin aimed at the Yugoslav fighters. What got Djilas into trouble after the war was his saying, "The more I delved into Soviet reality, the more my doubts multiplied. . . ." He was shocked when a Red Army commander confided to him that not until Communism had triumphed in the whole world would wars acquire their ultimate bitterness and slavery.

In 1954 Tito removed him as president of the Federal People's Assembly, stripped him of his decorations, and sentenced him to jail, in the same cell he had occupied in 1937. Undaunted, Djilas continued to write; his book *The New Class* was smuggled out to publishers in the West, and this prolonged his third confinement in cell or house arrest. His presence in our supplement would have asserted the independence that will not bow down.

One of Tito's master strokes, begun while World War II was still in progress, was to form brigades of women, eighteen-year-olds from the different republics, to repair the railroads. After the fighting, brigades were formed of both men and women, numbering in the thousands, youths who had to devote a year to public works. They have built factories, hydroelectric dams, and, ultimately, the national throughway, 681 miles long, from the northwestern to the southernmost tip of Yugoslavia, directed by Army engineers. The teenagers, of course, come from the six republics, and the highway is named "Brotherhood and Unity." I spoke to the colonel in charge: "How about sexual irregularities?" I asked. He smiled. "They live in separate barracks some miles apart. We want them to get used to each other and we work them hard. They dance on Saturday night after a long week. Not many pregnancies." "Well, it may not be the most efficient way to build a road," I said, "but it seems a good way to build a nation."

From Belgrade I headed northwest overland across the vast, well-cultivated Serbian plain for Zagreb and my meeting with Miroslav Krleza, the Croatian encyclopedist, playwright and poet. Had the Croatians the choice, they would have given him, not Andric, the Nobel Prize. I spent happy hours in the Zagreb Film studios watching the animated films, the first foreign ones to receive an Oscar. Then on to Ljubljana, the capital of Slovenia, center of the graphic arts, and the site of some of the recent discoveries in Illyrian archaeology. I had with me my flyrod, and two Slovene friends, Jacka Stula, a prominent editor (whom I first met in San Francisco), and his wife, a museum curator, arranged that I should have the chance to use it. A fishing license was procured at the Hunters' Club with this byplay. I paid a fee of $10.00, and asked what dry-fly should I use. "You're using a dry-fly?" "Yes." "Too early." The clerk handed me back $5.00. My friends drove me up the valley that leads to Lake Bled and the snow-capped Julian Alps, at their foot the Sava Bohinjka, a swift deep river, a landscape of breathtaking beauty with old castles or ruined country houses on the high points, cement pillboxes guarding every pass, and small shrines with fresh cut flowers for the Partisans who had met their deaths here as they drove back the Italians and Germans.

I had a second exposure in Yugoslavia in January 1963, when the Ford Foundation asked me to join Neil Chamberlain, the economist, and the Ford representative, Stanley Gordon, on a commission to select thirty mature men and women out of those who had applied for grants of $8,000 for informative visits of six or seven months in the United States.

"Exposure" is the right word, for we flew to Europe in one of the bitterest winters on record. We were diverted to Zurich as all airports in Yugoslavia were closed, went on to Vienna and there boarded the once-famous Orient Express for the overnight run to Belgrade. The inlaid wood of the ancient sleepers creaked, and mine must have transported many a bulky archduke or -duchess, for there was a deep furrow in the mattress. I noticed that as we passed through small villages the stationmasters saluted.

For part or most of our twenty-one days it snowed, the temperature stuck at zero, and in the Harem in Skopje (now a museum), it was so frigid that I was driven out in three minutes. I don't mean we did our selecting in harems, though a warm one would have been a relief. Some 150 applicants had already been screened at the six major universities and we were to choose with the aid of our interpreter from their favored candidates, beginning in Belgrade. The hearings took place in the rector's offices at 9:30 A.M. and preceding them we were served with slivovitz (Yugoslav firewater), Turkish coffee, and biscuits. Then the candidates presented themselves, one at a time, to explain *in English* where each wished to go, and specifically, why. The first to come before us in Belgrade was a woman judge in her early forties, an expert on international law. She was good to look at, obviously intelligent, spoke excellent English — and had consulted our USIA office in planning her mission. She would begin in New York at the time of the General Assembly at the United Nations, then spend six weeks at the Harvard Law School; after Christmas, go to the University of Chicago, and take her last weeks at Stanford. (We were unanimous in approval.) "Please, if accepted, could I bring my fourteen-year-old daughter with me?" We deferred to Stanley, who shook his head. "Perhaps for the Christmas holiday, only." (He had warned us that in preceding grants couples had been permitted to come, and had simply enjoyed themselves as tourists.)

The next was a burly operator in his fifties who obviously had little English. Some one had written his short speech which he had memorized phonetically. It sounded like this: "I am Vexprtin Redymedcloors. Ivilgo Chicgo vorkviv hartcheffurnmarkz verrygut hartcheffurmarkz. . . ." If this big guy really was an "expert" as he claimed, he might be a good choice for Hart, Schaffner and Marx.

The third candidate was a well-dressed young architect. In Communist countries, contractors and architects are supposed to work as a unit. The man before us was an independent, one of the two ablest mavericks in Serbia. His firm had won competition after competition but the only buildings which the state had actually paid them to construct were out of the country, such as the Yugoslavian pavilion at the Brussels World's Fair. Like the woman judge he had used the USIA files in his preparation and in clear English he named the

American firms he wished to consult and the cities whose architecture he intended to study. "Yes."

We traversed the length and breadth of the country and once again I was unprepared for its beauty and for how far, in the rivalry between nationalism and Marxism, unity had prevailed. We traveled by train except for one wild night when our only progress through the blizzard from Split up the Adriatic was on a bouncy little vessel whose sugar-and-water champagne helped us forget the motion. I recall how in Macedonia the sun broke through and we watched the kids coasting on one ski or a tin tray, and the Rector of the University whizzing by on an old-fashioned sled. The Danube was a yellow solid sheet of ice, which we crossed on our way to Novi Sad. This small town had been the last refuge for the Serbian government when the Turks swept by on their way to Hungary; for nearly two centuries it had been sustained by the Venetian fleet, and its museum and branch university held historic paintings and manuscripts.

Our testing concluded in Slovenia, where we accepted the last of thirty-one candidates. The intent of the Foundation was for us to select men and women of influence — lawyers, teachers, artists — who in their half year in the United States would better understand our republic, and at the universities we met those whose perspective had definitely been changed by the experience. My friends the Stulas were waiting for us at Ljubljana: we all dined together and on Saturday night attended a performance of *Don Carlos* in the little bandbox of an opera house, where the role of Philip II was sung by Basil, a splendid bass on loan from Belgrade. Sunday Mrs. Stula gave us a private showing of the Illyrian antiquities in the museum. The Illyrian alphabet has never been deciphered; the language lingers on in the names of the rivers. The most prized object was the situla, a bucket made of thin bronze plate, only nine and a half inches high, and on it is shown in three friezes the spiritual and physical life of the Illyrians.

"Such fragments seem very scarce for a people who once spread from the Adriatic to Switzerland," I remarked.

"Yes," said Mrs. Stula ruefully, "and you know where the finest collection resides? In the Peabody Museum at Harvard. An Austrian grandduke spent his life and fortune gathering it, and on his death, it was Harvard that made the only serious bid. . . ."

I wondered then, and wonder still, if Yugoslavians, those talented, fiercely independent people, may not be a hope for the future if they preserve the unity which Tito instilled. I used to smile as I saw the American diesel locomotives, and the trolleys rattling about Belgrade with "Washington, D.C." thinly painted over — all part of the aid, together with the shipbuilding expertise which we gave them when they began their post-war industrialization. The "humanization" of Communism was begun by Tito. Although he punished Djilas for going too far, he permitted Serb, Croatian, and Slovene artists to paint as they pleased, to travel freely, and to sell abroad. Kadar, who rode into Budapest with the Russian tanks at the time of the rebellion, has quietly, temperately made Hungary the showcase of the satellites, its consumer goods and abundance of food, a model. The Czechs have evoked quick pride in the victories of their tennis players and permitted the young stars to invest their prize money — as much as $300,000 — abroad. The Poles, with their Solidarity, the secret ballot, and the expulsion of rapacious politicians, have set an example for people everywhere. The Polish debts cause me to wonder if the future ever-rising demands on both the Soviets and ourselves for economic aid may not compel a reciprocity, instead of the war Stalin predicted, and a reduction of military extravagance, perhaps in my lifetime.

And I learned a lesson: how recklessly a fanatical minority in the United States, by applying pressure to a handful of Congressmen, can throw our foreign relations to the winds. Among the minorities we harbor are a minute and angry band of Croatians who would like to disrupt Yugoslavia. They found a way to influence Wilbur Mills, once the powerful chairman of the Ways and Means Committee in the House, which caused him to cancel the "favored nation trade treaty" with Yugoslavia in 1962. President Kennedy had assured Kennan of the continuance of that treaty, and our Ambassador had so assured Tito. When it was at the point of being revoked, Kennan's personal appeal to the President and his flight to Washington to remonstrate with Congressman Mills were of no avail. The goodwill fostered by one of our foremost diplomats was destroyed by an alcoholic forced to leave Congress in disgrace, a man who had never been outside the United States.

I call it a godsend that as Walter Lippmann passed his zenith George Kennan became our moderating voice. Kennan is a slender, fine-looking man of great composure. Under President Truman he had risen to a position of highest importance as director of the Policy Planning Staff: he had played a key role in the Marshall Plan, in our relations with Germany, and in opposing our advance beyond the 38th Parallel in Korea. But his views were not congenial with those of Dean Acheson, and when John Foster Dulles replaced Acheson as Secretary of State it shortly became apparent that he regarded Kennan as "a very dangerous man." Kennan rightly requested a leave of absence, without pay, and moved to Princeton, where J. Robert Oppenheimer welcomed him as an affiliate in history at the Institute for Advanced Study. State's loss was the *Atlantic*'s gain, and he wrote his first papers for me: "Training for Statesmanship" (May 1953) and "The Illusion of Security" (August 1954).

Some time later I had the pleasure of listening to him in Oxford at a luncheon given for him and his calm Norwegian wife, Annelise, by Isaiah Berlin. Kennan was then in the midst of a series of lectures scrutinizing the misunderstanding and errors — on both sides — which had complicated the West's relations with Lenin. Isaiah told me they were brilliant and that he had been urging Kennan to write a history of the Russian Revolution. Never before had I listened to an American explaining so rationally that in doing things disagreeable to our interests the Russians might be reacting to irritants in our own behavior. I was struck by Kennan's honesty and by his beautiful choice of words.

This memory was still in mind when my editorial associate, Emily (Wendy) Beck, Samuel Eliot Morison's daughter, alerted me that Harvard had invited Kennan to deliver a second series on the increasing difficulty in dealing with Stalin. It was a most valuable tip. I attended eight of his talks, which attracted an overflow audience in Memorial Hall. They were so fair-minded, so penetrating in insight and characterization that I asked the diplomat to let me bring the two series together in a book.

"But they are only lectures," he protested.

"They're more than that; they are absorbing and very informative. Many Americans should read them. Besides, they'll earn you some money."

"None of my books have done that. What do you mean?"

I took a flyer. "Not less than forty thousand dollars."

"Good heavens!" said Kennan. "That would throw my taxes completely out of control. . . ."

"But you don't have to touch the royalties. They can be placed in a trust fund for the education of your younger children." That appealed to him and the trust was set up.

Russia and the West under Lenin and Stalin appeared after Kennan's appointment as Ambassador to Yugoslavia and it lifted the curtain on many disputed events. The Book-of-the-Month Club distributed

237,000 copies, we issued eleven printings, and the foreign rights were snapped up. Surprisingly, an admirer on the West Coast bought the film rights for a documentary, $10,000 advance and another $50,000 when completed. (Alas, the film never was.) In the spring of 1962, on my first visit to Belgrade, I dined with the Kennans, and presented to George a royalty statement showing $108,000 in the fund for the education of the children. "It's unbelievable," mused the author. Said Annelise, "George, the next book you write *will be for us*."

It was to sound out that next book that I invited myself to Princeton after the Kennans' return. George had told me that he'd kept a journal from his first year in the Foreign Service. "I write it when traveling or depressed," he said. He permitted me to read it and it is a fascinating blend of observation, sad or hard truths, and the self-misgivings which assail us all. Princeton is lovely in the autumn, and as we walked the book took shape: a narration of the assignments which had taken him all over Europe and his evolving philosophy as an American diplomat, 1925 to 1950.

In the book, volume I of his *Memoirs*, one follows steps which led from his anonymity to authority. His start in the Foreign Service was uncertain: he was first a vice counsul in Hamburg, then a secretary of legation in Riga, one of the listening posts of Communist activity. With a growing conviction that he was ill equipped, Kennan was about to resign when a friend reminded him that the State Department would willingly transfer him to Berlin for intensive study of Russian, Chinese, or Arabic. Those two years in Berlin, during the twilight of the Weimar Republic, were one of Kennan's happiest interludes: he mastered Russian, extended his knowledge of Germany, and he fell in love with his mainstay, the delightful Annelise.

In 1933 when the United States recognized the Soviet Union — the last of the great powers to do so, as Czarist Russia was the last to recognize us — the Kennans were assigned to reopen Spasso House, our long-shut Embassy. They arrived ahead of Ambassador William Bullitt and other members of his staff; their only form of transportation was an Indian motorcycle and sidecar, and I like to think of the two of them slithering through the Moscow snow. All beginnings are memorable, and this must have been fun. With the Ambassador came Theodore White, his military attaché, an Air Force captain, for Bullitt insisted that he must have his own plane. White, the only American ever to be granted a pilot's license by the Soviets, had been at St. John's Military Academy with Kennan. Humor arrived in the person of Charles Thayer, future author of books on diplomatic life, who would teach Cossack officers a wild game called polo. And a friendship that was to be lifelong began with Charles ("Chip") Bohlen, like Kennan a freshly trained "expert."

After a brief stint in Vienna, which repaired his health, Kennan returned to Moscow, where it became his duty to attend the purge trials, day by day, and to write analytical dispatches about the vicious process which in the Army alone was to liquidate or exile one-third of the field officers above the rank of colonel — "a sort of liberal education in the horrors of Stalinism," as he called it. It was this prolonged observation of Stalin's ruthlessness that made Kennan so invaluable on his third assignment to Moscow under Ambassador Averell Harriman, 1944 to 1946. The good feeling toward the Soviets had evaporated when their brutality toward Poland was understood. In answer to a starry-eyed inquiry from the Department, while the Ambassador was away, Kennan dictated in cold blood an 8,000-word telegram to the State Department, which he dispatched in five installments. President Truman read it. Secretary of the Navy Forrestal made it required reading for hundreds, if not thousands, of officers in the armed services, and, as George said, "My official loneliness came in fact to an end. . . . My reputation was made. My voice now carried."

Kennan's telegram of February 22, 1946, is a unique document, from which I shall quote some of the most forceful passages. It begins:

In view of recent events, the following remarks will be of interest to the department.
I.   Basic features of postwar Soviet outlook, as put forward by official propaganda machine.
     A.   The USSR still lives in antagonistic "Capitalist encirclement" with which in the long run there can be no permanent peaceful coexistence. As stated by Stalin in 1927 to a delegation of American workers:
     "In course of further development of international revolution, there will emerge two centers of world significance: a socialist center, drawing to itself the countries which tend toward socialism, and a capitalist center, drawing to itself the countries that incline toward capitalism. Battle between these two centers for command of world economy will decide fate of capitalism and of communism in entire world. . . ."
     D.   Intervention against USSR, while it would be disastrous to those who undertook it, would cause renewed delay in progress of Soviet socialism and must therefore be forestalled at all costs.
     E.   Conflicts between capitalist states, though likewise fraught with

danger for USSR, nevertheless hold out great possibilities for advancement of socialist cause, particularly if USSR remains militarily powerful, ideologically monolithic, and faithful to its present brilliant leadership. . . .

So much for premises. To what deductions do they lead from standpoint of Soviet policy? To the following:

A. Everything must be done to advance relative strength of USSR as factor in international society. Conversely, no opportunity must be missed to reduce strength and influence, collectively as well as individually, of capitalist powers. . . .

At the bottom of the Kremlin's neurotic view of world affairs is traditional and instinctive Russian sense of insecurity. Originally, this was insecurity of a peaceful agricultural people trying to live on vast exposed plain in neighborhood of fierce nomadic peoples. To this was added, as Russia came into contact with economically advanced West, fear of more competent, more powerful, more highly organized societies in that area. But this latter type of insecurity was one which afflicted rather Russian rulers than Russian people; for Russian rulers have invariably sensed that their rule was relatively archaic in form, fragile and artificial in its psychological foundation, unable to stand comparison or contact with political systems of Western countries. For this reason they have always feared foreign penetration, feared what would happen if Russians learned truth about world without or if foreigners learned truth about world within. And they have learned to seek security only in patient but deadly struggle for total destruction rival power, never in compacts and compromises with it. . . .

This is admittedly not a pleasant picture. Problem of how to cope with this force is undoubtedly greatest risk our diplomacy has ever faced and probably the greatest it will ever have to face. . . .

Soviet power, unlike that of Hitlerite Germany, is neither schematic nor adventuristic. It does not work by fixed plans. It does not take unnecessary risks. Impervious to logic of reason, and it is highly sensitive to logic of force. For this reason it can easily withdraw — and usually does — when strong resistance is encountered at any point. . . .

In Russia, party has now become a great and — for the moment — highly successful apparatus of dictatorial administration, but it has ceased to be a source of emotional inspiration. Thus, internal soundness and permanence of movement need not yet be regarded as assured. . . .

Our stake in this country, even coming on the heels of tremendous demonstrations of our friendship for Russian people, is remarkably small. We have here no investments to guard, no actual trade to lose, virtually no citizens to protect, few cultural contacts to preserve. Our only stake lies in what we hope rather than what we have. . . .

Much depends on health and vigor of our own society. World communism is like malignant parasite which feeds only on diseased tissue. This is the point at which domestic and foreign policies meet. Every courageous and incisive measure to solve internal problems of our own society, to improve self-confidence, discipline, morale, and community spirit of our own people, is a diplomatic victory over Moscow worth a thousand diplomatic notes and joint communiqués. If we cannot abandon fatalism and indifference in face of deficiences of our own society, Moscow will profit — Moscow cannot help profiting by them in its foreign policies.

I doubt if any such downright and explicit assessment of a foreign power, once our ally, has ever been recorded by a junior officer. We reprinted it in full in his *Memoirs*, volume I.

This was the first of Kennan's momentous warnings, and it has been followed by others as recurring crises have confronted us. I think of his anonymous article "The Sources of Soviet Conduct" in *Foreign Affairs*, his recommendation of "containment," by which he did *not* mean *containment only by military force*. I think of his re-monstrance in the *New York Times* of December 2, 1973, when first the meaning (and the humiliation) of our dependence upon Arab oil was seen in the light of the future. I think of his "grand design of American foreign policy" in his terse book *The Cloud of Danger*, published in 1977, in which he asks, "Must our relations with the Soviet Union be increasingly militarized, poised for the ultimate showdown of armed strength, or can we break out of the straitjacket of military rivalry?"

A recent and forceful appeal to Russians and Americans was Kennan's leading article in the *Atlantic* for January 1981, entitled "Stop This Madness!" Speaking before the Second World Conference on Soviet and East European Studies, held in Garmisch, Germany, this is the heart of his argument:

Modern history offers no example of the cultivation by rival powers of armed force on a huge scale that did not in the end lead to an outbreak of hostilities. And there is no reason to believe that we are greater, or wiser, than our ancestors. It would take a very strong voice, indeed a powerful chorus of voices, from the outside, to say to the decision-makers of the two superpowers what should be said to them:

"For the love of God, of your children, and of the civilization to which you belong, cease this madness. You have a duty not just to the genera-tion of the present; you have a duty to civilization's past, which you threaten to render meaningless, and to its future, which you threaten to render nonexistent. You are mortal men. You are capable of error. You have no right to hold in your hands — there is no one wise enough and strong enough to hold in his hands — destructive powers sufficient to put an end to civilized life on a great portion of our planet. No one should wish to hold such powers. Thrust them from you. The risks you might thereby assume are not greater — could not be greater — than those which you are now incurring for us all."

But where is the voice powerful enough to say it?

There is a very special tragedy in this weapons race. It is tragic because it creates the illusion of a total conflict of interest between the two societies. It tends to conceal the fact that both of these societies are today confronted with internal problems never envisaged in the ideologies that originally divided them. In part, I am referring to environmental problems: the question whether great industrial societies can learn to exist without polluting, exhausting, and thus destroying the natural resources essential to their very existence. These are not only problems common to the ideological worlds; they are ones the solution of which requires each other's collaboration, not each other's enmity.

George Kennan would have been extraordinarily articulate in any profession. The eight momentous years of his career in the Soviet Union have made him not only our elder statesman but a cautious prophet whom every foreigner of consequence wishes to consult when he comes to the United States.

CHAPTER

XIX

Men who know their future is limited are drawn closer in friendship. On his recovery from that ominous operation in Philadelphia, Dick Danielson's devotion to the *Atlantic* and to me was touching. He accepted his frailty with humor. "I swallow eighty-four pills a day," he said laughingly, but when he neglected to do so he was vulnerable. I was standing beside him at the sharp corner of my secretary's desk when he suddenly blacked out. I supported him as he slid to the floor. I realized then how gaunt that big frame had become.

For Christmas he and Barbara gave me a membership in Tihonet, a famous little trout club on the cranberry bogs of Cape Cod, but before the season opened, a second fall on the tiles of his bathroom had broken Dick's hip. He was undaunted when, with his cane, we drove down to the old clubhouse. Mrs. Besse, the housekeeper, helped him into his Wellingtons as I mounted the rods, and then at the lip of his favorite stream, "the ADM," I launched the small aluminum canoe, he gingerly lowered himself into the discomfort of the bow seat, and I began to paddle slowly upstream. Two hours as the sun set was about his limit. I remember one trip when I had launched the canoe and was returning to the car for the paddles; in the seconds while my back was turned, Dick had fallen to his knees in the act of hooking a good rainbow, "Isn't he a beauty!" he said. "He came to my first cast."

As long as he lived Dick maintained his concern for the magazine. On his death in 1957 neither of the sons wanted the responsibility, and his married daughter, Marion Danielson Campbell, became our new president. She had a cool financial judgment and considerable editorial experience, having been a manuscript reader for me, and, during the war, an assistant to Herbert Elliston on the *Washington Post*. She managed her happy domestic life in New York with her husband and two sons and on her trips to Boston watched over her mother as she watched over our prosperous development.

Beginning with the foreign supplements in 1952 we had steadily diversified the content of the magazine. The Centennial issues not only reached a larger public, they showed that our readers welcomed a thorough examination of such provocative subjects as psychiatry and mental health conservation or the Catholic Church in America. Having agreed on the topic, the staff suggested writers and possible angles of approach. It was a team effort, more exciting than anything attempted in earlier days; Emily Flint carried the heavy burden of make-up; Crockett alerted the advertising agencies to what was coming up; Don Snyder and Frank Herbert calculated the size of press run. There was considerable suspense in it because one never could be sure.

At this time one of our older employees suffered a bad accident. When Marion discovered that her medical expenses and convalescence had all but wiped out her savings, she was shocked, said something must be done about it, and shortly she, Snyder, and our lawyer worked out a company-financed insurance and pension plan to cover everyone.

This was now possible because we were solidly in the black and the pension could be paid for out of earnings. In those good years we also bought our buildings on Arlington and Marlborough streets — which we had been renting since Sedgwick sold the company — at a cost of $400,000, again out of earnings, and as I stepped down in February 1966 our reserves in bonds and cash were close to half a million. At this time Don Snyder compiled a meticulous record, "Ten Years of the A. M. C.," Fiscal 1955–64." It shows that year by year, our Atlantic books — the Press — *averaged* an annual profit of $80,000 and that the *Atlantic*, which hit a high of $272,809 in 1960, *averaged* an annual profit of $170,771, before taxes, over the decade. That twelve-page report took many hours — many years — to conclude. I treasure it as a record of accomplishment and integrity.

Of course, it came as a surprise that I was to be replaced. True, I had passed sixty-five, but with things humming, who would have thought of retiring? In the mid-summer of 1964 Marion came to our cottage at Beverly Farms for a quiet talk, and in her direct way told me that she had chosen my successor, Robert J. Manning, the Assistant Secretary of State for Public Affairs under Presidents Kennedy and

Johnson. After twenty-four years in office I should *not* have felt surprise; I had written in *Jubilee* that "one reason the *Atlantic* has survived is that it has changed its editors more frequently than its rivals." But I did feel chagrin.

"How long," she asked, "do you think it will take for him to learn the ropes?"

"Not more than three years, or less than two."

I was getting used to the idea as she stressed how much Charlie Morton admired him, how Manning had made his reputation covering the White House for *Time*, and in his three years in charge of Henry Luce's London Bureau. I asked what long-term plans she had for the magazine. "Well, after Bob Manning, who is taking Don's place, has had his run, I think we'll probably sell it."

I remembered meeting Manning when he was a Nieman Fellow at Harvard. Now when I went to Washington I was impressed by his eagerness, and he won me when he said that throughout his career, to edit the *Atlantic* had been his dream. We talked about the supplements, about London, about fly-fishing, which he loved, and I made a mental note to propose him for the first opening at Tihonet. I had no way of knowing how his years with Henry Luce had fitted him for the change, but I felt we could work out the transition amicably.

Because of my involvement with several Atlantic authors whose books were in progress, Marion suggested that I continue to edit manuscripts for the Press, with a small peg but a reasonable commission on any book earning over $5,000. My salary as editor-in-chief even in the best years had never exceeded $35,000, and when I needed more I had the royalties from my books and my lecture fees. This was a way to wind down; to move into comfortable quarters on the third floor back, with the loyal Miss Albee to handle my correspondence, and the typing and retyping of my lectures and books, was a temptation, and a saving grace. It proved more productive and longer-lasting than either Marion or I could imagine.

In the third floor back, between the concentration on manuscripts, I had intervals of reverie. The respect for law was obviously evaporating as the emphasis on violence was played up in the press, in fiction, films, and on TV. "It is impossible to under-estimate American taste," as Henry Mencken once said. After the students' demonstrations, and the Weathermen's bombs, violence became an addiction, spectacular, shocking, but acceptable and salable — so long as it didn't happen to the spectator. The Watts riots in California were not so much racism as the result of plain misery, but in their attempt to restore order the police were reviled as "pigs." There was talk downstairs of doing a supplement on police, and by coincidence the *Atlantic* received three short stories, unquestionably authentic, by a sergeant on the Los Angeles police force. They hung fire for a couple of months until it was decided not to include fiction in the forthcoming supplement, at which point Miss Adams, who had more confidence in them than the other readers, sent them up to me.

They struck me as the real thing, deliberately purified for the magazine, and in my letter to the author I said I suspected they were chapters of a novel — and if I was right I should like to read it. My guess was correct.

In came an outsize manuscript, the narrative of three recruits who enter the Police Academy in the same class, how they are trained, and their initiation on the force — rich, raw material by a man who had studied Hemingway and was himself capable of power. For five months Sergeant Joseph Wambaugh and I worked on the revision, cutting out episodes that rightfully belonged in the next book, and improving the transitions among the three careers. Then, outward bound on a speaking trip, I took with me a contract for this novel, entitled *The New Centurions*, and a check for an advance royalty of $3,500. Wambaugh needed editing and he and his young wife, Dee, were grateful for my interest when they dined with me at the Town House in Los Angeles.

The next day he drove me out to their home in the tiny suburb of Walnut: I saw where he jogged at sunrise, the studio in the shopping center where Dee gave drawing lessons, and I met their two boys. Joe had been twelve years on the force, serving by preference in Hollenbeck, the Mexican quarter in Los Angeles. "They're great people, the Mexicans," he told me. "Good workers and honest. If they go on a bust and get caught, they'll admit it. I respect them."

Joe and Dee were vacationing in Mexico when I wired them that a major book club had chosen *The New Centurions* for the January selection. The novel had been out two weeks when Chief of Police Davis wrote me an angry letter, stating that Joe had overlooked a clause in his contract requiring him to submit anything he had written to his superiors for approval, and that Wambaugh would be censored at a hearing. I replied that he should be proud of his sergeant; the novel did full justice to police anywhere and was being read with delight — by police — and many thousand others. If he would ask any librarian, he would learn it was an honor to be distributed by the Book-of-the-Month Club. The hearing never took place, as the City Council of Los Angeles voted a resolution commending Sergeant Wambaugh — and his editor — for publishing a novel of such fidelity, at a critical time. . . .

Joe had no further need of me after his second novel, *The Blue Knight*; the paperback sale was enormous and he became a millionaire, independent enough later to buy back the film rights of *The Onion Field* and produce the picture as he felt it should be done. I shall remember his younger self, taking his degree and teaching himself to write at night school, and parting with the force with such reluctance after thirteen years. He and Dee remembered me with a card on my eightieth birthday.

The writer who consoled me for our loss of Wambaugh was a black. I have told how in his last year at the Harvard Law School James Alan McPherson found the time to write short stories, and some kind benefactor had advised him to show them to me. He brought me three, and with natural curiosity I asked how in the world he'd been able to do them with the bar exams three months away. "The first year was the really hard one, Mr. Weeks," he said shyly, "not the last."

The stories were exceptional. So right they were that I hoped Bob Manning would accept them, as he did, two of them within the week. Our check for $1,400, I learned later, James carried in his pocket for a fortnight to feel its glow before endorsing it to his mother in Savannah.

After receiving his degree he decided to spend the summer working on a newspaper in Roxbury while he went on with his writing. Once a week James came in town to lunch with me in the small café at the Ritz-Carlton; this was the beginning of our friendship and the shaping of his first volume of short stories. One of them, "The Gold Coast," is the illumination of his own experience as a janitor in Cambridge; another, "A Solo Song: For Doc," is the portrait of a shrewd and aging waiter James admired during the five summers when he himself was a waiter on the Great Northern. What distinguishes McPherson's stories are the characters, the flick of irony, the naturalness of the dialogue, and the absence of bitterness. As the publication of *Hue and Cry* approached, James wrote, "Certain of the people happen to be black, and certain of them happen to be white; but I have tried to keep the color part of most of them far in the background where these things should rightly be kept. I have tried to say . . . what I have seen of humanity: the good, the bad, the predictable things, and some things not so easily understandable or predictable. I have tried to make sense for myself, of some of the more serious problems (ideas?) of my generation. . . ." That this book was distinctive was soon recognized: James received a grant from the Rockefeller Foundation and at the annual meeting of the American Academy of Arts and Letters he was given an award. The message was clear: go on writing.

James determined to teach rather than practice law; first at the University of Iowa (where, as he wrote me, "some of my Freshmen have never known a black much less been taught by one"), then at the University of California at Santa Cruz, at the University of Virginia and then recalled to Iowa. Manning made him a Corresponding Editor and James's articles about Chicago's Blackstone Rangers and the gouging of the blacks by Chicago landlords could only have been written by a discerning lawyer, with fellow sympathy.

James teaches composition to those who aspire to write, and the reading of their manuscripts takes time away from the writing of his own. His promising pupils began submitting their stories to the *Atlantic,* and one of them, Breece Pancake from West Virginia, had two of his accepted before McPherson's second collection of stories, *Elbow Room,* came off press in 1977. This is a mature book: the characterization objective, the dialogue strong, the emotions ranging from the shyness of young love to the courage and adjustment of a mixed marriage. The most significant appraisal was by Ralph Ellison, the novelist: "To my mind McPherson ranks with the most talented and original of our younger writers. The title story alone reveals more about the spiritual condition of Americans during the 1960s than is to be found in most novels."

Elbow Room was nominated for a National Book Award but to our disappointment the honor went to a novel. On April 10, 1978, James wrote me:

> If I am able to do a better book, and if you will continue working with me, I hope that some day, even if I never receive any awards (to be honest, I've had more than my share already), someone searching through the records of this time in the country's history will wonder how it was that two people from backgrounds as different as ours could find enough in common to sustain a friendship for so long a time. The man who can explain that will have grasped the real meaning of this country's promise.

A week later James won the Pulitzer Prize for Fiction, ten years after his first visit to the *Atlantic.* It is very rarely awarded to a volume of short stories.

Dr. Johnson called the essay "a loose sally of the mind," a facetious definition and one that does less than justice. The essay is captious, rather than "loose" — as owlish as T. S. Eliot, as didactic as Francis Bacon, as sentimental as Charles Lamb. In my youth I thought Robert Benchley was side-splitting, but he never grew beyond self-mockery and does not seem so amusing today. Bernard de Voto could be sharp and observant, as when he wrote about the myth of the taciturn Yankee or Westerners who had designs on our public lands. Clarence Day memorialized his parents with utmost charm, and Edmund Wilson became the finest scholar-critic of his time. But none of my contemporaries wrote — or writes — with the grace, judgment, and *the range of feeling* of E. B. White. In these bomb-haunted years he remains himself, and the essay, given up for dead by the journalists, became a glory in his hand. His weekly "Notes and Comment" in the *New Yorker*, his pages in *Harper's* "Easy Chair" (which I envied), his "Farewell" to Harold Ross, his evocation of Fred, his favorite dog, are aspects of White's versatility.

Here is Fred as he appears in White's essay "Bedfellows":

I am lying here in my private sick bay on the east side of town between Second and Third avenues, watching starlings from the vantage point of bed. Three Democrats are in bed with me: Harry Truman (in a stale copy of the *Times*), Adlai Stevenson (in *Harper's*), and Dean Acheson (in a book called *A Democrat Looks at His Party*). I take Democrats to bed with me for lack of a dachshund, although as a matter of fact on occasions like this I am almost certain to be visited by the ghost of Fred, my dash-hound everlasting, dead these many years. In life, Fred always attended the sick, climbing right into bed with the patient like some lecherous old physician, and making a bad situation worse. All this dark morning I have reluctantly entertained him upon the rumpled blanket, felt his oppressive weight, and heard his fraudulent report. He was an uncomfortable bedmate when alive; death has worked little improvement — I still feel crowded, still wonder why I put up with his natural rudeness and his pretensions. . . .

Anyway, it's pleasant here in bed with all these friendly Democrats and Republicans, every one of them a dedicated man, with all these magazines and newspaper clippings, with Fred, watching the starlings against the wintry sky, and the prospect of another Presidential year, with all its passions and its distortions and its dissents and its excesses and special interests. Fred died from a life of excesses, and I don't mind if I do, too. . . .

When the Academy of Arts and Letters conferred its Gold Medal for Essays and Criticism on White it did so in these words:

If we are remembered as a civilized era it will be partly because of E. B. White. The historian of the future will decide that a writer of such grace and control could not have been produced by a generation wholly lacking in such qualities, and we will shine by reflection in his gentle light. Of all the gifts he has given us in his apparently casual essays, the best gift is himself.

Every editor covets the books of a very few authors he wishes he might have published. Andy White is one of mine.

Thornton Wilder was a second whose books, had the dice rolled my way, I might have published. Rumor had it that in his twenties, preparing for a year at the American Academy in Rome, Thornton had laid out on graph paper his own map of the literary and historical sites in the Eternal City. His mind fed on history: we see it in *The Cabala*, his first book, where he reincarnates the death of Keats in Rome, watched over by the faithful Severn in that little room at the foot of the Spanish Steps. We see it in his first novel, where he finds or invents the legend of *The Bridge of San Luis Rey* in Peru. *The Bridge*, with its Old World flavor, is the book which might have brought Wilder into our fold for, as I have told, I had written him after the publication of *The Cabala* asking to see his next manuscript, which I hoped we might serialize in the *Atlantic*. In came the nearly complete novel of *The Bridge* and, as the First Reader, I was sure we had a prize — and perhaps the possibility of publishing it as a book afterward. But I was outvoted, two to one, by my seniors, Mr. Sedgwick and his assistant, Miss Converse, who, for reasons I have never understood, could not see it for the *Atlantic*.

Our friendship deepened in spite of this rejection. In 1937, when our directors were deliberating over the choice of a new editor, Wilder, to whom I offered the editorship, urged me to assert my claims.

Like a great navigator he fixed his mind on one constant star: he believed in immortality, in particular, the immortality of writers. This was why he felt it important to transpose the tragedy of John Keats into our own era, why he transplanted Madame de Sévigné to Peru in his novel of South America, why he turned to Caesar and Cleopatra in that fine novel of his maturity, *The Ides of March*. With his gift for characterization, Wilder would take the body of fact about a young poet or an aging emperor and by the power of imagination reanimate them for our appreciation.

In 1942 when this country was rallying from the defeat at Pearl Harbor, Thornton produced his finest play, *The Skin of Our Teeth*, a thrilling reminder of man's ability to survive, in which he links the past with the present. In each of the three acts his characters seem doomed, first by the return of the Ice Age; in the second, by a flood greater than that which Noah survived; and in the third, by a war of extermination. But his people are dogged.

As the ice is closing in, Antrobus says to his wife, "These people don't take much. They are used to starving. . . . Maggie, these people never give up. They think they will live and work forever." In the second act, as the Ark is sailing away from Atlantic City, Mrs. Antrobus calls out to her husband: "George Antrobus! Think it over! A new world to make — think it over!" And in the third act, when the men have wearily returned from the war, Ivy explains, "The author means that just like the hours and stars go by over our heads at night, in the same way the ideas and thoughts of the great men are in the air around us all the time and they're working on us, even when we don't know it. . . . That's all we do — always beginning again! Over and over again. Always beginning again."

In the autumn of 1950 Thornton came to Harvard to deliver the Charles Eliot Norton Lectures. There had been eminent predecessors in that lectureship, T. S. Eliot and Robert Frost among them, but I dare say that Wilder's talks penetrated more deeply into the thinking of the students who were twelve years old at the time of Pearl Harbor and who had grown up in the nuclear atmosphere of a Cold War. His words sank in. He took for his theme American loneliness.

I asked him if I might publish three of his lectures, those on Thoreau, Melville, and Emily Dickinson, in the *Atlantic*, and after a moment of hesitation he said, "Yes, on one condition: a lecture, when written, becomes rigid. I should like to add in italics the thoughts that occurred to me as I was walking to the auditorium, and the further ideas that sprang to mind even as I was reading from my notes." I encouraged him to insert these amplifications and they were particularly revealing in what he said of Thoreau.

"I must tell these young people who are hurrying by me," he began, "that Thoreau finally lost his battle — the typical American battle of trying to convert a loneliness into an enriched and fruitful solitude." He told them that through his long quest Thoreau heard the closing of three doors: the door to Love, closed when at the age of thirty-four Thoreau wrote of the woman he loved, "The obstacles which the heart meets with are like granite blocks which one alone cannot remove. . . . We meet but to find each other further asunder." The door to Friendship closed when, again in his Journal, he describes his relation with Emerson as "one long tragedy." And, as the years passed, Thoreau increasingly mourned his lost youth and the intoxication which nature had afforded him then — but no longer.

"Yet," cried Thornton, his voice rising, "millions have testified to the powerful clarifications that he brought back from Walden Pond. And all his triumphs came from his embattled individualism, from pushing it to the limits that border on absurdity, and from facing — 'face to face' — the loneliness consequent upon it!"

In 1960 I felt proud when I was asked to make the presentation to him of the first gold medal which the MacDowell Colony Association now presents annually to one of its illustrious alumni. At the end of the ceremony Thornton shook my hand. "Ted, you were too generous. People don't say things like that anymore."

Toward the end of his life, while on a visit to Florida, Thornton walked into a popular restaurant to find that no table was available. "May I have your name, please?" asked the head waiter. "Thornton Wilder." Pause. "Aren't you the man who wrote *Hello Dolly!*" "Yes, I did have something to do with it." That was enough. He was soon seated, the word spread, and instead of the quiet meal he had anticipated, he spent the rest of the noon autographing menus. It is pleasant to think that *Dolly* took such good care of him and his sister Isabel at the close.

My friendship with Walter Lippmann began with an admiration I never lost and became an easy, shared affection. Our happiest companionship was in Maine where he shed that invisible suit of armor which protected him against criticism in Washington. We competed: I played his and Helen's best ball for 25¢ a hole on the harborside links at Southwest Harbor, and whatever advantage I won was lost in the afternoon on the close-cut croquet lawn back of their camp. As a golfer Walter had a methodical swing, rarely looked up and was seldom in trouble — not easy to beat. At croquet Helen was a tigress, speeding shots accurately through the narrow English wickets and whacking an ineffectual ball like mine into the shrubbery. No matter who was my partner, I dragged us down, to Helen's delight.

The Lippmanns' camp was built for privacy. There was the main cabin with living room, dining room and a royal suite, and, spaced along the shore, separate cabins for additional guests and at the end of the row Helen's garden of delphinium and roses, their bedroom and Walter's workshop. In the morning guests amused themselves until copies of the New York papers were delivered shortly before lunch. Happily my visits frequently coincided with those of the Henri Bonnets, the French Ambassador and Ellie, his delightful wife, a born tease. Walter doted on them both and they made a long stay; Henri deep-sea fishing through the midday and after supper everyone trying to beat Ellie at cards. At whatever game she was a wizard, as her husband was not, but there was the evening when Henri could not miss and as the score was added she proclaimed, "Henri — the King of Can-astra!"

Probably because of our relaxed intimacy Walter confided in me in some of those periods when he rebelled against the pressure of writing his column, "Today and Tomorrow." I think that even as a young man he marshaled his thoughts with incredible speed, but such books as *Drift and Mastery* and *A Preface to Politics* were not composed with the deadline which pressed upon him three times a week in Washington, and recurrently he felt the urge to return to the book writing of the early years, and to a spaciousness which his memory exaggerated. The first time he sought my advice was in September of 1949 when, at the end of their summer holiday, he and Helen dined with us in Boston. In the course of the meal he remarked that no one had written a really searching history of American foreign policy and I asked why he wasn't uniquely qualified to do it. He stared at the prospect, enlarged on it when Fritzy and Helen left the table, and from Washington sent me a three-page layout beginning:

Washington, D.C.
September 20, 1949

Dear Ted:

I have been jotting down some ideas for the work I mentioned to you at your house. At present I conceive the title as some variation on the idea of "The Rise of the U.S.A. as a World Power." It would be in three volumes divided as follows: Vol. I To the Rejection of the Treaty of Versailles; Vol. II To the Enactment of the Neutrality Act; Vol. III From the Manchurian Affair to the Present Time. Now for a little more detail. . . .

But, having weighed the time and research necessary for the project, Walter decided not to do it.

I have already alluded to his leave of absence from the column in the autumn of 1951 when he began writing the first chapters of *Essays in the Public Philosophy* and when Helen wrote my wife to keep a lookout for a suitable house conveniently close to Cambridge. I was never sure how ready she was to surrender the sense of power they shared in the Capital and abroad. By coincidence, as I emerged from their guestroom at Woodley Road, she and I met at the head of the stairs. Her cheeks were flushed and she said to me with tears in her eyes, "You may think he's an easy man to live with — but he isn't."

In retrospect, had Walter pulled out to write the two- or three-volume history of American foreign policy and had it become important, a reference work, "a classic," would it have been as important as the influence his column continued to exert on millions of readers for years? He wrote at a perilous time when, like it or not, we discarded our isolation forever, when, as he said to me in a long prospectus, "the unpreparedness of the western allies determined the high political strategy of the war — the decline of Britain and of the French and western European empires, the dependence on Russia, and the appearance of only two great powers (both of them non-European)."

In the tributes to him at the memorial service, 1975, in the National Cathedral in Washington I said, "He nagged our national conscience" as no other writer ever has done. He made us face and think out the hard realities, and from time to time he held up one individual's accomplishment as in these splendid words, written after the retirement of Justice Oliver Wendell Holmes:

There are few who, reading Judge Holmes' letter of resignation, will not feel that they touch a life done in the great style. This, they will say, is how we live, and this is how to stop, with every power used to the full, like an army resting, its powder gone but with all its flags flying. Here is the heroic life complete, in which nothing has been shirked and nothing denied — not battle or death, or the unfathomable mystery of the universe, or the loneliness of thought, or the humors and the beauties of the human heritage. This is the whole of it. He has had what existence has to offer: all that is real, everything of experience, of friendship and of love, and the highest company of the mind, and honor, and the profoundest influence — everything is his that remains when illusion falls away and leaves neither fear nor disappointment in its wake.

The book that gave Lippmann the most distress was his last, *Essays in the Public Philosophy.* It began with a premonition, as he observed the political and military weakness of France, and the complacency of Britain in the late 1930s, and our own uncertainty as to whether we should or should not go to their aid. He became convinced that the democratic process had weakened to the point where it could no longer conduct war or support a just peace, and, as was characteristic, his analysis of failure was more telling than his solution. His doubts were enlarged by the lowering of standards and the departure from law which he observed during the McCarthy scourge when the final chapters were being written. He knew that his book would be read as a repudiation of democracy. When Curtis Cate and I went to Southwest Harbor to help him with the final editing in September 1954, I felt that he was still not confident of the latter chapters. The inner struggle had been intense, and when the manuscript was finished, he called his friend and classmate, Dr. Carl Binger, to reserve a room for him at the Massachusetts General Hospital, where for three weeks he recuperated.

It was not in Walter's diffident character to write about himself, but he was willing that someone should write his biography and ready to help the writer. The first candidate to present himself was a Canadian who had made Lippmann the subject of a doctoral thesis and for whom I secured a grant to study Walter's correspondence. When this arrangement did not prove promising, we turned to the late Richard Rovere, the Washington correspondent for the *New Yorker*. After a year of preliminary study Rovere found that the double burden was more than he had strength for, and he recommended Ronald Steel. In drawing the contract, Louis Auchincloss, Walter's lawyer, inserted a special clause. The Lippmanns had requested this was to be a cerebral biography concerned as briefly as possible with their private lives, and to enforce the point a jury was named of Auchincloss, George Kennan, and Arthur Schlesinger, Jr., to decide whether the biographer had gone too far in the personal passages.

Steel was a young, respected historian, author of three books, the best known, *Pax Americana*. He commended himself to Walter in the initial interviews; the contract, containing the jury clause, was signed in 1969, and the delivery date set for January 1, 1973. This was a misjudgment by all of us; it was not realized what an immense amount of Lippmann's prose had to be assimiliated by a man too young to have experienced the conditions under which Walter's early books were written.

For his sources Steel had the cards of notation the Canadian, Gary Clarkson, had compiled from Walter's correspondence at the Yale University Library and for which he was reimbursed; the Oral History up to 1950, which Dr. Allen Nevins had taken down for the Columbia University archives, Lippmann's twenty-four books, uncounted editorials in the *New Republic* (of which Walter was cofounder) and the *New York World*, many speeches, the articles in *Vanity Fair* and the *Atlantic*, and 4,500 columns of "Today and Tomorrow." That was a prolonged assimilation.

At the outset there was a natural tendency for Steel to match his interpretation of events against Walter's, and when I pointed out the inappropriateness of such rivalry Ronald's revision was a just balance between his hindsight as an historian and Walter's foresight as an observer.

Ronald's interviews with the Lippmanns in Washington became friendly and disarming. The sensitive time for the Lippmanns were the years 1935–1936, when Walter had written *A Preface to Morals* and had realized — and revealed — that his first marriage was a bleak failure. In this vulnerable period, he fell in love with Helen Armstrong, the wife of his best friend, and the anguish he and Helen went through before their divorces and remarriage was what they wished to shield. Until the day came when Helen said impetuously to Steel, "You really ought to read Walter's love letters; they show a poetic side of him no one knows. Four of them are in my safe deposit box." When she gave her consent to Auchincloss, the biography ceased to be strictly "cerebral."

Steel took nine years to complete the writing and the final version was rightly held to a single volume. I am sure there was exasperation in the hundreds of letters, the many pages of queries and suggestions I sent to him, and there was moderately little exasperation in what came back to me. Too few readers are aware of the long thought and toilsome detail that go into distinguished biographies. I wish Walter had lived to read it all. The last time I took him out to dine in New York, four years before the book appeared, he asked me, "Are the reviews good?"

To see one's other self slip away, beyond hope, is prolonged sadness. I realized when I went abroad to lecture at the Salzburg Seminar in the spring of 1968 that this would be my wife Fritzy's last trip with me. An aorta operation had not given her the relief we hoped for. We spent Easter weekend in Vienna and as we sat listening to *Rigoletto* in the new Opera House, beneath the music a still voice said, "Last time."

Back on Beacon Hill there were spells when she forgot where she was. After I caught her in the center of Charles Street walking against the traffic I sought help. Two sisters from Nova Scotia spelled each other by day, and I cooked supper. We joked about a new book I might do, "Seven-Minute Meals for Men without Women," and we spent the early evening listening to the records of Cole Porter, Gershwin, and Kern we had danced to when we were young lovers. We went to our cottage in Beverly Farms, and in late afternoon I would drive us to Wingaersheek Beach or the Cathedral Pines. She slept in my arms until the night before she died on July 25, 1970.

At the Memorial Service I tried to say in two paragraphs what she had meant to us and to her friends and neighbors, and David McCord, who loved her dearly, gave a touching eulogy. Not long before, Peter Davison had published his poem "North Shore" in the *Atlantic*; it encompassed, better than I can say, our forty-five years of happiness, my grief and feeling of desolation which followed.

NORTH SHORE
(for Charles Hopkinson)

1   THE EMBARKATION FOR CYTHEREA

The sun is high. Young Saxons shouldering oars
Trample the shaven lawn. Platoons of girls
In organdied profusion follow them,
Flowers of Boston's bright virginity,
Cool limbs beneath frail garments. At the pier,
Piled high with picnic baskets, cutters ride
The hospitable swell, their halyards eased
Yet eager to spread sail. Across the strait
The islands rise like rain-clouds from the sea.
Here on our hill the house, after its crowded morning,
Will sleep till dusk. Then we expect them home,
Their wine all drunk, their faces gorged with sun,
Guiding their ships with briny headsails furled,
To quiet moorings.

2   THE RETURN

Many years have passed.
The house and I still wait for their return.
Shutters keep out the sun, chairs lie in shrouds,
The Chinese vases rattle with dry leaves.
Angry with age, but waiting, I keep watch
High in the eastern wing, my spyglass cocked
To sight the flicker of those homeward sails.
Perhaps they are all dead? I have not heard
A youthful voice for years. When will they come?
The sea still glimmers, empty of islands now.
The lawns are empty. Over the weathered house
Gulls hover, wailing their disdainful cry.
At night the house is silent, and the wind
Steals out each dawn to comb a barren sea.

In June 1971, before I got into the thick of editing the biography of Walter Lippmann, Leverett Saltonstall called at my office to discuss the possibility of a memoir which his family had been urging him to write but about which he had his doubts. He brought with him a chronology of his forty years in public office, copies of speeches, three lectures he had delivered at Pennsylvania State University, and a sheaf of short anecdotes, gathered by an assistant. He told me that Henry Laughlin, the head of Houghton Mifflin Company, had looked them over, without encouragement. There is spice in trying to get at something one's nearest rival may have missed.

"Suppose we make another approach," I suggested. "If you can give me an hour or so, I'd like to ask some questions." Lev assented, put on his hearing aid, and I called in Miss Albee. Saltonstall had been in politics all his life, beginning as alderman in Newton, representative in the Massachusetts Legislature, its Speaker, war Governor, and for four terms in the United States Senate under Presidents Roosevelt, Truman, Eisenhower, Kennedy, and Johnson. I knew nothing of parliamentary procedure, and except for a successful struggle to change the Massachusetts censorship law I had never been involved in state politics. "How could you afford to go into politics?" I began. "Did you have an inheritance?" Yes, from his grandmother Brooks. I asked if the family had always been Republican. No, his great-grandfather, also a Leverett, was a Democrat when elected president of the Massachusetts Senate. But his father's lifelong friendship with Theodore Roosevelt, which began when they were clubmates at Harvard, had swung father and son to the Republican Party. . . . Miss Albee was taking down his answers in shorthand.

Those meetings were to continue each week for three and a half years, with time out for the Saltonstalls' summer holidays at North Haven. Lev's memory was reliable and his speaking style easy, candid, colorful — and emphatic when aroused. This was my first attempt to edit an "as told to" book. My ingenuous questions sometimes made him laugh but they pushed him to spell things out and reminded him of incidents or opposition he'd half-forgotten. I had to respect his modesty about himself, his reluctance to criticize people but not policies, and what grew on me was the intensity of his devotion to his wife, Alice, often referred to as "my missus," to Harvard, and to the nation.

In Boston, as I knew, he was a walking legend. When James Michael Curley baited him by referring to him as a man "with a Harvard accent and a South Boston face," it boomeranged; Lev won the election and ever after the state re-elected him for the Saltonstall grin and jaw. Tears came to his eyes when he told how, during the war — "and even today" — people stopped him in the street to thank him for what he had done for a son in service. He was war Governor when the cable came to the State House telling that his undergraduate son, Peter, had been ambushed and killed in Guam and, as he explained to us quietly, he had driven himself back to Dover to share the grief with Alice. It was his chauffeur who told me that when he called for the governor the following morning to bring him to a memorial ceremony for a young Marine, killed in action, not a word was said about Peter on the drive or in Lev's address.

In Washington at the outset Saltonstall was devoted to the Navy and in time became the ranking Republican on the Armed Services and Appropriations committees, and sponsor of the National Science Foundation. On Capitol Hill "Salty" earned a reputation for the diplomacy he exercised when a piece of legislation, differing in a number of points, had passed the House and Senate and gone to conference for compromise. Studying the two versions at home, Lev would draw a line through ten points in the House version he thought dispensable and check a balancing number he believed the Senate would surrender. At the next meeting in the conference his forethought was usually approved, and they got down to the nitty-gritty differences. His method was so sensible it became known as "doing a Saltonstall."

When the manuscript was finally typed I wrote this at the conclusion of my preface:

It is a measure of a politician in Washington to name the men he most admired (and who in turn admired him). Saltonstall's list was topped by President Eisenhower, and General George C. Marshall; it included Admiral Rickover, whom Leverett pushed through for the rank of admiral when the submariner would otherwise have been "plucked" by the Navy Board; it included "Vinegar" Joe Stilwell, with whom Saltonstall paced the deck in the dawn hours before the atom bomb tests at Bikini; it included Sen. Richard Russell of Georgia, Saltonstall's opposite number on the Armed Services Committee (Russell, returning after a long illness, as he scanned the Appropriations Bill, exclaimed, "Damn it, Lev, you got just the bill you wanted and you had only one-third of the votes"), and Senator Lyndon B. Johnson. They had been working together on a piece of legislation and when the Saltonstall version seemed preferable, "Lev" sent Lyndon a note saying he didn't want to double-cross him. Johnson said in an aside to one of Saltonstall's aides, "Tell Lev he wouldn't know how to double-cross anyone."

Saltonstall's account of these men and of the admiration he felt for them gives us an insight on American integrity, theirs and his.

It was a bitter disappointment when our associates at Little, Brown declined to accept *Salty* and my juniors at the Atlantic, also in a mood of economy, would not do it on their own. There are times when a publisher has a duty to print what is admirable and in the public interest even though it may not break even; such was the case here and the turn-down was a narrow-minded judgment of which I was ashamed. When Tom Winship, the editor of the *Boston Globe*, heard the verdict he too was indignant, stepped in and decided to publish *Salty* partly as a serial and then in a well-designed book with many photographs — and I had the fun of attending the autographing parties with the Senator. The integrity of Leverett Saltonstall glorifies public service.

The election of John F. Kennedy in 1960 was a rejuvenation. He was our youngest President and like T.R. he brought buoyancy back into the White House. At his inauguration, with Robert Frost beside him, Kennedy in his crisp, epigrammatic sentences reminded us of our obligation; he spoke with the same determination on his visit to Berlin and he did not hesitate to compel Khrushchev to remove the missile sites from Cuba. I doubt if we realized what a symbol of trustworthy America Kennedy had become in his thousand days.

His assassination, followed by the murder of his brother Robert, was a disgrace of our national spirit and a shock to the world. Ten years later Nixon and Agnew, "Mr. Clean," were our Executives. Such a decadence in the electoral process makes one wonder if Walter Lippmann's grieving at the end of his life about "the ungovernability of man" was right.

In *Credos and Curios*, the papers of James Thurber, which his wife published posthumously, she quotes his memorable lines: "Let us not look back in anger, nor forward in fear, but around in awareness." Those words remind me of the rallying power of this country in a crisis. Read the roll of those who were in authority or in service in 1941 and 1942: FDR, Stimson, Marshall, Harry Hopkins, Vannevar Bush, Eisenhower, King, Nimitz, Halsey and Spruance, MacArthur and Patton, John McCloy, Bob Lovett, Forrestal and Patterson, Arnold, Spaatz, Eaker, Doolittle, and Curtis, the Texans, Will Clayton, Jesse Jones, and Milo Perkins, Bob Sherwood, Archie MacLeish, and Elmer Davis, Senators Taft, Truman, Russell, Byrd, and Johnson. How many more that I have forgotten composed the actual "elite" which Lippmann was searching for in his troubled book *Essays in the Public Philosophy*.

Is it in our power to elect or attract such men to government service in the years of jeopardy ahead? I pray so, for we shall need them. We enter a period of financial distress, of doing without, probably of famine. We, with our evident food surplus, with our sovereignty in technical equipment, with our vanity in possessions, and our precedent for giving aid, will have little warning of what may be demanded of us by our allies, and by those impoverished nations whose economy is inadequate and whose population is exploding. The People's Republic of China will probably take care of itself but it sets an example of the overcrowding and underfeeding which I dread; between now and the year 2000, the population of China will have increased by a number equal to our entire population as I write. Were I Lord of the Universe I should forbid the making and selling of nuclear weapons, whether by France, the Soviet Union, he United States, or whoever, and I would apply the money saved to restoring the good earth. Where to plant 30,000 nuclear warheads without hurting anyone would be quite a problem. Much simpler to discharge the lot into outer space.

AFTERWORD

I began this book with the statement that publishing is a gambler's profession; it still is and the stakes are larger than they were fifty years ago. Two of the more successful gambles in my experience occurred in Boston. In 1925 Herbert Jenkins, an editor at Little, Brown, read in *The Times Literary Supplement* that a war novel was a runaway success in Germany. War novels were supposed by then to be dead but on the impulse Jenkins cabled Erich Maria Remarque making the blind offer of an advance royalty of $1,000 for the American rights of *All Quiet on the Western Front*. A New York publisher, who also had not read the book, bid $500. Jenkins's won, and Little, Brown realized on that shot in the dark over half a million (hard dollars).

The second gamble, made by Henry Laughlin, then head of Houghton Mifflin, was for a known quantity. It was public knowledge that Winston Churchill was writing a history of the Second World War and that Henry Luce had purchased with a large wad the serial rights for an illustrated version in *Life*. It was thought there would be at least two volumes. Money had to talk and there was the additional courtesy of charming the Prime Minister. Laughlin proved capable of both. As it turned out there were not two volumes but six, and Houghton's investment of an advance of $250,000 produced book revenue of over $4,000,000 and subsidiary income of over $1,000,000.

While I am speaking of finances I must stress a dispiriting factor. Because of the stringency of the tax laws, those of my contemporaries, Richard Simon and Max Schuster, who founded an immensely successful house, and Bennett Cerf and Donald Klopfer, who founded Random House, felt it necessary to sell out so that their families would receive a lucrative inheritance. Bennett and I had desks side by side when we were working for Horace Liveright. I judge him the most versatile (remember his fight to release *Ulysses* by James Joyce from the clutches of our Customs) and the most exuberant, skillful publisher I have known. Cerf attracted able editors and Nobel Prize winners, Sinclair Lewis and William Faulkner; he put together a conglomerate of three other firms, including Alfred A. Knopf, whose founder he profoundly admired. He once laughingly referred to all this as "the U.S. Steel of publishing," and it was worth $34,000,000 when sold to RCA. Many smaller houses have followed that course and the wonder in my mind is whether, once in the conglomerate, they have retained the initiative, the personal quality that is characteristic of such surviving independents as Scribner's, Harper & Row, Houghton Mifflin, Doubleday, McGraw-Hill, W. W. Norton and New Directions?

It is beyond question that thanks to the conspicuous example of Alfred Knopf in the 1920s books in hard covers today are better designed and better printed than in the past. Alas, they are also more rife with typos and errors of fact because good proofreaders (and editors) are in short supply.

In 1923, when I began, the sunburst of American novelists, Sinclair Lewis, John Dos Passos, F. Scott Fitzgerald, Thornton Wilder, and Ernest Hemingway, shortly followed by John Steinbeck and William Faulkner, brought to an end the long sovereignty of British writers. The flow is now the other way. But fiction is spotty; the bomb has had an unsteadying effect. From England I enjoy the versatility of Graham Greene, John Fowles, Iris Murdoch, V. S. Pritchett, and Geoffrey Household, and here, the all-around virtuosity of Robert Penn Warren and the novels of Saul Bellow, John Updike, Louis Auchincloss, and Philip Roth.

As I grow older, biography and history mean more to me: it is a field in which Iris Origo, Agnes de Mille, Barbara Tuchman, Cecil Woodham-Smith, Elizabeth Longford, and Catherine Drinker Bowen have excelled with style, understanding, and judgment. And not too much Freud.

It used to be thought that only the most popular titles in hard covers could be reprinted in cheaper editions. Then in 1942, with all publishers' lists to choose from, the government began distributing paperbacks overseas in the Armed Services Editions and in very large printings. This was a gold mine to be exploited in peace and here is where the gambling — it is called "auctions" — for a new writer of a sexy or sensational novel has pushed the guarantee up to preposterous figures. At the same time paperbacks, serious or light, are the only economy in a college education; they provide a good living for an army of pulp, and a few talented writers, and they dismiss the notion that motion pictures and TV would kill reading. For a long time to come I foresee an irrepressible minimum of young people who believe that words are jewels to be polished.

Where we have advanced in magazine publishing is in the wider spectrum of periodicals like the *National Geographic, Scientific American, Archaeology,* the *Smithsonian,* and the *Bulletin of Atomic Scientists,* to name but five. Where we have sunk is to the depths of vulgarity. Charlie Morton used to say that a woman should not look like a cow. The cows that are spread out each month in *Playboy, Penthouse,* and the like may excite lonely males or adolescents waiting for a haircut; as an example of repetitious prurience they are hard to beat. Let's change the subject.

I am proud of my alumni, the younger men who served with me during my fifty-seven years. I begin with John Walcott of Cambridge: John came to us fresh from Harvard, tall, modest, a trustworthy First Reader whose comments I quoted at staff meetings. John's needless death in World War II — he was sideswiped by a truck — saddened us and ended a promising career. Chester Kerr, an Eli, took control of the Press and was skilled in editing novelists James Hilton, Ann Bridge, and H. E. Bates; but the OWI called him to Washington and at war's end he became an editor at the Yale University Press, where he proved to be conspicuously the best in that field. Today, busy as ever, he is reviving in New Haven the famous Boston trademark of Ticknor & Fields.

Seymour Lawrence came to the Press in 1952 as the *Atlantic* was moving into my big years, and he brought an enterprise, a love of publishing, and a talent for personal persuasion. Sam endeared himself to Edwin O'Connor in the early stages of *The Last Hurrah,* and he scored his triumph with Katherine Anne Porter. Her short stories were among the very best; she was included in several O. Henry collections and Harcourt Brace published three volumes of her stories for the fastidious. But Katherine Anne made a reputation for nonproduction; for over twenty years it was known that she had a novel in progress which she would not finish. Sam acquired the contract for us, installed her in an inn at Rockport, Massachusetts, and urged her on until only a small wedge remained to be written. Without her knowledge he submitted a typed copy — still lacking the wedge — to the Book-of-the-Month Club, and when they accepted it on condition it be finished, she had the incentive she needed. *Ship of Fools* was at last published in 1962, became an instantaneous success, and Katherine Anne at last had more money than she could live to spend. This troubled her: "I don't want to leave a damn penny," she said, "to either of my husbands!"

Curtis Cate joined the magazine in 1954 with a resourcefulness that made him singularly valuable. His father, as I have mentioned, had been an ambulance driver with the French, who settled his family in Senlis in 1919, with the result that his oldest son became European in thought and language and after his years at Harvard and Oxford was eager to have a tryout with us. He was an acquisitive editor and proved his value as our correspondent in Paris, where his friendship with Carlton Lake, his approach to Isak Dinesen and José Ortega y Gasset, his correct appraisal of de Gaulle, his admiration for the Imagists, and his articles on Simone de Beauvoir and the rise and decline of Françoise Sagan gave a Parisian accuracy to our contents.

It was our custom to give summer tryouts to promising undergraduates. Whitney Ellsworth read manuscripts for us for three weeks before doing his stint in the Army, and on return proved to be bright, perspicacious with a keen nose for what would be provocative. He was a spark at our editorial meetings but there was one incurable problem: he preferred New York to Boston. At an opportune moment he jumped at the chance of publishing the *New York Review of Books* where his success was our loss.

Peter Davison, son of the poet Edward Davison and a poet himself, took charge of the Press when Sam left to establish his own firm. Some publishers sidestep poetry, but Peter attracted or held good poets such as Stanley Kunitz, who won the Pulitzer Prize in 1959. Peter was editorially responsible, with the assistance of Esther S. Yntema, for the emergence of L. E. Sissman as a regular contributor to the *Atlantic* in both poetry and prose. Like Wallace Stevens, Sissman, in a career of high-pressured business, managed to fence off interludes for his writing. His better poems, in the late 1960s, appeared after his first bout with Hodgkin's disease, when he realized the grim limitation of time. In Peter's preface which graces *Hello, Darkness*, Sissman's collected poems, which won the National Book Critics Circle Award, Davison writes, "Born in the twenties, bred in the thirties, bewildered and polarized by the war, stunned by the evasions of the fifties, and coming of age, if ever, in the sixties, he [Sissman] concluded:

> *I warm myself in isolation. . . .*
> *I hide*
> *Out in my hideout from the memory*
> *Of our unlovely recent history. . . .*
> *I see,*
> *By luck, a leisurely and murderous*
> *Shadow detach itself with a marine*
> *Grace from an apple tree. A snowy owl,*
> *Cinereous, nearly invisible,*
> *Planes down its glide path to surprise a vole.*

"The poem is dated 1969, when New England saw not only a southward wave of snowy owls, but signs that the Vietnam war would not quickly cease to be murderous."

Peter himself is a pastoral poet, happiest on his farm in Essex County or on his visits to the chronicler of the far north and deep sea, Farley Mowat, Canada's favorite author. Or, again when editing *Beautiful Swimmers* by William W. Warner, that most human, succulent account of watermen, blue crabs, and the Chesapeake Bay which was in its eighth printing when awarded the Pulitzer Prize in 1977. And it was Peter who spaced and encouraged the intensive program of Dr. Robert Coles, the psychiatrist with special dedication to children.

Peter, like a good editor, has his eye on the long shot. At the close of negotiations for a contract with Senator "Pat" Moynihan's agent, Peter asked if there were any promising novels in the shop. Why yes, as a matter of fact, there was one, a first novel about the skulduggery in the sale of modern art, by a young American living in Ireland, a very cleverly written story sure to take a high bid in paperback. The advance in hard covers was $100,000 — for a first novel. Peter closed the deal when he returned to Boston. The novel, *Provenance*, by Frank McDonald, was provocative, climbed as a best seller, and in the auction for the paperback rights it fetched $750,000. Even if you divide by ten to compare with the advances in 1923, that is a lot more money than Hemingway received for *The Sun Also Rises*.

Editing is effective in inverse proportion to the number who decide. On numerous occasions throughout our fifty-five-year association with the editors of Little, Brown and Company, we have felt more confident about books whose chances they thought were dubious. At the outset they could and did exercise a veto, but this was changed in the early 1930s when we kept unearthing authors — Mazo de la Roche, Ann Bridge, Mari Sandoz, Agnes Newton Keith — whose success surprised them. Alfred McIntyre, for instance, voted against our awarding Mazo the Atlantic Novel Prize in 1927, and in disputed judgments thereafter we had the option of printing at our own expense titles we believed in.

Each side of our combination has respected the other's initiative. In 1937 George Kennan submitted an immature manuscript to Little, Brown and it was rejected; twenty years later when I persuaded Kennan to let us publish his excellent lectures, *Russia and the West under Lenin and Stalin*, there was no thought, probably no remembrance, of who came first. We have lived together, I surmise, with more forbearance than exists in most partnerships; there is inevitable friction over details — book jackets, when to apply more advertising — rarely a case like *Salty* when a worthy book is dismissed by an overbearing instinct for economy. What saves the partnership is mutual respect and the confidence of a young editor like Upton Brady, Davison's successor, that the Atlantic has long attracted writers of quality whose books should be encouraged, even when they needed as much editing as he and Peter have given this.

One needs consultants for such a book. I am very grateful to Mrs. Vladimir Nabokov for permission to quote her husband's poem "Softest of Tongues" and his letters, and for her advice; Sir Isaiah Berlin and Joan Bright Astley checked my reminiscences of England; Alfred Kazin and Richard McLanathan amplified my account of the Soviet Union and Neil Chamberlain helped to remind me of my visits to Yugoslavia; I have long relied on those brave women, Agnes Newton Keith and Agnes de Mille, and I am thankful for Anne Morrow Lindbergh's sensitive interpretation of Charles' philosophy; Wendy Morison Beck could help me as no other about her father, Admiral Samuel Eliot Morison; Sir Sacheverell and Francis Sitwell have approved my pages on Sir Osbert and Dame Edith Sitwell. I am grateful to Oscar Handlin for his illuminating letter about Ralph McGill, and to Mary Lynn Smith, Ralph's second wife, for her helpful reminders. I thank John Bush for permission to quote from the papers and letters of his father Vannevar Bush; Mrs. James B. Conant kindly reviewed the pages concerning her husband; Barbara Rex encouraged me in what I said about Catherine Drinker Bowen and before his death I thanked the late John H. Powell, Jr. for his firm, fair judgment of Kitty's *Miracle in Philadelphia*. I welcomed the advice and additions Cynthia Morton Hollingsworth gave me about her father, Charles Morton; finally I speak from the heart in blessing those of my Old Guard: Donald Snyder, Emily Flint, Kay Ellis Vickers, Louise Desaulniers, Virginia Albee and Natalie Greenberg, for their unfailing attention, their prodding and, so often, the right advice.

INDEX

315

Bohlen, Charles, 285
Bolte, Charles, 101
Bone, James, 55–58
Bonnet, Henri, 298–299
Bonnet, Mme. Henri (Ellie), 298–299
Borghese, Elisabeth Mann, 206
Bowen, Catherine Drinker, 3, 223–231, 309
Boyd, Julian, 230
Bracken, Brendan, 55, 78
Bradbury, John, 176
Bradley, David J., 128–129
Brady, Upton, 313
Breit, Harvey, 205
Bridge, Ann, 313
Briggs, Le Baron R., 141
Bright, Joan. *See* Astley, Joan Bright
Bromfield, Louis, 143
Brooks, Lawrence, 176
Brooks, Paul, 274
Brooks, Van Wyck, 157
Brown, John Mason, 143
Browning, Miles, 110, 112
Bryant, William Cullen, 266
Buchan, John, 149
Buck, Paul, 48
Buck, Pearl, 20
Bulgakov, Valentin, 255
Bullen, William, 176
Bullitt, William, 284
Burns, Richard F., 222
Bush, Vannevar, 3, 91–94, 96, 98, 164–166, 219
Butler, Harold, 50
Butlin, Billy, 188

Cabot, Charles C., 35, 139
Cabot, Godfrey, 140
Caldwell, Erskine, 245
Campbell, Marion Danielson, 289–291
Campbell, Roy, 151
Camus, Albert, 119, 123
Canfield, Dorothy, 82
Carson, Rachel, 94
Carter, Bernard S., 86, 89
Carter, Hodding, 171
Cate, Curtis, 205, 235, 311
Cecil, Lord David, 151
Celler, Emanuel, 25
Cerf, Bennett, 125, 309
Chagall, Marc, 207, 251
Chamberlin, William Henry, 8–10
Chandler, Raymond, 3, 157–161
Chaudhuri, Nirad C., 205–206

Chauncy, Henry, 142
Chayefsky, Paddy, 241–244, 247, 248–249, 256–259
Church, Caroline, 6
Churchill, John Spencer, 56
Churchill, Sir Winston, 308
Ciardi, John, 83–84, 268
Clark, Grenville, 100, 140, 141
Clark, Leonard, 268
Clark, Mark, 86
Clarkson, Gary, 301
Clay, Henry, 52
Clay, Lucius, 201
Clemens, Samuel, 10, 126–127
Cloud, Dudley, 220
Cloud, Jeannette, 20
Codman, Charles, 30, 85–89
Codman, Mrs. Charles (Theodora), 86, 88
Cohn, David L., 6–7
Coke, Sir Edward, 229
Cole, Edwin M., 219
Coles, Robert, 263, 312
Colefax, Lady Sybil, 51, 151
Collins, Sir William, 184
Commager, Henry Steele, 103
Compton, Arthur H., 26
Conant, James Bryant, 4, 91, 135–137, 138, 141, 164, 189–190, 212, 216–218, 237
Connolly, Cyril, 73, 75, 270
Converse, Florence, 6
Cowden, Roy, 143
Cowles, Gardner, 45, 124
Cox, Gardiner, 206
Crankshaw, Edward, 233
Creswick, Richard, 51, 68–70
Critchell, Laurence, 81–82, 120
Crockett, Leslie B., 123, 290
Crockett, Mrs. Leslie B. (Kay), 123
Croly, Herbert, 45
Crosby, Harry, 265
Crowther, Geoffrey, 73, 139, 152, 154
Curley, James Michael, 179, 196, 208, 209, 304
Curtis, Harriet, 176
Curtis, E. P. (Ted), 88
Cushing, Archbishop Richard, 28

Dabney, Virginius, 171
Danielian, N. R., 126
Daniels, Danny, 133
Daniels, Jonathan, 171
Danielson, Barbara, 5, 35, 50, 120, 289

McCloy, John, 214, 237
McClure, S. S., 4
McClusky, Clarence W., 11
McCord, David, 20, 37, 212, 303
McCormick, Anne O'Hare, 43
McDonald, Frank, 312
MacDonald, James, 66
McDonald, Torbert, 193
McGill, Ralph, 3, 50, 51, 71, 72, 79–80, 171–175, 176
McGill, Mrs. Ralph (Mary Elizabeth), 174
McGinley, Phyllis, 236
Machell, Roger, 184
McIntyre, Alfred, 47, 122, 313
McLanathan, Richard, 251–252
MacLeish, Archibald, 21, 24, 43–44, 49, 53, 98, 138, 154, 266
MacLeish, Mrs. Archibald (Ada), 154
MacLeish, Roderick, 207
McPherson, James Alan, 3, 178, 293–294
McRae, John, 104
Madariaga, Salvador de, 68
Mahoney, Daniel, 101
Mailer, Norman, 246
Mangelsdorf, Paul, 140
Manley, Albert, 176
Mann, Thomas, 43, 206
Manning, Robert J., 290–291, 293, 294
Markel, Lester, 153
Marquand, John P., 21, 89, 96, 126, 204
Marsh, Jordan, 208
Marshak, Samuil, 247
Marshall, George, 138–139, 156, 190, 237, 305
Marshall, James, 25
Martin, Donald, 105
Martin, Joseph, 97
Marvell, Andrew, 75, 269
Masefield, John, 68, 69–70, 145, 182–183
Matthiessen, F. O., 141
Matthiessen, Peter, 123
Maugham, Somerset, 21–22
Maurois, André, 21
Medina, Harold, 211
Mehta, Ved, 144–145
Mencken, Henry, 125, 157
Meštrović, Ivan, 277
Meyer, Agnes, 43
Meyer, Cord, Jr., 101, 123
Meyer, Eugene, 43
Michener, James, 30

Miller, Arthur, 245
Mills, Wilbur, 282
Milosz, Czeslaw, 235
Moore, Brian, 123
Moore, George, 75, 151
Moore, Henry, 207
Moravia, Alberto, 119
Morgan, J. P., 115, 119, 121
Morison, Samuel Eliot, 3, 103–114, 206
Morison, Mrs. Samuel Eliot (Priscilla), 114
Morrison, Kathleen, 276
Mortimer, Raymond, 75
Morton, Charles W., 36–42, 121, 125, 128, 205, 207, 233, 234, 291, 310
Morton, Mrs. Charles W. (Mildred), 37–39
Mosher, John, 38
Moynihan, Daniel Patrick, 312
Mumford, Lewis, 242
Murchie, Guy, 185
Murdoch, Iris, 309
Murray, John, 184
Murray, Mrs. John (Diana), 184
Murrow, Edward R., 190–191
Mutch, Margaret, 27

Nabokov, Vladimir, 3, 12–14, 313
Nagumo, Chuichi, 110–111
Nehru, Jawaharlal, 8, 210
Nervi, Luigi, 214
Nevins, Allen, 301
Niebuhr, Reinhold, 237
Nixon, Richard, 174
Nock, Albert Jay, 24–25
Nordhoff, Charles, 3, 28–30

Ober, Harold, 227
O'Connor, Edwin, 3, 123, 193, 196–198, 207–210, 310
Ogden, Archibald G. (Archie), 120
Olson, Charles, 85
O'Malley, Frank, 207
Oppenheimer, J. Robert, 99, 102–103, 164, 192, 283
Origo, Iris, 309
Osland-Hill, Edward, 60
Ozawa, Jisaburo, 107

Page, Walter Hines, 239
Palfrey, John, 225
Pancake, Breece, 294
Pasternak, Boris, 243, 252
Patterson, Eugene, 173

321

241–261; reception of delegation of Soviet writers (1960), 274–276; trip to Yugoslavia (1961), 276–282; special reports on psychiatry in America (1961, 1962, 1964), 262–264; retirement from *Atlantic Monthly* (1964), 290–291; lecture tours continue, 142–145, 192

Weeks, Mrs. Edward Augustus (Fritzy), 35, 148, 151, 156, 182, 186, 187–189, 211, 275, 302–303

Weeks, Mrs. Edward Augustus. *See* Adams, Phoebe-Lou

Weeks, Edward (grandson), 220

Weeks, Edward Francis (Ted) (son), 35, 206, 219, 220

Weeks, Sara (daughter), 35, 206

Weeks, Sinclair, 138, 139, 212, 216

Welch, Joseph Nye, 191

Wells, Anna Mary, 11

Welty, Eudora, 3, 6, 119

West, Jessamyn, 3, 120

West, Rebecca, 51

Wharton, Edith, 157

White, E. B., 38, 39, 233, 295–296

White, Katharine, 38, 39

White, Theodore, 284

White, William Allen, 48–49

Whitehead, Alfred North, 97–98, 164, 239

Whitman, Alden, 114

Whitman, Walt, 74, 75, 267

Whitney, George, 138, 139

Whittier, John Greenleaf, 10, 267

Wigglesworth, V. B., 94

Wilbur, Richard, 270

Wilder, Thornton, 151, 246, 296–298, 309

Williams, W. E., 73

Willis, Harold, 30

Willkie, Wendell, 45, 47

Wilson, Arthur, 214

Wilson, Carroll, 98

Wilson, Edmund, 119, 210, 275, 295

Wilson, Mrs. Edmund (Elena), 275

Wilson, Kenneth, 210

Wilson, Robert Cade, 98

Wilson, Woodrow, 97, 239

Winship, Laurence, 50, 51–52, 55, 58, 59, 65, 66, 71, 72, 79, 81

Winship, Thomas, 306

Wister, Owen, 89

Wolfe, Edward, 6

Wolff, Robert Lee, 48

Woodham-Smith, Cecil, 309

Woods, Betty, 49

Woollcott, Alexander, 19–20

Wouk, Herman, 194

Wren, Sir Christopher, 56–57

Wyeth, Andrew, 274

Wylie, Elinor, 268, 269

Yates, Richard, 123

Yeats, William Butler, 75

Yntema, Esther S., 311

Youngert, Eugene, 218

Zerina, Vera, 250